Interpreting
Kant's *Critiques*

Interpreting Kant's *Critiques*

KARL AMERIKS

CLARENDON PRESS · OXFORD

OXFORD
UNIVERSITY PRESS

Great Clarendon Street, Oxford OX2 6DP
Oxford University Press is a department of the University of Oxford.
It furthers the University's objective of excellence in research, scholarship,
and education by publishing worldwide in
Oxford New York
Auckland Bangkok Buenos Aires Cape Town Chennai
Dar es Salaam Delhi Hong Kong Istanbul Karachi Kolkata
Kuala Lumpur Madrid Melbourne Mexico City Mumbai Nairobi
São Paulo Shanghai Taipei Tokyo Toronto

Oxford is a registered trade mark of Oxford University Press
in the UK and in certain other countries

Published in the United States
by Oxford University Press Inc., New York

© in this volume Karl Ameriks 2003

The moral rights of the author have been asserted
Database right Oxford University Press (maker)

First published 2003

All rights reserved. No part of this publication may be reproduced,
stored in a retrieval system, or transmitted, in any form or by any means,
without the prior permission in writing of Oxford University Press,
or as expressly permitted by law, or under terms agreed with the appropriate
reprographics rights organization. Enquiries concerning reproduction
outside the scope of the above should be sent to the Rights Department,
Oxford University Press, at the address above

You must not circulate this book in any other binding or cover
and you must impose this same condition on any acquirer

British Library Cataloguing in Publication Data
Data available

Library of Congress Cataloging in Publication Data
Data available
ISBN 0-19-924731-5
ISBN 0-19-924732-3 (pbk.)

1 3 5 7 9 10 8 6 4 2

Typeset by Kolam Information Services Pvt. Ltd.
Printed in Great Britain on acid-free paper by
T.J. International Ltd., Padstow, Cornwall

ACKNOWLEDGMENTS

I thank the editors at Oxford University Press, and especially Peter Momtchiloff, for their invaluable assistance with this volume. On innumerable specific points I am heavily indebted to my colleagues at Notre Dame, and to the audiences for whom earlier versions of many of the chapters were presented. A major inspiration for this volume comes from the interests and questions of my students over the years, and I especially hope that this book can be of help to them and other students of Kant in the future.

I acknowledge permission to reprint materials from the following publications:

Introduction (and Chapter 11): portions of 'On Being Neither Post- Nor Anti-Kantian: A Reply to Breazeale and Larmore Concerning "The Fate of Autonomy"', *Inquiry* 46 (2003), 272–92.

Chapter 1: 'Kant's Transcendental Deduction as a Regressive Argument', *Kant-Studien*, 69 (1978), 273–85.

Chapter 2: 'Recent Work on Kant's Theoretical Philosophy', *American Philosophical Quarterly*, 19 (1982), 1–24.

Chapter 3: 'Kantian Idealism Today', *History of Philosophy Quarterly* 9 (1992), 329–42.

Chapter 4: 'The Critique of Metaphysics: Kant and Traditional Ontology', in *The Cambridge Companion to Kant*, ed. Paul Guyer (Cambridge: Cambridge University Press, 1992), pp. 249–79.

Chapter 5: 'Kant and Short Arguments to Humility', in *Kant's Legacy: Essays in Honor of L. W. Beck*, ed. Predrag Cicovacki (Rochester, NY: Rochester University Press, 2000), pp. 167–94.

Chapter 6: 'Kant's Deduction of Freedom and Morality', *Journal of the History of Philosophy* 19 (1981), 53–79.

Chapter 7: 'Kant on the Good Will', in *Grundlegung zur Metaphysik der Sitten*, ed. Otfried Höffe (Frankfurt: Klostermann, 1989), pp. 45–65.

Chapter 8: 'Kant and Hegel on Freedom: Two New Interpretations', *Inquiry* 35 (1992), 219–32.

Chapter 9: 'Zu Kants Argumentation zu dritten Abschnitt der Grundlegung', in *Systematische Ethik mit Kant*, ed. Carsten Held and Hans-Ulrich Baumgarten (Freiburg: Alber, 2001), pp. 24–54.

ACKNOWLEDGMENTS

Chapter 10: '"Pure Reason of Itself Alone Suffices to Determine the Will"', in *Immanuel Kant: Kritik der praktischen Vernunft*, ed. Otfried Höffe (Berlin: Akademie Verlag, 2001), pp. 99–114.

Chapter 11: 'On Schneewind and Kant's Method in Ethics', *Ideas y Valores* 102 (1996), 28–53.

Chapter 12: 'How to Save Kant's Deduction of Taste', *Journal of Value Inquiry* 16 (1982), 295–302; and 'Kant and the Objectivity of Taste', *British Journal of Aesthetics* 23 (1983), 3–17.

Chapter 13: 'New Views on Kant's Judgment of Taste', in *Kants Ästhetik/Kant's Aesthetics/L'esthétique de Kant*, ed. Hermann Parret (Berlin/New York: Walter de Gruyter, 1998), pp. 431–47.

Chapter 14: 'Taste, Conceptuality, and Objectivity', in *Kant Actuel*, ed. F. Duchesneau, G. LaFrance, and C. Piché (Montréal/Paris: Bellarmin/Vrin, 2000), pp. 141–61.

CONTENTS

Introduction: The Common Ground of Kant's *Critiques* ... 1

Part I: The First *Critique* and Kant's Theoretical Philosophy ... 49

1. Kant's Transcendental Deduction as a Regressive Argument ... 51
2. Recent Work on Kant's Theoretical Philosophy ... 67
3. Kantian Idealism Today ... 98
4. The Critique of Metaphysics: Kant and Traditional Ontology ... 112
5. Kant and Short Arguments to Humility ... 135

Part II: The Second *Critique* and Kant's Practical Philosophy ... 159

6. Kant's Deduction of Freedom and Morality ... 161
7. Kant on the Good Will ... 193
8. Kant and Hegel on Freedom: Two New Interpretations ... 212
9. Kant's *Groundwork* III Argument Reconsidered ... 226
10. 'Pure Reason of Itself Alone Suffices to Determine the Will' ... 249
11. On Two Non-Realist Interpretations of Kant's Ethics ... 263

Part III: The Third *Critique* and Kant's Aesthetics ... 283

12. How to Save Kant's Deduction of Taste as Objective ... 285
13. New Views on Kant's Judgment of Taste ... 307
14. Taste, Conceptuality, and Objectivity ... 324

Index ... 345

Introduction

The Common Ground of Kant's *Critiques*

1. Interpretive Prolegomena

Like the well-known and continually frustrating academic search for 'the historical Jesus', the interpretation of Kant's philosophy can be said to be undergoing a 'third wave' in our time.[1] The first wave of Kant scholars offered extensive synoptic treatments, culminating with Hermann Cohen's three volumes on the three *Critiques*; later, Norman Kemp Smith and H. J. Paton provided relatively abbreviated English versions of this largely apologetic and historical approach. In a second period, in the heyday of positivistic analytic philosophy in the 1960s, the work of outstanding original thinkers such as P. F. Strawson, Wilfrid Sellars, and Jonathan Bennett introduced a very different approach, emphasizing a critical reconstruction of arguments that were sometimes connected only loosely to the original text but very effectively engaged central issues in contemporary analytic philosophy (e.g. the private language argument, the linguistic turn, the verification principle). However noteworthy its irreversible achievements, this second period remained caught at times in its own particular interests, somewhat like the 'second-wave' mid-century theologians, whose very concern to be modern (in this case, 'existential') may now seem to some readers to be the most outdated feature of their work. The new Kantians' focus on rigor and current issues came with the cost of leaving most of the original context of Kant's work out of sight, and of usually going only so far as to consider the first of Kant's three *Critiques*—and, even then, only a little more than half of that work, or, in the case of practical philosophy, little more than the first half of the *Groundwork*.

The contemporary third wave of Kant scholars, represented in the United States by interpreters such as Henry E. Allison and Paul Guyer, and in part anticipated by the work of leading postwar German philosophers such as Dieter

---

[1] Cf. John P. Maier, *A Marginal Jew: Rethinking the Historical Jesus*, vol. 2 (New York, 1994), 1. All this, of course, is the work of later generations of historical scholars trying to reconstruct the significance of an original 'master', and it is of a very different character than the lively disputes among successors who began writing when the master, or at least his immediate students, were still alive. The story of Kant's *immediate* reception has its own biblical parallels, and it is the focus of my earlier study, *Kant and the Fate of Autonomy: Problems in the Reception of the Critical Philosophy* (Cambridge, 2000).

INTRODUCTION

Henrich and Gerold Prauss, stands in the shadow of its illustrious predecessors, but it has the special merit of combining the historical concerns of the nineteenth century with the demands for clarity and relevance raised in the twentieth century.[2] With all this progress, however, each era has also made the interpretive process much more intimidating for its successors. It is no wonder that it is only in very rare cases that individual contemporary scholars have managed to complete separate volumes like Cohen's on the main topics of each of Kant's three *Critiques*. The abundance of accumulated scholarly material and the general drive toward specialization has resulted in a fractured situation in which most work on Kant continues to focus on one *Critique* at a time, and typically on only a relatively small portion of the text. Despite Kant's own wide-ranging systematic interests, there have been remarkably few attempts to present—in one surveyable volume and from the perspective of one author—a unified and non-elementary treatment of fundamental issues in all the main branches of the Critical philosophy.

This situation has long struck me as very unfortunate, given the frequent experience of finding key steps in central arguments in Kant's main writings that appear to have a close relation to arguments from his other works. Even without appealing to such experiences, it would seem evident a priori that an internal comparative approach deserves serious attention—and so it is all the more striking that so far it has been relatively neglected in the literature. Since Kant himself obviously designed his Critical system with a unified approach to philosophy in mind, it is hard to believe that the many similarities in the arguments of the *Critiques* are either accidental or incidental.

This point has to be balanced, of course, with a recognition of significant—and often still overlooked—changes in Kant's thought during his central Critical years. The basic form of the *Critique of Judgment* (1790), for example, was not even envisioned when the *Critique of Pure Reason* was first published (1781). It is also important to acknowledge that drives for architectonic unity can be distorting—not only in Kant but also in his interpreters. Each of the three *Critiques* has its own distinctive topics, and it would be foolish to expect exactly the same

---

[2] See e.g. Henry E. Allison, *Kant's Transcendental Idealism: An Intrepretation and Defense* (New Haven, 1983), *Kant's Theory of Freedom* (Cambridge, 1990), *Kant's Theory of Taste: A Reading of the Critique of Judgment* (Cambridge, 2001), and *Idealism and Freedom: Essays on Kant's Theoretical and Practical Philosophy* (Cambridge, 1996); Paul Guyer, *Kant and the Claims of Taste* (Cambridge, Mass., 1979), *Kant and the Claims of Knowledge* (Cambridge, 1987), *Kant and the Experience of Freedom: Essays on Aesthetics and Morality* (Cambridge, 1993), *Kant on Freedom, Law, and Happiness* (Cambridge, 2000); Dieter Henrich, *The Unity of Reason: Essays on Kant's Philosophy*, ed. R. Velkley (Cambridge, Mass., 1994), and *Aesthetics and the Moral Image of the World: Studies in Kant* (Stanford, Calif., 1992); Gerold Prauss, *Erscheinung bei Kant: Ein Problem der 'Kritik der reinen Vernunft'* (Bonn, 1971), and *Kant über Freiheit als Autonomie* (Frankfurt, 1983), including a chapter on 'Kants Theorie der ästhetischen Einstellung'. In referring to Kant's *Critique of Pure Reason*, I use the standard references to the A (1781) and B (1787) editions, and the Norman Kemp Smith translation (London, 1929). References to Kant's *Critique of Practical Reason* are to the volume (V) and page of *Kant's Gesammelte Schriften* (Berlin, 1900–) and to the Mary Gregor translation in *Kant's Practical Philosophy* (Cambridge, 1996).

INTRODUCTION

approach to the theoretical issues of the *Critique of Pure Reason*, for example, as to the moral issues of the *Critique of Practical Reason*, or the aesthetic issues of the *Critique of Judgment*.

Nonetheless, it is important to try to understand the main sections of the *Critiques* as sharing not only a common general philosophical position but also several very similar argumentative structures. Once one is sensitive to these similarities—and also attentive to relevant differences and intervening changes—it becomes possible to find significant support for interpretations of difficult aspects of one text by appealing to patterns of argument found elsewhere in Kant's work. All too often, interpreters have pinned a very peculiar position on one part of Kant's system that may seem a plausible reading when looking at only a few sentences or paragraphs but can suddenly appear highly questionable when one steps back to consider the broader patterns and key developments of Kant's thought.

I came across this phenomenon somewhat by accident while researching my first book, *Kant's Theory of Mind*, and puzzling over several bold and unguarded claims in the literature about Kant's views—for example that particular remarks about the 'I of apperception' by themselves either completely deny or implicitly entail claims that we certainly know our own self as a subject. It turned out that these claims were typically 'based' on a hasty use of tiny portions of the text, and they can be shown to be in clear conflict not only with the full development of the *Critique* (especially the nuanced discussions of the latter half of the work, and the systematically interconnected revisions for the second edition), but also with a wide range of highly relevant evidence from lectures and other writings.[3] It also turned out that questions like this about the Critical theory of the self are very closely intertwined with developments in Kant's position on philosophical methodology in general, and with the central issue of our spontaneity in particular. The main clue to understanding a crucial development in Kant's Critical views on our freedom (see Part II below) lies in connecting a key pattern of changes in formulation between the two editions of the first *Critique* (1781 and 1787) with key changes in his style of argument between the *Groundwork* and the second *Critique* (1785 and 1788). Once these connections are seen, the natural question that arises is, why have they not been noticed more generally? One partial explanation may be that Kant is typically taught in courses where the instructor is forced to focus solely on Kant's theoretical philosophy and its core texts, or on his practical philosophy and its core texts. This has led to a culture in which most of those who teach Kant do research almost entirely in only the one sphere or the other. Hence it may not be so surprising after all that even scholars who have worked on Kant for a long time might neglect important connections between his arguments concerning freedom in these two very different contexts—even though

---

[3] See the Preface to the expanded and revised 2nd edn of my *Kant's Theory of Mind: An Analysis of the Paralogisms of Pure Reason* (Oxford, 2000).

freedom is explicitly a 'keystone' concept for Kant (see the Preface to the *Critique of Practical Reason*), and therefore obviously cannot be treated properly by considering only one part of philosophy.

2. The Basic Structure of the *Critiques*

The features of Kant scholarship that have just been reviewed strongly reinforced my desire to put together a collection of writings concerning central topics of all three *Critiques*. In this way, issues and interpretations that are hard to follow in the context of one of Kant's works can easily gain illumination from related studies of other aspects of the Critical philosophy. Readers familiar with only one or two of the texts can thereby also be encouraged to begin to explore further on their own the various ways in which Kant's other works might be of help in deciphering difficult aspects of each of the *Critiques*.

2.1 Kant's Four Step Transcendental Procedure

Underlying all my interpretations of particular issues is a simple hypothesis about the basic structure of Kant's transcendental philosophy: namely, that it aims primarily at providing a regressive account of the necessary conditions of human experience. Thus, the *Critique of Pure Reason* sets out the necessary (or a priori) conditions of theoretical experience; the *Critique of Practical Reason* sets out the necessary conditions of 'pure practical', i.e. moral, experience; and the *Critique of Judgment* sets out the necessary conditions of pure 'purposive' experience, in particular of the aesthetic phenomenon of pure judgments of taste. This 'simple hypothesis' is hardly a revolutionary idea, but the way that it continues to be overlooked or resisted in many interpretations of Kant's main works makes it a thought that is still worth emphasizing.

The collection of essays that follows devotes one section each to a selection of writings on Kant's accounts of theoretical, practical, and aesthetic experience. The sequence of chapters approaches the main concerns of Kant's system in a way that parallels the systematic and chronological order of the three *Critiques*. Although the essays were formulated originally in very different contexts, they exhibit a common approach in interpreting the major connections and distinctions that Kant's transcendental investigations draw between what he takes to be the three main kinds of human experience. Before considering any of the differences, it is best to review some of the most basic common features of Kant's system.[4] The first

---

[4] In *Kant and the Fate of Autonomy*, I argue that this fourfold structure also provides a helpful template for understanding and evaluating the main German philosophers who immediately succeeded Kant. Cf. my 'On Being Neither Anti- nor Post-Kantian: A Reply to Breazeale and Larmore on "The Fate of Autonomy"', *Inquiry*, 46 (2003), 272–92.

INTRODUCTION

move in unpacking my 'simple hypothesis' about Kant's transcendental philosophy involves taking the structural kernel of his system as a whole, and also of each of its three major parts, to comprise four basic steps:

1. a starting point in common experience (E);
2. a transcendental derivation (TD) from this of various pure forms, categories, or principles;
3. an ultimate metaphysical account of all this in turn as making sense only on the basis of transcendental idealism (TI); and, finally,
4. a guiding idea and concluding argument that these first three steps are the essential prerequisites for vindicating the ultimate goal of human autonomy (AUT), in various key practical and methodological as well as theoretical senses. (In schematic form: E only if TD, and this only if TI; and then, given E and TD, AUT also only if TI.)

2.2 The Modesty of the Critical System

Note that on this reading the ontological doctrine of transcendental idealism enters into the Critical philosophy at a third stage, only *after* the second step, when the existence of *pure* forms of knowing (in a broad sense) has already been secured. That is, contrary to what is assumed by some other interpreters, transcendental idealism is not at all taken to be tantamount in meaning to the procedure of a transcendental deduction of necessary forms of experience, but rather is introduced as a logically subsequent doctrine that starts from the conclusions of *prior* transcendental arguments for such forms. It is meant to offer an explanation for these forms and a resolution for otherwise insoluble conflicts in related general claims about the world—once their existence has been established. (This implies, incidentally, that the doctrine is not clearly relevant for any contexts that appear to concern mere empirical matters—and yet many interpretations of Kant proceed as if his idealism is to be applied straightaway to such contexts.)

In most general terms, this reconstruction means that I read Kant as offering a 'metaphysics of experience', but one in which both key terms of this well-known phrase take on a meaning that may not be so well-known. First, Kantian 'experience' is not defined in terms of private so-called 'Cartesian' representations, but instead designates a cognitive situation occurring, roughly speaking, at a level no lower than that of the core perceptual judgments of common sense. Second, the Critical 'metaphysics', even while it criticizes its scholastic predecessors, remains fundamentally rationalist: in its epistemology it requires certain and pure principles for empirical knowledge (or morality, or taste) that take us beyond a completely naturalistic framework, and in its transcendental idealist ontology it implies a kind of immaterialism, i.e. an insistence on a non-spatio-temporal character for things in themselves (which turns out to be a crucial condition for the satisfaction of the prime aims of morality and taste).

Kant's versions of rationalism and immaterialism are doctrines that can be overlooked because sometimes it is assumed that the only options to empiricism and materialism are the more radical alternatives of a *dogmatic* rationalism, i.e. an epistemology relying on a heavy presumption that theoretical reason can positively determine substantive features of things all on its own, entirely apart from sensible considerations, and a *spiritualistic* immaterialism, i.e. an ontology that theoretically ascribes all sorts of specific (e.g. psychological) and independent powers to what is non-spatio-temporal.

For these reasons and others, including an explicit self-characterization of his philosophy in these terms in one of his metaphysics lectures, I have characterized Kant's distinctive kind of rationalist system as, in general, a relatively moderate or 'modest' one.[5] By this term I do not at all mean to deny that Kant is extremely interested in developing what would seem to us nowadays to be a much too ambitious and elaborate system. Like many traditional philosophers, Kant is notorious for all sorts of hasty claims to have solved philosophy's basic problems in a 'certain' and 'complete' way. My point is simply that, despite these claims, the 'system' that Kant actually *sets out* is not 'dogmatic' or radically rationalist, and it has numerous significant limitations that distinguish it as *relatively modest* in comparison with that of his major predecessors and successors. Looking back, there are many obvious ways in which Kant's epistemology and ontology is not as radical as that of earlier philosophers such as Aquinas, Descartes, Hume, Berkeley, Spinoza, and Leibniz. Unlike them, he clearly does not contrast our 'manifest image' with a system of detailed and allegedly certain theoretical claims about ultimate reality as purely theological, mechanistic, psychologistic, spiritualistic, monistic, or monadological. Moreover, just as surely, he does not make the kind of incredibly strong methodological and metaphysical claims found in his immediate successors: Reinhold, Fichte, Schelling, and Hegel. He is of course responsible for suggesting to them the very idea of a fundamentally autonomous rational system—one that would put autonomy at the heart of its notion of reality in general, as well as at the ground of its view of philosophical methodology and of the role that philosophy should play in culture in general. But there is an awful lot that depends on exactly how the notion of autonomy is developed in detail; and once the details are attended to, I believe it can be shown that there are many specific ways in which Kant's conception of our autonomous rationality is both

---

[5] See *Kant and the Fate of Autonomy*, 37; cf. *Lectures on Metaphysics/ Immanuel Kant*, ed. and tr. Karl Ameriks and Steve Naragon (Cambridge, 1997), III, and *Kant's Theory of Mind*, 7–8. A somewhat similar approach is found in Rae Langton, *Kantian Humility: Our Ignorance of Things in Themselves* (Oxford, 1998) (see below, Ch. 5).

more modest and more appealing than that of his successors, even if it no doubt has flaws of its own.[6]

This modesty can be specified by comparing the approach of other philosophers with the three basic structural components of Kant's system on this reading: (1) its non-absolute basis (E); (2) its limited development (TD); and (3) its restricted scope (TI). First, since the Kantian *basis* is 'experience' (see e.g. B218), in the sense of putative empirical knowledge (*Erfahrung*), it has what I would call a relative rather than an absolute certainty; that is, it does not have the kind of totally indisputable certainty that a 'Cartesian' skeptic finds in the mere existence of representations. This point is all the more obvious when one looks at the second and third *Critiques*, which make sense only on the *presumption* of some kind of valid experience in morality or aesthetics, an experience that is 'higher' than any so-called Cartesian basis because it is meant to reflect everyday core beliefs and involves substantive non-egocentric claims.

Second, since Kant's arguments from this basis to specific categories or pure principles depend on claims about pure forms of intuition or judgment that are not themselves deduced from an absolute basis such as the mere notion of representation (or of willing or feeling in general), it follows that the *development* of his system inherits the 'merely' relative certainty of its basis as well as a specific dependence on the irreducible given aspects of the additional claims just noted. Thus, ('second level') claims about the applicability of the pure categories of perceptual experience, or of the fundamental formulations of the pure principle of morality, or of the basic conditions of genuine judgments of taste, all presuppose that there are common and ordinary ('first level') perceptual, moral, or aesthetic experiences had by beings with something fundamentally like our basic—and ultimately contingent—specific forms of sensibility (i.e. space and time) and pure sensitivity (i.e. in moral respect and aesthetic appreciation).

Third, the *scope* of Kant's metaphysical claims is sharply limited by his doctrine of transcendental idealism. What reality is specifically like 'in itself' theoretical philosophy is largely forbidden to say in any positive way, although, to avoid contradiction, what we supposedly must assert with certainty is that it is not spatio-temporal as such. For Kant this specific idealist ontological doctrine is the necessary condition that makes it possible for his theoretical philosophy to introduce a general metaphysical *distinction* between known phenomena and *thinkable* noumena (which saves us from otherwise allegedly inescapable antinomies); for his practical philosophy to employ pure practical considerations to *determine* what is otherwise merely thought in a largely empty and hypothetical way (and thus to assert that as rational beings we all should posit God, freedom, and immortality); and for his aesthetic theory to *interpret* the apparent excess

---

[6] See the works cited above in n. 4.

of satisfying subjectively purposive phenomena that we actually experience as an unexpected 'symbol' of a deep harmonious intersection between the phenomenal patterns of the empirical world and an underlying noumenal moral 'substrate'.[7]

2.3 Modesty and the Regressive Approach

It is remarkable how often the moderate but still significant nature of Kant's approach in the first steps of his system appears to this day to be missed by readers of the *Critique of Pure Reason* (and of my reconstruction of it) simply because they presume that there are only two basic alternatives for Kant's transcendental arguments. These are: either to pursue a *strongly progressive* program, i.e. one with a 'super-deduction' that begins with a so-called Cartesian foundation of *pre-judgmental* states (such as sense data, unclear ideas, or mere 'private representations') in order to ascend then to a proof of 'objectivity' and an external world after all; or, in a direct reversal, to pursue a *strongly regressive* program, i.e. one that bypasses the Transcendental Deduction, assumes specific pure principles such as Newton's laws, and then merely adds to this an abstract account of the faculties involved in this knowledge and an explanation of how the ultimate metaphysical ground of such a science requires the doctrine of transcendental idealism.

I am driven to the hypothesis that there is something like a fatal attraction to think simply in terms of these two extremes; for, when I write that Kant should be read as assuming 'experience' in a relatively 'thick' rather than 'thin', or so-called Cartesian, sense, sometimes it is still thought that this must be tantamount to saying that Kant is always already starting with specific pure or scientific claims that contain much more than the mere fact that there is commonsense experience.[8] This is unfortunate because, although I have used the term 'regressive' ever since my initial characterization of the basic structure of Kant's Deduction, I have never maintained that it is 'strongly' regressive, i.e. that the arguments of the *Critique* must start originally from any higher-level contentious premises such as the truth of *objective a priori* principles or presumptions about any specific physical system. All that is presupposed with my view of the regressive form and commonsense starting point of Kant's arguments (at the most fundamental layers of his transcendental philosophy) is that there is some objectivity to our experience, that some of our states (of a basic kind, i.e. perceptual, moral, aesthetic) are

---

[7] In *Kant and the Fate of Autonomy*, I supplemented this point by arguing that the base, development, and scope of later Idealist systems differ strikingly from Kant's. They all insist on a much less relative basis, a much more tightly connected and unified development of principles, and a denial that the scope of their system leaves any major features of reality undetermined.

[8] See e.g. Daniel Breazeale, 'Two Cheers for Post-Kantianism: A Response to Karl Ameriks', *Inquiry*, 46 (2003), 239–59.

INTRODUCTION

not mere private events but can be justified and are true or false. (This point about Kant's argumentative method is of course in no conflict with allowing that from the start Kant personally never had any doubt about the truth of many pure principles.)

In calling my approach 'regressive' I do *not* mean that it is just like what Kant calls the regressive approach of the *Prolegomena*.[9] That work has a peculiar abbreviated structure, focused mainly on presenting the ultimate *idealistic results* of the first edition of the *Critique of Pure Reason* and defending them from misunderstandings. It therefore largely eschews the details of transcendental argumentation, totally skips the crucial Transcendental Deduction of the categories, and begins with premises that presuppose not only experience but also specific pure and scientific principles. Such a focus is understandable in the *Prolegomena* because its approach is limited and popular, not ground-laying. It is intent above all on defending the original *Critique* against the harsh reviews that focused on the doctrine of transcendental idealism—a doctrine that, whatever its other troubles, properly begins at a point in the argument that already contains premises with pure objective truths. All this is compatible with allowing that there is a more basic but still in some sense regressive argument in Kant's more fundamental discussions in the *Critique*, one that goes from ordinary experience to the original need for pure components.

The very first step of the *Critique*, the mere general characterization of 'experience', starts at a more basic level than the *Prolegomena*. It is thus still a distance from even offering an argument—as Kant does later, in the second step of his system (in the Transcendental Deduction and after)—that specific pure principles (going far beyond mere common sense) are not mere assumptions but can be shown to be necessary. They are needed for us to fill out and give a substantive, informative backing to the presumption of specific kinds of objectivity. For example, Kant argues, and does not simply assume, that the common notion that there are objective and not merely subjective time sequences ultimately requires an appeal to universal principles such as the Second Analogy's general law of causality.[10] Even if the Transcendental Analytic's arguments for such principles are not entirely disconnected from Kant's interest in Newtonianism, they do not (and cannot, if they are to be non-circular) themselves presume any

---

[9] Kant, *Prolegomena to Any Future Metaphysics That Will be Able to Come Forward as Science*, §5, note. Cf. Ch. 1 below, and *Kant and the Fate of Autonomy*, ch. 1. With respect to the Transcendental Aesthetic, there is considerable overlap between Kant's discussion in the *Critique* and that in the *Prolegomena* (and also in his *Inaugural Dissertation*), but this fact does not affect my main point.

[10] One understandable cause of confusion here is the fact that Kant speaks very early on (B5) of our being in 'possession' of certain modes of a priori knowledge, such as the principle of causality. Such talk can be taken as a reminder of what Kant believes is true and commonly believed, and not as something obviating the philosophical project of working out a non-question-begging argument for such a principle. (Otherwise the Second Analogy need not even have been written.)

specific scientific principles. They are aimed explicitly at defending various philosophical principles that are much more general, ones that any developed account of spatio-temporal experience would have to use, were it like Newton's or not.

2.4 The Regressive Approach and Skepticism

If this general interpretation is correct, then there can be, after all, already in the central structure of the first *Critique*, a distinctive and highly relevant moderate alternative to both the strongly progressive and the strongly regressive approaches. On the modest regressive interpretation, the ultimate argumentative starting point of each of the *Critiques* is thicker than a 'mere Cartesian' foundation but much thinner than any claim to an already present natural, moral, or aesthetic science; the original idea is simply that we have some valid everyday theoretical, or practical, or aesthetic judgmental experience.[11] The initial *definition* of experience, and the common manner in which it is recognized in ordinary life, need not contain any explicit pure components. These components are rather something that come to awareness as such only upon philosophical reflection and argument.[12] Moreover, although I have sometimes expressed Kant's reliance on experience in this way in terms of phrases such as 'common sense' or 'common knowledge', this is not meant to imply that Kant had any sympathy for the specific methodology of the 'popular philosophy' of his day or similar movements.[13] Terms such as 'common' or 'ordinary' are admittedly vague, but they have a certain appropriateness, and starting from them does not mean abdicating systematic philosophy's distinctive reflective capabilities and critical duties. Unfortunately, these points were widely misunderstood even in the first years of Kant's reception, a fact I have given an account of elsewhere.[14] But an equally important

---

[11] At the heart of this approach is a general claim that might qualify, like the *cogito*, as 'a priori' in a harmless sense; for the claim that we have experience at all does not itself—in any non-circular way—depend on any *specific* 'path' of experience. See Philip Kitcher, 'A Priori Knowledge', *Philosophical Review*, 89 (1980), 3–23.

[12] There are, of course, some complications here. One is Kant's argument in the Deduction about 'necessity' in our very notion of a perceptual object (B142). I do not want to deny the importance of this passage, but I believe that the meaning of 'necessity' there has to do with a contrast to sheer arbitrariness and a merely subjective as opposed to objective pole of thought, and this is not yet specifically to claim that there is a pure component such as the categories, which plays a universal role throughout experience. On the contrary, the need for the Transcendental Deduction arises in large part from the gap between a general statement that there is some kind of objectivity and a specific conclusion that this is, and must be, made possible for us by the categories. Another complication has to do with the fact that in many basic contexts Kant does help himself to one kind of 'pure' premise, namely mathematics. But even then this presumption is not equivalent to immediately saying that mathematics in this sense has objective validity; until further investigations are conducted it might be pure in meaning, but irrelevant in application, just like some of the Ideas of the Dialectic (see B147).

[13] See my 'Kant on Science and Common Knowledge' in *Kant and the Sciences*, ed. E. Watkins (Oxford, 2001), 31–52.

[14] See *Kant and the Fate of Autonomy*, especially the Introduction and chs. 1–2.

fact that recent research has unearthed is that there was a cell of early readers who were already remarkable clear about Kant's regressive approach. Expressing the view of a significant circle in Jena, Friedrich von Herbert wrote to J. B. Erhard on October 7, 1794 that 'Kant's entire system can be expressed in the hypothetical proposition, "If experience is... then". That experience is, is thereby presupposed, postulated, or however one calls it. Now if a skeptic were dumb and shameless enough to say, "But is there experience?" there is really no answer...'[15]

In saying that Kant begins with this kind of experience and then seeks, in a moderate way, simply to uncover its necessary conditions in a regressive procedure, my interpretations contrast with those that assimilate Kant's work to other recent traditions and assume that he must, above all else, be aiming at the radical project of a refutation of modern skepticism, one that works up in a strong progressive way from a minimal base of brute psychological states, e.g. simple theoretical ideas, completely empirical desires, or merely sensory aesthetic feelings. Because I follow Kant's own special understanding of the notion of experience, my approach does not connect the *Critiques* directly with these common discussions of skepticism. (Nonetheless, my approach is compatible with allowing that Kant was concerned with skeptical problems about the claims of the *higher* faculty of reason, and that relevant skeptical difficulties can arise *after* one accepts the principles of the Critical philosophy and tries to apply them in a concrete way.[16]) Since Kantian 'experience' is not a matter of undergoing bare sensory representations ('blooming, buzzing consciousness') but rather is characterized by judgment (*Erfahrung*, in the sense of 'putative empirical knowledge', or, less misleadingly, 'cognition', since it is compatible with falsehood; see A58/B83), it is something that already makes a claim to an objective status of some kind—e.g., 'the sun warms the stone', 'this kind of intention is wrong', 'this appearance is beautiful'.[17] On this reading, since a modern skeptic typically accepts arguments that start only from 'mere representations' (rather than experience in any objective sense), it is admittedly not clear that any such skeptic need be moved by Kant's main arguments or any simple extension of his approach.[18]

---

[15] Cited in Manfred Frank, '*Unendliche Annäherung*' (Frankfurt, 1997), 507.

[16] See Stephen Engstrom, 'The Transcendental Deduction and Skepticism', *Journal of the History of Philosophy*, 32 (1994), 359–80; and Paul Franks, 'Does Post-Kantian Skepticism Exist?' *Internationales Jahrbuch des deutschen Idealismus/International Yearbook for German Idealism*, 1 (2003), 141–64.

[17] There are of course peculiarities in each of these domains, especially in the case of aesthetics. As Rudolf Makkreel has reminded me, Kant does not literally speak of 'aesthetic experience', and this is understandable because it is not a way of discriminating perceptual objects into natural kinds. Also, although there is a special kind of pure component in aesthetic judgment, the judgment has the logical form of a common empirical judgment, and it does not yield the kind of general a priori principles found in the basic judgments of Kant's theoretical and practical philosophy. See Part III below.

[18] For a very helpful review of the recent tradition of (primarily) British philosophical literature, which in general begins by focusing on transcendental arguments aimed at skepticism, see Robert Stern, 'Introduction', *Transcendental Arguments, Problems and Prospects* (Oxford, 1999), 1–11.

INTRODUCTION

This point is connected with the common objection that, if Kant is allowed to have objectivity already in his premises, then his whole transcendental project is trivialized. As was noted, above, however, it is easy to show that Kant's regressive approach remains distinctive and significant because it does much more than simply reiterate that there is objective experience of various types. It goes on to argue, in considerable detail, for numerous necessary and universal structures for such experience, structures that are not immediately evident and that are quite substantial and controversial. Moreover, these structures also suggest a more general framework which is such that, even if the very specific claims that Kant himself makes turn out to be questionable (which is hard to deny), one can easily imagine more fine-tuned 'successor' families of similar but very interesting and more defensible claims that can be constructed in the 'spirit' of his project.[19]

For one popular and radical line of Kant interpretation, such a result is intolerable insofar as the whole aim of modern philosophy, and of Kant as well, is presumed to be something like the project of working outwards from one's own mind, via an 'objectivity argument', to a demonstration of the existence of the physical world. The tendency to overlook Kant's own moderate regressive approach may thus be explained as arising in part from the general presumption that, if philosophers are not making a kind of 'strong' theoretical argument—something that would directly defeat skepticism from an extremely thin or so-called Cartesian foundation—then their whole project is not very interesting anyway, is not genuinely foundational or 'transcendental' in a good sense, and so it does not matter much what else is going on. The desire to defeat skepticism in this way from the ground up is remarkably widespread, and in our own time it has been reinforced by influential reconstructions such as Strawson's and Rorty's. Whatever its sources and intrinsic interest, I have tried to rebut the *interpretive* presumptions of the strong reading in a number of ways.[20] In addition to repeating that a moderately regressive form of argument clearly matches the headings of Kant's own Transcendental Deduction, which explicitly center on establishing not objectivity as such but rather the objectivity of the *categories* (see §26), given that there is experience, I have stressed that there are a number of understandable reasons why readers could nonetheless have been confused on this basic point.

---

[19] See Michael Friedman, 'Philosophical Naturalism', *Proceedings and Addresses of the American Philosophical Association*, 71 (1997), 7–21.

[20] See Part I below, and *Kant and the Fate of Autonomy*, ch. 5; 'Problems from Van Cleve's Kant: Experience and Objects', *Philosophy and Phenomenological Research*, 63 (2002), 196–202; and 'Idealism from Kant to Berkeley', in *Eriugena, Berkeley and the Idealist Tradition*, ed. Stephen Gersh and Dermot Moran (Notre Dame: Ind., 2003). Some of these points are recognized by others in those parts of the *Transcendental Arguments* volume that refer to specific Kant texts, e.g. Quassim Cassam, 'Self-Directed Transcendental Arguments', 84. Quite apart from Kant, of course, there can remain much intrinsic value in exploring the various kinds of arguments that contemporary philosophers offer against many different types of skepticism, and these are covered very helpfully in *Transcendental Arguments*.

INTRODUCTION

2.5 Obstacles to the Regressive Approach

The sources of confusion here are at once deeply textual, systematic, and historical, but the main problem remains the widespread idea that Kant is starting simply from 'private representations'.[21] There is no doubt that Kant speaks about representation as basic in some sense, simply as the most general term for all components of mental life (A320/B376), and that his extremely influential immediate successor Reinhold made this notion the explicit and supposedly sufficient foundation for his best known and most ambitious system (the theory of the *Vorstellungsvermögen*). The term also plays a central and very different role in some of Kant's expressions of transcendental idealism, as when he says that all we know are representations—but here the term is meant to contrast in a global way with 'thing in themselves' and does not mean anything like individual 'Cartesian' sense data. Unfortunately, interpreters from the eighteenth through the twentieth century have often conflated Kant's transcendental use of the term 'representation' in this way, i.e. as an abbreviation for what the whole sphere of our theoretical knowledge can reach, with a crude empirical use—in other words, as standing for a set of primitive psychological acts.

When Kant himself attempts to characterize the popular notion of representation (A320/B376), he makes quite clear that it is a very primitive term, possibly signifying something as simple as either a bare sensation or 'idea' on its own. Hence it is immediately evident from the most basic and best-known principles of his epistemology ('intuitions without concepts are blind' (A51/B75), and 'the only use which the understanding can make of these concepts is to judge by them' (A68/B93)) that, strictly speaking, 'representation' by itself cannot mean a genuine cognitive state. For Kant a state can become a cognition, something that can be justified or unjustified, true or false, only when it has passed beyond the situation of being a mere psychological representation (the kind of representation that he believes occurs in lower animals) to that of being a cognitive aspect of something that has the logical form of a judgment, i.e. the complex and distinctive epistemic synthesis that Kant believes cannot be found in the many other species of representing beings that are 'lower' than us.

All this is also a reason, I believe, for not even saying that Kant's starting point is mere 'self-consciousness' or the 'unity of our self-consciousness'. 'Self-consciousness', for example, can designate a state of merely passive inner sense, an act of reflection, a sense of indeterminate social unease (in English), or an attitude of immediate confidence (in German)—and in none of these cases does there have to be any judgment or claim that such and such is the case. From such a meager basis, Kant ultimately neither can nor does make a transcendental argument for

---

[21] See e.g. James Van Cleve, *Problems from Kant* (New York, 1999), and Breazeale, 'Two Cheers for Post-Kantianism'; and cf. my essays cited above in nn. 4 and 20.

necessary structures. On the other hand, there surely can exist 'thick' states of 'self-consciousness' that happen to include a specific kind of cognitive representation, a claiming to *know that* something is true about one's self—and from such states Kant can and does go on to make arguments, for example that this may require categories or pure principles. Note that in that event, however, the focus specifically on the self does not do the essential work, and the conclusions can follow simply from the general conditions of the cognitive unity of an act.

Nonetheless, it might well be asked: what about the indisputable fact that Kant does frequently discuss self-consciousness, especially near the beginning of the Deduction—doesn't that mean that some kind of Cartesian basis is present after all? I would argue in just the opposite way: that Kant's discussion of self-consciousness there is most naturally understood as rather a key step precisely in his distinctive *non*-Cartesian strategy. This strategy is strongly emphasized throughout the B edition, especially in the wholescale revision of the Paralogisms. It involves repeatedly arguing that self-knowledge is not fundamental (heuristically or epistemologically) or privileged, but is subject to the same basic structures as knowledge in general. (See B160, which explains that the Deduction concerns 'the unity of the synthesis of the manifold, without or within us'.) What the B Deduction is repeatedly saying—unlike what Descartes, Leibniz, and even the pre-Critical Kant argue—is that *even* the self *knows* (as opposed to merely senses or intuits or has a general concept of) itself *only* via the general rules of synthesis that govern all experience, all putative knowledge claims.[22]

One much discussed example of such a knowledge claim is the mere self-conscious or apperceptive representation of a state that is understood as being 'for' the representing subject. This is not a brute ontological or psychological event but is something with semantic significance, a *claim* that there truly is something specific there 'for me'.[23] To understand the mere idea of such a 'thick' representation, one does not immediately have to decide whether it specifically involves a physical or spatial or other kind of non-solipsistic object. The main point is that, however one goes on to characterize these states, they are always apperceptions and not mere episodes of 'inner sense'. Thus, they are still quite distinguishable from the mere existence of a fuzzy Cartesian image or a bare Humean idea, or any merely clarified or associated or activated concatenation of these. That we in fact (supposedly) must have knowledge of outer spatial things, and never of merely pure inner things, is of course something Kant is eventually very concerned with, but the key argument for this in the *Critique* does not come until long after the Deduction, in the B edition Refutation of Idealism. Confusion may arise here

---

[22] This is a major theme throughout my *Kant's Theory of Mind*, especially chs. 3 and 7.
[23] See my 'Kant and Guyer on Apperception', *Archiv für Geschichte der Philosophie*, 65 (1983), 174–86; 'The Ineliminable Subject: From Kant to Frank', in *The Modern Subject*, ed. K. Ameriks and D. Sturma (Albany, NY, 1995), 217–30; and *Kant and the Fate of Autonomy*, ch. 5.

simply because, even though neither 'representation' nor 'apperception' means specifically *spatio-temporal* putative knowledge, Kant can and does go on eventually to argue that we have no actual states of apperception, or even representation, that *we can examine* that do not already bring with them this kind of knowledge in some way. That is, whenever we try to reflect on something like 'bare' sense data within us, we already understand this reflection itself to be part of the experience of a particular spatio-temporal being, and so at that point the data are obviously not altogether 'bare'.

2.6 Advantages of Modesty in the *Critiques*

In this context the vagueness of the phrases 'bring with' and 'in some way' is intentional and is meant to leave room for a way in which a natural objection to Kant's system can turn out to reveal one of its advantages. Contrary to what is sometimes presumed, Kant's transcendental approach does not insist on an absurd and absolutely 'tight' objective structure for any of the domains of experience. Kant does insist on a plethora of overarching universal principles, but he is quite aware of the fact that even theoretical experience seems 'subjective' at times, i.e. not absolutely rule-bound in a *direct* way, since there are waking thoughts that something 'merely appears to be so', as well as dreams and mental states more primitive than any kind of judgmental experience. Similarly, he realizes that not all of our practical experience involves acting from duty, i.e. for the sake of moral principles, since there are also merely prudential acts, as well as evil acts, indifferent acts, and acts too primitive to be rule-guided in any clear sense. And he knows that not all of our aesthetic experience turns out to be a pure estimation that something is naturally beautiful—since there are also complex ('dependent') judgments about art, about the sublime, and about the non-beautiful, as well as 'aesthetic' feelings of sense that are too primitive to claim any kind of validity.

For all these reasons, it is possible to argue that Kant has a relatively sensible and moderate approach in all the domains with which he is concerned. He has a way of arguing that all experience involves some pure rules, while at the same time he can leave a place for types of experience that make implicit reference to, but do not directly instantiate, the higher forms of objectivity in their domain. The important thing to see is that, on the regressive interpretation, Kant can allow such non-directly rule-governed interludes without having to fall back into the project of trying to build our paradigmatic cognitive states, from the bottom up, out of materials that are completely primitive. Each of the *Critiques* thus has room for three levels of mental life: (1) a crude domain of mere sensation, striving, or feeling; (2) a directly objective level of theoretical, moral, or aesthetic judgment, each with various pure as well as empirical elements; and (3) a mixed level (with numerous subforms), where one judges merely that something appears, say, warm, or practically attractive, or aesthetically appealing to oneself. The third level expresses only how matters 'really seem', and thus it explicitly connects the domains of both objectivity and subjectivity. Yet it does so in a way that is still fundamentally on the objective side insofar as a qualified claim about a state of affairs is still a claim, something with syntactic and semantic structure.[24] Without denying the sheer sensory existence of dimensions of our life that are much more primitive than objective judgment, Kant's system shifts our attention beyond the primitive 'given' of level (1), to spheres where we can move from our original fundamentally objective interpretation of matters at level (2), to take a 'step back' to characterize ourselves in a qualified quasi-objective state at level (3). Hence his discussions of apperception as self-representative (and not only judgmental in general), of practical intentions as leaving room for incorporating maxims that may not be rationally approved, and of aesthetic judgment as involving a special interaction of faculties that is precisely not present in all perception.

Interpretations that avoid the regressive approach are especially susceptible to missing these points. If one supposes, as they do, that Kant is out to defeat forms of skepticism by deducing a form of objectivity directly from the basic notions of representation, or willing, or imaginative sensitivity, then it can seem that the whole apparatus of Kantian principles must determine us from the very first step. We can always represent, or will, or perceive with imagination, and so, if objectivity comes immediately with these capacities, it is unclear how we could ever go wrong, ever be mistaken in a Kantian world. Thus it might seem, as it actually has to many interpreters, that in Kant's system there is no understandable room for perceptually encountering mere subjective time sequences, or for genuinely willing mere subjective, i.e. non-moral, ends, or for finding natural objects that are synthesizable by our perceptual faculties but not beautiful.

On the regressive interpretation, by contrast, such problems seem unlikely from the start. If the first *Critique* is understood regressively as starting with the notion that we have some objective experiences (see Part I below), but that representation by itself is not objective, then this already leaves understandable room for a domain of our theoretical life that is not immediately rule-governed. Similarly, if the second *Critique* (see Part II below) is understood as starting with the notion of a rational moral law that is disclosed to us only as a 'fact' because there is nothing in the mere concept of a free human will that entails the effectiveness of this law, then this already leaves understandable room for a domain of our life that is practical but does not obey moral rules. And if the third *Critique* is understood, as I propose (see Part III below), as taking beautiful

---

[24] See my discussion of this theme in the work of Prauss, Chisholm, and Sellars, in 'Contemporary German Epistemology: The Significance of Gerold Prauss', *Inquiry*, 25 (1982), 125–38. There I discuss the basic idea that talk about appearances is parasitic upon talk about things at an empirical level, but in the next section of this Introduction I argue that this idea also has an important application at the metaphysical level.

INTRODUCTION

forms to be appearances that contingently instantiate a particular kind of accord that fits in especially well with, but is not equivalent to, the general harmony of faculties required by all perception (because this accord happens to allow the harmony to function at a level that is most satisfactory in general), then this already leaves room for a domain of sensory life that does not disclose beauty.

Obviously, many specific questions can be raised about proposals like these, but I hope that they give some indication of how the essays that follow are guided, at least implicitly, by interpretive ideas that are meant to have a bearing on all of the *Critiques* at once. Before sketching the topics of the individual chapters, however, more needs to be said about the most perplexing feature of Kant's Critical philosophy, his idealism.

3. A Not Unrealistic Idealism

The greatest stumbling block for most readers of Kant is no doubt his transcendental idealism, and the problems here might seem only to get worse when that doctrine is approached as it is on my interpretation, with an 'everyday' regressive starting point followed by steps with significant metaphysical implications. To put it mildly, for some readers it may not be easy at first to see how such an approach is consistent with Kant's doctrines that we do not know things in themselves,[25] that our empirical knowledge is exhausted by spatio-temporal determinations that are merely phenomenal, and that non-spatio-temporal things in themselves affect our sensibility. In addition, even if all these notions can be shown to be consistent, it may appear unclear how a regressive interpretation can do justice to the positive intent of Kant's discussion of idealism, which many readers have taken to be dominated by a 'refutation' of skepticism requiring an argument not beginning with any objective claims.

3.1 The 'Refutation of Idealism' as a Regressive Argument

My own response to these difficulties is spelled out in the treatment of the details of several texts discussed in the chapters that follow (as well as in other recent writings[26]); but behind these specific interpretations there is an implicit and more

---

[25] I will always be treating this claim with the implicit restriction that it is meant to exclude only positive *determinate* theoretical knowledge of things in themselves. I take it that Kant does allow theoretically that there are things in themselves and that we can be sure that there are some specific features they do *not* have (e.g. of being spatio-temporal in an absolute sense). Moreover, we can think that, no matter what, they must be in accord with the general categories, and we can also use rational arguments concerning pure practical reason to license more specific positive determinations of some features of things in themselves (e.g. that there is at least some uncaused causation). See below, Chs. 4 and 5, and cf. Van Cleve, *Problems from Kant*; Robert M. Adams, 'Things in Themselves', *Philosophy and Phenomenological Research*, 57 (1997), 801–26; and Langton, *Kantian Humility*.

[26] See the works cited in n. 20 above.

general perspective that it may be helpful to make fully explicit right from the beginning. This perspective aims to defuse common worries about Kant's idealism by distinguishing issues at the level of empirical knowledge and at the level of metaphysics, while still employing a unified regressive strategy for handling questions about how Kant conceived our relation to outer items in these two different senses.

At the empirical level, many unnecessary interpretive problems can arise from simple misunderstandings of Kant's famous Refutation of Idealism (B275-9). For example, this text is often thought of, or even referred to, as a 'refutation of skepticism'—and yet it is quite clear that Kant gave serious thought to the particular title that he finally chose. Hence the position that is the target of Kant's argument here must be clearly delimited from the start, and, in particular, the sense in which it concerns a specific form of 'idealism', rather than skepticism as such, must be determined. Fortunately, this is not very difficult, since in his thesis statement, as well as in his presentation of the argument and the immediate explanatory note on it, Kant is explicit about the limited issue that he is discussing. The Refutation's thesis is that the 'empirically *determined*' consciousness of oneself proves the 'existence of objects in *space* outside of me' (Thesis, B275; my emphasis). Its proof goes through the middle step of discussing what is required for this 'determination' of time, and it concludes (for better or worse—I am focusing here on how the argument is intended and am not evaluating its persuasiveness[27]) that this is possible for us only by reference to a 'permanent' outer (i.e. spatial) thing. Note 1 to the proof then immediately explains that the refuted type of 'idealism' in question is an epistemological position which holds that 'the only immediate experience is inner experience, and that from it we can only *infer* outer things' (B276).

All this shows that traditional skepticism is never directly the issue here. What is at stake are rather two different models of knowledge. The model of what Kant calls 'psychological idealism' (B xln) claims that we know inner matters 'immediately' and can 'only infer' from these to what is outer. Kant's own model holds that, on the contrary, to know at least some determinate facts about oneself, one must first know (again, always in the sense of 'cognitive experience', *erfahren*, which allows for being fallible) something about what is 'outer', i.e. that there is something spatial and therefore something empirically distinct from one's own representations. Thus, even the Refutation turns out to presume the same kind of commonsense objective attitude that the regressive interpretation in general imputes to Kant. This implies that for anyone starting from a fully skeptical position, with nothing more than one's own representations, and no knowledge at

---

[27] See *Kant's Theory of Mind*, ch. 3, for a critical analysis of this argument and its relation to other texts such as the A edition.

all, no 'determination' of oneself, there is no direct connection with Kant's argument.[28] Kant's argument explicitly presumes that there is some kind of elementary factual knowledge, some kind of temporal determination. Then it asks whether this comes in the form of knowledge of inner things always preceding that of outer things, or whether it is rather the case that inner temporal knowledge is always (or at least sometimes—Kant might have more cautiously argued) parasitic on outer temporal knowledge. Kant's conclusion (note that this is a *specific conclusion* and not the same thing as the *more general* objective starting point) is nothing other than that outer knowledge must come first. This result is a very significant reversal of the so-called Cartesian tradition, but the most remarkable point is that the argument always moves at a level in which some knowledge is presumed, and there is simply a regressive question being raised about whether in the first instance this knowledge has to be of something spatial. All this is consistent with allowing the existence of merely subjective states 'prior' to such knowledge, as long as it is understood that these states as such are not themselves known and used as a ground for inference.

There are many reasons why some readers might miss these points. One is that Kant speaks about what our 'consciousness' or 'experience' requires, and these are terms that have fundamentally non-cognitive meanings for many readers. Hence the hasty empiricist might easily overlook the fact that when Kant uses these terms he is generally speaking of 'determined' consciousness, i.e. cognitive experience, and not brute sense data. Nonetheless, the main text is explicit on this point, and in a footnote Kant reiterates: 'but through inner experience I am conscious of my existence in time (consequently also of its determinability in time) and this is more [NB] than to be merely conscious of my representations' (B xln).

This point might have been better appreciated were it not for another source of confusion, the fact that Kant indicates in this footnote that his discussion is meant to meet the 'scandal' (B xln) of the problem of an external world. This can make it look as if a direct argument against radical skepticism is intended after all. But the first sentence of this footnote makes it clear that Kant's 'proof' is aimed at nothing other than what he calls 'psychological idealism', i.e. the position directly

---

[28] A response to skepticism can no doubt be *indirectly* connected with Kant's Refutation. For example, the argument of the Refutation may make the typical philosopher interested in skepticism reflect on the ambiguity in starting with anything like a 'Cartesian basis', and to appreciate the importance of the fact that this basis must be understood as either including inner experience in Kant's sense or being restricted to something much more primitive (typically, the skeptic tries in bad faith to have it both ways, to combine the psychological immediacy of the latter with the epistemic accomplishment of the former). If the basis is specified as including the former 'thicker' notion, then it becomes subject to the argument of Kant's Refutation; and if it specified as restricted to only the latter 'thinner' notion, then the Refutation can thereby indirectly force the question of whether that is an appropriate starting point. The fact of our fallibility about particular external claims cannot by itself justify using the thinner basis, because this point is also appreciated on the alternative, 'thicker' approach. Moreover, the thinner approach cannot be defended as withdrawing to a safer, more modest level of claims, for it is withdrawing from the cognitive level of claim-making altogether, and thus it has an extremely artificial relation to our actual consciousness.

countered in the main text by the regressive strategy explained earlier. Moreover, there is an obvious source for Kant's talk of 'scandal' and his special irritation here: namely, the fact that the highly influential figure F. H. Jacobi had just written a book insisting that the claim that there are outer things must be literally a matter of 'faith' (B xl, note a).[29] Kant's reaction is not surprising in this context, since his Critical work is totally opposed to mixing mystical or religious language in this way with fundamental theoretical issues.

More generally, Kant's deep uneasiness with the invocation of 'faith' here is an indication of his commitment to getting completely beyond the old polar options of thinking that our access to basic truths must be through either strict proof from a precognitive basis (simple representations, brute sense data) or some kind of special quasi-religious 'leap'. The relevant but all too neglected third option is to allow that in fact there can be some objectivity that we all accept and realize that we accept, and that it is perfectly in order philosophically (even if it is not a matter of taking up the most challenging of tasks) to start from this acceptance. Once the role of this perspective in his thought is appreciated, it is not surprising to find that Kant ignores solipsism and stays focused on what he calls 'our mode of perceiving', which he presumes is 'peculiar to us, and not necessarily shared in by every being, though certainly [N.B.] by every human being' (A42/B59). This is similar to the regressive way in which the second *Critique* takes the categorical authority of morality to be a basic 'fact of reason'. As such a 'fact', it is not deducible from any skeptical or 'neutral' basis; and as rooted immediately in 'reason', it is independent of any special individual 'faith', or even any extra acts of rational postulation like those in Kant's own arguments concerning the implications of the idea of the highest good. Likewise, the third *Critique*'s treatment of taste is aimed at those who are interested in working non-reductively in this domain from a phenomenon of judgments that are taken to have some kind of common 'validity'.

3.2 The Regressive Approach and Transcendental Idealism

Kant believes there is no reason to expect that his initial objective and common-sense attitude toward the basic facts of these domains will be undermined by his own merely 'formal' or 'transcendental' idealism, since this is a metaphysical doctrine that concerns a different level of issues. It aims not to deny or give a

---

[29] 'Faith' is the central theme of a major book by Jacobi, published in 1787, *David Hume über den Glauben, oder Idealismus und Realismus*. Jacobi appropriated Hume's doctrine of belief for an anti-rationalist version of Christian fundamentalism, immediately setting Kant's teeth on edge. Jacobi did not have a trustworthy grasp of Kant's distinction between empirical and transcendental externality, but his work played an extremely important role in forcing thinkers of the period to compare Kant and Spinoza. See my 'Idealism from Kant to Berkeley', and 'Kant, Fichte, and Short Arguments to Idealism', *Archiv für Geschichte der Philosophie*, 72 (1990), 63–85.

further internal description of the objectivity of experience, but rather (given the assumption that it exists) to make it 'intelligible' (B41) globally by putting it in a context that can allow philosophers to meet the puzzles about it that are generated upon reflection. To be a strong 'non-Cartesian' empirical realist, and to conclude, as Kant's Refutation does, that within our experience outer knowledge precedes inner knowledge, is still not to say whether the determinate contents of that knowledge must be transcendentally real rather than ideal. This is a matter to be resolved only in a further step, by a metaphysical consideration of the ultimate nature of the main features that we can determine of the empirical domain, namely space and time. Eventually, Kant holds that theoretical philosophy requires a non-psychological but still idealistic interpretation of *these features*. Hence he calls his position a 'formal' idealism, i.e. a position that denies only the absolute reality of these formal determinations and not the existence of things themselves. This is a radical conclusion, but it is important to keep in mind that Kant believes it is one that is required only because of difficulties that arise after reflection—in what I called step three of his system—on very specific a priori spatio-temporal features characteristic of our empirical domain. These are therefore difficulties that can be determined *only after* spelling out (in what I called steps 1 and 2) the *Critique*'s general objective starting point and its implications.

In the practical realm, Kant's idealism appears to arise at a slightly later point. Even though the most basic principles that the Critical moral theory develops are also a priori, they do not essentially involve space and time, and hence they do not themselves generate an argument for transcendental idealism in the way that the spatio-temporal antinomies and epistemological perplexities of theoretical reason do.[30] Nonetheless, Kant makes it clear that transcendental idealism is needed for the practical domain as well, and that, even though it comes in at a later point in the course of exposition, it has a kind of metaphysical priority. The doctrine is revealed to be an essential precondition for our *holding onto* pure practical reason after reflection, because supposedly it alone can provide room for the kind of absolute freedom that Kant assumes we all suppose any accountable action requires. Given the Newtonian revolution and Kant's argument for a universal law of causality, there is no room for uncaused causes within experience. Hence freedom is possible only if there is, as transcendental idealism says, something more than the features of spatio-temporal experience. (This assumption is criticized in the essays that follow, but nothing in this criticism affects the point that at the level of interpretation Kant should be understood as arguing regressively in the second *Critique*.)

In the domain of aesthetics, the doctrine of transcendental idealism plays a less central role, but eventually it is also explicitly invoked in the third *Critique* (see

[30] On this point I disagree with John Rawls' very important and influential account of Kant in *Lectures on the History of Moral Philosophy*, ed. B. Herman (Cambridge, Mass., 2000), p. 239.

especially §58). The doctrine remains at least consistent with the *Critique of Judgment*'s opening reprise of the first *Critique*'s empirical realism about ordinary perception. Kant's backing of the universal significance of the pure claims of taste has some similarities with his earlier considerations about space and time as our basic and universal forms of perception, but the 'universality' of taste does not by itself strictly require transcendental idealism. The doctrine is invoked later, however, in a positive way that invokes themes of the second *Critique*, when it is introduced as the best way to make sense of the deeper moral dimensions of pure aesthetic sensitivity and the idea that this sensitivity points to a 'noumenal substrate'.[31] In sum, in all three *Critiques* Kant introduces his doctrine of transcendental idealism only in a context in which some kind of objectivity in our experience is already presumed.

3.3 Things in Themselves as a Common Ground, Not a Transcendent Inference

Even if all this reveals how a regressive interpretation of Kant's system as a whole can fit his general non-Cartesian approach to empirical knowledge and, at the very least, leave some room for exploring the notion of transcendental idealism, there remain many thorny details concerning another major challenge that Kant's idealism presents for anything like common sense, namely his metaphysical doctrine of things in themselves. The traditional difficulties here concern, first, the internal and external coherence of the idea of such things, then problems in seeing how such things could ever be asserted to exist, and finally the issue of understanding how, from a purely theoretical perspective, Kant can claim that there actually exist such things and that they affect us. These very complicated issues obviously cannot even begin to be covered in any detail here, but in this introductory discussion it may be possible to indicate the general contours of my

---

[31] The second and third *Critiques* are also very similar in emphasizing two very basic forms of 'optical illusion' (V: 116–17) that Kant believes are found in those who lack an appreciation for transcendental idealism. Because of the intensity of the feeling of moral respect, we might suppose that here it is sensibility rather than reason that guides our proper everyday judgment. Kant's idealism, however, allows us to reverse our perspective and to regard even this feeling as rooted in a deeper, non-empirical ground, a noumenal acceptance of morality that has empirical feelings and phenomenal judgments as its derivative expressions. Similarly, the intensity of a genuine aesthetic feeling may mislead the empiricist into thinking that it is the ground of the judgment of taste, whereas the transcendentalist can regard that feeling as well as rooted in something deeper, in this case a special interaction of faculties that has various empirical feelings and phenomenal judgments as its derivative expressions (§9). This 'harmony' also has an analog in the first *Critique*, for it is nothing other than a special variety of the general harmonious combination of basic perceptual faculties that is thematized in the *Critique of Pure Reason*. In fact, insofar as it is tied directly to perceptual contexts, the 'pure' element of taste is not so much like the second *Critique*'s noumenal moral will—which can be understood as accepting morality for its own sake in a way that does not need any spatio-temporal characterization—as like the pure element of a typical judgment of experience in the first *Critique* (e.g. 'the river pushed the boat down the stream'), which necessarily combines a pure principle (causality) with a spatio-temporal specification and empirical instantiation.

perspective in a way that can at least explain why these well-known problems have not seemed totally overwhelming to me.

Matters can seem insuperably difficult, no doubt, *if* one begins, as many do, with the presumption that *in general* a thing in itself (even when its existence is denied, or when it is affirmed in a serious ontological sense and not reduced to a matter of a mere methodological perspective)[32] must be understood as being a peculiar kind of wholly *transcendent* entity *by definition*, something that could be approached only by building all sorts of tenuous argumentative bridges from appearances within us. An alternative approach—and one that I see as reflecting Kant's own historical and logical trajectory—is to leave open the thought that sometimes it can be proper to *start* instead with things in themselves, so that the relevant question becomes: What *else* might there be to talk about? In other words, in some contexts (and, I will argue, in fact the most common ones) it can be talk about appearances (in some non-trivial sense), rather than about things, that calls for explanation.

Before developing this approach, however, it must be noted that in *some* contexts for Kant there is no getting around thinking of a thing in itself that is transcendent in a strong sense, one that involves existence clearly separate from the whole realm of sensible appearances and human theoretical knowledge. It is evident from the *results* of Kant's work, and especially the implications of his practical doctrines, that he holds that there are a number of different kinds of such transcendent things in themselves—and that this is not an unusual belief.[33] God, as the coordinator of the highest good, is taken to be properly thought of as a thing in itself that is not literally a part of the world but is in an intricate one-way causal relation to the cosmos. Finite selves, such as the moral persons that human beings take themselves to be, have a closer relation to the empirical domain. Whereas it would seem that Kant's God (I mean the 'classical Critical' God, i.e. the pre-*opus postumum* deity of the postulates) might easily exist without there ever having been any other concrete beings, the thing in itself that is a finite self's soul and free will might need some sensible being to affect and to 'attach' to at some point, although it certainly cannot (for Kant) be strictly identical with or dependent on its mere sensible effects.

---

[32] See above, n. 25. In a helpful Introduction in *Idealism and Freedom* (p. 5), Henry Allison begins a discussion of those who are critical 'of anything like what Karl Ameriks has termed a "short argument" to transcendental idealism from the mere conception of an epistemic condition'. He goes on to criticize other interpreters and to reformulate his own reading of transcendental idealism so that it is expressed not merely in terms of an epistemic condition and includes reference to the role of specific forms of intuition; but he does not, as far as I can see, directly argue against my preference for a metaphysical reading of Kant.

[33] Since the first issue here is simply whether we might coherently think about such things, and not whether we can offer compelling theoretical arguments about them, the evidence of Kant's lectures on metaphysics and philosophical theology, and their lengthy discussion of traditional 'transcendent' metaphysical and theological concepts, is also very relevant.

INTRODUCTION

The most relevant implication of these points here is that they count against any interpretation that takes Kant's notion of a thing in itself in general to be either totally negative or simply the notion of some 'ordinary' aspect of or standpoint on empirical things. Unfortunately, once it is granted in this way that there can be some things in themselves, such as God and finite free wills, that are only loosely related to sensible appearances, this may seem to make it even harder to understand the relation between 'ordinary' things in themselves (i.e. those concerning merely physical objects) and sensible appearances. Nonetheless, for items in this realm of 'non-personal' being, Kant presents no doctrines of pure practical reason that would imply that they have a fully separate existence like that of God or other souls, which are beings that might well exist at some point 'unattached' to sensible things altogether. Thus, as far as reason leads us, 'non-personal' things in themselves (if there are any) at least do not appear to *have to be as* separate from experience as other things in themselves. This is a result that at least says something, but unfortunately it still does not tell us very much; hence Stanley Cavell's vivid (but not quite literally meant) response to Kant's metaphysics: 'thanks for nothing'.[34]

Can we say anything more positive about this realm—for example, something very simple about how to think of its quantity? On this question Kant is at times explicitly agnostic: empirically, we use our theoretical knowledge to divide items in line with the determinations of space and time, but however that division ends up,[35] it is in principle not to be assumed to be isomorphic to the pattern of ('ordinary') things in themselves.[36] Moreover, there are no promising theoretical arguments for concluding that these 'things' constitute an all-inclusive singularity, or that they amount to a plurality of beings.

A kind of agnostic response to these issues seems understandable, but it cannot be the last word, given that Kant also has deep substantive commitments that count against ever accepting some logically possible options. In particular, if it is allowed that there might be only one thing in itself, then a situation like solipsism or Spinozism appears to follow, and we know that Kant definitely did not want these options left open. But if he excludes them, what might his ground be? And, whatever it is, how can he use it without violating his own claims about the fundamental limits to our knowledge of things in themselves?

---

[34] Stanley Cavell, *In Quest of the Ordinary: Lines of Skepticism and Romanticism* (Chicago, 1988), 31.

[35] There are also problems with counting ultimate 'things' even at the empirical level in Kant's system. Some of Kant's language points to an interaction of innumerable tiny forces, but other considerations suggest that he might allow that the total sphere of physical interaction is one entity, a cosmic field. The Critical philosophy has its own special problems here, but since contemporary physics and ontology run into many of the same conundrums, or worse, there is no special reason to press this issue against Kant.

[36] The trouble with asserting an 'isomorphism' of members at the phenomenal and noumenal levels is that this would conflict with transcendental idealism's implications for our theoretical ignorance about particular noumena. See Ch. 2 below, n. 7, and cf. Van Cleve, *Problems from Kant*, ch. 10, and John Findlay's much too neglected *Kant and the Transcendental Object* (Oxford, 1981).

INTRODUCTION

I believe that the proper way to begin to understand Kant's views here is to recognize that from the very beginning of his career he always starts from, and holds to, the fact that there is a real interaction of finite substances. From the beginning, he explicitly distances himself from Berkeley, Leibniz, Spinoza, Malebranche, Hume, and others whose systems he takes to deny such interaction.[37] Moreover, Kant thinks that interactionism is not only the best philosophical theory, but also the position that ordinary people all hold, just as he thinks we all hold that human beings all 'certainly' have the same basic forms of sensibility. In a deep sense, he assumes it to be literally the common position that should be the starting point for all sensible philosophical work. Although Kant allows that 'logically' the solipsistic idealist's hypothesis cannot be defeated, he proceeds from what he takes to be a common ground on which this hypothesis is irrelevant: we are finite beings always believing that we are affected by at least some other finite beings, and we recognize that other personal beings also hold that. Kant does not mean that this common ground is a matter of 'faith', something that we make an effort to hold onto or that requires a special intuitive faculty or complex speculative or emotional attitude. While he believes that all alternatives to this view can, after full philosophical examination, be shown to have serious difficulties, he does not claim that this process of examination is logically conclusive, and it is not how he supposes that people in general arrive at, or ever need to arrive at, the common ground.

3.4 The Metaphysical Dimension of the Common Ground

This may all seem sensible enough if understood merely at an empirical level, but Kant also takes the notion of interaction to have some kind of deep significance at the level of metaphysics, to signify a truth that ultimately cannot be spelled out in ordinary spatio-temporal terms. Is not this kind of claim vulnerable to the external criticism of being a form of old-fashioned dogmatism, or to the internal criticism that it is precisely the kind of position that Jacobi and others took to be directly ruled out by transcendental idealism's own restrictions?

These are perplexing issues, but I believe there is a natural but neglected way to find a consistent response available for Kant here, one that goes along lines that are distinct from, but still very close to, the regressive response discussed earlier concerning the empirical problem of external knowledge. If the thought of our fundamental metaphysical relation to external things in themselves affecting us involves a knowledge claim that is an *inference* from empirical givens within us, then the situation does seem dire. On Kant's own account, all our theoretical

---

[37] See below, Chs. 4 and 5, and *Kant's Theory of Mind*, ch. 3. Cf. Eric Watkins, 'Kant's Theory of Physical Influx', *Archiv für Geschichte der Philosophie*, 77 (1995), 285–324. See also *Lectures on Metaphysics Immanuel Kant*, 5–6.

causal inferences are restricted to an employment of the Second Analogy, and its principle is restricted to contexts where all the items are empirical. If somehow, literally miraculously, we did get an exemption to use the principle in this situation, then it would seem that we could know things beyond experience in a way that makes pointless the *Critique*'s whole effort to restrict our theoretical knowledge.

For Kant there is an alternative, however, to appealing to the dogmatism or inconsistency of using particular transcendent inferences. The solution is to reiterate the regressive approach discussed earlier and to note that, although in ordinary life its starting point tends to be understood originally in empirical terms, its core idea can be expressed in a way that does not depend on any specific empirical, i.e. spatio-temporal, details. Because of its independence from spatio-temporality, this core idea (one might think of it as the residue of a kind of Kantian 'realist' phenomenological reduction) is for Kant a general *metaphysical* thought: we each implicitly assume, and we accept that others similarly assume, that we are finite and receptive beings, and so there is something not entirely in us that allows us to come into direct contact with something other than ourselves.

Theoretically, of course, we could go on to rehearse various speculative doubts about this idea, in a spirit similar to those that are raised in the *Meditations*, and could then construct a response like the one that Descartes offers—but that is not in fact what any of us do, and it is not what Kant ever does or proposes. To be sure, by the eighteenth century, alternatives to even this minimal form of interactionism are hardly unheard of, hardly a matter of sheer madness, an abdication of reason, or a fascination with evil demons. The followers of Spinoza, Leibniz, Hume, and others offer ingenious systems with revisionist philosophical hypotheses about non-interactionist ways to consider and in effect think away 'the world'—but Kant does not follow their path for a moment, and it is not clear that he is proceeding improperly. A similar strategy can be employed for responding to objections to Kant concerning matters such as the problem of other minds, or worries about how the phenomenal side of one's own self lines up with its unknown and inaccessible aspects. In such cases it is only fair for a Kantian to hold that, if there are *no specific* reasons to say that things are definitely unlike what we ordinarily suppose, we have a right to go on and continue to believe what we all already do believe. That is, it is not fair to make a special objection to Kant simply because he—like all other philosophers—has not come up with an airtight metaphysical argument about such matters as how to 'prove' other minds, or other beings at all.

Here some might be tempted by the thought of a reliance on *practical* reason as the ultimate Kantian foundation for the claim that there is something metaphysically external. I would hesitate to encourage such a proto-Fichtean interpretation, because (1) Kant does not explicitly argue in this way; (2) it could make externality insecure for all those who are not thinking properly of their practical rationality;

INTRODUCTION

(3) Kant's appeals to practical reason (in its fundamental pure sense) appear rather to presuppose various theoretical doctrines that would make a practical argument to externality redundant, since his theoretical argument for transcendental idealism (which is the condition for holding on to pure practical reason) involves an already *non*-practically secured space for absolute freedom in a realm of external things in themselves; and (4) it is not clear how such a practical argument could succeed by itself, since phenomenal markers are needed to pick out the relevant appearances that are worthy of being treated as involving metaphysical externality. If such markers are taken to be by themselves sufficient, it would seem that the turn to the practical is not needed; and if they are not so taken, choosing to emphasize any particular instance would seem arbitrary.

The alternative to this approach, the regressive strategy, does not say that there is a *ground* for the claim of metaphysical externality in an *immediate* deliverance of our pure practical reason. Instead, it says that, while our general commonsense and practical commitment to other beings does in fact bring 'with it' the thought that there is really something out there, absolutely speaking, this thought is already accepted in a more basic form that does not have to involve specific practical claims. The idea of a basic theoretical acceptance of metaphysical interactionism thus does not provide a specifically 'practical foundation', but it can make it at least understandable that in ordinary practical life we do not have to begin second-guessing and then find a proof (in a purely practical argument) to respond to a general worry that there is nothing 'out there' after all.[38]

3.5 The Coherence of Metaphysical Interactionism

Before going on to describe how Kant's metaphysical interactionism can properly proceed, some additional radical objections to its very idea still need to be considered and disarmed. Even if it is allowed that there is an acceptance of metaphysical interactionism in Kant that can be distinguished from any kind of ordinary knowledge claim resting on particular empirical or a priori *inferences*, or special intuition ('faith'), and even if this acceptance is taken to reflect a truly common 'belief' (I use this very vague word here only for lack of a better term; it is meant to signify a positive 'doxastic attitude' but not anything involving special effort or reflection), there are those who would object that the *content* of the belief is internally unsustainable. The most familiar form of this objection comes from a kind of concept empiricism, from those who suppose that terms such as 'plural' and 'causal' (hence 'finite' and 'passive') and 'thing' can have only a sensory meaning for Kant. This objection picks up understandably on Kant's own strong

---

[38] Although it would be highly anachronistic, one way to understand this idea may be to think of it as in part a transcendental theoretical marriage of some of the ideas of Alvin Plantinga (on 'basic beliefs') and Ludwig Wittgenstein (on 'certainty').

emphasis on sensible experience, but the obvious problem with such an objection is that it wholly discounts the center of Kant's philosophy, his Metaphysical Deduction and account of the categories. Precisely because he is not an empiricist, and precisely because he has an account of the origin of these pure concepts that traces them to logical forms that are not restricted to sensory contexts, it is easily possible for him consistently to introduce terms not determined by any sensory evidence.

Despite its obvious limitations, the empiricist reading of Kant has sources in various strands of the text that can easily mislead readers. Kant has a tendency to abbreviate his position (e.g. B298/A239), and often he will simply call some terms 'meaningless' when it is very clear on reflection that he must mean no more than what we would express by saying they do not yield a warranted theoretical claim about a particular individual. Concepts without demonstrable matching intuitions cannot be totally meaningless, or 'empty' in the radical sense of being equivalent to nothing, for on Kant's own theory many of them can be easily distinguished from each other. The unschematized ideas of substance, quantity, quality, and so forth are not the same as each other, and hence must have some differences in content. Otherwise, there would be no way to make sense of Kant's initial account of the relation of these ideas to the pure forms of judgment, an account that totally abstracts from any particular type of intuition. This is precisely what sets up the problem of the Transcendental Deduction of the categories, which is the task of showing how concepts that have an origin and formal meaning apart from sensory intuition can nonetheless have a necessary application to the objects of our particular kind of intuition.

Another influential source of confusion here is a misunderstanding of the images of Kant's 'Copernican' turn. At first, Kant's discussion of this idea does seem to say that we should think simply in terms of representations and concepts 'within us' rather than in terms of any objects and truths that are there independently, outside of us. But a closer reading reveals that the text's main point is merely to indicate, in anticipation, a way of thinking that 'would agree better with what is desired, namely, that it should be possible to have knowledge of objects a priori' (B xvi). In other words, the real issue here is how to make sense of our objective a priori *knowledge*, and this very question presupposes a context in which it is allowed that there is knowledge of objects ('that experience in which they can be known... for experience itself is a species of knowledge', B xvii) and, at some point, even pure knowledge. The Copernican thought is introduced simply as a clue to Kant's eventual proposal for the best explanation of this fact. Kant's ultimate answer, of course, is that the pure *forms* of sensibility, and all the particular cognitions that they determine, are transcendentally ideal (and in this sense *they* are not independent of 'us' in general). This may be a remarkable conclusion, but it is compatible with starting with, and holding onto, all sorts of undisputed empirical facts, as well as with never taking back the thought of an actual metaphysical relation to a non-ideal 'matter' of things (a 'matter' that is not theoretically determinable by us, and is not meant to serve in any way as a 'standard' for measuring claims within the empirical realm). In other words, even Kant's 'Copernican turn' is in no way a reduction of things to a mere figment of empirical minds.

3.6 The Regressive Approach and Metaphysical Interactionism

All the same, even if it is not internally incoherent to ascribe to Kant a position called 'metaphysical' interactionism, it may seem wrong for him to introduce such a seemingly mysterious complication, especially if it is denied that it is rooted in any special inference or intuition. Is there anything that can be said in behalf of Kant's *affirming* an actual, and not merely possible, form of interaction (in a non-practical, non-personal context) in a concrete *non-empirical* sense? I think that there is, but it is simply a matter of further clarifying the regressive strategy already introduced, while continuing to distance oneself from the 'inference' model that might seem to be the most natural way to understand the route to things in themselves.

If Kant were to present his position as an argumentative inference (either inductive or deductive) from sensations, and especially as a claim thereby to know with certainty something *specific* and transcendent, then he would be subject to all sorts of strictures from Hume, Jacobi, and his own *Critique*. But Kant's 'formal idealism' is not set out as such an inference, or even as an inference to something new at all. Kant starts by going along with the common thought that there are things distinct from us. Then he subtracts from the intrinsic characterization of those things whatever features turn out not to be able to be consistently ascribed to them in that way. Finally, he concludes not that there is nothing, but rather that some 'matter' (not in a physicist's sense, but just in the commonsense starting-point sense of 'something or other out there') still exists, and it is such that it cannot in itself have the specific spatio-temporal 'forms' that our experience manifests. There is nothing absurd in saying all this while continuing to believe that distinct thing(s) in themselves definitely exist in contact with us, but that theoretically 'we know not what' they are like otherwise in a positive way. Moreover, although the nature of these things is not within the specific content of our empirical knowledge, they do not have to be thought of as 'strongly' transcendent in the way in which Kant thinks (on practical grounds) that God is, or that our souls might be, i.e. able to exist in some contexts that are completely out of touch with sensory existence. The main point here is that there is nothing in any of Kant's arguments about the ideality of spatio-temporality that ever involves taking back the most fundamental aspect of his starting position, which is simply the metaphysical claim that we are receptive to other things and there is something more than our individual finite being.

This metaphysical understanding of Kant's starting point fits the fact that, in developing all sorts of ways (everyday, scientific, and philosophical) to determine features of our specific kind of experience for the purpose of the prediction and empirical explanation of other things, we never have a good reason for *insisting* that these *specific* spatio-temporal facts literally characterize things in themselves. On reflection, we can learn to hold that there is a huge store of highly useful theoretical common knowledge of this sort that *might not* at all reveal the ultimate nature of things as such, even while we recognize that this precaution still leaves us, in contrast, completely certain about our initial thought that confronting us there exists something *simpliciter*, i.e. in itself. (Think of how Aristotelian 'knowledge' functioned until Newton, and think of what might have been if nothing like Newton or Einstein had been.) *For a while*, we could of course also *suppose* that the empirical determinations that we obtain do reflect the ultimate inner nature of things—if not exactly, then at least in principle, or 'confusedly'. The mere transcendental distinction between the thought of how things appear and how they are in themselves is not yet a transcendental idealist claim about specific features, a claim that these features of experiences are definitely *not* features of things in themselves. But Kant does go on to take the step of transcendental idealism, and this involves the additional and very strong claim that for us any belief in a traceable 'reflection' of things in themselves in appearances must be wrong, since the Antinomies supposedly show that the spatio-temporal pattern central to the features determining our theoretical knowledge is such that it cannot be the same as the intrinsic structure of things. (The Transcendental Aesthetic argues that transcendental realism about space and time is pointless and mysterious, but the clinching argument for Kant's idealism seems to me to require the Antinomies.) The persuasiveness of this particular argument is not of concern here. The main point for the prior issue of interpretation is simply that, even if his most radical idealist claims are left unquestioned, Kant is in a situation where he has not given, and does not mean or need to give, the slightest ground for doubting that we are always, all along, literally in touch with things in themselves, with the fact of their existence confronting us.

To recapitulate: Kant's starting thought is that non-personal thing(s) really affect us. For us this thought may come initially with specific empirical accompaniments, but none of them are essential to it. The thought then can be transformed from an ambiguous general claim that there is some finite interaction into a statement specifically about interaction with a definitely *non*-empirical meaning. The final step is a firm one, however, only when it is established, in the last stages of Kant's argument, that the interaction cannot be fully accounted for in what we call empirical terms, because there is something fundamentally

INTRODUCTION

non-ultimate about the specific spatio-temporal features that define empirical explanation for us. Unlike his talk about God or freedom, Kant's talk about ordinary, i.e. non-personal, things in themselves is in a sense theoretically direct, even if it is also in a sense opaque. That such things are there at all seems to be given to us in a kind of direct reference and immediate thought. That these things cannot be in themselves similar to the empirical (i.e. spatio-temporal) features that we are familiar with from the first is a point that we come to see only after considerable reflection (although Kant believes that a similar point is already at least implicit in our first common practical thoughts about freedom). So in one sense they are right with us, and yet what they are remains beyond us. Or to put the point poetically, Hölderlin said that God is 'near and hard to grasp' (*Nah ist/ und schwer zu fassen der Gott*), but Kant would more likely say this about 'ordinary' things in themselves—and also that we all do and should believe this.

This metaphysically described starting point is similar to, but distinct from and in a sense more basic than, the empirically described regressive starting point discussed earlier, because it entails *only that* there are other *being*(s) that affect us. It does not itself make the basic claim of the empirical level that we have some *determinate* knowledge about empirically distinct facts, i.e. determinations of either temporal or spatial features. There is nothing in the metaphysical starting point alone that conflicts with this claim, however, and there is even some sort of positive connection between the two claims. Kant appears to think that, whenever there is some empirical knowledge and empirical affection, there is some kind of belief in a metaphysical relation, too (i.e. that we are receptive to things in themselves)—although the reverse claim need not be held. It is likely, for example, that Kant pictures the situation of brute animals as one in which representing subjects in themselves are also affected by real things in themselves, but in such a way that, although some kind of representations arise, empirical knowledge and cognitively determined appearances do not result.

Having said all this, I am not denying that philosophers might well continue to ask questions such as: How do we know that we aren't merely manufacturing everything out of our own secret resources? Or, how do we know that we are not any more than a part or aspect of one all-inclusive being? However, *if* Kant's prime offense is simply that he does not think that he or others should spend much time on such worries, then it can hardly be objected that in this respect his position, his *merely formal* idealism, is the one that must sound overly speculative and absurd to common people.

This is about as far as my apologetics for transcendental idealism go. I do not go so far as to endorse Kant's own confident claims that (1) space and time *must* be ideal; (2) 'psychological idealism' has been refuted a priori; and (3) morality, and even our common belief about or attachment to it, *clearly* requires the doctrine of transcendental freedom. Nonetheless, I believe we would do well to remain guided by Kant's even more basic ideas that (1) experience in a cognitive sense is the best starting point for philosophy; (2) it is productive to work from this starting point to seek relevant necessary truths and philosophical framework principles for experience in general, and for each of the more specific basic varieties of human experience, as well as for the ('moderate') interconnection of all our branches of common knowledge; and (3) the development of such principles should leave room for important truths that may transcend any completely empirical or natural determination (e.g. that there are subjects of experience and non-relative values, and perhaps inner natures of physical things that are too subtle for our science ever to be able to grasp, even in principle).

In addition, although I am not endorsing Kant's doctrine of the ideality of space and time, or its claim that we are fundamentally receptive in a sense that not only has a transcendental epistemological dimension (expressing a general structural characteristic of sensible knowledge) but also requires concrete metaphysical relations (affection by things in themselves as non-spatio-temporal), I believe that Kant deserves more credit than he is generally given for appreciating the different levels that are involved here. Some common criticisms of Kant seem to suggest that he means his metaphysical 'story' about things in themselves to be a relevant 'explanation' of the general process of our cognition, or even that it is introduced precisely as a supernatural mechanism to make sense of specific given facts, and ultimately in a way that undercuts their common validity.[39] Sometimes such a story is objected to not only on the grounds that there aren't any accessible 'gears' here of the sort that would be needed for any genuinely helpful explanation, but also because things in themselves are supposedly beyond concepts altogether, and so never could be part of an 'explanation' that might be accurate in principle, even if in fact we could never use it.

Kant, however, does not make either of these mistakes. First, he can consistently hold that talk about things in themselves is not absurd or mere empty words, beyond concepts altogether, because (as was noted above in Section 3.5) we can think of them intelligibly, even if not very informatively, in terms of all the unschematized categories. Second, whatever the structure is of these things in themselves, Kant never proposes that that is where we should expect explanations of specific facts in our experience. On the contrary, these are all to be explained (insofar as *we can use* the term 'explanation' meaningfully) autonomously, by the details of the regressive accounts provided by transcendental arguments or other modes of ascertaining what empirical knowledge demands 'from within'. Such accounts may not explain everything (to say that a general causal law is needed for our empirical knowledge to have a justified temporal order is not to say why there

---

[39] See e.g. John McDowell's critique of 'the transcendental story', *Mind and World* (Cambridge, Mass., 1994), 3–6, 41–4. In other respects I gather that McDowell's approach, especially in his more recent work, has many parallels to the regressive interpretation.

is such a law at all), but to do their work they do not have to wait in suspense for transcendent details that some day might fill in gaps within our explanations of empirical events as such. The metaphysical acceptance of things in themselves, or even, on practical grounds, of specific characterizations of some of them (e.g. as free), is never meant to interfere with, or take the place of, the details of ordinary epistemology, science, and action theory. Like the endless speculative battles about universals and particulars, Kant's discussion of what is in itself can 'leave everything as it is' outside the classroom—except insofar as his specific arguments about space and time contest the position of those dogmatists who would go so far as to insist on dogmatic speculative claims, such as that they have proofs that refute the fundamental preconditions of pure morality.

3.7 Things in Themselves and Appearances

There is no space here to test this interpretation on all of Kant's self-interpretive claims, but the basic strategy can be exhibited by considering his famous remark that it would be absurd to think 'there can be appearances without anything that appears' (B xxvif). On other interpretations, this remark can look, at best, like an endorsement of a very bad inference. One might at first imagine that it means: 'Here are some items that are really (empirically) appearing, and now we are going to *infer* beyond them and say that there must be something else, a totally different thing, "that appears" and is not itself an appearance at all.' It is not hard to see how this inference seems very bold and questionable, especially for a philosophy such as Kant's, which regularly questions causal inferences beyond experience. Alternatively, one might take the passage to be totally anodyne, and not bold at all but simply an indication of two sides of the same item. This is as if it were saying, at most, that an appearance *is* a thing that appears, and that the value of having two different expressions—'appearance' and 'thing that appears'—may be only that the first can remind us of the 'subject pole' of experience, that for which there is an appearance, and the second can remind us of the 'object pole', the fact that there is something that appears. But this anodyne reading is inappropriate in at least two ways. First of all, it seems compatible with an extremely weak 'object pole'. We might just as well say, even with a rainbow, a pink elephant, or a round square, that notionally there is an appearance to or for a subject, and also a 'thing that appears'—and yet the 'thing that appears' is then nothing more than the wholly subjective appearing rainbow or elephant. A transcendental distinction between appearances and things in themselves does not need to be introduced for marking such a shallow difference.

Secondly, the anodyne reading goes against Kant's clear intention in this section of the text, which is to make a general remark about the notion of a thing in itself that will fit in with his heavily metaphysical views, expressed here as well as elsewhere in the *Critique* (B xxviii; cf. A538/B566 f.), which allow for particular non-spatio-temporal things in themselves, such as noumenal agents with an absolutely free will. These wills are 'things that appear' insofar as they have sensible effects, and yet they are precisely not themselves to be *equated* with any mere 'appearances', even if, for each of these wills, there are appearances that have to be very closely related to it as *its* effects and as the proper expression of its fundamental personal identity. (It is in this sense that human actions, which are freely and non-empirically caused and also fit into a lawful empirical series of effects, can concern, as Kant says here, 'one and the same being', since the being's 'empirical character' is the result of its own 'intelligible character'—and yet these two characters are still not the very same thing, since one grounds the other.) It is crucial that in this case the term 'appearance' does not have the mere positive meaning of designating 'an actual process of appearing', but rather is being used, above all, to indicate a negative sense of 'appearance'. That is, the term is meant as a reminder that all the phenomenal effects of our will appear in accord with empirical laws, and in that sense are phenomenally determined—and yet, precisely because Kant's transcendental idealism about space and time teaches that such appearances are *mere* appearances, it turns out that this phenomenal determination does not entail absolute necessitation and is not indicative of the ultimate nature that the will can have as a thing in itself insofar as it is free. (Note also that, just like Sellars' notion of the 'manifest image', being a 'mere appearance' in *this* sense does not at all imply being psychological or private—even though, at the empirical level, Kant does distinguish between private mere appearances, or illusions, and public determinate phenomena.)

All this implies that, when Kant says here that an 'appearance' requires 'a thing that appears', he has in mind more than the truism that any appearance can be called a thing that appears. Ultimately Kant has in mind the thought that whenever he goes so far as to understand something as an appearance in the transcendental sense of a *mere* appearance (and it is only with such a meaning that the phrase even warrants a special philosophical use and an account), he is taking this also to imply the existence of something that is truly a thing in itself and *not* a mere appearance. And it implies this not because there is a causal inference from the appearance to the thing, but rather because, throughout Kant's discussions, the notion of a thing is always basic, and the notion of a mere appearance is to be understood as derivative, as something introduced because of a feature that cannot sustain the status of being a proper characterization of the thing *simpliciter*.

Note that by itself this point is not, and does not need to be, an argument that there *are* any such mere appearances, let alone that space and time specifically are mere appearances. It is simply a reminder that, *if* some thing or some feature is regarded as a mere appearance, then this makes sense for us only in a context where there is at least something else that is not regarded as a mere appearance, but as a thing *simpliciter*. All this is consistent with Kant's constantly believing in the importance of his specific arguments about space and time as appearances, and even with his wanting us to think about their consequences here—but the point about the derivative nature of appearance talk in general is still not equivalent to any such specific arguments.

3.8 Appearance as 'Non-Fraudulent' on a Metaphysical Reading of Kant's Idealism

Nonetheless, there is a residual worry here that may be the deepest source of resistance to Kant's idealism, namely the fear that calling something metaphysically a 'mere appearance' in this way implies taking away its reality altogether.[40] One standard reason for suspecting that this is what Kant is up to can be dismissed very quickly. The language of the 'Copernican Revolution' has led some readers to think that reality as such for Kant might be relative to what is in minds. It is worth emphasizing again (see Section 3.5 above) that nowhere does Kant assert such a position, let alone begin to make an argument for it. He does not absolutize minds, but instead notes that the thing in itself even of our own mind could be, as far as we know theoretically, something ultimately *non-mental* (B427–8). While Kant may argue that sensible features are in various ways relative to mind, he never argues that things as such are mind relative. He often reminds us that the items of *empirical knowledge* go only so far as empirical principles can reach (which is not the same as what we could actually perceive), but he does not ever make the very different and general ontological claim that 'to be is to (perceive or) be perceived'.[41]

There are also positive reasons to think that a complete dismissal of reality in ordinary experience cannot be what Kant's idealism means. Note that in general the notion of an appearance is the notion of something that really appears and exists in some way but is possibly based in something more fundamental.[42] Consider an ordinary example. We say of jaundiced, i.e. yellow-appearing, persons that they appear to be sick, because they really do appear jaundiced,

---

[40] This seems to be McDowell's greatest worry about Kant. He speaks of the empirical world seeming 'fraudulent' on Kant's metaphysical account (*Mind and World*, 44). More specifically, though, he says that it is its 'claim to independence' that comes to seem 'fraudulent', and he immediately glosses this as a matter of its not being 'genuinely independent of us'. I argue below that the central implication of Kant's idealism is indeed to question the independence of empirical features, but this non-independence need not lead to a sense of fraud, since it is not a matter of their being thought to be dependent on us, in any ordinary sense, but is rather a function of their having to have an additional real ground beyond themselves. So we get more, rather than less, reality than we expected.

[41] For more details, see my 'Idealism from Kant to Berkeley'.

[42] Cf. M. Heidegger, *Being and Time*, tr. J. Macquarrie and E. Robinson (New York, Harper and Row), §7A, 'The Concept of Phenomenon'.

and our hypothesis is that the jaundice is a sign of real sickness in the person ('illness', for short). But we need not think that jaundice itself is an illness, even if there really is sickness whenever jaundice exists. Now consider that, in a new 'bioworld', jaundice might no longer be an effect of illness at all, although the best informed people in that world would continue to assume that it is. (This is somewhat like what actually happened when specialists long assumed that ulcer effects were the result of a certain kind of inner physical situation that we now know was not the real cause.) In such a situation, the truth is that jaundice is a 'mere appearance' of illness—but this would do nothing to take away the empirical reality that is jaundice. The problem, in other words, is not 'jaundice realism' but 'jaundice–illness realism'. The mistake of 'jaundice–illness realism', and the reason that the phrase 'mere appearance' could become appropriate here, has to do not with the nature of jaundice as an actual appearance, but simply with a misunderstanding of its relation to a reality that is more fundamental in a straightforward way.

Now consider that we similarly might think that a person's actions are thoroughly determined, i.e. not absolutely free, because each of its empirical acts has a lawfully connected empirical antecedent, a causing cause that in each case (that we empirically determine) also appears as itself a caused cause, and in this way it has an in principle predictable 'empirical character'. But then we might also come to change our minds and truly believe (perhaps simply by being reminded by Kantian practical considerations) that this person is free after all, on account of an inner non-empirical faculty which has causes that are not themselves (externally) caused. This pure faculty of will is responsible for an uncaused causing that defines its intelligible character, which in turn is the source of its thoroughly lawful empirical character.[43] We can then allow that this person really continues to *appear* determined in everyday life (insofar as it has only caused causings in its discernible empirical history), and at the same time we can say that this determinism is a 'mere appearance'. The appearance of the determined empirical character is still there, just like the appearance of jaundice, but our extra thought, the inference that this is an effect of *complete* determination, of *only* caused causes, is wrong, just as, in the bioworld I hypothesized, it is in fact false that the jaundiced person is literally ill, despite all the evidence.

Note that appearances that are 'mere appearances' in this way can still be very important and not 'fraudulent'. Facts about jaundice can be more relevant than truths about illness in contexts where the question is what color to wear on a given day. In the case of freedom in the context of Kant's transcendental philosophy,

---

[43] The best account of this scenario, presented simply as a coherent possibility, and not with any sympathy for it as a likely truth, remains Allen Wood, 'Kant's Compatibilism', in *Self and Nature in Kant's Philosophy*, ed. A. Wood (Ithaca, NY, 1984), 57–72.

appearances are similarly important. Presumably Kant believes that, when a free and good person does a deed of intrinsic moral worth, such as properly providing empirical help to another person, the goodness of the act may be rooted in something non-empirical. Nonetheless, it also has something to do with the first person having a genuinely helpful *empirical* character and the other person truly receiving this help empirically, in accord with the usual phenomenal laws. Hence, even if for Kant the ground of unconditioned value is beyond space and time (in the ultimate commitment to a good will), nothing in the doctrine of the transcendental ideality of space and time requires taking away the vivid empirical reality of our life as empirical characters—or the genuine value that this reality has in the context of its taking on a particular shape ultimately because of a particular ground that is more fundamental than it. Everything in Kant's moral theory and regressive strategy speaks for holding onto and affirming that these empirical situations of common life truly have value and therefore do exist. Mistakes arise only when, as in the case of jaundice, we make improper inferential claims about the *ground* of the appearances. The mistake is to say, for example, that the ultimate ground of the value lies basically in the empirical effect. Similarly, it would be wrong to say that a person who constantly appears to have determined, i.e. empirically lawful, actions cannot be ultimately free, or that the ultimate ground of a non-personal being must be a finite number of spatial material bits or a real infinite number of spatial material bits. In other words, the Kantian idealist is distinguished, strictly speaking, not by a negative claim about experience as such, but by a refusal to affirm a metaphysical hypothesis that spatio-temporal features characterize the ultimate nature of things. This is both a practical belief about personal beings, and a more basic theoretic belief about beings in general, one that is brought in to eliminate the inconsistencies in characterizing things in terms of spatio-temporal bits alone.

There is another kind of relation between appearances and the things that appear through them that is relevant here. We say, for example, that someone's beauty or happiness appears in their smile. In this situation, the appearing smile is an indication of something greater than it, namely, the person's total happiness or beauty, but the relation is not merely, or perhaps not at all, a relation of cause and effect but rather of part and whole. A particular smile can express or exhibit one's happiness or beauty in such a way that it is literally part of the beauty or happiness itself. (The jaundice case that I introduced was originally intended to be unlike this—although, for all I know, in our world the biological facts may be such that a jaundiced appearance is best understood as itself part of the ill person's illness and not a mere sign of illness.) Similarly, in the example of the good intelligible character and the effect of good empirical action, there can be a part–whole relation. The empirical action is, after all, a crucial *part* of the total *goodness* in this situation, a goodness that includes the non-empirical good will (even if on

Kant's moral theory the relation of the value of the empirical action to the particular value of moral *worth* may still be one of effect to cause, since only a free and noumenal will can have the property of such worth). The empirical action can also be considered as part of the total identity of the being as a *person* (persons, unlike mere souls, or mere bodies, are a special combination of intelligible and empirical features),[44] and so in that way too there would be some kind of a part–whole relation between an appearance and a thing and itself. I am not sure what to say of non-personal contexts, since Kant does not give examples that illustrate how the relation of a non-spatio-temporal and non-personal aspect of a thing in itself to its spatio-temporal appearance can be thought of in terms of a part–whole relation. Nonetheless, even in this case the appearance–thing in itself relation is not necessarily one of total separation, since the appearance of a person's will is an empirical effect that must exist in order to be really affected. This is one more reason to believe that the reality of features of the empirical domain does not become 'fraudulent' simply because of Kant's idealism.

3.9 Ideality as a Kind of Non-Independence

At this point it might begin to look as if even my metaphysical reading of things in themselves has become suspiciously anodyne. If things in themselves and appearances can be in such cozy relations as cause and effect, or even part and whole, why introduce such a threatening term as 'ideal' in contrast to 'real'? Why not simply say: Kant holds that empirical characters and concrete spatial forms are *fully* real, and he also happens to think that there are additional realities: namely, intelligible characters for persons and (necessarily) features more basic than spatio-temporality for non-personal beings? The answer is that 'fully real' is a strange and ambiguous phrase. It could mean 'real at all'—and then it is immediately clear that there need be no denial that appearances, in some sense, are real (e.g. as components of acts of thought, or at least as physiological phenomena). Or it could mean something much more complicated, such as 'really has a nature of a certain supposed kind, a kind implying not merely some form of existence, but a special kind of relation to grounds, a relation that allows it to exist with a very significant degree of independence from other beings'. On my reading, the more complicated reading is the relevant one: Kant's denial of transcendental realism is meant not as a denial of the reality of the empirical as such, but rather as a denial of a certain way of thinking about its relation to grounds. For Kant, it is the typical mistake of transcendental realism to take the concrete existence of spatio-temporal features as unconditioned, with the thought that either they are themselves fully independent existences, or they are direct modifications of such existences—as in

---

[44] See *Kant's Theory of Mind*, ch. 4.

Leibniz's theory of monads,[45] or Newton's theory of space and time as directly rooted in God, or a radical empiricist theory that roots them in the independent existence of particular mental acts, acts that each exist absolutely and need nothing outside them for their being. The error of this dogmatic realism is not that it denies that spatio-temporal features have a kind of concrete reality, but that it assumes a false relation of this reality to grounds, namely, the special relation of having no further kind of ground at all outside of the mental being that it inheres in or is.

This implies that the dogmatic realism that Kant opposes is not quite like the jaundice case discussed earlier. With transcendental realism about space and time, the mistake involves a false claim about being unconditioned *by anything* outside, whereas with jaundice-illness realism the mistake involves a false claim which allows that there is an outside condition but happens to misidentify what that condition is. In the jaundice-situation, as I described it in the new bioworld, it is true that people really have jaundice, i.e. a particular kind of yellow appearance, and that there is some outside ground for this, and yet there is no real underlying jaundice-illness. In this situation, even if talk of jaundice-illness is warranted (insofar as in that world all the empirical evidence is for it), the fact is that 'in itself' (so to speak; this is meant only as an analogy) the jaundice-illness is not real but ideal.

Despite this difference, the jaundice-illness examples remain in important ways similar to the Kantian examples. A sensible body really appears spatio-temporal, and yet there is no spatio-temporality in itself and therefore no underlying 'materialism-illess'. Likewise, a phenomenally lawful empirical character really appears and seems only to have non-free causes, yet in itself there need not be any 'determinism-illness'. Whether or not the justifications for these Kantian claims are very convincing, the main point stands that, even if we were to go so far as to accept their truth and a metaphysical reading of things in themselves, this reading would not take away empirical reality as such. All that would happen is that a new interpretation would be accepted concerning the borders of our existence. Thus, although there are all sorts of incidental differences between Kant's idealism and the jaundice example, there remains a basic analogy with Kant's transcendental idealism that dissolves the worst worries: accepting the unreality of the alleged illness does not make the original appearance itself a 'fraud', since it undercuts not the reality of our experience itself but only the extravagant claim of a certain kind of interpretive inference beyond it.

---

[45] The issue here is not the independent existence of space and time as such, since Leibniz clearly denies that, and yet Kant still denies that this saves Leibniz from transcendental realism. The crucial question is whether spatio-temporal features turn out to be reducible to mental features of monads, as with Leibniz, or whether, as with Kant, they can have a distinct non-mental ground.

INTRODUCTION

It is true that in the jaundice case the reason for speaking of the non-reality of the illness has to do with a contingent truth (in the modified bioworld), whereas Kant's reason for calling his case a matter of the non-reality of an illness (determinism, materialism) has to do with what he thinks is a sound *pure* philosophical consideration. Whereas the jaundice-illness turns out not to be real simply as a matter of fact, in the other cases it is presumably an a priori matter that absolute claims about determinism and spatio-temporal ultimacy turn out to be untrue. None of this, however, affects the basic fact that on my metaphysical reading even Kant's 'mere appearances' maintain a genuine form of existence and truly characterize our common experience. Furthermore, Kant's idealism is more like realism than traditional forms of idealism, because it stresses that empirical features are grounded in the natures of things in themselves in a way that involves a real interaction among finite entities, and it insists that we should not assume that these things are intrinsically mental in character. The dogmatist's mistake is simply to take an extra fateful step and to mischaracterize these features as having a fully independent kind of being that they do not have, as if they were attached to unconditioned beings of pure reason rather than conditioned and interacting concrete beings. For Kant, the ideality of spatio-temporal features involves not only the truth that they are dependent, but also a truth about the way they are dependent, since they cannot be reduced to features of particular minds, as in empiricism and other forms of rationalism (e.g. the monadology).

3.10 Retrospect

To describe Kant's path to idealism in this way may be to understand it, if one wishes, as a kind of non-empiricist radicalization of Locke, the Locke for whom there remains something non-mental beyond the nominal essences that we can determine in experience. It can thus be understood not as any kind of egocentrism, but as something like what happened elsewhere in the process of philosophical reflection in the course of the scientific revolution, when one kind of sensible property after another lost its independent ontological status for good objective reasons. For those who stayed free of the peculiar positions of skepticism and psychological idealism, this development never meant that there were no external things left. It meant only that many properties previously thought to be fundamental had to be delegated to the status of being 'mere appearances' of what remained as even more fundamental. Kant repeatedly compares his own procedure explicitly with this process,[46] and he also distinguishes himself from it, but only insofar as he thinks that others stopped *too soon* in the process. That is, they kept holding, directly or indirectly, onto a spatio-temporal characterization of

---

[46] See A45/B62, and *Prolegomena*, First Part, Remark Two.

INTRODUCTION

things in themselves, while he thought it could be shown that even this sensible characterization was no longer tenable.[47] Kant said this not because he held that there are no things (beyond us) at all, or because he claimed theoretical insight into a new special type of things, such as monads, but rather because, for better or worse, he held that there surely is something confronting us, and about all that we can say for sure about it is that *in itself* it cannot be spatio-temporal.[48] In sum, Kant's idealism is a non-anodyne position, and hence it is not easy to justify; but if my reading is correct, it is not subject to the objections of 'egocentrism' that have most bothered readers. This is because these worries have had little to do with Kant's actual position, since his 'idealism' is so non-'Cartesian' and so unlike other philosophies that have been covered by this term.

4. Preview

The chapters that follow are divided into three parts which consider in turn the three *Critiques* and the three basic areas of Kant's work: theoretical philosophy, practical philosophy, and aesthetics.

4.1 Kant and Theoretical Philosophy

Part I consists of a selection of five of my main essays on Kant's theoretical philosophy. The first essay presents my initial regressive reading of Kant's Transcendental Deduction of the categories on the basis of a detailed analysis of the B edition version and a critique of influential non-regressive interpretations by Wolff, Strawson, and Bennett. My interpretation stresses difficulties in using the Deduction directly to meet traditional empiricist concerns about skepticism, and it also argues that the concluding stages of Kant's argument are not easily separated from substantive aspects of his notions of space and time as ideal forms. This essay is influenced very much by the early work of Dieter Henrich, and it discusses how his stress on the 'two-part' structure of the Deduction bears on important ways in which Kant's argument is closely related to the form and content of the Transcendental Aesthetic as well.

---

[47] There are several complications here, of course, most of which concern the need always to posit something in addition to mere presence in space and time as a kind of 'force'.

[48] Wilfrid Sellars is perhaps the most reliable interpreter for tracking the deeper similarities between Kant's views and various developments in scientific realism. His own system, however, favors a realist program that ultimately has serious reductionist implications for the items of the 'manifest image', and he properly does not claim that Kant is committed to such a program. See e.g. his *Science and Metaphysics* (London, 1968); and cf. Michael Friedman, *Kant's and the Exact Sciences* (Cambridge, Mass., 1992). Kant's own position is strikingly unlike typical versions of scientific realism insofar as it leaves room for some sort of reality completely beyond whatever we expect that our science can ever determine. The modesty in this position is such that some might argue that recent scientific developments make it even more 'realistic' than typical 'realism', because there are no confident presumptions here about what science can achieve.

INTRODUCTION

The second essay is influenced very much by the work of Gerold Prauss, and it consists largely of a survey of interpretations of Kant's Transcendental Deduction and transcendental idealism. It distinguishes a wide variety of non-regressive interpretations of the Deduction and indicates some of their limitations. More positively, it explains how Prauss's highly original discussion of Kant's notion of appearance in experience helps with understanding details of the complex Critical conception of judgments of perception. The survey of work on transcendental idealism gives special attention to the early Kant scholarship of Prauss and Henry E. Allison, but it does not endorse their preference for what seems to be a relatively non-metaphysical reading of Kant's doctrine.

The third essay discusses in more detail the general features of many arguments in contemporary philosophy that are often understood as versions of Kantian idealism. I argue that these arguments are in fact quite distinct from Kant's own understanding of transcendental idealism because, unlike them, it depends essentially on the notion of our specific forms of intuition. The essay also attempts to mediate between non-metaphysical and metaphysical readings of Kant's idealism presented in interpretations by Allison and Paul Guyer. The essay ends with a discussion of special difficulties that arise in Kant's crucial arguments about space and time in the Antinomies, and it proposes that understanding transcendental realism as a specific way of absolutizing the forms of experience may offer the best strategy for making sense of the contradictions that Kant claims to find in dogmatic positions.

The fourth essay contains a brief survey of the first *Critique*'s Transcendental Dialectic, but it is devoted primarily to a treatment of Kant's changing views on the fundamental question of how to arrive at a theoretical account of the unity of the world that overcomes the shortcomings of occasionalism, theories of pre-established harmony, and naïve versions of the doctrine of 'physical influx'. The essay stresses that, although it is very difficult to determine Kant's exact route to a distinctive and stable position on interactionism, the topic is clearly of fundamental importance in all stages of his work, and throughout all of them he favors the affirmation of real interaction between finite things. The essay draws on ideas and materials from lectures by Kant used in my initial work on Kant's theory of mind (1982),[49] and it also relies heavily on several newly found sets of notes from Kant's lectures on metaphysics (published in German only in 1983, and translated in 1997, with several corrections to the German edition).

The fifth essay offers an extended analysis of the problems of idealism and interaction as treated in Rae Langton's recent monograph, *Kantian Humility* (published in 1998). I endorse Langton's highly analytic and metaphysical approach, and her thought that Kant's notion of things in themselves has much to do

---

[49] See the first edition of *Kant's Theory of Mind* (Oxford, 1982).

INTRODUCTION

with a conception of the intrinsic natures of things. Nonetheless, I find difficulties in Langton's own argument that transcendental idealism, in the sense of an insistence on our ignorance of things in themselves, is to be understood as resting basically on the consequences of the mere receptivity of our experience. There are historical and systematic problems with this reading, difficulties concerning key features in the development of Kant's treatment of space, time, and interaction. In some ways the reading appears remarkably close to an influential interpretation of Kant by his German idealist successors (and some versions of the contemporary 'merely methodological' interpretation of transcendental idealism) that I have criticized earlier under the heading of the so-called 'short argument to idealism'.[50] Here, as elsewhere, I find systematic links between this 'short argument' and a non-regressive reading of the Deduction, links that count against each of them as satisfactory interpretations of Kant's intentions.

4.2 Kant and Practical Philosophy

Part II begins with an essay (Chapter 6) concerning a pivotal development in Kant's practical philosophy, one that confirms the central role of judgment and experience in Kant's philosophy. I argue that Kant's first major work in practical philosophy, the *Groundwork of the Metaphysics of Morals* (1785), suggests a very intriguing but ultimately unsatisfying argument for the existence of freedom and the validity of morality, one that starts at first from a mere consideration of the general nature of human judgment and activity. I then argue that, for a wide variety of inadequately appreciated considerations having to do with refinements in his epistemology and theory of mind between the two editions of the first *Critique*, Kant's second major work in practical philosophy, the *Critique of Practical Reason* (1788), adopts a very different and explicitly more regressive strategy. Thus, I conclude that there is a 'great reversal' in Kant's position, contrary to the readings of scholars such as Paton, Beck, and Henrich, who have argued that there exists a deep continuity in these major texts, either because there is also something like a regressive strategy already in the *Groundwork*, or because there is also a non-regressive strategy carried forward into the second *Critique*. My reading stresses that Kant's discussion in the second *Critique* makes fully explicit, for the first time, that the 'experience' lying at the basis of his practical philosophy is not anything as general as the apparent spontaneity of the mind in the process of judging or willing as such, but instead involves a kind of absolute freedom that can be grounded *only* regressively through the specific premise of a binding form of *moral* experience (called 'the fact of reason'). This is, of course, a very substantive and controversial premise, and also one that Kant

[50] See my 'Kant, Fichte, and Short Arguments to Idealism', and cf. Ch. 3 below.

insists is sustainable only on the basis of the metaphysics of transcendental idealism worked out in his prior theoretical philosophy.

In evaluating Kant's approach, I explain first how his final strategy regarding freedom has the merit of fitting some of the most sophisticated developments in his Critical philosophy of mind, and in particular his objections to the Cartesian tradition.[51] In this way his mature work contrasts favorably with the more dogmatic approaches of many of his predecessors, immediate successors, and contemporary admirers. Kant's approach here also fits the 'moderate' pattern of his general transcendental strategy, insofar as it can hardly be taken to be aimed at defeating skepticism (this time of a practical form), since the moral skeptic is defined precisely by a rejection of the substantive premises of Kant's argument. Despite these advantages, I note that there are also methodological respects in which in this practical domain Kant's regressive approach is less satisfying than it is in the theoretical domain. Whereas ordinary people are not theoretical skeptics, and hence arguments that cannot defeat such skepticism need not be a 'real' problem in common life, it seems clear that many ordinary and decent people are deeply skeptical about the specific kind of moral experience that Kant insists on using as a foundation in his second *Critique*. Moreover, unlike his transcendental account of cognitive experience, Kant's account of practical experience has the extra burden of presuming the controversial doctrine of transcendental idealism (i.e. of presuming both that such a doctrine is needed and that it can be independently established) rather than being simply one step in an argument toward that doctrine.

The second essay of this section (Chapter 7) focuses on a normative question central to the beginning of Kant's *Groundwork*, the concept of a good will. After distinguishing three varieties of the concept that can be constructed from Kant's writings, and criticizing several recent readings concerning them, I conclude that one can make the best sense of Kant's intentions here by connecting the good will not to an individual act or perfect attitude, but to the entirety of one's character. Once this is done, however, there remain some very hard-to-understand basic features of Kant's notion of character: his account of temptation, and his claim that we all can and should go through a fundamental moral conversion.

The third essay (Chapter 8) contrasts my metaphysical reading of Kant's notion of freedom with recent accounts of freedom offered by Allen Wood in a book on Hegel and by Henry Allison in a book on Kant. Wood argues that Kant's account is more concerned with the metaphysics of causation than Hegel's and is therefore weaker, whereas Allison proposes and defends an understanding of freedom in Kant that plays down the role of causality and metaphysics. Against both of these interpretations I argue for the relevance of causality and metaphysics to discus-

---

[51] For more details, see the Introduction to the 2nd edn of my *Kant's Theory of Mind*.

sions of free action. I also argue in part with Wood against Allison on the issue of the meaning of Kant's theory, and in part with Allison against Wood on the issue of the relative coherence and defensibility of Kant's theory in contrast to Hegel's.

The fourth essay (Chapter 9) provides a detailed critical account of the beginning of the argument of part III of Kant's *Groundwork*, the section of his writing in which he seems to come closest to offering a direct proof of our absolute freedom. I contend that there are several ambiguities and missteps in what seems to be Kant's main line of argument here, but I take this not to count against my earlier interpretations or Kant's own wisdom. On the contrary, realizing that there may be such fundamental flaws in this part of the *Groundwork* is the easiest way to understand why Kant never directly refers back to it, and why (according to my account) he reversed his method of presentation so dramatically in the second *Critique*.

The fifth essay (Chapter 10) provides a more detailed account of how the treatment of the 'fact of reason' in the second *Critique* can be read as an explicit reversal of Kant's earlier procedure. In now clearly insisting on disallowing any route to a claim of absolute freedom that does not rest on the moral law, Kant reaches a position that puts the least strain on the notion that came to dominate the second edition of his first *Critique* (1787): the claim that we have no privileged theoretical knowledge of the self, not even of its absolute spontaneity. The downside of this result is that Kant also calls freedom the 'keystone' of his Critical philosophy, the center of his effort to help rebuild all philosophy, life, and culture around the notion of autonomy. Without any theoretical argument or uncontroversial practical foundation for this keystone concept, Kant's insistence on autonomy can appear vulnerable. Thus, it is no surprise that Kant's system was heavily revised by his immediate successors, who were desperate to find new and stronger ways to undergird the autonomy that they were even more enthusiastic about than Kant himself. (This theme is explored in my earlier study, *Kant and the Fate of Autonomy*.)

The sixth essay (Chapter 11) turns to questions about the ultimate nature of the content of Kant's ethical theory. I criticize aspects of the very influential constructivist reading of Kant's ethics, originated by John Rawls and his students and employed in Jerome Schneewind's important treatment of the history of modern ethics. I indicate historical and systematic reasons for allowing a much more positive relation between Kant's ethical theory and moral realism. As with his theoretical philosophy, Kant's arguments against the metaphysical tradition here can be understood as anything but global and complete, and as aimed primarily at very specific forms of dogmatic objectivism or relativism in ethics. In an addendum to my original discussion, I point out some ways in which this realist approach can begin to respond to the most obvious objection to it (raised recently

INTRODUCTION

by Charles Larmore[52]): namely that it may not do justice to Kant's special emphasis on self-legislation. I argue that Kant's notion of autonomy does not in fact have the overly subjective implications that are commonly ascribed to it by its opponents—and that also are often assumed, or even glorified, by many who call themselves followers of Kant.

4.3 Kant and Aesthetics

The essays of Part III focus in a similar way on interpreting Kant as using the regressive presumption of a kind of 'objective' experience, in this case the presumption of the third *Critique* that there are valid judgments of taste. The first essay (Chapter 12) combines two earlier articles, in which I argue that there is a way of reconstructing Kant's account of taste such that it has a plausible deduction, but one that involves understanding natural beauty as an objective feature disclosed in a particular kind of pure appreciation of sensible forms.

The second essay (Chapter 13) defends this position in response to a direct critique of it by Hannah Ginsborg, from the perspective of a subjectivist reading of Kantian taste. The critique provides an opportunity for clarifying ways in which my objectivist reconstruction does not have the kind of unwelcome consequences that it might at first seem to have. There is a way of reading Kant's argument that shows how taste can be called objective for reasons that are not tied to either the kind of objectivity associated with science and a mere knowledge of causal relations, or to the specific kinds of rationalist doctrines that Kant was mainly trying to warn against insofar as he was very reluctant (as he obviously was) explicitly to call his theory an objectivist one.

The final essay (Chapter 14) is a defense of my reading against another set of objections, including some recently articulated by Paul Guyer. Here I elaborate ways in which the objective nature of Kantian taste is also connected with another feature that is often denied of it, namely a fundamentally conceptual character. In saying that Kant's argument presumes that taste is objective and conceptual, I do not mean that this is to take it to be all objective and all conceptual. Since it is rooted in human perception, taste must involve sensation and feeling, and in this sense it is obviously subjective and intuitive as well. This does not mean, however, that we should think that Kant (insofar as his aesthetic theory insists on valid judgments) means to deny a sense in which it also needs to remain both objective and conceptual, as these terms are commonly understood now.[53] Kant's discussion of 'aesthetic experience' here is also especially important because it concerns a

---

[52] See Larmore's discussion of my brief presentation of this position in *Kant and the Fate of Autonomy* in his 'Back to Kant? No Way', *Inquiry*, 46 (2003), 260–71.

[53] For this reason I do not qualify my position as 'quasi-objective', as Allen Wood has recently qualified his own position (which in other ways is similar to my view; see below, Ch. 12) in saying that aesthetic truths 'are not objective truths, however, in the sense that they are not about the properties objects have irrespective

level of a posteriori and particular judgment that is relatively neglected in his other writings. Although I do not go into detail concerning other related features of the third *Critique*, such as the characterization of judgments of natural purposiveness and systematicity in the physical sciences, I do point out how the general structure of Kant's discussion here fits in well with my overall interpretation of him as a 'moderate' philosopher regressively seeking universal features of particular kinds of presumed experience.

5. Postscript: Kant and the Conflict of Interpretations

I conclude this introduction with a brief comment on the fact that these essays concern the topic of 'interpreting Kant's *Critiques*' in the double sense that they offer a series of textual interpretations of their own and they do so by surveying and reacting to a wide range of interpretations offered by others. At times, this kind of approach can be frustrating, and the desire can arise for more of a focus directly on the philosophical issues themselves, or on their treatment in the primary texts alone. Such a reaction is certainly understandable, but I believe it is not an unfortunate accident or a matter of mere personal style that these essays have ended up giving so much attention to interpretive disputes.

Ever since the original publication of the Critical philosophy, its complexity and significance have put it at the center of an intense debate among followers, revisionists, and outside interpreters.[54] The extremely ambitious and systematic character of Kant's philosophy naturally lends itself to synoptic visions, and this inevitably leads not only to countless disagreements on particular issues, but also to competing metaphilosophical reflections about what any large-scale philosophy like this can hope to accomplish in modern times.[55] Elsewhere, I have argued that these points are interconnected, and that the recent 'historical' and 'aesthetic' turns in philosophical writing that have come deeply to affect even analytic philosophy are rooted in basic features of modern philosophy in general and in reactions to fundamental difficulties in interpreting Kant in particular.[56] Kant's

---

of our subjective experience of them and also in the sense that they cannot be proved or confirmed by rational argument or empirical evidence' ('The Objectivity of Value', in *Unsettling Obligations* (Stanford, Calif., 2002), 183). I argue that there are many non-aesthetic features with both of these characteristic that are still commonly regarded as objective, even if they of course do not have exactly the same kind of objectivity as some features that have nothing to do with experience.

[54] Why this happened is a major theme of *Kant and the Fate of Autonomy*.

[55] See e.g. the very different Kant-inspired perspectives offered by Robert Brandom, Allen Wood, and Karl-Otto Apel in *What is Philosophy?*, ed. C. P. Ragland and Sarah Heidt (New Haven, 2001).

[56] See my 'Text and Context: Hermeneutical Prolegomena to Interpreting a Kant Text', in *Kant verstehen/Understanding Kant*, ed. D. Schönecker and T. Zwenger (Darmstadt, 2001), 11–31; 'Reinhold über Systematik, Popularität und die "Historische Wende"', in *Philosophie ohne Beinamen. System, Freiheit und Geschichte im Denken C. L. Reinholds*, ed. M. Bondeli and A. Lazzari (Basel, 2003), 303–36 ; 'Hegel's Aesthetics: New Perspectives on its Response to Kant and Romanticism', *Bulletin of the Hegel Society of Great Britain*, 45/6 (2002), 72–92.

diagnosis of our times as 'an age of Criticism' (A xin) is now more appropriate than ever before. Contemporary philosophy increasingly tends to present itself not as a particular science, but as a uniquely autonomous and argumentative mode of reflection—one that, more than any other, must be open to testing all given authorities and disciplines, while subjecting itself to special self-scrutiny.

Attempts to turn modern philosophy into a totally rigorous 'program' have been repeatedly attempted, but without true success, even if numerous particular writings along this line have provided invaluable lessons. Up to now, the distinctively philosophic process of universal critical reflection has found no better 'method' than that of remaining a basically interpretive response (rather than being merely descriptive or explanatory, in any genuinely scientific sense) to the most influential self-interpretations of its own past. It is an open question whether Kant's ideas (even more than those of Descartes, Nietzsche, or someone such as Wittgenstein) will long continue to play the special role that they have, for decades and decades, in molding all at once the most basic issues of philosophical dispute throughout contemporary theory, practice, and aesthetics. But the fact is that the Critical philosophy has so far played an extraordinarily influential role in all three of these basic areas of experience and philosophy, and so it is not an insignificant task to try to put together the beginnings of a coherent general interpretation of its most basic points. The goal of this effort is not to call nostalgically for a return to a past system, but rather, in an age of ever increasing specialization, to bring together a full spectrum of conflicting perspectives so as to stimulate our interpretive community's awareness of its origins and its potential as a whole. In this sense, this work is meant to be 'Kantian' above all not because of the defense of any particular substantive doctrine in the *Critiques*, but because it hopes to serve Kant's own ultimate goal as a scholar: the development of autonomy through the 'severe criticism' (A xvi n.) that is needed in trying to do justice simultaneously to the common ground of ordinary experience, the advances of science, and the demands of morality.

Part I

The First *Critique* and Kant's Theoretical Philosophy

– 1 –
Kant's Transcendental Deduction as a Regressive Argument

Considerable study has been given in recent years to the question of transcendental arguments in general and to Kant's transcendental deduction in particular. Recent analytical studies of Kant have approached his work with a pronounced interest in the former general issue and with broad theories about the way the first *Critique* as a whole should be interpreted. As a consequence, there has been a tendency to pass over the complex details of Kant's own discussion of the structure of transcendental argumentation. Indicative of this situation is the absence of any detailed treatment of the second edition version of the transcendental deduction. In this paper I shall argue that, once Kant's revisions in the second edition are given their due, his transcendental deduction of the pure concepts of the understanding can be seen to have a surprisingly clear structure and one that is at variance with contemporary interpretations. My main objective is to give a fair representation of that structure, but in so doing I will argue that it has been misrepresented in a fundamental and common way by Kant's most distinguished recent commentators—Peter Strawson, Jonathan Bennett, and Robert Paul Wolff. Whereas their interpretations see Kant's deduction as aiming to provide a proof of objectivity which will answer skepticism, I will argue that on the contrary it is necessary and profitable to understand the deduction as moving from the assumption that there is empirical knowledge to a proof of the preconditions of that knowledge.[1]

I

Transcendental deductions are not familiar entities. It is only natural to exploit whatever examples we have of them in order to cast light on the notorious difficulties of Kant's deduction of the categories. Yet surprisingly little attention

---

[1] I believe my specific exposition of the structure of the deduction is unique, but in the older secondary literature there are parallels to it as well as to the current line of interpretation I oppose. See Hans Vaihinger, *Kommentar zu Kants Kritik der reinen Vernunft*, vol. I, 2nd edn (Stuttgart, 1922), 384–450.

has been paid to Kant's explicit designation of the argument of the Transcendental Aesthetic as a transcendental deduction (B119). In a remarkably systematic paragraph added in the second edition, Kant explains what he means by a 'transcendental exposition' and how it is that his analysis of space is one. Briefly, Kant declares a transcendental account of a particular representation (B) to be one which shows how B explains the possibility of a kind of synthetic a priori knowledge (A). Such an account has two parts:

(1) For this purpose it is required that such knowledge does really flow from the given concept, (2) that this knowledge is possible only on the assumption of a given mode of explaining the concept. (B40)

This means that the transcendental deduction in the Transcendental Aesthetic in particular must show (1) how the science of geometry 'really flows' from the representation of space, and (2) how geometry is possible only if that representation has a particular (in Kant's view, ideal) nature. This suggests that a transcendental deduction of a particular type of knowledge demonstrates its necessary and sufficient conditions. The demonstration of the sufficient conditions would be given in showing how the knowledge 'really flows' from a given representation; a demonstration of necessary conditions would come in explaining the nature that a representation essential to that knowledge must have—in this case it comes in Kant's argument that geometry is possible as a science only if the representation of space is an a priori intuition, which is possible only if space is transcendentally ideal.

If an argument of this structure is to be found in Kant's Transcendental Analytic, it seems we should expect an account of the necessary and sufficient conditions of the type of synthetic a priori knowledge formulated in the propositions of the Principles of the Analytic, e.g. that 'all alterations take place in conformity with the law of the connection of cause and effect' (B232). This is quite a strong claim; it is the claim that Kant not only is providing an account of what must be the case if the causal maxim is to be valid, but that he is also aiming to provide a sound argument which has that maxim as its conclusion. Commentators have not shrunk from ascribing such a difficult project to Kant's Analytic, and their interpretations appear to be backed by Kant's famous remark in the *Prolegomena* (paragraphs 4 and 5) that the *Critique* employs a synthetic or progressive and not merely an analytic or regressive method, i.e. that it presents arguments which do not merely assume synthetic a priori knowledge and demonstrate its presuppositions but which have synthetic a priori principles as their conclusions. So it would *seem* that Kant's description of one part of a transcendental exposition as involving a demonstration of how knowledge 'really flows' from a representation is equivalent to the claim that a transcendental deduction must include an argument which moves deductively to a synthetic a priori principle from premises merely elucidating a particular kind of representation. However, if this is the case, we should be able to find such a progressive argument in Kant's transcendental deduction of geometrical knowledge. In fact, immediately after explaining the two elements of a transcendental exposition, Kant gives us two paragraphs, the second of which obviously addresses itself to the treatment of necessary conditions of geometrical knowledge ('not otherwise than insofar as the intuition has its seat in the subject only'), and this suggests that the preceding paragraph is the account of sufficient conditions. But it is no such thing: the paragraph merely characterizes geometrical knowledge as synthetic a priori and argues that only if the representation of space is an a priori intuition is this knowledge possible. So instead of the expected progressive argument there is only another regressive explanation of necessary conditions for a type of knowledge.

It should be recalled that at this point in Kant's transcendental exposition all that is even alleged to have been shown is that geometry involves synthetic a priori propositions and this requires an a priori intuition of space, though it may also be assumed from the 'metaphysical exposition' of space that we are in possession of an a priori intuition of it (just as the later 'metaphysical deduction' shows we are in possession of pure concepts). It is difficult to believe that Kant could have mistaken these points for a progressive argument as characterized so far. What Kant has proved at most is something of the logical form: *A* only if *B*, *B*. (Note that A, the characterization of geometry as synthetic a priori, does not entail that geometry is true of the world, nor does it involve specific claims about Euclidean geometry.) It would be unjustifiably uncharitable to assume that he took this to be an argument establishing the truth of *A*. It is only fair to recommend that Kant's requirement that a transcendental exposition show how knowledge 'really flows' from a representation not be construed as having to involve a progressive argument in the sense of a deductive proof with a synthetic a priori principle as its conclusion and the mere having of a representation as its premise. There are other considerations backing this interpretive proposal. Kant speaks elsewhere of the 'objective' and 'subjective' lines of a transcendental deduction (Axvii), the latter tracing synthetic a priori knowledge back to its 'original germs' or 'sources' in the human mind (A97, A786). It thus may be possible to take the 'subjective' (as opposed to the 'objective' and regressive) part of a transcendental exposition simply to relate a particular type of a priori knowledge to specific faculties, activities or types of representation of the mind,[2] without providing a deductive

---

[2] Here I agree with J. Hintikka's argument that a genuinely Kantian transcendental argument requires a 'dynamic' element, that it must involve 'showing how it is due to those activities of ours' that knowledge is obtained ('Transcendental Arguments: Genuine and Spurious', *Noûs*, 6 (1972), 275). But I do not agree that we must regard the 'psychological apparatus' of the first edition as 'the very gist of the Kantian arguments' (p. 276).

argument going from the description of a mere representation to a conclusion which is an objective synthetic a priori principle. To say that knowledge 'really flows' from a particular representation, one should not have to be able to deduce the knowledge from the nature of the representation.

This interpretation not only makes sense of the first part of the transcendental deduction of the Aesthetic; it can also provide a general lesson for reading Kant's transcendental arguments: what at first may appear to be presented as a (non-trivial) deductive argument demonstrating that mere representations are logically sufficient conditions for knowledge is better understood as an essentially regressive argument. Confirmation for this thesis is to be found in the transcendental exposition of time (B48). Incomplete as the exposition is, Kant's intentions at least are clearly no more than to 'exhibit the possibility' of a body of knowledge—obviously this is to supply necessary, not sufficient, conditions. I will argue that the transcendental deduction of the Analytic bears out this general theory and so demonstrates a formal correspondence with Kant's earlier (regressive) argument for idealism. It will also be shown that, contrary to recent interpretations, the deduction of the categories has a material dependence on Kant's doctrine of transcendental idealism.

II

The best way to substantiate the theory that there are significant formal correspondences between the Aesthetic and the Analytic would be to find that the proof structure of the deduction of the categories parallels that of the transcendental deduction in the Aesthetic. In its most skeletal form the central argument of the Aesthetic (with respect to space) has this structure: the science of geometry (A) requires synthetic a priori propositions which in turn require pure intuitions (B), and these are possible only if transcendental idealism is true. In this way the Aesthetic gives a transcendental explanation of how a body of knowledge (A) is possible only if a particular representation (B) has a certain nature. The argument of the Analytic would have a parallel structure if it is of the form: empirical knowledge ('experience') is possible only if the 'original synthetic unity of apperception' applies to it,[3] which is possible only if pure concepts have validity, and this in turn requires that transcendental idealism be true. Such an argument would be transcendental in that it too would explain that a body of knowledge is possible only if there are representations (pure concepts) of a certain kind. The subjective aspect of the deduction, like that of the Aesthetic, could lie simply in the description of the nature and type of representations involved, e.g. in the demonstration

---

[3] This formulation is an incomplete representation of my interpretation. Later it will be shown to be an essential part of Kant's argument that the unity of apperception applies universally to all our representations only because of the nature of our forms of sensibility.

of the appropriateness of their being a priori, and would not include the strong claim that the mere possession of certain representations (not cognitive by definition) entails a body of knowledge.

The interpretation of the Aesthetic given here follows rather directly from Kant's text and is hardly controversial. The proposed interpretation of the Analytic, however, appears at the very least to be directly contrary to the approach of the best known recent analyses (which I will refer to jointly as the 'received interpretation', *RI*). The major departure of this interpretation is that it takes the *Critique* to accept empirical knowledge as a premise to be regressively explained rather than as a conclusion to be established. Peter Strawson, Jonathan Bennett, and Robert Paul Wolff have insisted at length that such an argument is undesirable, uninteresting and not representative of Kant's best intentions.[4] They all represent the transcendental deduction as basically aiming to *establish* objectivity, i.e. to prove that there is an external and at least partially lawful world, a set of items distinct from one's awareness, and to do this from the minimal premise that one is self-conscious. Whereas these interpretations see the transcendental deduction as showing that one can be self-conscious only if there is an objective world of which one is aware, my interpretation takes Kant essentially to be arguing that for us there is objectivity, and hence empirical knowledge, only if the categories are universally valid. I will defend this interpretation with the following three-part argument. First, reasons will be given for rejecting the *RI*, then objections to my alternative interpretation will be countered, and finally an account will be given of the data that have appeared to justify the *RI*.

III

There are two general reasons for being dissatisfied with versions of the *RI*: their representations of the transcendental deduction do not yield what they promise, a (non-trivial) valid argument, and it is highly unlikely that they reflect Kant's intentions. To clarify these charges it is necessary to make explicit the various formulations of the argument held to be at the heart of the transcendental deduction.

According to Strawson, the major argument of the deduction is 'to establish that experience necessarily involves knowledge of objects, in the weighty sense' (p. 88), and to do this not from the 'disappointing' assumption that 'experience is necessarily of an objective and spatio-temporally unitary world' (p. 85). Strawson expresses the deduction as 'the thesis that for a series of diverse experiences to

---

[4] Peter Strawson, *The Bounds of Sense* (London, 1966); Jonathan Bennett, *Kant's Analytic* (Cambridge, 1966); Robert Paul Wolff, *Kant's Theory of Mental Activity* (Cambridge, Mass., 1963). All quotations without citation in the following section refer to these works.

belong to a single self-consciousness it is necessary that they should be so connected as to constitute a temporally extended experience of a unified objective world' (p. 97). One could object that this formulation is a distortion of Kant's view, since he held it is contingent that consciousness is temporal, but it would hardly do to reject Strawson's interpretation on the basis of this dubious doctrine. More significant is the fact that the formulation indicates how strong a claim the transcendental deduction is being expected to support. Strawson's version is no weaker than the thesis that there cannot be a self-conscious subject without an objective world. So expressed, the argument is certainly saved from triviality, but its objective is so bold that, not unsurprisingly, many have been unable to find adequate grounds for it.

The reasons for rejecting Strawson's argument have varied. Though it has been argued by some that such transcendental arguments in general cannot succeed against an obstinate skeptic,[5] I will restrict my critique to objections against Strawson's specific formulation of the transcendental argument. What is claimed to be shown is that the fact of encountering a series of temporally experienced items entails that one has the ability to distinguish 'subjective' from 'objective' items, i.e. from items 'conceived as distinct from particular subjective states of awareness of them' (p. 89). However, as Graham Bird has pointed out, the notion of 'items conceived as distinct from *particular* states of awareness of them' is inadequate because items could pass Strawson's test for objectivity and still merely be properties of one's mind.[6] If 'particular' means 'any one particular', then enduring states of mind turn out to be 'objective' (my anger, for example, may be distinct from a particular awareness of it); on the other hand, if 'particular' means 'all particular', then the looks and sounds of things become 'subjective' (for how are we to understand the blueness of a flower, for example, independent of any references to states of consciousness?). Even if there is a way to iron out the wording of Strawson's conclusion, a decisive objection can be made by noting a peculiarity of his route to the conclusion:

It was agreed at the outset that experience requires both particular intuitions and general concepts. There can be no experience at all which does not involve the recognition of particular items *as* being of such and such a kind. It seems that it must be possible, even in the most fleeting and purely subjective of impressions, to distinguish a component of recognition, or judgement, which is not simply identical with, or wholly absorbed by, the particular item which is recognized, which forms the topic of the judgement.

---

[5] Barry Stroud, 'Transcendental Arguments', *Journal of Philosophy*, 65 (1968), 241–56. I agree with Stroud's criticism of Strawson, not his interpretation of Kant. Stroud assumes Kant's purpose in the transcendental deduction is that of a refutation of idealism, that Kant means to establish the objective validity of concepts in general.

[6] Graham Bird, 'Recent Interpretations of Kant's Transcendental Deduction', *Kant-Studien*, 65 (Sonderheft, 1974), 1–14.

... the recognitional component, necessary to experience, can be present in experience only because of the *possibility* of referring different experiences to one identical subject of them all. Recognition implies the *potential* acknowledgement of the experience into which recognition necessarily enters as being one's own, as sharing with others this relation to the identical self. It is the fact that this potentiality is implicit in recognition which saves the recognitional component in a particular experience from absorption into the item recognized ... (pp. 100–1)

As Ross Harrison has observed, there is a crucial shift here in the meaning of 'component of recognition'.[7] At first the component designates the necessity that there be a general or descriptive and not only a demonstrative element in judgments. It is unclear why this should imply the necessity of a 'recognitional component' in the quite different sense of a distinguishable subjective portion of experience. It seems that a sense data experiencer could have all that Strawson's original premise requires, a component of recognition in the first sense, without being in contact with an independently existing world.

Other advocates of the *RI* also fail to construct a significant valid argument out of the materials of the deduction. Bennett's analysis includes no less than four accounts of the transcendental deduction:

1. The aim of the deduction is ostensibly to disprove the Humeian conclusion that 'objectivity and causality are at any moment liable to collapse' (pp. 100–1).
2. This is done by arguing not merely that 'concepts can be applied only in a causally ordered realm' (a typical regressive formulation) but 'by showing ... there cannot be experience which is not brought under concepts at all' (p. 102).
3. 'The central argument in the transcendental deduction has to do with the ownership of mental states', i.e. employs the premise that 'every representation is someone's' (p. 103). (This 'central argument' Bennett claims is in the first three paragraphs of the second edition version. The last ten paragraphs are treated as peripheral; this may explain Bennett's view that the second edition is 'only marginally clearer.')
4. 'What Kant ... repeatedly offers to prove in the transcendental deduction is that all experience must be of a realm of items which are objective in the sense that they can be distinguished from oneself and from one's inner states' (p. 131).

These are radical theses, since Bennett expressly uses 'experience' in the sense of consciousness, not knowledge, though he adds Kant's 'modest asservation' that

---

[7] Ross Harrison, 'Strawson on Outer Things', *Philosophical Quarterly*, 20 (1970), 213–21. Cf. Richard Rorty, 'Strawson's Objectivity Argument', *Review of Metaphysics*, 24 (1970), 207–44.

'all suppositions about experience must concern experience... which is accompanied by self-consciousness' (p. 106). The term 'supposition' is important; it reflects Bennett's awareness that Kant entertains the logical possibility of representations which, although they are 'nothing to' the owner, might be had in a 'subhuman' way without implying or giving knowledge of objectivity (pp. 104–5). Bennett thinks that Kant properly excludes this possibility because 'states which one could not know oneself to be in... cannot intelligibly be made a subject for speculation' (p. 105). This claim (properly qualified) fleshes out the third account of the deduction but trivializes others; if only those states which one could know oneself to be in are under consideration, obviously 'experience' must be brought under concepts and there will be no 'experience' of a collapse of objectivity. Only Bennett's fourth account promises an interesting argument, yet this version is one that Bennett himself says is not proven in the deduction. He contends the conclusion that consciousness implies that objectivity is established only in the Analytic of Principles, that there are only 'illegitimate' attempts to derive it in the Analytic of Concepts (p. 130). (The charge of 'illegitimacy' is but a consequence of the *RI*'s insistence that Kant is trying to establish that experience is objective and its chagrined discovery that he frequently defines it to be so.) Thus, none of Bennett's versions provide an account of the text of Kant's transcendental deduction itself which yields a non-trivial argument with a good claim to soundness.

Wolff's interpretation is more concerned than the others with seeing the whole *Critique* as built around an argument that 'the categories are conditions of the possibility of consciousness itself' (p. 94). Wolff even claims 'the deduction will not work unless the categories are viewed as "the necessary conditions of any consciousness whatsoever"', (p. 159) a view which at the least conflicts with Kant's intentions, since Kant emphasizes the dependence of the deduction on the specific nature of human consciousness. Wolff is determined to construct out of Kant's text a progressive argument showing that knowledge "really flows" from "the mere fact of consciousness" in a deductive way. This commits him not just to the already questioned thesis that there cannot be consciousness without an objective world, but also to the claim that consciousness without empirical knowledge is a logical impossibility. (Sometimes, Wolff does say the aim is to establish 'the *possibility* of empirical knowledge as a necessary condition of consciousness' (p. 112), and perhaps he means this to be equivalent to the earlier thesis.) Wolff treats Kant's pronouncements to the contrary as 'incompatible' with 'the central argument' and holds that 'Kant finally states in absolutely unambiguous language that we cannot be conscious of an unsynthesized manifold' (p. 158).[8] In fact, Kant's text is not so clear:

---

[8] In Section V, I argue that Kant does not believe any of *our* representations are unsynthesized, for the categories are 'universally valid'. But unlike Wolff, I point out that this belief has an essential dependence on Kant's theory of our forms of sensibility, on the contingency that our senses are as they are.

For even though we should have the power of associating perceptions, it would remain entirely undetermined and accidental whether they would themselves be associable; and should they not be associable, there might exist a multitude of perceptions, and indeed an entire sensibility, in which much empirical consciousness would arise in my mind, but in a state of separation, and without belonging to a [one] consciousness of myself. This, however, is impossible. For it is only because I ascribe all perceptions to one consciousness (original apperception) that I can say of all perceptions that I am conscious of them. (A121–2)

Note that what Kant is calling impossible is not the existence of any consciousness which is not self-conscious and does not imply 'appearances which fit into a connected whole of human knowledge'. What Kant is denying is the possibility of having a 'multitude of perceptions', an 'entire sensibility' which is 'in my mind' while there is no 'one consciousness of myself'. This is an acceptable though trivial denial if all it excludes is the sense of saying many states can belong to one consciousness while there is no one subject who has those states. If Kant meant to make a stronger claim (perhaps Wolff is right in thinking that Kant did, but then it is significant that the passage occurs only in the first edition), the claim is unfounded. Wolff emphazises the last sentence of Kant's statement as if it clinches his case, but that sentence is equivalent to saying, if I am conscious of *X, Y, Z*, then there is one consciousness of *X, Y, Z*. For this inference to work, *X, Y, Z* must be my perceptions, not just any perceptions, and so the inference is just equivalent to the above mentioned trivial denial. As Kant's own considerations in the Paralogisms indicate, it is not evident that the having of a series of perceptions requires that one subject have 'all perceptions'.[9]

Whatever their differences, the advocates of the *RI* agree in striving to find in Kant's transcendental deduction an argument deducing empirical knowledge from consciousness and its conditions. Since even those who have wanted to find such an argument in Kant have failed to construct a significant valid one, it should be determined whether Kant himself was really concerned with developing such an argument. Though there are some prima facie indications to the contrary, which will be dealt with later, the overwhelming evidence is that Kant did not put forth the transcendental deduction as having the aim the *RI* imputes to it. Kant nowhere states that it is to give the sufficient conditions of empirical knowledge or is a proof that there is an objective world. What Kant says he is doing is providing a deduction of the categories, a proof of *their* objective validity, which, since they are pure concepts, can be done only by showing their a priori applicability to experience, i.e. by showing that they are part of the (necessary) conditions for the

---

[9] See Ben Mijuskovic, 'The Premise of the Transcendental Analytic', *Philosophical Quarterly*, 23 (1973), 156–61. Mijuskovic shows that Wolff's candidate for the premise of the deduction cannot be correct. His own view is that Kant's ultimate premise is time consciousness, but this view is independent of his valid critique of Wolff, and is not supported by the final version of the deduction.

possibility of experience (A93, A95, B169), where 'experience' is defined as 'empirical knowledge' (B147, B161, etc.). The question to which Kant addressed his argument is whether appearances universally obey pure synthetic principles. His answer was expressly dependent on the use of the notion of 'possible experience'. He says there is no direct proof, for example, from the concept of an event or happening to the legitimacy of the causal maxim; the argument of the Analytic must invoke the characteristics that an event needs to be empirically knowable in order for it to establish the maxim (B765, B815).

IV

Kant's own statements about the nature of the transcendental deduction support the earlier account of its structure which was proposed as an alternative to the *RI*. But the claim that the deduction should be treated as having this structure cannot rest on this appeal to authority. It must be shown that it is plausible and significant for an argument to have this form—a matter all proponents of the *RI* have doubted. In response to these doubts, I will clarify the form of the deduction on my interpretation and show that the deduction so construed, as employing the possession of empirical knowledge as a premise, is nonetheless not trivial.

The first task is best achieved by taking care of a natural objection to the interpretation given in Section I. There it was proposed that Kant's transcendental deductions are in general best regarded as having a regressive and not a progressive form. Yet it was also said that a typical progressive argument would have a synthetic a priori principle as its conclusion. Now if the essence of the transcendental deduction is the argument that empirical knowledge is possible only if the categories are applicable, and hence only if some synthetic a priori principles are true, it would appear that the deduction is progressive after all. Furthermore, the argument appears to move deductively to its conclusion from premises non-trivially entailing it, since 'experience' is not defined as involving synthetic a priori principles. Despite these considerations, it can be shown that the proposed interpretation is a genuine alternative to the *RI* and that there is good reason for calling the deduction regressive. What complicates matters here is the relativity of the terms 'progressive' and 'regressive'. It is not adequate to define the former as involving a demonstration of the sufficient conditions of something and the latter as a demonstration of necessary conditions, because in general one and the same argument demonstrates both necessary and sufficient conditions (if x implies y, x is a sufficient condition of y and y is a necessary condition of x). However, once the epistemological concern of transcendental arguments is taken into account, I believe adequate distinguishing definitions of 'progressive' and 'regressive' are available: a regressive argument would show that y is a necessary condition of knowledge x; a progressive argument would show that z is a sufficient condition of knowledge x, where z is a type of representation not defined as epistemic. These definitions have the merit of making just the distinction advocates of the *RI* would also recognize. When I argue that the deduction is regressive as just defined, this is to say that it is not progressive in their sense; that is, it is not a radical argument from a premise not assuming the possession of knowledge. This does not put me into conflict with Kant's claim in the *Prolegomena* that the *Critique* has a progressive form, for his criterion of 'progressive' refers not to the premise but to the conclusion of the argument. It can be agreed that the deduction is progressive simply in the sense that it proceeds toward the establishment of synthetic a priori principles.

The most common objection to regarding the transcendental deduction as regressive is that this would render it trivial. To paraphrase Strawson, doesn't an argument which uses empirical knowledge as a premise just present the skeptic with conclusions which can have no more strength than its questionable assumptions? The first reply to this question is that not every interesting argument has to be a refutation of extreme skepticism. Secondly, there are different levels of triviality and the transcendental deduction is not formulated as trivially as it might be. On this interpretation Kant's premise is not, as is often assumed,[10] Newtonian and Euclidean science, but is the relatively weak assumption of some empirical knowledge. Furthermore, the conclusion of the argument is relatively strong. The argument is not the circular claim that experience (empirical knowledge) requires mere objectivity; it is the claim that such experience requires the universal validity of a number of a priori concepts.[11] So the argument does move from a relatively weak premise to a relatively strong conclusion, and while the argument so contrued perhaps does not have to move as far as the *RI* version of it does, it still makes a substantive claim. What makes this regressive argument vulnerable is not that it argues for so little but that it claims so much. Later I will show that it is only by making considerable metaphysical assumptions that Kant

---

[10] See e.g. S. Körner, 'On the Kantian Foundation of Science and Mathematics', in *The First Critique*, ed. Terence Penelhum and J. J. MacIntosh (Belmont, Calif. 1969), 97–108; and T. D. Weldon, *Kant's Critique of Pure Reason*, 2nd edn (Oxford, 1958), 75. It has been called to my attention that an extensive demonstration that Kant's argument in the Aesthetic does not depend on Euclidean geometry is given by T. B. Humphrey, 'The Historical and Conceptual Relations between Kant's Metaphysics of Space and Philosophy of Geometry', *Journal of the History of Philosophy*, 2 (1973), 483–512.

[11] A failure to appreciate this point is manifest in M. Gram's recent and typical interpretation: 'In order to show something transcendentally, we must be able to show something about experience in the strong sense [= empirical knowledge] while being restricted to an . . . argument [which] must rely on the weak sense [= mere consciousness] of "experience"' ('Must Transcendental Arguments Be Spurious?', *Kant-Studien*, 65 (1974), 304–17). Gram concludes that transcendental arguments are therefore impossible, but he neglects the relevant possibility of an argument from one strong sense of experience to another, i.e. from empirical knowledge to the validity of the categories. Compare S. Körner's worry that an 'analytic' transcendental deduction would be trivial: 'If a transcendental judgement were analytic, it could certainly establish what can be deduced from our philosophical presuppositions of whatever kind they might be, but it could never justify these presuppositions' ('On the Kantian Foundation', 98). Once again, it can be asked why the assumption is made that a transcendental deduction must be absolutely presuppositionless.

manages to complete the deduction, but whatever possible weaknesses this may indicate in Kant's strategy, it at the same time lays to rest the most common objection to that strategy.

V

At this point it may appear a sheer mystery how the *RI* has received the support it has. It would be improper to suggest that the only basis of the *RI* is the penchant of contemporary philosophers to make out of Kant's philosophy a radical refutation of skepticism. There are two prominent features of the text which strongly suggest there is a progressive argument in the deduction. The first is the emphasis on the fundamental importance of the 'transcendental unity of apperception', the thesis that representations must be capable of being my representations and must meet the conditions of being elements within the unity of consciousness. This point, more than anything else, has been responsible for the view that Kant meant to deduce the validity of the categories from the 'fact of consciousness'. Even in the second edition, Kant begins the deduction with a discussion of the unity of consciousness and the 'many consequences' that follow from it (B132–3). However, it is not clear that developing the consequences of the 'original unity of apperception' is equivalent to drawing out the implications of the mere having of representations. If it were, the deduction would appear to have the progressive structure of an argument for consciousness as a logically sufficient condition of the validity of at least some objective concepts. But Kant immediately distinguishes 'original apperception' from 'empirical apperception' (B132) in such a way that only the latter designates the mere having of representations. 'Empirical consciousness' as such is not argued to have any implications with respect to the objective validity of concepts. On the other hand, 'the transcendental unity of apperception is that unity through which the manifold given in an intuition is united in the concept of the object. It is therefore entitled objective and must be distinguished from the subjective unity of consciousness, which is a determination of inner sense...' (B139). Kant makes it clear that the transcendental unity of apperception is a necessary condition of empirical knowledge; representations which cannot be unified as mine cannot be representations which amount to knowledge (B137). If it is also the case that the condition that representations agree with the transcendental and not merely the empirical unity of consciousness just means for Kant that they are objectively related, then 'original apperception' would be a sufficient condition of empirical knowledge as well, though by definition and not because of any progressive argument. In paragraph 19 of the second edition Kant does say that the 'objective unity of given representations' is precisely what 'indicates their relation to original apperception' (B142). 'Original' and 'objective' unity of apperception are here interchangeable terms for Kant.

Hence, one cannot argue that the deduction is progressive simply because it begins with a discussion of the unity of consciousness and its conditions, for there is strong evidence that the unity which concerns Kant is not that given with the 'fact of consciousness' but is that involved when there is 'objective' consciousness, i.e. experience in his sense.

There is a further important reason for not regarding ordinary consciousness as the starting point of Kant's argument. Such a perspective makes unintelligible the structure of the deduction in the second edition. If the *RI* is right, the demonstration in paragraph 20 that intuitions are subject to the categories should complete the deduction, for if the starting point of the argument is the consideration of just any representations that come before consciousness, any proof that representations are subject to the categories should be conclusive. However, Kant insists that the deduction's purpose is 'fully attained' only later, in paragraph 26, 'by demonstration of the a priori validity of the categories in respect of all objects of our senses' (B145). This statement expresses Kant's view that the aim of the deduction is the proof not of mere objectivity but of the validity of the categories, and also makes clear that the central issue of their validity is settled only after paragraph 20. Contrary to what is assumed by recent analytic interpretations, the later paragraphs are meant not as a mere spelling out of the subjective circumstances involved in the application of the categories, but as a continuation of the basic argument of the deduction.[12]

The 'beginning' of the deduction concerns the use of the categories for representations already unified in one intuition. Kant's early discussion repeatedly focuses on 'the manifold of representations in *an* intuition' (B133, 135, 139). In paragraphs 20 and 21 he capitalizes 'Einer' to indicate his concern with the unity of one intuition. This point stands out in the German but is somewhat lost in the translation,[13] though it is obvious once attention is given to the footnote to B144, which states that the proof 'so far rests on the represented unity of intuition' (cf. B155 n., 160 n.), and to the repeated statement of paragraph 20 that the argument concerns 'the manifold ... so far as it is given in a single empirical intuition'. Kant's argument to this point is that representations in one intuition are unified by consciousness, that the logical functions of judgment just are the ways consciousness unifies representations, hence these representations must be subject to

---

[12] This point and much of the analysis in the following section is indebted to Dieter Henrich, 'The Proof Structure of Kant's Transcendental Deduction', *Review of Metaphysics*, 22 (1969), 640–59. Cf. also G. Prauss, *Erscheinung bei Kant* (Berlin, 1971), 277.

[13] The essential two-part structure of the proof is somewhat hidden from English readers because of weaknesses in Smith's otherwise excellent translation. The pivotal sentence in paragraph 21, B144, should read: 'Thus in the above proposition a beginning is made of a deduction of the pure concepts of the understanding; and in this deduction *so far*, since the categories have their source in the understanding alone, independently of sensibility, I have abstracted from the mode in which the manifold for an empirical intuition is given, *in order to* direct attention solely to the unity ...'

these functions. The argument depends heavily on the general validity of the 'metaphysical deduction' and its claim that 'the same function which gives unity to the various representations in a judgement also gives unity to the mere synthesis of various representations in an intuition' (B104). Here I will focus not on that difficult claim but on Kant's remarkable belief that still more has to be established for the transcendental deduction to be complete.[14]

The concern of the second part of the deduction is indicated in the title of paragraph 26: 'Transcendental deduction of the *universal* possible employment in experience of the pure concepts of the understanding'. Kant's earlier argument that the categories apply to representations which are unified in *an* intuition leaves open the question whether the categories apply to representations not so united. Kant has argued that the unity of an intuition depends on the 'original unity of apperception', but if this in turn is just the objective unity of experience, it is natural to inquire whether there are representations which 'may present themselves to our senses' not in conformity with the categories. In particular, one might wonder whether it is necessary for the elements of mere perception (prior to their unification in the thought of a singular item, an intuition) to be in agreement with the 'logical forms of judgment', whether, as Kant puts it, the 'empirical synthesis of apprehension' must conform with the 'intellectual synthesis of apperception' (B162 n)—a question which Kant takes not to have been resolved earlier. It is very significant that Kant's answer here is not to directly invoke the conditions of the unity of consciousness, but to argue along lines set down by the Aesthetic, which had shown that all *our* representations must be in space or time and that we are a priori certain of the unity of space and time. Kant now argues that, since all unity (and hence this unity too) 'presupposes a synthesis which does not belong to the senses' (B160 n.) but to the understanding and its categories, 'everything that is to be represented as determined in space or in time must conform' to the categories (B161). It is thus the universality and unity of space and time, not the unity of consciousness as such, which is invoked to guarantee the 'universal validity' of the

---

[14] Obviously, much hinges on the metaphysical deduction, for the ultimate success of Kant's argument depends on his properly identifying specific pure categories necessary for judgments and properly coordinating these with a set of principles which are unique and basic with respect to our spatio-temporal experience. I am not assuming that Kant succeeds on this task. S. Körner has gone so far as to claim that this task is in principle impossible ('The Impossibility of Transcendental Deductions', *Monist*, 51 (1967), 317–31), but in view of Eva Schaper's response ('Arguing Transcendentally', *Kant-Studien*, 63 (1972), 101–16), Körner's argument cannot be taken to be decisive. This issue, and Schaper's specific arguments against Körner, are independent of any theses about what Kant meant, but I do believe Körner has seriously misconstrued Kant's strategy. According to him, Kant's transcendental deduction is 'aimed at showing that and how a priori concepts are applicable or possible, [and] examines only the schema which has been established by the metaphysical exposition of this particular schema. It thus does not examine a schema the uniqueness of which has been demonstrated. [Hence, Kant fails] even to *consider the need* for interpolating a uniqueness demonstration' (Körner, *Impossibility*, 323). This is quite a strong charge, for, as has been argued above, the explicit aim of Kant's transcendental deduction is to establish the categories as necessary conditions of experience, and to do this is precisely to argue for their unique validity.

categories for us. In this way Kant's deduction in the Analytic depends on the doctrine of idealism in the Aesthetic, for only the thesis that space and time are forms of the mind, dependent on it and a priori knowable, can justify the certainty that they are unities determining all our representations.

These points can shed light on the second feature of Kant's text which might appear to lend support to the *RI*. In paragraph 13, Kant considers the possibility of

> appearances so constituted that the understanding should not find them to be in accord with the conditions of its unity. Everything might be in such confusion that, for instance, in the series of appearances nothing presented itself which might yield a rule of synthesis and so answer to the concept of cause and effect. (B123)

Because of this passage, the transcendental deduction has often been read as essentially having the purpose of showing against Hume that we can be certain of a lawful and therefore objective world. On this view the deduction's aim is to establish the causal maxim and in this way to prove there is something to be distinguished from the arbitrary sequences of one's mental states. However, an alternative interpretation is possible, and there are reasons for believing that Kant saw that the transcendental deduction was not designed to establish the causal maxim from scratch. The possibility of a world of chaotic representations which Kant mentions in paragraph 13 can be understood as presenting not the traditional problem of skepticism, but rather the problem which the two-part structure of the second edition deduction explicitly raises, namely whether the scope of the categories extends to all our representations or just to a subset already considered objective by definition. This interpretation might also explain why, in the pivotal paragraph 20 of that deduction, Kant reminds the reader to refer back to paragraph 13. While the *RI* takes the notion of representations not subject to the categories as something directly contrary to the central argument of the *Critique*, something the mature Kant supposedly could not have seriously entertained, it is easier (especially in view of the preservation of the section in the second edition) to take it simply to represent the logical possibility, which Kant continued to stress, that our sensibility might have been such that what is given our senses would not be determined as it is by unified pure forms of sensibility.

I will conclude my critique of the *RI* by analyzing those passages in the deduction itself which have supported the belief that Kant's primary concern is to reply to the skeptic and establish the objectivity of experience by proving the causal maxim. In the first edition, Kant does argue that 'appearances are themselves actually subject to a rule', for otherwise the 'reproducibility of appearances', which is itself 'necessary to experience', would be impossible (A100). Kant's conclusion is that 'all appearances stand in thoroughgoing community according to necessary laws and therefore in a transcendental affinity', and that without causality perceptions would 'be without an object, merely a blind play of representations' (A112,

A114). This suggests that somehow Kant was trying to argue that the necessity of some order among representations is tantamount to the validity of the category of causality. But the 'affinity' that Kant argues for is not at all equivalent to the reign of the principle of universal causality. The requirement that the world not be such that cinnabar is 'sometimes red, sometimes black, sometimes light', is a requirement that can be met without the law of causality applying to all objective appearances. On the other hand, a world could be so arranged that it universally obeyed strict causal laws and yet was so various that no adequate 'affinity' of appearances would be available to human observers. Affinity can be either a stronger or a weaker condition than causality, and it really is not essential to Kant's main argument for the objective validity of the categories *in general*, a fact which is evident from Kant's omission of the topic in the second edition. The phenomenon which it was supposed to explain in the first edition, the empirical reproducibility of appearances, is passed over in the second edition as an 'only subjective' and secondary feature (B140).

The second edition also alone gives an appropriate discussion of the 'necessary' relation that objects of experience have. The example that the first edition gives of the thesis that 'the relation of all knowledge to its object carries with it an element of necessity' (A104) is the concept of a triangle, which provides a rule for uniting and reproducing representations of it. This suggests that the necessity involved in objective representations is equivalent to the relation of logical necessity between the concept of a thing and its defined constituents (e.g. 'three straight lines'). In the second edition Kant rectifies this suggestion by noting that the 'necessary unity' of representations which he means to prove signifies not that representations 'necessarily belong to one another', but that 'they belong to one another in virtue of the necessary unity of apperception in the synthesis of intuition' (B142). What Kant argues is not that individual representations have a necessary tie with one another, but that for representations really to be representations of one item it is necessary that they be thought of as combined in an object, and this just is for them to be unified in accordance with the logical form of judgment.

In conclusion, it should be emphasized that I have argued only that a regressive interpretation of the transcendental deduction is supported by evidence of Kant's intentions and by recognition that such an argument need not be trivial, question begging, or tied to the scientific presuppositions of Kant's day. I have not contended that the deduction so construed, as moving from empirical knowledge to the universal validity of the categories, is valid. But as noted before, the progressive interpretation has failed to find a valid argument in the deduction, and if one is to be found it seems only proper to proceed by first testing that proof structure which is best aligned with Kant's own avowed and considered strategy.

– 2 –

Recent Work On Kant's Theoretical Philosophy

SINCE M. J. Scott-Taggart's 1966 survey,[1] there has been an explosion of fruitful work on Kant that has made it impossible to provide a similarly inclusive and manageable review today.[2] Thus I have found it necessary here to exclude discussions of Kant's practical philosophy,[3] as well as of the helpful studies that the last decade has finally brought to the aesthetic and methodological issues of the period of Kant's third *Critique*.[4] And even with respect to the first *Critique*, it is possible only to mention that there have been great clarifications of such familiar topics as Kant's account of mathematics,[5] intuition,[6] and

---

[1] M. J. Scott-Taggart, 'Recent Work in the Philosophy of Kant', *American Philosophical Quarterly*, 3 (1966), 171–209, and amended version in L. W. Beck (ed.), *Kant Studies Today* (LaSalle, 1969).

[2] To get some idea of the scope of extant work on Kant, readers should consult Gerold Prauss (ed.), *Kant: Zur Deutung seiner Theorie von Erkennen und Handeln* (Cologne, 1973); Pierre Laberge, 'Dix années d'études canadokantiennes (1968–78)', *Philosophiques*, 5 (1978), 331–80; and R. C. S. Walker, *A Selective Bibliography on Kant*, 2nd edn (Oxford, 1978), as well as the lists in *Kant-Studien* (which include, for example, over 500 items for 1975 alone).

[3] Some of these are reviewed in Zwi Batscha (ed.), *Materialen zu Kants Rechtsphilosophie* (Frankfurt, 1976); Rüdiger Bittner and Konrad Cramer (eds.), *Materialen zu Kants 'Kritik der praktischen Vernunft'* (Frankfurt, 1976); and Karl Ameriks, 'Kant's Deduction of Freedom and Morality', *Journal of the History of Philosophy*, 19 (1981), 53–79.

[4] Some of these are reviewed in Jens Kulenkampff (ed.), *Materialen zu Kants 'Kritik der Urteilskraft'* (Frankfurt, 1974); Karl Ameriks, '*Kant and the Claims of Taste* by P. Guyer', *New Scholasticism*, 54 (1980), 241–9; Wolfgang Bartuschat, 'Neuere Arbeiten zu Kants *Kritik der Urteilskraft*', *Philosophische Rundschau*, 18 (1971), 161–82; and Werner Stegmaier, 'Kant's Theorie der Naturwissenschaft', *Philosophisches Jahrbuch*, 89 (1980), 363–77.

[5] See e.g. Gordan Brittan, *Kant's Theory of Science* (Princeton, 1978); Rainer Enskat, *Kants Theorie des geometrischen Gegenstandes* (Berlin, 1978); R. P. Horstmann, 'Space as Intuition and Geometry', *Ratio*, 28 (1976), 18–30; Ted Humphrey, 'The Historical and Conceptual Relations between Kant's Metaphysics of Space and Philosophy of Geometry', *Journal of the History of Philosophy*, 11 (1973), 483–512; Philip Kitcher, 'Kant and the Foundations of Mathematics', *Philosophical Review*, 84 (1975), 23–50; Ulrich Majer and Rainer Stuhlmann-Laeisz, 'Das Verhältnis von Mathematik und Metaphysik in Kants Theorie der Naturwissenschaft', *Grazer Philosophische Studien*, 5 (1975), 165–88; Charles Parsons, 'Kant's Philosophy of Arithmetic', in *Philosophy, Science and Method*, ed. S. Morgenbesser, P. Suppes, and M. White (New York, 1969), 568–94; and J. E. Wiredu, 'Kant's Synthetic A Priori in Geometry and the Rise of Non-Euclidean Geometries', *Kant-Studien*, 61 (1970), 5–27.

[6] See e.g. Moltke Gram, 'The Crisis of Syntheticity: the Kant–Eberhard Controversy', *Kant-Studien*, 71 (1980), 155–80; J. Hintikka, 'On Kant's Notion of Intuition', in T. Penelhum and J. J. MacIntosh (eds.),

causality.[7] Similarly, it can be only noted in passing that some neglected and especially difficult topics have begun to receive due attention, e.g. Kant's account of empirical concepts,[8] and the positive aspects of his treatment of rational psychology[9] and rational theology.[10]

Significant as these topics are, recent discussions continue to be dominated by what Ralph Walker[11] has called the two 'central issues' of the *Critique*, namely transcendental idealism and transcendental arguments. Scott-Taggart began his survey by drawing attention to the first issue and by reviewing the historical work which more and more had stressed the rationalist and metaphysical side of Kant's philosophy. He could hardly have anticipated how popular Strawson and others would make the second issue, and how this would bring with it a reapplication of Kant to the classical concerns of empiricism. In reviewing the discussion of both of these issues, I will be implying that we have come full circle now. The recent attempts to tone down Kant's discussion of idealism, and to formulate his transcendental approach mainly in terms of a solution to the problem of the

The First Critique (Belmont, Calif., 1969); J. Hintikka, 'Kantian Intuitions', *Inquiry*, 15 (1972), 341–5; Wilfrid Sellars, *Science and Metaphysics: Variations on Kantian Themes* (London, 1968); Manley Thompson, 'Singular Terms and Intuitions in Kant's Epistemology', *Review of Metaphysics*, 26 (1972), 314–43; Ian White, 'Kant on Forms of Intuition', *Proceedings of the Aristotelian Society*, 79 (1978–9), 123–35; T. E. Wilkerson, 'Things, Stuffs and Kant's Aesthetic', *Philosophical Review*, 82 (1973), 169–87; and K. D. Wilson, 'Kant on Intuition', *Philosophical Quarterly*, 25 (1975), 247–65.

[7] See e.g. H. E. Allison, 'Kant's Non-Sequitur: An Examination of the Lovejoy–Strawson Critique of the Second Analogy', *Kant-Studien*, 68 (1977), 367–77; L. W. Beck, *Essays on Kant and Hume* (New Haven, 1978); Gerd Buchdahl, *Metaphysics and the Philosophy of Science* (Cambridge, Mass., 1969); D. P. Dryer, 'Kant's Argument for the Principle of Causality', in P. Laberge, F. Duchesneau, and B. Morrissey (eds.), *Proceedings of the Ottawa Congress on Kant in the Anglo-American and Continental Traditions* (Ottawa, 1976); Jeffrie G. Murphy, 'Kant's Second Analogy as an Answer to Hume', *Ratio*, 11 (1969), 75–8; Wrynn Smith, 'Kant and the General Law of Causality', *Philosophical Studies*, 32 (1977), 113–28; James Van Cleve, 'Four Recent Interpretations of Kant's Second Analogy', *Kant-Studien*, 64 (1973), 71–87; and James Van Cleve, 'Substance, Matter and Kant's First Analogy', *Kant-Studien*, 70 (1979), 152–61.

[8] R. E. Aquila, 'Kant's Theory of Concepts', *Kant-Studien*, 65 (1974), 1–19; R. E. Aquila, 'The Relationship between Pure and Empirical Intuition in Kant', *Kant-Studien*, 68 (1977), 275–89; R. B. Pippin, 'Kant on Empirical Concepts', *Studies in the History and Philosophy of Science*, 10 (1979), 1–19; and Michael Benedikt, 'Kritische Erwägungen zur jüngeren englischsprachigen Kantliteratur', *Philosophische Rundschau*, 17 (1970), 1–27 at 27 n.

[9] Karl Ameriks, *Kant's Theory of Mind* (Oxford, 1982); R. E. Aquila, 'Personal Identity and Kant's "Refutation of Idealism"', *Kant-Studien*, 70 (1979), 259–78; Alfons Kalter, *Kants vierter Paralogismus* (Meisenheim, 1975); J. L. Mackie, 'Kant on Personal Identity', *Grazer Philosophische Studien*, 10 (1980), 87–90; S. C. Patten, 'Kant's Cogito', *Kant-Studien*, 66 (1975), 321–41; Wilfrid Sellars, 'This I or He or It (the Thing) Which Thinks', *Proceedings of the American Philosophical Association*, 44 (1970–1), 5–31; Wilfrid Sellars, 'Metaphysics and the Concept of a Person', in *Essays in Philosophy and its History* (Dordrecht, 1974), pp. 214–43; and Michael Washburn, 'Did Kant Have a Theory of Self-Knowledge?', *Archiv für Geschichte der Philosophie*, 58 (1976), 40–56.

[10] Pierre Laberge, *La Théologie Kantienne précritique* (Ottawa, 1973); Josef Schmucker, *Das Problem der Kontingenz der Welt* (Freiburg, 1969); Josef Schmucker, 'On the Development of Kant's Transcendental Theology', in L. W. Beck (ed.), *Proceedings of the Third International Kant Congress* (Dordrecht, 1972), 495–500; Allen Wood, *Kant's Rational Theology* (Ithaca, NY, 1978); and Francois Marty, 'Bulletin d'études kantiennes: le problème metaphysique dans la philosophie de Kant', *Archives de Philosophie*, 34 (1971), 81–124.

[11] R. C. S. Walker, *Kant* (London, 1978).

external world, have run into so many problems that a return to something like the metaphysical school of interpretation may be expected.

1. Transcendental Idealism and the Thing in Itself

Most recent discussions of Kant's distinction between appearances and things in themselves fall into either one of two large groups. First, there are those who deny that the distinction is meant as a distinction between two different objects. These interpreters generally go on to defend some way of still understanding the designation of the spatio-temporal items of our knowledge as 'mere appearances'. Secondly, there are those who believe that Kant did mean his distinction to refer to different objects. Generally, these interpreters go on to argue that for this reason there are great philosophical weaknesses and inconsistencies in Kant's *Critique*. Hardly any interpreters defend the doctrine of the old textbook version of the *Critique*, the doctrine of a real distinction between a set of spatio-temporal and dependent appearances and a set of ultimately real things in themselves that are unknowable by us.

An important anticipation of the first group of recent interpretations is to be found in Graham Bird's work. Bird proposed that, in speaking philosophically of something as a thing in itself, we are not speaking of a thing that is other than an appearance (as can happen when we speak empirically about an object as opposed to its mere image): we are simply considering the thing no longer from a merely empirical perspective but rather from an epistemic one, and in particular from one that is 'transcendental' because it reveals certain a priori components.[12] This suggests not only that things in themselves and appearances are ontologically identical, but also that the philosophical consideration of things in themselves is just a philosophical consideration of them as appearances, i.e. as items of knowledge.

This approach to Kant obviously could absolve him from the charge of hypostatizing a second world, but by itself it does not give a full explanation of the doctrine of the unknowability of things in themselves, or of the passages that seem to speak positively about distinguishing things in themselves from appearances. The interpretation thus is to be filled out either by explaining more about how the proper transcendental perspective on things differs from some *improper* (and hence empty) view of them as things in themselves, or by developing some further and *proper* notion of what it would be to regard things as things in themselves—without multiplying entities or running afoul of Kant's limitations on our knowledge. These alternatives allow us to divide our first group of recent interpreters into two subclasses: those who take the first option and criticize even

---

[12] Graham Bird, *Kant's Theory of Knowledge* (London, 1962), 36 ff.

any separate *idea* of a thing in itself, and those who defend a distinct and intelligible sense in the idea of *considering* items *as* things in themselves rather than as appearances.

A strong example of the first subclass of interpreters is to be found in Arthur Melnick's treatment of transcendental idealism. Melnick argues that it is only proper to be a transcendental idealist, in the sense that objects are to be treated as phenomena because 'involved in the very concept of an object is that it is a way of organizing our experience'. That is, 'there is to be found in the transcendental deduction an analysis of an object (as essentially an epistemic notion) that in itself suffices to establish the point that an ontology cannot be a feature of the world itself but must refer to how a subject's experience is connected to his judgmental apparatus'.[13] Kant's idealism is acceptable once it is understood that 'he is making a point about the dependence of the *concept* of an object on the *notion* of a (judging) subject, not any point about the dependence of the existence of objects upon the existence of a subject'.[14]

This interpretation has the merit of distinguishing Kant's view from some absurd kinds of idealism, and it can be used to point out the genuine empirical realism in his philosophy. However, Melnick offers little textual evidence for his intepretation here, and there are obvious grounds for challenging it. It would be odd if Kant's idealism rested simply on the analysis of the concept of an object, for then Kant's arguments in the Aesthetic and the Antinomies would seem pointless, and yet it is precisely these arguments that we know represent Kant's own route to idealism. Melnick prefers to treat Kant's idealism as not resting essentially on the notion of forms of intuition and the peculiarities of space and time. He argues that to hold otherwise would be to hold that sensible intuitors with other kinds of sensibility could know things in themselves, and yet 'Kant does not think the objects of [such] an alternative sensible intuition are in any respect things in themselves'.[15] One trouble with this argument is that it does not distinguish between alternative kinds of sensibility that are without a priori forms and alternatives that do have such forms. It could be that, for reasons similar to those he offered for space and time, Kant would believe that the second kind of alternative would involve transcendental ideality. On the other hand, he gave no clear reason for saying that the first kind of alternative must involve transcendental ideality, and if he could have given such a reason, it is remarkable that he didn't do so in those parts of the text that most emphasize the idealism doctrine.

What especially distinguishes Melnick's interpretation is his radical idea of how we are to take the notion of a thing in itself. For him it is 'the notion of a non-

---

[13] Arthur Melnick, *Kant's Analogies of Experience* (Chicago, 1973), 133–4.
[14] Ibid. 145.
[15] Ibid. 153.

epistemic concept of what it is to be an object. It is an alternative conception of what is involved in being an object, the idea, namely, of a concept of an object that would have sense apart from any reference to how the experience of a subject hooks up epistemically to his intellectual (judgmental) structure'.[16] Thus, 'a thing in itself is not a different kind of thing... but rather a different kind of concept of a thing';[17] in fact, it is 'the notion of a concept quite literally incomprehensible to us'.[18] That is, since for Melnick we find on analysis that the notion of an object must be necessarily related to our forms of knowing, it is claimed that the notion of an object independent of such a relation is an absurdity.

However Melnick might back his analysis, it remains hard to see why it should be pinned on Kant, for it seems to conflict both with what Kant meant in stressing that we *can think* things in themselves, and with what we know about his belief that God can comprehend and know things in themselves. The closest thing to an appreciation for this problem in Melnick is his peculiar treatment of the idea of an intellectual intuition of things in themselves. His explanation of why we lack such an intuition is not the traditional one that we simply fail to have it because we are passive and finite, but is rather that we necessarily fail to have it because it's something that can't be had at all. That is, if we had such an intuition of an object, then we would have to be epistemically related to it, and so it couldn't be fully independent of us and couldn't be a thing in itself.[19] Once again, whatever intrinsic merit this line of reasoning may have, it goes quite counter to Kant's apparent views and makes it very hard to understand the way in which these views really were presented (namely, with all the passages that contrast our knowing with God's).

Others have expressed views quite similar to Melnick's, although their interpretations are not worked out in as much detail. Ralf Meerbote, for example, has held that 'to say things in themselves are unknowable is... merely to say that... objects in order to be known must satisfy particular conditions of knowledge',[20] and that to call spatio-temporal objects appearances in a transcendental sense 'means no more and no less than that objects, in order to be knowable, must be subsumable under particular a priori conditions'.[21] A similar view is expressed at one point by Hintikka, although he stresses that these 'a priori conditions' must

---

[16] Ibid. 152.
[17] Ibid. 154
[18] Ibid. 152.
[19] Ibid. 154.
[20] Ralf Meerbote, 'The Unknowability of Things in Themselves', in Moltke Gram (ed.), *Kant: Disputed Questions* (Chicago, 1967), 168.
[21] Ibid. 69; cf. R. P. Horstmann, 'Conceptual Schemes, Justification, and Consistency', in P. Bieri, R. P. Horstmann, and L. Krüger (eds.), *Transcendental Arguments and Science* (Dordrecht, 1979), 266; Paul Guyer, '*Kant: An Introduction* by C. D. Broad', *Philosophical Review*, 87 (1979), 640–7 at 643; and D. P. Dryer, 'Critical Notice: W. H. Walsh, *Kant's Criticism of Metaphysics*', *Canadian Journal of Philosophy*, 7 (1977), 413–23 at 420.

reflect structures of our 'knowledge seeking *activities*'.[22] All these views share the assumption that (even if things in themselves and appearances are not distinct objects) Kant could see no distinct and positive sense in *considering* objects *as* things in themselves. Moreover, it would seem that, even if Kant did tie the unknowability of things in themselves (which he speaks of as but a *theoretical* unknowability for *us*) very closely to the doctrine of a priori conditions of experience, he still meant that claim to be something to be inferred from the doctrine, and not something that is simply identical in meaning to it.

Jonathan Bennett has offered an interpretation that is similar to those studied so far, but is more open to acknowledging that at least sometimes Kant himself uses the term 'thing in itself' as if it were a consistent notion of something that is really distinct from appearances and unknowable.[23] Bennett insists, however, that 'Kant has no business using any such notion', and that he 'has no right to make even agnostic or negative uses' of phrases such as 'real in itself'.[24] The grounds for Bennett's insistence lie not merely in his own systematic views, but in his beliefs about the basic meaning of the *Critique*. That meaning supposedly rests in a doctrine which Bennett calls 'concept empiricism' and which 'implies that we can understand only statements which have implications for possible experience'.[25] Unless it is made trivial, this doctrine verges on conflating claims about what is required for justification with claims about what is required for meaning, and, as others have noted,[26] there are fortunately good grounds for withholding its ascription to Kant.

The peculiarity and vulnerability of Bennett's approach shows up in a typical way in his treatment of the specific question of Kant's understanding of the meaning of 'reality'. On the basis of the fact that Kant provides a schematic and phenomenal definition for this term, Bennett states that it is an 'empirical concept' for Kant,[27] and so Kant can never mean to be contrasting the realm of appearances (which meets this definition) 'with any possible subject of investigation or even of conjecture'.[28] This implies that if a concept has an empirical use, then it is merely empirical. Yet the very passages that Bennett refers to in order to back his view, namely Kant's remarks about the 'real in appearances'

---

[22] J. Hintikka, ' "Dinge an Sich" Revisited', in Gerhard Funke (ed.), *Akten des 4. Internationalen Kant-Kongresses*, 3 vols. (Berlin, 1974–5), 89.

[23] Jonathan Bennett, *Kant's Dialectic* (Cambridge, 1974), 191; cf. John Hoaglund, 'The Thing in Itself in English Interpretations of Kant', *American Philosophical Quarterly*, 10 (1973), 1–14 at 14.

[24] Bennett, *Kant's Dialectic*, 52; cf. Lauchlan Chipman, 'Things in Themselves', *Philosophy and Phenomenological Research*, 33 (1973), 489–502 at 497; Gottfried Martin, 'A Lifetime's Study of Kant', *Synthese*, 23 (1971), 2–17 at 13 ff.

[25] Bennett, *Kant's Dialectic*, 52.

[26] D. P. Dryer, 'Bennett's Account of the Transcendental Dialectic', *Dialogue*, 15 (1976), 118–32; Paul Guyer, '*Kant's Dialectic* by Jonathan Bennett', *Philosophical Review*, 85 (1976), 274–82; Allen Wood, 'Critical Notice: *Kant's Dialectic* by Jonathan Bennett', *Canadian Journal of Philosophy*, 5 (1975), 595–614.

[27] Bennett, *Kant's Dialectic*, 49.

[28] Ibid. 56.

(B207 ff.),²⁹ can be used against him, for such phrases would be pleonastic if Bennett's view were accepted. The natural way to take Kant's remarks is rather as referring implicitly to a contrast between phenomenal and other senses (not theoretically determinable by us) of 'reality'. If Kant had not accepted such a distinction, then his own deep beliefs in God, an afterlife, and other non-empirical items would be entirely senseless. As Aquila has noted, 'Kant by no means concludes that there is no distinction between two sorts of existence claims [empirical and transcendent]; he merely observes that we lack [theoretical] criteria for determining the truth value of one of the sorts of claims'.³⁰

Some of the difficulties discussed so far disappear when we move to the second subclass of recent interpreters, those who say that, although for Kant there are not two objects involved, there are still two transcendental and *intelligible* aspects or points of view that are called for by his doctrine of things in themselves and appearances. Such a 'double aspect' interpretation can be found in work by H. E. Matthews, H. E. Allison, and Gerold Prauss.

Matthews' interpretation begins with the now familiar claim that 'Kant does not mean by an appearance or representation [in a transcendental sense] a particular type of thing such that it exists only in the mind. To talk about appearances is to talk about things from a particular point of view, namely as they are experienced by human beings'.³¹ Matthews moves toward new ground when he says that, although 'things in themselves . . . will be the very same things that we perceive', still when they are considered as such, they are to be 'considered from some other point of view than that of human experience'.³² Here the reference to an 'other point of view' seems to involve not merely a verbal but a real and intelligible possibility. To speak of things as appearances is thus to contrast them with a significant possibility; it is not to say merely that they are subject to a priori conditions, nor is it to contrast them with an (allegedly) absolutely incomprehensible idea of considering them apart from such conditions. Unfortunately, Matthews does not explain which other perspective(s) on things is the view on them as things in themselves. If any such view would do, then

---

²⁹ References in the text with 'A' or 'B', as is customary, refer to the first or second edition of the *Critique of Pure Reason*, as translated by N. K. Smith. Other references will be to the volumes of the *Akademische Ausgabe* (AA) of *Kants' Gesammelte Schriften* (Berlin, 1900–). This edition is still incomplete, and significant new material has been published recently. See J. Hintikka, ' "Dinge und Sich" Revisited', in Gerhard Funke (ed.), *Akten des 4. Internationalen Kant-Kongresses*, 3 vols. (Frankfurt, 1974–5), i. 86–96; Gerhard Lehmann, 'Zur Frage der Systematik in Kant's Metaphysikvorlesungen', in Gerhard Funke (ed.), *Akten des 4. Internationalen Kant-Kongresses*, 3 vols. (Berlin, 1974–5), i. 140–54; and Gerhard Lehmann, 'Die Vorlesungen Kants in der Akadamieausgabe', *Zeitschrift für philosophische Forschung*, 31 (1977), 283–9.
³⁰ R. E. Aquila, 'Things in Themselves and Appearances: Intentionality and Reality in Kant', *Archiv für Geschichte der Philosophie*, 61 (1979), 293–307 at 304; cf. Merold Westphal, 'In Defense of the Thing in Itself', *Kant-Studien*, 59 (1968), 118–41.
³¹ H. E. Mathews, 'Strawson on Transcendental Idealism', *Philosophical Quarterly*, 19 (1969), 204–20 at 208.
³² Ibid.

it would seem that all views, including ours, could be called views of things in themselves (and the 'double aspect' collapses into one). On the other hand, if there is some one privileged view, then there would be grounds for suspecting that Kant's talk about our view as dealing merely with phenomena is not as realistic in a commonsense way as Matthews believes.

Matthews' interpretation is also characterized by a detailed attempt to dismiss any idea that Kant is committed to facts 'which might be verified by non-empirical means'.[33] He presents Kant's belief in freedom as having to do with the mere adoption of a 'practical view';[34] he states that for Kant the proposition 'God exists' is neither true nor false;[35] and he recommends that any talk about our being affected by distinct things in themselves is to be translated into the observation that affection is a feature that 'helps define our human mode of experience'.[36] These claims are not entirely new, but they are controversial, and it is especially hard to understand why Kant was so negative about compatibilism and atheism, unless he believed that they deny what are important and real facts, even if they are not empirically verifiable ones.

The writings of Henry Allison go beyond Matthews in attempting to give more of an account of why and how we can be interested in specific kinds of considerations of objects as other than appearances for us. Allison arrived at a double aspect interpretation only after revising his own earlier views. He began by focusing not on the distinction between things in themselves and appearances, but rather on the distinction between the transcendental object and the thing in itself. His initial conclusion was that the former stands for the idea of a necessary unity among representations, whereas the thing in itself is understood by Kant not as such a mere idea but as a distinct cause of appearances.[37] Precisely because he interpreted Kant in this way, Allison criticized him for having only a 'half-emancipated' theory, for not seeing that transcendental philosophy requires only the notion of a transcendental object. (Allison thus also stated that for Kant to say something is necessary for experience is '*ipso facto*' to say it is subjective.[38]) In his later writings Allison has shifted to saying that it is not a 'two object' but rather a double-aspect view that Kant holds, 'for the most part'.[39]

---

[33] H. E. Matthews, 'Strawson on Transcendental Idealism', *Philosophical Quarterly*, 19 (1969), 204–20 at 208, 210.

[34] Ibid. 211.

[35] Ibid.

[36] Ibid. 217.

[37] H. E. Allison, 'Kant's Concept of the Transcendental Object', *Kant-Studien*, 68 (1959), 166–86 at 178; cf. Donald Gotterbarn, 'Objectivity without Objects: A Non-Reductionist Interpretation of the Transcendental Object', in Gerhard Funke (ed.), *Akten des des 4. Internationalen Kant-Kongresses*, 3 vols. (Berlin, 1974–5), ii. 196–203; and Horst Seidl, 'Bemerkungen zu Ding an Sich und transzendentalen Gegenstand in Kants "Kritik der reinen Vernunft"', *Kant-Studien*, 63 (1972), 306–13 at 311.

[38] H. E. Allison, 'Kant's Transcendental Humanism', *Monist*, 55 (1971), 182–97 at 192.

[39] H. E. Allison, 'The Non-Spatiality of Things in Themselves for Kant', *Journal of the History of Philosophy*, 14 (1976), 313–21 at 317; cf. Allison, 'Kant's Transcendental Humanism', 194.

Here his discussions are especially helpful because they try to reconcile such an intepretation with Kant's remarks about space and time, the Antinomies, and the nature of affection.

Allison's treatment of space and time is unique in stressing and approving the fact that Kant did insist on claiming the non-spatio-temporality of things in themselves. Allison notes that this claim follows immediately on the traditional interpretation, and he argues that it also follows on the double aspect theory, for in that case to consider things as appearances is to consider them as spatio-temporal, whereas to *consider* them rather as in themselves is precisely not to consider them that way. A familiar difficulty here is how this claim can be compatible with Kant's remarks about the unknowability of things in themselves. Allison responds that there is no problem here, because the claim of the non-spatio-temporality of things in themselves is an analytic judgment, and Kant's restriction is to be taken as dealing simply with 'synthetic judgments about the real nature of things'.[40] This point is explained further in the analysis of the Antinomies, which claim that things in themselves not only can be (or are most likely to be), but also must be, non-spatio-temporal. Here Allison argues the doctrine of the phenomenality of space and time is to be seen as derivable independently of the controversial steps of the specific thesis and antithesis arguments, and can be said to follow from the fact that 'the conception of the physical world as a whole existing in itself is intrinsically incoherent'.[41] The basic argument is that 'the concept of an absolutely existing world of sense is purported to be empirical . . . as such the concept must be subject to rules of reference. But the object to which it refers, while purportedly empirical, violates the conditions of experience'.[42] It is not so clear to me that this claim can be accepted without an arbitrary restriction on 'experience' or a reference back to the specific arguments of the Antinomies after all.

In his most recent work Allison has taken on the especially difficult problem of Kant's positive remarks about things in themselves and affection.[43] Allison's view on these remarks is that they simply show how intelligible and necessary the consideration of objects as things in themselves was for Kant; they do not prove that such consideration must involve distinct objects. Here his view (like Prauss's) rests largely on a passage at B xxvi, where Kant notes that the *same* items can be seen as phenomena and things in themselves; and on passages from the *Opus Postumum*, where Kant calls the idea of a thing in itself 'not the thought of an extra object, but just an abstraction'.[44] The first passage may not be as conclusive

---

[40] Allison, 'Non-Spatiality', 320.
[41] H. E. Allison, 'Kant's Refutation of Realism', *Dialectica*, 30 (1976), 223–53 at 239.
[42] Ibid. 243.
[43] e.g. A251f.; B306; *AA*, IV.314.
[44] *AA*, XXII.31; cited in Gerold Prauss, *Kant und das Problem der Dinge an Sich* (Bonn, 1974), 60; cf. Hinrich Fink-Eitel, 'Kants Transzendentale Deduktion der Kategorien als Theorie des Selbstbewusstseins', *Zeitschrift für philosophische Forschung*, 32 (1978), 210–38 at 225.

as it appears, because it involves the special context of freedom, where it is important (and proper, given his practical philosophy) for Kant to maintain that there can be an identity between the being who appears in phenomenal and empirically determined action, and the one who in a transcendent way is an absolute source of this action. Such a view does not require that *in general* all phenomena and associated noumena are to be said to involve the very same objects. The second passage is more striking, but it comes from an even odder context (the scribblings of 1801), and in any case it still may be proper to hold that, while the *thought* of a thing in itself is not the thought of an object distinct from phenomena, there can be extra considerations in Kant's philosophy that would lead one to claim that in a sense there are objects (e.g. God) distinct from phenomena.

In developing his account of affection, Allison at first asserts merely that 'others' (P. Lachièze-Rey, B. Rousset, G. Prauss) have 'decisively repudiated' the traditional two object or 'double affection' theory,[45] but then he goes on to build his own account and to suggest that others have not gone far enough. Whereas Prauss, for example, speaks of certain 'relapses',[46] such as Kant's remark in his response to Eberhard to the effect that the thing in itself is not the matter of experience but rather its ground,[47] Allison contends that even in such passages Kant can be taken to mean simply that 'the thought of the affecting object as ground or cause of our representations is a merely analytic truth'.[48] One problem here is that Allison's own interpretation of the transcendental object might be taken to allow us to make sense of our having representations, and even objective representations, without having to admit any other really affecting being.

In order to find the most developed argument for the double aspect interpretation, one must turn to the writings of Gerold Prauss. Although Prauss admits he is interested primarily in a systematic reconstruction of what Kant *ought* to have said,[49] he provides a most impressive textual basis for the double aspect interpretation. First, he presents a precise quantitative and linguistic study of Kant's uses of the phrase 'thing in itself', and he notes that in the overwhelming majority of cases Kant uses not the mere phrase *Ding an sich* but rather *Ding an sich selbst*. He claims that the latter should in turn be seen as an abbreviation for *Ding an sich selbst betrachtet*, and he concludes that the phrase 'thing in itself' in its full meaning is adverbial rather than adjectival; it is meant to designate a special way of looking at things, and not to hypostatize a special kind of thing. However, as various

---

[45] H. E. Allison, 'Things in Themselves, Noumena, and the Transcendental Object', *Dialectica*, 32 (1978), 41–76 at 65.
[46] Prauss, *Kant und das Problem*, 103.
[47] *AA*, IV.215; cf. *AA*, IV.459.
[48] Allison, 'Things in Themselves', 72, 76.
[49] See Gerold Prauss, *Erscheinung bei Kant: Ein Problem der 'Kritik der reinen Vernunft'* (Berlin, 1971), 175; and Prauss, *Kant und das Problem*, 41, 75, 204.

reviewers have indicated,[50] there are some passages that rather imply the traditional adjectival interpretation (B164, A504/B532 f.), and the fact is that Kant makes little use, even at the very end of his career, of the full phrase that Prauss takes to be the key. Moreover, even if the adverbial formulation were taken to be the main one in Kant and ordinary usage, this alone would not resolve the issue of its philosophical meaning.

Secondly, Prauss places much weight on the few specific passages that do seem explicitly to express the double aspect view.[51] It turns out that these passages occur in the same special contexts that were discussed in the review of Allison, and so the qualifications noted then become all the more important. Another difficulty is that, in insisting that Kant must mean 'thing in itself' and 'phenomenon' to refer to the same object, Prauss may be overinfluenced by a point that occurs in other interpretations, namely that, 'if we want to distinguish a human standpoint on the world from other possible standpoints, then we [still must] imply that they are all standpoints on the same world'.[52] The limitation of this truism is that it can show only that ultimately there can be but one *world*; it doesn't show that the ultimate components of that world are to be aligned in a one to one identity or correspondence relation with the items we distinguish as phenomena.

Thirdly, Prauss makes much use of passages that occur in Kant's treatment of the problem of arriving at an objective meaning from givens that are merely subjective appearances, and he emphasizes the statement that 'appearances that are determined by categories are phenomena' (A248; see also A20/B34: appearance 'is the undetermined object of empirical intuition').[53] It is remarkable how similar (but more detailed) Prauss's reading of such passages is to what one would expect from Melnick, for Prauss states that the very determination of objects by inescapable a priori conditions is what Kant means by calling them 'phenomena' in a transcendental sense.[54] Thus, Prauss also finds it unfortunate that Kant generally expresses his idealism as if it were rather tied to the idea that we have ultimately contingent forms of sensibility. Prauss therefore emphasizes those few places (A114, A581/B609) where Kant speaks as if the transcendental ideality of an object does follow simply from its being something we can determine by our judgmental (as opposed to sensory) apparatus.[55] In reply, one might hold that these passages are rare for a good reason, that they are mere slips which fail to reiterate the general emphasis that Kant gives to his notions of space and time. Moreover, even if Kant

---

[50] Beck, 'Meta-Critique', 297; Claudius Strube, '*Kant und das Problem der Dinge an Sich* von Gerold Prauss', *Zeitschrift für philosophische Forschung*, 30 (1976), 487–90.
[51] See Gerold Prauss, *Erscheinung bei Kant: Ein Problem der 'Kritik der reinen Vernunft'* (Berlin, 1971), 22; and Gerold Prauss, *Kant und das Problem*, 27, 32.
[52] Mathews, 'Strawson', 209; cf. Prauss, *Kant und das Problem*, 31.
[53] Cf. Prauss, *Erscheinung bei Kant*, 21, 24; Bird, *Kant's Theory of Knowledge*, 6.
[54] Prauss, *Kant und das Problem*, 57–8.
[55] Ibid. 38, 59, 184; Gerold Prauss, 'Zum apriorischen Entwurf', *Philosophische Rundschau*, 22 (1976), 190–9 at 196.

says that determined appearances *are* phenomena, this need not mean that the categorial determination of them is what their phenomenality consists in; Kant may have meant to indicate merely an extensional rather than an intensional equivalence. Here Prauss would also have to deal with the problem of Kant's remarks that we can 'think' things in themselves, since there is a pure meaning to the categories independent of space and time and their phenomenality. Like Melnick, Prauss has no sympathy with this idea, but he does not develop a detailed rebuttal.[56]

Where Prauss goes far beyond Melnick is in his explanation of how the recognition of the categorial determination of phenomena (or of what he calls 'the projection of the transcendental object') is only one half of the project of transcendental philosophy. (Baum and Horstmann's review strikes me as unreliable here because it misses this point.[57]) The other half is to explain what it would be to consider these same objects (transcendentally) in themselves, that is, not as they are determined by our a priori forms. With a fine flair for drama, Prauss himself emphasizes the difficulty of this project. He stresses that on his view such a consideration is not to lead to a view of something that is literally a 'non-appearance', nor to a revelation of new contents in objects, for it is essential to Kant that all the content we can know is subject to the categories.[58] Nonetheless, Prauss thinks a kind of distinct sense can be given to considering objects as things in themselves. This is simply to consider them as something that is in some way transcendentally independent of us, and Prauss explains that such consideration comes down to a matter of recognizing rather than cognizing (*anzuerkennen ohne zu erkennen*) objects.[59] I suspect what he means is that, no matter how responsible our understanding may be (transcendentally) for the meaning of objects, for the structures they have that can be asserted truly or falsely, still the fact that objects exist, and that on particular occasions we obtain truth rather than falsity, is not a matter that is wholly up to our 'judgmental apparatus'.

Prauss concludes his study with a discussion of the problem of affection, which he gives a treatment that is similar to the one already discussed in relation to Allison. Prauss adds that to state the problem in a fair and interesting manner is already to refer to entities under something more than a merely empirical description. He believes this is to bring in the experiencing subject as an active source of

---

[56] Prauss, *Kant*, 146 n.
[57] Manfred Baum and R. P. Horstmann, 'Metaphysik und Erfahrungstheorie in Kants theoretischer Philosophie', *Philosophische Rundschau*, 25 (1979), 62–91 at 88; but cf. Günther Maluschke, '*Kant und das Problem der Dinge an Sich* von Gerold Prauss', *Kant-Studien*, 67 (1976), 586–93; Werner Marx, '*Erscheinung bei Kant* und *Kant und das Problem der Dinge an Sich* von Gerold Prauss', *Philosophisches Journal*, 84 (1975), 422–6; Robert Pippin, '*Erscheinung bei Kant* by Gerold Prauss', *Journal of the History of Philosophy*, 12 (1974), 403–5; Robert Pippin, '*Kant und das Problem der Dinge an Sich* by Gerold Prauss', *Journal of the History of Philosophy*, 14 (1976), 374–8.
[58] Prauss, *Kant und das Problem*, 38, 134.
[59] Ibid. 145–6, 83, 133; cf. Prauss, *Erscheinung bei Kant*, 91.

intentionality, as a complex of *Sinngebilde* or semantic vehicles which are unlike mere objects in that they can be true or false. What Prauss here does not enter into is a consideration of recent analyses such as Sellars', which point toward a rather different and naturalistic (functionalistic) account of the 'active' (*leistende*) experiencing subjectivity that he takes to be ultimate.[60]

If we turn now to the second group of recent interpreters, those who hold that Kant did subscribe to the two object theory of appearances and things in themselves, we find that for the most part they differ simply in the intensity of their disapproval of such a view.

Perhaps the most extreme example of this kind of position is to be found in a series of articles by Moltke Gram, who has refurbished Jacobi's old charge both that Kant requires distinct things in themselves and that his own theory simultaneously forbids such entities. According to Gram, Kant requires such entities because of the doctrine of space and time as forms of intuition; if we were affected by ultimately real spatio-temporal features rather than transcendent things in themselves, it could not be held that space and time are mere forms. It is also part of Kant's doctrine that we cannot know things in themselves, and so Gram holds that Kant is caught in a contradiction; for the doctrine of affection requires that we are not merely under some kind of causal influence by things but that we are made to *perceive* matters, and hence to understand them under some description. Gram concludes that to say we 'are affected by a thing in itself when we perceive anything would imply that we perceive objects that satisfy certain descriptions. And this would contradict the claim that we cannot be perceptually acquainted with things in themselves'.[61] As others have noted, there appears to be something missing in this argument, for the fact that things in themselves cause us to understand matters under a particular perceptual description does not mean that they must cause us to understand them under a description that we can say applies to things in themselves.[62] From the acceptable fact that the affection relation must in one sense be an epistemic relation, in that its effect has to do with a being in a state of knowledge, Gram seems to have jumped to the questionable claim that this epistemic state must be transparently about things in themselves.

A different kind of contradiction in Kant is asserted by T. E. Wilkerson. Wilkerson begins by carefully formulating and then quickly rejecting interpretations such as Matthews'. The main basis for this rejection is surprising, for what Wilkerson stresses at first is not that Kant was committed to the idea of metaphysical entities beyond experience, but rather that Kant's theory of experience

---

[60] Prauss, *Kant und das Problem*, 121, 213; but cf. Gerold Prauss, *Einführung in die Erkenntnistheorie* (Darmstadt, 1980).
[61] Moltke Gram, 'The Myth of Double Affection', in W. H. Werkmeister (ed.), *Reflections on Kant's Philosophy* (Gainesville, Fla., 1975), 29–33 at 30; cf. Moltke Gram, 'How to Dispense with Things in Themselves', *Ratio*, 18 (1976), 1–16 and 107–23 at 10 and 107.
[62] Aquila, 'Things in Themselves', 301.

supposedly reduces objects to collections of sensations, in which case there would not be any independent empirical beings that would be around to be numerically identified with things in themselves.[63] Wilkerson appears quite oblivious to the ways Allison, Bird, and others have explained in detail how Kant can be consistently committed to an empirical realism distinguishable from Berkeley's,[64] and how all the passages that speak of bodies as 'mere appearances' should be read in a transcendental rather than empirical manner. It is typical that Wilkerson claims his view is backed by passages such as the one in which Kant says 'nothing is really given us save perception' (A493/B521).[65] This remark shows not that Kant thought we can *know* only our perceptions, but simply that he believed that in one sense we aren't directly given external items. As other passages demonstrate, Kant clearly thought of our empirical knowledge as bound only by the laws of science and not by what can be collected in our sensations (A226/B273).

Wilkerson also regards Kant as committed to talking about various noumenal entities, especially in his practical philosophy,[66] and he charges that this conflicts sharply with the critical philosophy; for 'if knowledge requires both concepts and intuitions ... we cannot say anything about noumena'.[67] This is not an uncommon view, but it is quite remarkable, for there is no clear reason why all sorts of metaphysical expressions could not be allowable, even if *we* don't have intuitions to *warrant* them, as long as we are not thereby *insisting* on any synthetic theoretical assertions.

A more moderate criticism of Kant as a two object theorist is to be found in Walker's recent book. Walker brings out how Kant's theory of experience goes beyond the kind of subjectivism Wilkerson imputes, for the necessary unity that is thought in the transcendental object must transcend all mere collections of sensations. Moreover, Walker explains how Kant believes that mere perceptions cannot be a sufficient basis for our understanding of the world, since our perceptions themselves are parasitic upon our grasp of the world.[68] Unlike Wilkerson, Walker also attends to the texts which indicate that for Kant talk of noumena is 'not nonsense' but only 'futile' and 'lacking in empirical application'.[69] Finally, Walker argues that transcendental idealism is perfectly appropriate insofar as it

---

[63] T. E. Wilkerson, *Kant's Critique of Pure Reason* (Oxford, 1976), 186.
[64] H. E. Allison, 'Kant's Critique of Berkeley', *Journal of the History of Philosophy*, 11 (1973), 42–63; R. E. Aquila, 'Kant's Phenomenalism', *Idealistic Studies*, 5 (175), 108–26; Myron Gochnauer, 'Kant's Refutation of Idealism', *Journal of the History of Philosophy*, 12 (1974), 195–205; M. D. Wilson, 'Kant and the Dogmatic Idealism of Berkeley', *Journal of the History of Philosophy*, 9 (1971), 459–75; M. D. Wilson, 'On Kant and the Refutation of Subjectivism', in L. W. Beck (ed.), *Kant's Theory of Knowledge* (Dordrecht, 1974).
[65] Wilkerson, *Kant's Critique*, 182.
[66] Ibid. 192
[67] Ibid. 195; cf. 198.
[68] Walker, *Kant*, 129.
[69] Ibid. 130

reminds us that 'we build for ourselves a picture of the world',[70] that is, that at all levels, from simple classification to complex theorizing, we have to rely on our synthetic activities and not on what merely follows with logical necessity from the given.

Walker moves toward criticism of Kant when contending that the scientific world we construct in this way should be taken as the 'best guess' of what there ultimately is. (Walker here approaches a familiar reading which I have given little attention, namely that the belief in things in themselves expresses a 'methodological' or regulative postulate underwriting our commitment to the attainment of an ideal scientific picture of reality.[71]) Walker claims 'this ought to be [but is not] admitted by Kant. For his official position is that we can know nothing at all about things in themselves (which certainly precludes knowing that things are not just what we take them to be)'.[72] It is difficult to know what to make of this charge, since Walker ignores the main reasons for Kant's view, such as the Antinomies, and does not explore the possibility that the restrictions about knowledge that Kant held were meant primarily for detailed synthetic claims that make determinate reference to specific noumena.[73] If he had attended to this possibility, Walker also might not have gone on to add his final charge, that Kant is inconsistent in allowing the claim that the self, in some ultimate sense, certainly exists.[74] Walker himself accepts the claim, but he thinks it must violate Kant's own restrictions; he does not consider how careful Kant is to avoid inflating the claim into an illicit theoretical affirmation about a particular *mental substance*.

An even less developed criticism of Kant's theory is to be found in the recent interpretations of W. H. Walsh. Walsh states that Kant 'continued throughout the period of the *Critique* to speak as if the concept of a thing in itself [thought through the pure category of existence] were entirely intelligible'.[75] Walsh then claims that when we try to speak about a transcendent thing in itself we say 'nothing determinate at all';[76] that when we entertain the notion that God is such a thing 'it is hard to see what positive work this concept performs';[77] and that

---

[70] Ibid. 129.
[71] Recent work closest to this view is found in Rolf George, 'Transcendental Object and Thing in Itself—the Distinction and its Antecedents', in Gerhard Funke (ed.), *Akten des 4. Internationalen Kant-Kongresses*, 3 vols. (Berlin, 1974–5), II. 186–95; Peter Krausser, 'Kant's Theory of the Structure of Empirical Scientific Inquiry and Two Implied Postulates Regarding Things in Themselves', in L. W. Beck (ed.), *Kant's Theory of Knowledge* (Dordrecht, 1974), 159–65; Jürgen Mittelstrass, 'Ding als Erscheinung und Ding an Sich: Zur Kritik einer spekulativen Unterscheidung', in J. Mittelstrass and M. Riedel (eds.), *Vernünftiges Denken* (Berlin, 1978), 107–23; and Nicholas Rescher, 'The Problem of Noumenal Causality in the Philosophy of Kant', in the *Primacy of Practice* (Oxford, 1973), 69–87.
[72] Walker, *Kant*, 130.
[73] Cf. Aquila, 'Things in Themselves', 313; and M. D. Wilson, 'On Kant'.
[74] Walker, *Kant*, 123.
[75] W. H. Walsh, *Kant's Criticism of Metaphysics* (Chicago, 1975), 80.
[76] Ibid.
[77] Ibid.

when it is proposed that independent reality be 'understood in terms of what an intuitive understanding might think', our reply should be, 'it could, but would that be wholly satisfactory?'[78] It is difficult to take these as insurmountable objections to Kant, for he would be the first to insist on the minimal theoretical detail that can be gained from the idea of things in themselves. The crucial question is simply whether we are required to think that there are such things; if we seem to run into contradictions by not saying so, and yet are not caught in inconsistency if we do say so, it seems obvious what we should say.

Rather than developing in principle arguments against the idea of distinct things in themselves, Walsh has tended toward registering his disinterest in the notion and to suggesting more and more that Kant himself may have been uncommitted to it even in his practical philosophy. (Sometimes these suggestions are hard to understand, for Walsh seems to be simply contradicted by the *Foundations*[79] when he says that Kant's moral theory required only that 'the world of the scientific observer and the world of the moral agent be different; it did not call for one to be superior in reality to the other'.[80]) When Walsh concludes that for Kant 'belief in free will is not a matter of speculation but of action', and that 'the objects in question [God, free will] are practical, not theoretical realities',[81] he is endorsing a familiar view of Kant, while in effect taking back his concessions to the two object interpretation. This move strikes me as premature, for even if (as Kant believed) we can't theoretically know or prove our freedom, and even if we in fact *come* to believe in it primarily in the context of 'action' rather than mere 'speculation', it seems that *what* we believe is still understood to be a fact, and a fact that on Kant's philosophy must go beyond the domain of the empirical. This is quite a significant issue, for the last comments from Walsh come from an important context, his response in a *Festschrift* for Heinz Heimsoeth devoted to the question of Kant's attitude toward metaphysics. Here Walsh surely deserves credit for the reminder that the metaphysical school of interpretation[82] led by Heimsoeth (the great influence of which is charted by Scott-Taggart and Funke[83]) can go too far, and that it would be a mistake to ascribe to Kant a metaphysics theoretically committed to the notion of a 'primordial spiritual being', or a 'true infinity of the spiritual world'.[84] But while Heimsoeth's view obscures how much the *Critique* insists on refuting

---

[78] W. H. Walsh, *Kant's Criticism of Metaphysics* (Chicago, 1975), 80.
[79] *AA*, IV.457.
[80] Walsh, *Kant's Criticism,* 166.
[81] W. H. Walsh, 'Kant and Metaphysics', *Kant-Studien*, 67 (1976), 372–84 at 380.
[82] See Moltke Gram (ed.), *Kant: Disputed Questions* (Chicago, 1967), 95–199.
[83] M. J. Scott-Taggart, 'Recent Work in the Philosophy of Kant', *American Philosophical Quarterly*, 3 (1966), 171–209 and amended version in L. W. Beck (ed.), *Kant Studies Today* (LaSalle, Ind., 1969), 1–71; Gerhard Funke, 'Die Diskussion um die metaphysische Kantinterpretation', *Kant-Studien*, 67 (1976), 409–24.
[84] W. H. Walsh, 'Kant and Metaphysics', *Kant-Studien*, 67 (1976), 372–84 at 381.

spiritualism, that is, a science of the intrinsic nature of fully mental and independent realities (A379–80), Walsh's comments can also obscure how much Kant simultaneously insisted on rejecting what he called materialism (A379, B420, *Prolegomena* §§46 ff.).

These remarks indicate that Kant was after a peculiar kind of third position, which ultimately identifies reality with a kind of being of which we can say little more (theoretically) than that it definitely is not like *either* the spatial–physical or the temporal–psychological being with which we are ordinarily familiar. As has been noted, such a view does not entail the existence of a second world, but it does require giving up any insistence on an isomorphism of phenomena and noumena. Kant's own language can be a bit misleading here, as when he speaks about each thing having an 'empirical character' that corresponds to an 'intelligible character' (A538/B566 ff.). Thus, Broad has objected that, 'although everywhere else he has been quite skeptical about this', 'Kant assumes in this part of his work that each distinguishable empirical substance is the appearance of a different thing in itself'.[85] Yet even if Kant says that each empirical character has some intelligible character behind it, this does not really require asserting a universal one to one mapping of phenomena onto noumena. And it is only proper for Kant not to assert this, for otherwise there would be a very significant breach in the doctrine of the unknowability of things in themselves.[86] Moreover, precisely this position seems to be the one endorsed by Kant when he said, 'it is a complete misunderstanding of the theory of sensible objects as mere appearances, to which something non-sensible must be attached, if one imagines or seeks others to imagine that what is meant thereby is that the super-sensible substrate of matter will be divided according to its monads just as I divide matter itself'.[87] This statement can be taken as pointing toward an 'agnostic' position, one that would be compatible with Kant's casual shifts between singular and plural references to the thing in itself, and that would nicely avoid the dogmatic extremes of holding that either there must be a complete identity of phenomena and noumena, or there must be a complete division and/or lack of correspondence between them.

Among recent interpretations, the only one that seems fairly satisfied with allowing Kant to be a two object theorist is to be found in a short but very dense article by Richard Aquila. Aquila devotes most of his effort to indicating ways in which the double aspect interpretation is not compelling. At various points I have already made use of many ideas similar to ones that he develops, such as the fact that Kant carefully altered his comments about unschematized categories to

---

[85] C. D. Broad, *Kant: An Introduction*, ed. C. Lewy (Cambridge, 1978), 277.
[86] Cf. Nicholas Rescher, *Conceptual Idealism* (Oxford, 1973), 119ff.
[87] *AA*, VIII.209 n.; translation from H. E. Allison (tr. and ed.), *The Kant–Eberhard Controversy* (Baltimore, 1973).

indicate that we are restricted not in thinking but only in claiming to know things in themselves through them (A147/B186; A247/B304).[88] One difference between our interpretations, however, is that Aquila is not interested in a double aspect theory even in the case of the self. He shows how 'it is compatible with the two object interpretation to maintain that a "phenomenal person" is to be identified not with a particular phenomenal object, but rather with a noumenal entity regarded as "ground" of at least some of the behavior exhibited by some phenomenal object'.[89] Ingenious as this idea is, Aquila seems in this case to be going further than Kant wanted to go, for it seems unnecessary to hold that *in general* Kant must assert a two object rather than a double aspect view. (Thus, B306 seems explicitly to allow the possibility of either a double aspect or two object relation between phenomena and noumena.) The fact that we don't *have* to say that in all cases there is numerical identity between phenomena and noumena, and even the fact that for Kant we can't assert that theoretically we know such identity exists, does not entail that, for all we know, it couldn't exist in some cases, or even for the most part.

Aquila rejects this option by emphasizing Kant's talk of a causal relation between phenomena and noumena,[90] and by arguing that, since things in themselves are non-spatial, and phenomena are spatial, phenomena and noumena can't be the same things.[91] Yet it might be that some kind of grounding relation between an intelligible character and an empirical character that belongs to it (as an aspect of ultimately the same thing) is not impossible; and it might also be that the second objection can be met by saying that objects are spatial simply in the sense that they are perceivable as spatial. Aquila considers precisely this possibility, but he contends that it leads to the absurdity that mere analysis could reveal something about things in themselves.[92] What he appears to be objecting to is the idea that then the mere fact that a thing appears to us in an F-way would tell us something about a thing in itself, namely that it is an F-appearing thing in itself. This is such a peculiar and minimal kind of information that it is not so clear to me that a Kantian must be bothered by this objection.

2. The Transcendental Deduction

Agreement has not been reached about the starting point or the conclusion of Kant's transcendental deduction, let alone the nature and validity of the path

---

[88] See Aquila, 'Things in Themselves', 303.
[89] Ibid. 306.
[90] Ibid. 300.
[91] Ibid.
[92] Ibid. 299.

between its end points. However, for a long time there has been a *semblance* of agreement among many writers on at least the first of these sets of issues. More specifically, throughout the discussion generated by Strawson, Bennett, and Stroud in the late 1960s,[93] there has been a kind of common assumption about Kant's aims. At the same time, this discussion has been marked by a strong preference for the broad issue of transcendental arguments in general, and by an interest in developing and criticizing examples of such arguments quite distant from what is offered explicitly in the *Critique*. These tendencies initally dominated only Anglo-American interpretations, but it is clear from some recent collections that they are also gaining influence abroad.[94]

Despite the importance of the vast body of literature in this vein, I shall pass over many of its details. Its story is probably familiar enough already,[95] and my primary aim here is rather to review the best of recent exegetical work. But something must be said about the distinctive idea that, since at least *The Bounds of Sense*, has widely been assumed to define what Kant was trying to do. This idea is that the transcendental deduction is to be read as a direct response to Humean skepticism and that, very roughly speaking, starting from a weak *premise* of something like the fact that we are conscious beings, Kant's main aim is to *establish* that there is an objective realm (what Strawson calls 'the objectivity thesis'). The number of interpreters who accept this general line (and who are then interested mainly in how successful arguments of this sort can be) is remarkable; only more remarkable is the proliferation, sometimes within the pages of a single interpretation, of different formulations of precisely what the end points of the argument are supposed to be.

In particular, it is worth noting some of the many different ways (with emphases added) that Kant's *premise* has been expressed by those working within this popular line of interpretation, viz. as: 'the is/seems distinction'[96] 'the *empirical* unity of apperception';[97] 'what must be *present* in every experience or awareness of oneself as having it';[98] 'the possibility of the *existence* [original

---

[93] P. F. Strawson, *The Bounds of Sense* (London, 1966); Jonathan Bennett, *Kant's Dialectic* (Cambridge, 1966); Barry Stroud, 'Transcendental Arguments', *Journal of Philosophy*, 65 (1968), 241–56.

[94] P. Bieri, R. P. Horstmann, and L. Krüger (eds.), *Transcendental Arguments and Science* (Dordrecht, 1979); K. Cramer, R. Bubner, and R. Wiehl (eds.), *Neue Hefte für Philosophie: Zu Zukunft der Transzendentalphilosophie*, no. 14 (Göttingen, 1978); Rüdiger Bubner, 'Kant, Transcendental Arguments, and the Problem of Deduction', *Review of Metaphysics*, 28 (1975), 453–67.

[95] A good overview has been provided by Jonathan Bennett, 'Analytic Transcendental Arguments', in Bieri *et al.*, *Transcendental Arguments*, 45–54; cf. Werner Becker, 'Erkenntnis und Erfahrung in der Transzendentalphilosophie', *Philosophische Rundschau*, 18 (1971), 190–206; Findlay, 'Kant and Anglo-Saxon Criticism'; Klaus Hartmann, 'Neuere englischsprachige Kantliteratur', *Philosophische Rundschau*, 22 (1976), 161–90.

[96] Leslie Stevenson, 'Recent Work on the *Critique of Pure Reason*', *Philosophical Quarterly*, 29 (1979), 345–54 at 345.

[97] T. E. Wilkerson, 'Transcendental Arguments', *Philosophical Quarterly*, 20 (1970), 200–12 at 200.

[98] Richard Rorty, 'Strawson's Objectivity Argument', *Review of Metaphysics*, 24 (1970), 208–44, at 208.

emphasis] of self-consciousness';[99] 'one's *thought* of one's numerical identity... what it means to *pass* from one state of representation to another',[100] 'the common property of *being* my experiences';[101] '*awareness* of successive mental states *as* mine';[102] 'the analytical proposition, that "I think" must be able to accompany all my thoughts... the *concept* of self-consciousness';[103] 'the role which self-consciousness plays in the *connection* of our experiences';[104] 'the *employment* of first person pronouns to express [non-vacuously] one's own identity';[105] 'the fact of our commitment to certain judgmental *abilities*... [i.e.] that we do make judgments about our continuing identity';[106] 'the *weakest* of all possible assumptions—the mere possibility of thinking "I think" '.[107]

Similarly, it has been said that the argument premises (i.e. is about the necessary conditions of) 'applying even the *minimal* notion of experience';[108] 'consciousness itself... our *awareness* of time';[109] 'thoughts that are *of* something';[110] '*conceptual* experience';[111] '*coherent* experience';[112] 'any coherent *question* about experience ever arising';[113] 'the *possibility* of the identity of the *thinking* self';[114] '*attributing* different experiences to a single temporally extended self';[115] 'the ability to *say* "I" on different occasions and mean the same thing by it';[116] '[being able to] *tell* whether or not my perceptions displayed any regularity';[117]

---

[99] Dieter Henrich, 'The Proof Structure of Kant's Transcendental Deduction', *Review of Metaphysics*, 22 (1969), 640–59 at 657; cf. Dieter Henrich, 'Die Deduktion des Sittengesetzes', in A. Schwan (ed.), *Denken im Schatten des Nihilismus* (Darmstadt, 1975), 55–112 at 83.

[100] Dieter Henrich, *Identität und Objektivität* (Heidelberg, 1976), 86; cf. also 167.

[101] Broad, *Kant: An Introduction*, 147; cf. Barry Stroud, 'Transcendental Arguments and Epistemological Naturalism', *Philosophical Studies*, 31 (1977), 105–15 at 112.

[102] R. E. Aquila, 'Two Kinds of Transcendental Arguments in Kant', *Kant-Studien*, 67 (1976), 1–19 at 5.

[103] Malte Hossenfelder, *Kants Konstitutionstheorie und die transzendentale Deduktion* (Berlin, 1978), 19, 148.

[104] Baum and Horstmann, 'Metaphysik', 74.

[105] G. W. Smith, 'The Concepts of the Sceptic: Transcendental Arguments and Other Minds', *Philosophy*, 49 (1974), 149–69 at 169.

[106] Paul Guyer, '*Identität und Objektivität* by Dieter Henrich', *Journal of Philosophy*, 76 (1979), 151–67 at 162.

[107] Paul Guyer, '*Kant's Criticism of Metaphysics* by W. H. Walsh', *Philosophical Review*, 86 (1977), 264–70 at 266.

[108] Leslie Stevenson, 'Recent Work on the *Critique of Pure Reason*', *Philosophical Quarterly*, 29 (1979), 345–54 at 348.

[109] Ben Mijuskovic, 'The General Conclusion of the Argument of the Transcendental Analytic', *Southern Journal of Philosophy*, 12 (1974), 256–64 at 358, 262.

[110] Stroud, 'Transcendental Arguments and Epistemological Naturalism', 112.

[111] Peter Hacker, 'Are Transcendental Arguments a Form of Verificationism?', *American Philosophical Quarterly*, 9 (1972), 78–85 at 82.

[112] T. E. Wilkerson, 'Transcendental Arguments Revisited', *Kant-Studien*, 66 (1975), 102–15 at 102.

[113] Eva Schaper, 'Arguing Transcendentally', *Kant-Studien*, 63 (1972), 101–16 at 115.

[114] Manfred Baum, 'Transcendental Proofs in the *Critique of Pure Reason*', in Cramer *et al.*, *Neue Hefte*, 3–26 at 24.

[115] Guyer, '*Kant's Criticism*', 266.

[116] Walsh, *Kant's Criticism of Metaphysics*, 56.

[117] S. C. Patten, 'An Anti-Sceptical Argument at the Deduction', *Kant-Studien*, 67 (1976), 550–69.

'[being able to] *secure* that identity [which]... our own various states of mind do not immediately manifest';[118] 'judgments which Hume never thought of doubting'.[119]

Obviously, these formulations can be arranged in a broad spectrum, ranging from propositions that make overt claims that are very weak in content, to ones that appear to make considerably stronger claims. I believe the quotations show that beyond a superficial sense of agreement there is an important unclarity permeating this line of interpretation, as well as an unfortunate tendency to conflate epistemological and ontological claims. Of course, it might be countered that many of the different formulations are compatible since they are not always meant to represent an ultimate premise, and so there are different premises that stand for different stages of the deduction. Nonetheless, at some point a commitment has to be made as to precisely what the ultimate premise is. Here a serious dilemma arises, for either a very weak premise is to be chosen, and then all the steps to the further and much stronger claims would need to be defended (more than they are); or a fairly strong premise must be taken as the starting point, in which case it becomes unclear how the distinctive aim of defeating skepticism can be met.

Beyond these difficulties is the fact that there is an obvious alternative line of interpretation which begins by following Kant's own frequent remarks[120] that it is experience (*Erfahrung*), in the general sense of empirical knowledge, that is the premise of his deduction. (It should be noted that *erfahren* is commonly used to mean 'to gain knowledge', and that *Erfahrung* and even *Erkenntnis*, unlike 'knowledge' in English, need not be true (A58/B83). Similarly, what is 'objective' can be delusive, so what is really being presupposed here is simply a structure that allows for the possibility of truth or falsity.[121]) This premise is cognitive, so it is stronger than any claim of the mere existence of attentive consciousness or self-consciousness. It is also more general than any of the many formulations that focus on the special conditions of personal identity or a real unity of consciousness. Because their premise already involves objectivity (but *not* anything as specific as Euclid or Newton), advocates of this kind of interpretation obviously also require a different view of the *conclusion* of the argument. Here the proposal is again to follow Kant's own comments closely when he speaks of this as a deduction of the *categories*, that is, of a special set of pure concepts, and not of empirical concepts in general (the 'objectivity thesis').

---

[118] Guyer, '*Kant: An Introduction*, by C. D. Broad', *Philosophical Review*, 87 (1979), 640–7 at 644.
[119] L. W. Beck, 'Towards a Meta-Critique of Pure Reason', in P. Laberge, F. Duchesneau, and B. Morrissey (eds.), *Proceedings of the Ottawa Congress on Kant in the Anglo-American and Continental Traditions* (Ottawa, 1976), 184.
[120] E.g. B161, B218, *AA* XI.315, XX.774.
[121] See Broad: *Kant: An Introduction*, 111; Ralf Meerbote, 'Kant's Use of the Notions "Objective Reality" and "Objective Validity"', *Kant-Studien*, 63 (1972), 51–8; Prauss, *Erscheinung bei Kant*, 62, 86.

It is remarkable how rarely this kind of interpretation has been presented recently.[122] The desire to see Kant as responding to Hume's radical skepticism probably has been responsible for much of the resistance to this alternative interpretation. But even if it were granted that Kant thinks he has some way of disproving some of what Hume may have thought, and that there may be doctrines somewhere in the *Critique* that could be used to deal with the problem of the external world, it cannot be simply assumed that the transcendental deduction is meant directly to solve that problem. Yet it is frequently objected that it would be improper and question-begging for Kant to begin here with the possession of empirical knowledge.[123] I think this is unfairly to prejudge the issue of whether it can be the validity of *pure* concepts that is Kant's prime concern, and it is also to forget the value of philosophical arguments without absolutely indubitable starting points. The non-triviality of a deduction construed as an argument concluding with the categories can be shown even by materials provided by the dominant interpretation. Thus, when Beck and Wilkerson each present their own five-step versions of the basic argument of the Analytic, they see few difficulties with the first two steps, which are meant to establish that our representations have some objective reference, and they suggest important amendments only for the later steps,[124] which involve more specific claims (such as the principle of causality). Even if one disagrees with their assumption about where the biggest problems lie, their discussions show indirectly how the premise of the alternative interpretation can serve as the starting point of a significant argument.

In addition to the viability of an alternative, there are intrinsic difficulties that plague the interpretation of the transcendental deduction as involving only premises such as the existence of self-consciousness or personal identity. For example, it has been argued that, even if it were granted that an act of self-consciousness requires a sense of some kind of object in contrast to it, this could be simply an enduring mental feature, or a mere abstract proposition, and so not a

[122] But see A. Phillips Griffiths, 'Transcendental Arguments', *Proceedings of the Aristotelian Society*, 43, suppl. (1969), 165–80 at 166; Stephan Körner, 'On Bennett's "Analytic Transcendental Arguments"', in Bieri *et al.*, *Transcendental Arguments*, 65–9 at 65; Melnick, *Kant's Analogies*, 45; Günther Patzig, 'Comment on Bennett', in Bieri *et al.*, *Transcendental Arguments*, 71; Jay Rosenberg, 'Reply to Stroud', *Philosophical Studies*, 31 (1977), 117–21 at 118; Wilfrid Sellars, 'Some Remarks on Kant's Theory of Experience', *Journal of Philosophy*, 64 (1967), 633–47 at 635; Charles Taylor, 'The Validity of Transcendental Arguments', *Proceedings of the Aristotelian Society*, 79 (1978–9), 151–65; and especially Karl Ameriks, 'Kant's Transcendental Deduction as a Regressive Argument', *Kant-Studien*, 69 (1978), 273–87; William Stine, 'Self-Consciousness in Kant's *Critique of Pure Reason*', *Philosophical Studies*, 28 (1975), 189–97; and Walker, *Kant*, 76.

[123] Aquila, 'Transcendental Arguments', 5, n. 7; W. H. Bossart, 'Kant's Transcendental Deduction', *Kant-Studien*, 68 (197), 383–403 at 387; Moltke Gram, 'Must Transcendental Arguments Be Spurious?' *Kant-Studien*, 65 (1974), 304–17 at 317; Guyer, '*Kant's Criticism*', 266; Schaper, 'Arguing Transcendentally', 115; Wilkerson, 'Transcendental Arguments', 204; and Wilkerson, 'Transcendental Arguments Revisited', 113.

[124] Wilkerson, *Kant's Critique of Pure Reason*, 50; Beck, *Essays*, 44.

distinct and concretely existing being.[125] Similarly, even if it were granted that our experiences are necessarily owned,[126] and that we must have an awareness of them as such,[127] it has been observed that it still seems all too possible for this to be compatible with chaos and without any entailment that there is an external world.[128] Moreover, both types of premise seem inappropriate because of points stressed by Kant himself. Mere self-consciousness would seem to be nothing more than the empirical unity of consciousness that Kant indicates does not as such require pure concepts (B139–40). And an a priori argument founded on the claim of personal identity would seem to be precisely what the Third Paralogism is meant to warn against. Finally, if it is insisted that Kant does aim to prove the existence of an external world, the most natural place to look for that project is in the Refutation of Idealism,[129] and this alone would seem to make the most popular interpretation of the deduction a story of something other than the deduction. This problem has been responded to in a revealing fashion by Wilkerson, who has gone so far as to pronounce the text of the Refutation of Idealism 'redundant', since supposedly Kant 'already provided a plausible refutation of idealism in the transcendental deduction'.[130]

Despite all these difficulties, there are some understandable grounds for the popular interpretation of the deduction. There are many passages in the first edition version which suggest a starting point that is not experience, as defined earlier, but rather something else designated by the 'bare representation "I think"' (A117 n.). There are also some indications that Kant was trying to answer Hume directly by arguing for some kind of a priori 'affinity', a core of objectivity necessary for all our representations (A121).[131] It is not insignificant, though, that most of the recent interpretations rest heavily on such first edition passages, and they play down the fact that the second edition brought with it a wholesale revision and an excision of references to 'affinity'. It could be argued that these changes are crucial and that the point of the second edition version is precisely to make clear that, insofar as the 'I think' is used as a premise of the deduction, it is

---

[125] Ross Harrison, 'Strawson on Outer Objects', *Philosophical Quarterly*, 20 (1970), 213–21; Henrich, *Identität und Objektivität*; Jeffrey Tlumak, 'Some Defects in Strawson's Anti-Skeptical Method', *Philosophical Studies*, 28 (1975), 255–64.

[126] For resistance even here, see Eddy Zemach, 'Strawson's Transcendental Deduction', *Philosophical Quarterly*, 25 (1975), 114–25.

[127] This is much more questionable for Kant; cf. James Van Cleve, '*Kant's Critique of Pure Reason* by T. E. Wilkerson', *Teaching Philosophy*, 2 (1978), 387–9.

[128] Broad, *Kant: An Introduction*, 130; Peter Rohs, '*Identität und Objektivität* von Dieter Henrich', *Zeitschrift für philosophische Forschung*, 32 (1978), 303–8 at 307; R. C. S. Walker, '*Identität und Objektivität* by Dieter Henrich', *Grazer Philosophische Studien*, 4 (1977), 189–97 at 193.

[129] Though there are problems even here—see Stine, 'Self-Consciousness', 194.

[130] Wilkerson, *Kant's Critique*, 82.

[131] Cf. H. E. Allison, 'Transcendental Affinity—Kant's Answer to Hume', in L. W. Beck (ed.), *Kant's Theory of Knowledge* (Dordrecht, 1974); Guyer, 'Kant on Apperception', 207; Prauss, *Erscheinung bei Kant*, 123.

meant to be equivalent to the *objective* unity of representation that occurs in judgment, and so the starting point of the argument cannot be something a radical Humean would have to accept. (For other examples of Kant's tendency to appeal to premises incompatible with radical skepticism, see B20, A165/B206.)

Nonetheless, there are arguments even in the second edition that do *seem* to begin with a mere 'same sounding consciousness', or subjective gathering of representations (B135). It is impossible to present a close study of such passages here, and I will note only one problem that has been much discussed recently. It has been observed that, if the passages are understood in the way that those who emphasize the first edition wish, then the conclusion that Kant draws about the universal validity of the categories appears to present a *reductio ad absurdum*. That is, if the premise is something like a mere gathering of representations in a same sounding consciousness, then Kant would seem committed to the wild idea that all our representations are (somehow simply in virtue of *being our representations*) judgmental, objective, and representative of a thoroughly causal realm. Of course, some qualifications are immediately in order, for as is sometimes noted, Kant speaks carefully of the conditions without which representation would be 'nothing to me' (B132), and so he is not to be taken to be arguing that representation *simpliciter* entails causality. But even then, there seem to be all too many *self-conscious* representations which indicate that, if Kant's argument is taken in the popular way, then it must be wrong. Indeed, the argument appears so clearly wrong that it becomes impossible to understand how Kant ever could have presented it, and so the problem could be turned into a *reductio* of the interpreters[132] who have stressed it. Yet even if this interpretation is rejected—and it is allowed that Kant, like all of us, recognizes self-conscious representations that by themselves do not imply universal causality—there remains the difficult problem of what is to be said, especially in Kant's philosophy, about such representations.

Recently this issue has been approached most directly by Gerold Prauss and L. W. Beck, but I believe their views are best appreciated only after a review of some important exegetical work by Dieter Henrich. In a very significant article that appeared in English in 1969, Henrich argued persuasively for the primacy of the second edition version of the deduction, and he drew attention to a feature of it that has been all too ignored or misunderstood, namely its basic division into two parts, one ending at §20 and the other concentrated in §26. Henrich shows how through §20 the proof of the categories is 'valid only for those intuitions which already contain unity', and thus Kant can say in §21 that the proof is not yet complete, because 'this statement...does not yet clarify for us the range within which unitary representations can be

---

[132] E.g. C. I. Lewis, *Mind and the World Order* (New York, 1929), 221; R. P. Wolff, *Kant's Theory of Mental Activity* (Cambridge, Mass., 1963), 299.

found'.¹³³ Henrich then explains how 'the restriction just made in §20 will be overcome in the paragraphs of §26, where it is argued that in our representations of space and time... we have intuitions which contain unity and which at the same time include everything that can be presented to the senses'.¹³⁴ So, whereas the first part of the deduction is meant only to explain that representations taken to be already combined in the unity of an intuition (as opposed to a mere sensation) must be subject to the forms of judgment and thereby (given the metaphysical deduction) to the categories, the second part of the deduction addresses the question of whether '*all* that may *present* themselves to our senses' must also be so subject (B159). Thus, it meets the issue raised in A90/B123, as to whether for us *really* can be appearances so 'constituted that the understanding should not find them in accordance with the conditions of its unity'.

By focusing on §26 and its crucial reference (B160 n.) to the forms of space and time (whose nature is what guarantees that all that is given us must in some way be subject to the categories after all), this account indicates a limitation in the interpretation that Kant is deducing everything simply from the notion of self-consciousness, and it simultaneously removes the embarrassing appearance for the alternative interpretation of having the deduction rest simply on a stipulation that objective judgment and the categories go together. The second stage of the deduction can now be seen as pointing to a way to meet those who note that there is more to our consciousness than explicitly unified intuitions, and that the crucial categories, such as causality, are tied up with types of judgment which it is not clear we must make use of, even if it is granted that they are necessary to such judgments when they are made.¹³⁵ By making the forms of intuition central, this construal of the deduction also brings it into a close connection with the surrounding discussion in the Transcendental Aesthetic and the Principles; the ultimate validity of the categories can be seen to be meant to rest on one long argument about how we must place items within one spatio-temporal framework, one realm of 'possible experience'.

These points generally have not been stressed by those who do discuss the two stages of the deduction. Henrich continues his article by using a late letter of Kant's to argue that the deduction could also have been carried out simply (if less perspicuously) by showing somehow that the forms of sensible intuition are derivable solely from self-consciousness in its need to have a concrete meaning for the categories.¹³⁶ An interpretation that in effect tries to apply this idea to §26 itself has also been sketched by R. Brouillet.¹³⁷ Similarly, Walker has contended

---

¹³³ Dieter, 'Proof Structure', 645.
¹³⁴ Ibid. 646.
¹³⁵ Melnick, *Kant's Analogies*, 51.
¹³⁶ Dieter, 'Proof Structure', 648.
¹³⁷ Raymond Brouillet, 'Dieter Henrich et "The Proof of Structure of Kant's Transcendental Deduction": Reflexions critiques', *Dialogue*, 14 (1975), 639–47.

that, although the deduction is presented in two stages, this is confusing and unnecessary, for the general conclusion supposedly follows simply from noting that all our 'apprehension' is 'like judging'.[138] Other treatments of the deduction focus on its two stage character but without a direct emphasis on the forms of intuition.[139]

The most important work along this line is Henrich's own short but very impressive book, *Identität und Objektivität*.[140] Henrich's book offers a two-stage approach to the deduction, but this time the stages are justified for systematic reasons and are not mapped onto phases of the text. The first stage of this reconstruction is given a textual basis in only a few notes from Kant's *Reflexionen* (especially R6350). It argues that the nature of judgment, and in particular the use of categorical subject–predicate propositions, requires an item that, unlike a simple sensation, can bear a number of predicates and so manifest an objective complexity. Henrich notes several limitations to this argument and stresses that by itself it cannot show that objectivity is any more than 'sporadic'.[141]

This last point parallels what was said earlier about the first stage of the B deduction. However, Henrich now insists that Kant thought the only way to complete the deduction, and to show that there is a 'thoroughgoing' connection of all that presents itself to us, is 'through the analysis of self-consciousness'.[142] Henrich ignores the text in the second edition to which he himself had drawn attention, and instead uses a passage in the first edition (A108) to develop what is in effect a version of the popular interpretation's account of the beginning and end points of the deduction. Although he begins by showing various ways in which the mere *unity* of consciousness would be an insufficient premise,[143] he goes on to claim that Kant must be arguing from the conditions of a subject's certainty that he is the same in transitions *over time*.[144] This starting point is said to have the virtue of revealing rules that (a) the subject must be aware of with a 'Cartesian certainty',[145] and that (b) must apply to all that can be presented to us. In this way a bridge is laid down for concluding to the 'universal validity' of the categories. Whereas the conditions of the synthesis in judgment could show (at best) only that in certain cases a complex object is required, the synthesis involved in our

---

[138] Walker, *Kant*, 78.
[139] For such treatments see Hans Wagner, 'Der Argumentationsgang in Kants Deduktion der Kategorien', *Kant-Studien*, 71 (1980), 352–65; Bossart, 'Kant's Transcendental Deduction', *Kant-Studien*, 68 (1977), 383–403; and George di Giovanni, 'Paragraphs 20 and 26 of the Transcendental Deduction', *Idealistic Studies*, 10 (1980), 131–45; but cf. Dryer, 'Bennett's Account', 419.
[140] For a fine English summary, see Guyer, '*Identität und Objektivität*'.
[141] Henrich, 'Proof Structure', 52.
[142] Ibid. 53.
[143] Thus, there are some (see Baum and Horstmann, 'Metaphysik und Erfahrungstheorie', 74) who have objected that Henrich's starting point is not Cartesian enough.
[144] Henrich, *Identität und Objektivität*, 74.
[145] Ibid. 86.

identity is supposedly all-encompassing, and so alone can demonstrate a thoroughgoing objective realm governed by accessible a priori rules.[146] Henrich notes that this still would not prove that it is specifically the categories given by the table of judgments that are required by the rules involved in our certainty of identity, but he thinks that 'much speaks' for believing that these are the same, and this is enough for a Kantian deduction to succeed.[147]

Despite its great ingenuity, deep problems in Henrich's analysis have not gone unnoticed. The claim that we must be certain that all data will be in accord with our being able to know our identity in the future is still suspect as a relic of Cartesianism and as in any case not compatible with Kant's critical view.[148] Moreover, it is not clear what sort of 'rules' Henrich can have in mind if they are allowed to be compatible with all data.[149] And even if an a priori synthesis of judgment were required by a necessary synthesis in the awareness of our identity, skepticism can remain undefeated since the first stage of the argument is faulty; as Walker has observed, even if judgment requires a 'complex particular', it is not clear why a blue qualia that is square would be insufficient.[150] In view of all these problems, it is hard to see why Henrich himself has turned so far away from the text of the second edition deduction, and its emphasis on the forms of intuition and the specific problem of categories.

If it is tied closely to the second edition, a two stage analysis of the deduction can avoid some of these problems and can have the merit of showing clearly how, contrary to Lewis *et al.*, Kant was quite aware of and quite concerned with accounting for items that initially are not taken explicitly as fully unified and determined by the categories. Prauss has called such items 'subjective objects', but here much more still needs to be said, for very different items might come under this heading. Consider, for example, acts such as questions and commands, acts which obviously are not direct assertions of an intuitive unity and so are in this sense distinct from the paradigmatic judgments that merely state 'objective objects'. In what seems to be a variation of the Lewis objection, Malte Hossenfelder has recently argued that such acts reveal a non-judgmental realm that disproves the conclusion of Kant's deduction.[151] Yet surely the reason such acts are not to be identified with simple judgments is not that they are independent of a judgmental element, but rather that they happen to involve more than mere judgment. The existence of such an extra and complex stratum of awareness is an objection to Kant's theory only if a radical version of the popular interpretation is

---

[146] Ibid. 95–6.
[147] Ibid. 108–9.
[148] Cf. Guyer, '*Identität und Objektivität*'; R. C. S. Walker, *A Selective Bibliography on Kant*, 2nd edn (Oxford, 1978).
[149] See Rohs, '*Identität und Objektivität*', 306.
[150] Walker, *Selective Bibliography*, 195.
[151] Hossenfelder, *Kants Konstitutionstheorie*, 125.

accepted, to the effect that the categories must directly and fully determine all aspects of consciousness in their manifest content. To this there is an obvious response, which has been formulated in a nice way recently by Guyer: namely, that at most Kant needs to hold only that all data 'in consciousness be *explicable* by judgments applying the categories, but not [that they be] *expressible solely* in such judgments'.[152]

A similar response can be made to examples such as association, the awareness of mere concomitance, and subjective temporal passage. These states are much closer to being describable as prejudgmental, and in their content they obviously need not involve a full application of the categories. Yet this hardly means that as events there could be no way that someone such as a psychologist could locate them within a thoroughly unified spatio-temporal framework. A like account can also be given to the example that Beck has focused on, namely dreams. These could be understood either as imaginative sequences which are enrichments of ordinary perceptual judgments, and in this way similar to the 'supra-judgmental' examples discussed above, or as simply another form of relatively prejudgmental states such as simple association. In either case, we have items that are still expressible in accord with the categories. Even if to dream of a three-headed monster is not quite directly to learn about oneself rather than a monster,[153] still it can be argued that there is a way in which the dream event, as a fact about oneself, rather than about any real monsters, could be fitted into an objective picture of the world. There is no reason to insist that Kant would require more than this.

Even if the different kinds of 'subjective object' discussed so far can all be reconciled with Kant's conclusion about the 'universal validity' of the categories, this does not mean that they must be specifically what he had in mind when approaching that conclusion. What Kant says he is discussing here is the realm of 'apprehension', the perception of sensory givens. He does not mention dreams, and even though Beck speaks of 'dreamingly-seeing a three-headed monster',[154] I suspect Kant would prefer to call this a state of imagination rather than sight. Kant was phenomenological enough to believe in a difference between an appearance in the general sense of any kind of idea before the mind, and an appearance in the specific sense of a self-manifesting given (cf. B277 n.). A case thus can be made for saying that it is the latter kind of appearance that is Kant's main concern in §26, and in fact it is this kind of item that Prauss seems to have had in mind when introducing the notion of a 'subjective object'. However, Prauss is opposed (and sees Kant as opposed) to reifying sense data, and so he takes the term 'appearance' (*Erscheinung*) to refer not to an independent item between subject and object but rather to the state of mind of the perceiver, the state that, in some sense, must lie at the basis of empirical cognitions when 'objective objects' are determined. Prauss

---

[152] Guyer, '*Identität und Objektivität*', 160.   [153] Cf. Beck, *Essays on Kant*, 54.
[154] Ibid.

makes a good argument for taking such states to be the best way to understand what Kant ultimately meant by 'judgments of perception' (as opposed to those of 'experience') and he holds that they are the key to the completion of the deduction, for §26 does speak of having as its aim the demonstration that the categories apply 'even' for 'perception' (B161).

On such an interpretation, the realm of subjective objects is thought of as tied not to a peculiar stratum of pre-or suprajudgmental items (such as mere association, dreams, or commands), but rather to a kind of consciousness that is present precisely in the most ordinary acts of objective perception; it is the purely subjective side of such acts. Prauss deserves credit for uncovering the significance of such elements in Kant's theory, but it may be going too far to say that they alone are relevant to the problem of subjective objects. Even though §26 does emphasize the terms 'apprehension' and 'perception', it would seem that the issue of 'universal' validity for the categories can also be understood as bearing on Kant's earlier discussion of merely subjective or empirical apperception, as when one word calls another to mind (B140). Prauss treats this passage, which occurs in the final revision of the work, as due merely to a confusion on Kant's part.[155] Another peculiarity of Prauss's interpretation is that it suggests the problem of §26 is not at all the extension of the categories from some to all external objects, but rather their extension from the external realm to the internal one.[156] But it would seem that the former question is also relevant to the completion of the deduction and would connect most naturally to the special reference to the all inclusive nature of our forms of intuition. Prauss does not give this reference much of a role, and as a consequence he presents some controversial readings, especially of B138.[157] He suggests that, in Kant's statement that the categories are conditions for 'all intuitions to become objects for me', the emphasis should be on the term 'all', and the passage is about how even the inner realm (of subjective objects in his sense) falls under the categories. But the specific context of the passage would seem to indicate that the emphasis is rather on the term 'object', and Kant's point is the familiar one that, until a pure synthesis, such as that involved in the intuition of space, is concretely employed, as in the outlining of a specific figure, no genuinely determinate (and in that sense objective) empirical knowledge is reached (cf. B147).

Although questions may arise with respect to the interpretation of such individual passages, they are secondary to the importance of Prauss's general idea for developing a sophisticated Kantian account of the subjective side of our perceptual life. Prauss demonstrates that a Kantian theory cannot ignore this issue, that it cannot construe this realm naively in terms of some kind of Cartesian inner

---

[155] Prauss, *Erscheinung bei Kant*, 225, 284, 314 n.
[156] Ibid. 273.
[157] Ibid. 263 n.

intuition, that it thus must construe the realm as also subject, in some kind of derivative way, to judgment and the categories, and yet that it must maintain the distinctiveness of a realm that is subjectively objective, as opposed to simply objectively objective. Prauss proposes that Kant's theory points toward taking this realm to be composed of instances of implicit judgments of perception all of the form, 'it seems to me that x'. (He does *not* argue for the converse of this.) In the course of explaining the difficulties that prevented Kant himself from clearly achieving this precise formulation, Prauss provides an elegant analysis of the logic of such judgments. In effect, he takes such judgments to be understood in a kind of topic neutral way. 'It seems to me that the sun warms the stone' is to be read as 'I have appearances that invite the interpretation (*die Deutung naheliegen*), "this is the sun, this is the stone, and this sun warms this stone"'.[158] Prauss contends that such judgments have just the characteristics which Kant's theory requires, namely, (1) of involving the categories without directly applying them; (2) of making a claim to validity which bears on only one's own immediate experience (he calls this feature 'subjective validity', a Kantian phrase which, as Beck has noted,[159] can be misleading); and (3) of having a necessary reference to what is subjective while still employing only terms whose content is borrowed exclusively from the external objective realm.

This analysis has many benefits, and it clearly fits in very nicely with Kant's desire, especially in his latest work, to maintain the integrity of a subjective, non-material realm, even while reversing the Cartesian tradition, which assumed that the mental, as opposed to the spatial, is best known. Yet, just as this analysis may not explain all that is going on at the end of the transcendental deduction, it also should not be assumed to capture all of what Kant understood by the realm of the mental. In particular, it is not obvious that Kant would accept the claim (expressed most recently by Beck) that 'we have no conception of an inner non-spatial subjective realm of mere representations'.[160] There are understandable reasons why Kant wanted to de-emphasize such a realm (think of how it complicates the proof of transcendental idealism), but, aside from such parasitic events as dreams and Praussian judgments of perception, there would seem to be the possibility of simple reflection (which need not make any direct cognitive claims) on one's abstract thought as such. (Such events were Kant's own main examples in his earliest discussions of 'inner sense'.) Of course, one might try to explain such abstract occurrences in terms of special states of the human brain or information system. But even if this were allowed, it is not clear that such events would have to be fully identified with the judgments that can be used to classify them.[161]

[158] Ibid. 234, 272, 318.
[159] Beck, *Essays*, 51.
[160] Ibid. 46.
[161] Cf. Prauss, *Erscheinung bei Kant*, 151.

Sometimes Prauss himself suggests a kind of distinction here by saying that the 'subjective objects' that are the perceptual judgments are *given* only in a 'higher order' (supposedly infallible) reflexive intuition.[162] But if this is the case, a question can arise as to whether the original inner event that occurs when one is able or inclined to express the judgment 'it seems to me that . . .' need be fully the same as what this reflective judgment says. The old problem of qualia thus can re-emerge, even in a Kantian theory that holds that all our awareness involves something expressible in judgment. Prauss comes closest to acknowledging this when he admits that Kant allowed a layer of pure feeling (perhaps also involving such items as aesthetic reactions) that may escape his specific analysis.[163]

Prauss does not appear especially interested in this issue, for he thinks the Kantian inner realm is composed not only of subjective objects, but also of something more important, which is clearly subjective and not objective at all. This is supposedly our absolutely spontaneous capacity for intentionality and interpretation, for which Prauss thinks a physicalistic account would be a *hysteron proteron*. He adds that this still does not rule out applying categories to such a fully subjective realm, but he believes that here the categories would have a very different kind of meaning, that the flux of this creative inner life involves substantiality and change in a very different sense from that of the external world.[164] These speculations are not so easy to follow, and my own impression is that, although Kant does speak about sheer flux in the inner realm, this is meant merely as an abstraction. A different kind of temporality and categorialization need not be implied, for at least at the phenomenal and individual level one could argue that all the *intelligent* aspects of consciousness, even acts of 'spontaneous' intentionality, are meant to be expressible (though not solely expressible) in accord with the spatially schematized Principles. For now, however, it must be conceded that here, as in general, it still is not so clear what Kant's own view really was—that is, whether the *Critique* points more toward views such as Sellars' or rather toward the more traditional German line of interpretation that Prauss is articulating now in its most sophisticated form.

Work on this project was made possible partly by a grant from the Alexander von Humboldt Foundation of West Germany.

---

[162] Ibid. 35, 241.
[163] Ibid. 313.
[164] Ibid. 301, 310.

– 3 –

Kantian Idealism Today

In the 1980s, the main focus of work on Kant's *Critique of Pure Reason* has shifted from reconstructions of his Transcendental Deduction of the Categories to controversies about the meaning of transcendental idealism.[1] The topic of the Deduction was especially prominent in the 1970s because of the impact of Dieter Henrich's famous article on the B edition version,[2] and because of the influence of commentaries like Strawson's, which could be seen as an instance of a broader, largely Wittgensteinian, fashion for constructing so-called transcendental arguments against skepticism. Interpretations along this line gave short shrift to Kant's idealism, but this pattern changed in the 1980s, in part because of Gerold Prauss's work and Henry Allison's commentary.[3] This development can also be seen as due in large part to the rise of another Wittgensteinian fashion, namely interest in the broad debate between realism and anti-realism, as developed in the work of philosophers such as Dummett, Sellars, Rorty, Putnam, and Bernard Williams.

More recently, Paul Guyer has issued a lengthy commentary which ends by challenging Allison on the interpretation of Kantian idealism, and which returns to an emphasis on the Deduction as seen from a broadly Strawsonian perspective, but now backed by a detailed narrative about how the whole Transcendental Analytic fits into the broad sweep of Kant's never ending '*Entwicklungsgeschichte*'.[4] Unfortunately, but not surprisingly, it must be said that, despite all this important new work, Kant scholarship has yet to have been overcome by consensus. Guyer has rejected, among other things, Allison's approach to

---

[1] For a review of earlier work on those topics, see my 'Recent Work on Kant's Theoretical Philosophy', *American Philosophical Quarterly*, 19 (1982), 1–24.

[2] D. Henrich, 'The Proof Structure of Kant's Transcendental Deduction', *Review of Metaphysics*, 22 (1969), 640–59.

[3] See G. Prauss, *Kant und das Problem der Dinge an sich* (Bonn, 1974); H. Allison, *Kant's Transcendental Idealism* (New Haven, 1984). Cf. n. 1 above for a discussion of other works by them, as well as my other discussions: 'Contemporary German Epistemology', *Inquiry*, 25 (1982), 125–38; 'Kant's Transcendental Idealism (review of Allison)', *Topoi*, 3 (1984), 181–5; 'Kant and Guyer on Apperception', *Archiv für Geschichte der Philosophie*, 65 (1983), 174–86.

[4] P. Guyer, *Kant and the Claims of Knowledge* (Cambridge, 1987).

idealism, and Allison has rejected, among other things, Guyer's approach to the Deduction.⁵

By focusing here on the issue of Kantian idealism, I aim to show how it is possible to develop a reading of Kant that appreciates the limitations pointed out in the major new lines of interpretation while incorporating what is best in each of them. Although my arguments will be presented primarily as interpretive hypotheses, as claims about how Kant's own intentions are most accurately represented, they also are meant as a first step toward some partial vindication of the value (which is not yet to say the truth) of Kant's own views. I suspect that current attempts to make Kant look more fashionable are not just historically questionable; they may obscure for us the strength of some traditional positions still present in the *Critique*.⁶

When approaching Kantian idealism, it is important to be aware, from the very beginning, of a peculiar feature of many discussions of the general idea of the 'Copernican Revolution' (e.g. in Putnam or in Bencivenga⁷) which simply bypass those *specific* features of our experience that most concerned Kant, viz. the characteristics of a prioricity and spatio-temporality and the apparent linkage between these two. It is true that Allison's important interpretation does *not* depend on this tendency, but to appreciate that interpretation, and to put it in proper perspective, I think it is helpful first to consider the pattern of what can be called a 'short argument' to idealism, i.e. one that passes over the Kant's own 'long' and complex argument to idealism and its appeal to the specific features of our pure intuition.⁸

The interest in a 'short' argument may be due in part to some tendencies in Kant's own work. Precisely these specific features do seem to be ignored, for example, if one poses the Critical problem of knowledge as the general problem of how to understand the relation between our representations and distinct objects, i.e. to 'inquire what new character "relation to an object" confers upon our representations' (A197/B242; this is a passage which can and should be compared

---

⁵ There is much to be learned from these approaches, but I agree with much of their criticisms of each other. Thus, like Guyer, I have argued (see n. 3 above) that Kant's idealism transcends the merely 'epistemic' reading which Allison and those of his ilk propose; and, like Allison, I have also argued that Kant's Transcendental Deduction transcends the worries about skepticism that interpretations like Guyer's have often stressed (although to a lesser degree recently).

⁶ In particular, talk of a 'Copernican turn' notwithstanding, there may be considerable traditional and defensible realism in Kant's ontology (see my 'The Critique of Metaphysics: Kant and Traditional Ontology', in *Cambridge Companion to Kant*, ed. P. Guyer (Cambridge, 1992). Likewise, talk of a 'Refutation of Idealism' notwithstanding, there may be considerable and understandable disinterest in skeptical problems in Kant's Analytic—on this point the recent work of Michael Friedman, for example, is very instructive.

⁷ Hilary Putnam, *Reason, Truth and History,* (Cambridge, 1981); Ermanno Bencivenga, *Kant's Copernican Revolution* (Oxford, 1987).

⁸ See my 'Kant, Fichte, and Short Arguments to Idealism', *Archiv für Geschichte der Philosophie,* 72 (1990), 63–85.

with Kant's similar initial formulation in his famous letter to Herz, February 22, 1772). Kant indicates a number of ways in which this problem could be approached (cf. the letter and A92/B125, and B167–8). Dogmatic realists could say that objects directly produce our representations—call this the ectypal hypothesis—or it could be held, conversely, that it is our representations that produce objects—call this the archetypal hypothesis (one variation of which might be understood as phenomenalism). Of course, there are also other possibilities. Under a broad realist heading here one can imagine variations such as harmony, 'pre-formation', or common cause theories. That is, there might be an agreement of representation and object that is due not to any direct relation between them, but rather to something else which arranges the agreement. Another, and more radical, option is to shift the question, as Kant's own Critical turn ultimately does, so that it is no longer necessarily about an agreement with objects as such, but rather is restricted to objects of *knowledge*, in particular to objects of our possible theoretical and synthetic knowledge. To understand Kant's approach properly, then, it first should be distinguished from all these other theories.

This is quite a task, and the first hypothesis alone involves considerable difficulties. One difficulty with the ectypal hypothesis which Kant no doubt recognizes, but does not always emphasize, is that by itself it is insufficient to explain the peculiarity of *epistemic* representation as such. To say that a particular representation somehow comes into being as the result of the world's impact or 'affection' is not yet to say how that representation comes to have the complexity requisite for being considered a human cognitive state, i.e. a state that does not simply 'match' the world in some sense—as a mirror image might match something—but is such that it can be true or false, justified or unjustified. Since Kant allows non-human beings—and perhaps humans as well, at times—to have sub-judgmental states which he calls representations but which lack these epistemic features, the question remains of how *our* representations become epistemically representative. The mere 'impact of the world' can occur with subjects lacking this kind of representation, so it is insufficient to explain what happens in our knowledge.

At this point it could seem relevant to stress an extra difficulty, namely the fact that any such causal account would appear at best to be able to explain only *contingent* effects. Hence, if one believes, as Kant does, that our representations include a priori knowledge, and that a prioricity brings *necessity* with it, then the ectypal hypothesis appears insufficient for an extra 'modal' reason. But while Kant does focus on precisely this consideration, it is not clear just why he had to focus on it—a fact that is often passed over in current interpretations. For example, one interpreter says that Kant believes 'properties that attach to things in themselves could at best be known to do so contingently, but not necessarily'.⁹ But, one can ask, how does Kant ever make intelligible 'even' any knowledge of ultimately contingent properties? It is true that Kant is most concerned with ruling out 'modal' knowledge of a *non*-contingent noumenal type, but it is not clear how he could ever allow such contingent knowledge, either.¹⁰

Another sign that he need not have focused so quickly on modal issues can be found in Kant's *Prolegomena* (§9), where, even in the context of arguing that a priori knowledge seems inexplicable on theories other than his own, Kant explains this by first remarking that accidents of objects cannot in any way intelligible to us ever 'migrate' into finite intuiting subjects. So even if there can appear to be a special difficulty in the case of a priori knowledge, where a subject is to know an object prior even to being exposed to it, what Kant is saying is that in general such 'migrating' is mysterious, and hence a problem remains in *non*-apriori cases. And this means that he has a *general* objection to empiricism—that it leaves unexplained not only a priori knowledge but also empirical knowledge in its simplest form. He must reject as insufficient any empiricism that supposes knowledge is to be explained, at base, just by a representation coming to 'copy' some object outside it because of the causal 'impression' of that object. But to put the problem this way is also to say that the difficulty is not with empiricism as such, but with ectypalism of any sort; for, even if the cause were a *non*-empirical object 'acting' in a non-empirical way, producing a state with a non-empirical, i.e. necessary, epistemic character, that alone would not explain our representative state.

If one moves on to an archetypal theory, it turns out that similar difficulties arise immediately, although Kant speaks often as if we could understand how a representation agrees with an object if only—unlike what is really the case in our situation—the representation did produce the object. Most likely Kant's confidence here rests on extra presumptions. He need not be thinking that making something is as such sufficient to bring knowledge of that thing with it—for, after all, on his view pre-judgmental beings can make many things without knowing them at all. He may rather have been implicitly thinking of the making subject here as quasi-divine, and then he might have assumed that any such being, who can literally create objects, would also have the supposedly lesser power of knowing them. In any case, in either the archetypal or ectypal situation, a causal relation does not, merely as such, solve the problem of knowledge.

A similar objection can be used against positing a common cause, say God, as the source of agreement between our representations and objects. Even if such a

---

⁹ Guyer, *Kant and the Claims of Knowledge*, 359. What I am saying is not that Guyer is blind to this point, but that it is typical that it is not being focused on.

¹⁰ I suspect Kant passes over this issue because he believes that all our putatively contingent knowledge is phenomenal and in part dependent on non-contingent knowledge (Guyer's own analysis of the central role of the principle of causality could be used to bring this out), so that the ideality of the non-contingent infects the contingent.

causal relation is posited, it still leaves unclear precisely why the resultant agreement is specifically an epistemic one. (This is Kant's main point against Leibniz and Occasionalism—positions from which Kant's own really is not so easy to distinguish.) Two 'clocks'—perhaps one 'running' in the mind, and one outside it—could 'agree' because of a pre-established harmony, and yet that would not be sufficient for us to understand how the first amounts to a *knowledge* of the second. Of course, as Kant stresses, the harmony by itself also would not explain any *necessary* agreement, but this should not obscure the fact that there remains the general difficulty of explaining any genuine epistemic agreement here at all.

Kant himself does not dwell on these general difficulties. Just as he does not pause long over the question of how *empirical* concepts gain sense and reference, but rather jumps ahead to ask how this works for *pure* concepts, so too the agreement in knowledge that concerns him (most famously in the Deduction) is the necessary agreement of pure representations with their putative objects. This concern remains constant despite the major development in his idealism when he shifts from holding, as he did in the *Dissertation*, that these objects could be and are non-empirical, to arguing, as he did in the *Critique*, that—for determinate theoretical purposes—they must be empirical.[11]

But even if Kant himself did *not dwell* upon the *general* problem of knowledge, his successors have often written, and continue to write, as if he did—and thereby they have fallen easily into distorting what is *meant* by transcendental idealism. They have done so by presuming that the 'Copernican Revolution' is nothing other than the general presumption that objects can be intelligible *only* as 'relative' to the *concepts*, or systems of concepts, or theories, that we 'impose'. In a way, this stress on the essential and distinctive role of concepts in knowledge could be regarded as just a natural development of the insight that a mere causal theory of our representation is inadequate. Something like 'synthesis,' whatever that is, is also needed. This insight is well taken; it is at the center of Kant's Deduction, and it has spelled the death of the 'given'—but what is mysterious here is that this epistemic point so often gets immediately inflated into a metaphysical claim about the mere ideality of whatever is conceptually represented.

This connection between ideality and the Kantian emphasis on concepts has been accepted even by astute current critics of popular Kantianism. Thus, against the apparent anti-realism of Putnam, Nicholas Wolterstorff has argued that Kant's talk of concepts as 'rules for ordering experience' ought not—i.e. despite what the 'Kantians' say—to lead us to conclude that 'since *goose* is one of our

---

[11] The transition to this position is signaled in Kant's famous letter to Herz, which has been interpreted in different ways recently by Wolfgang Carl and Lewis White Beck, in *Kant's Transcendental Deductions*, ed. E. Förster (Stanford, Calif., 1989). For a fine mediation of their views, I have benefited from a paper by Predrag Cicovacki.

concepts, reality apart from us does not come with geese in it'.[12] Wolterstorff's point here is not about the objective *empirical* meaning or reference of the concept of goose (I trust he sees that Kant is no skeptic or subjectivist about that), but rather is about its absolute ontological status. Wolterstorff's presumption, like Putnam's, appears to be that for the Kantian something takes on an ideal character *already* from the fact that it is represented by one of 'our concepts', i.e. just from the fact that it is part of our theory for 'ordering experience'—although usually it is added that this character is connected with some particular feature of our conceptual capacity, e.g. with our theories having to be incomplete in scope, or underdetermined in evidence, or ultimately indeterminate in reference. On such an interpretation, then, that which is not ideal (in the supposedly Kantian transcendental sense) would have to be something that transcends the concepts of all our possible theories.[13]

As Guyer has noted, interpreters such as Graham Bird, Gordon Nagel, and Ralph Walker have all considered one or the other version of this interpretation as central to transcendental idealism. And this is not a new development;[14] similar lines of interpretation can be found in Kant's very first interpreters, and on through Hegel and his contemporary sympathizers.[15] There are of course significant differences *within* this line of interpretation, but such interpretations still all have something important in common in that they define the 'transcendentally real' simply as something that transcends our *conceptual* capacities as such. They thus agree in giving an *epistemic and non-specific* definition to the doctrine of transcendental idealism. Here the 'transcendentally real' has no special ontological status—indeed, it may be, and usually is, taken to be an empty category, for reality might well have nothing that in principle goes beyond all our *possible* concepts. No doubt, those who immediately reject the 'thing in itself' are usually thinking in these terms. But there is another type of 'epistemic' interpretation of idealism, one that is unlike all these in so far as it understands the transcendentally real rather as that which would transcend our *specific* cognitive faculties. In particular, given Kant's fundamental doctrine that for us objective cognition requires conception joined with intuition in warranted judgment, this view takes Kant's transcendental idealism to arise not from the nature of concepts or

---

[12] N. Wolterstorff, 'Realism vs. Anti-Realism', in *Realism, Proceedings and Addresses of the Catholic Philosophical Association*, 59 (1984), 62.

[13] Such an interpretation can be held in a 'modest' form, which declares that there *could* be meaning to the concepts of such transcendent objects, though in principle we can never reach that meaning; or it can be held in a radical form, which declares that ultimately the very idea of such objects must be regarded as in general meaningless, or at least as wholly meaningless to us.

[14] See my 'Hegel and Idealism,' *Monist*, 74 (1991); cf. P. Guyer, 'The Rehabilitation of Transcendental Idealism?' in E. Schaper and W. Vossenkuhl (eds.), *Reading Kant* (Oxford: Basil Blackwell, 1989), 140–67. This paper by Guyer is a version of parts of what was presented later at the end of his book, as well as earlier at an APA colloquium with Allison in 1985.

[15] Cf. R. Pippin, *Hegel's Idealism* (Cambridge, 1989), and the discussion of it in my 'Hegel and Idealism.'

theories as such, but rather from specific features connected with the nature of our kind of *intuition*. Thus, this view, which occurs prominently in Allison's work, ties Kant's idealism essentially to his doctrine of the a prioricity and the ubiquity for us of the pure forms of spatial and temporal intuition.

This variant has a major advantage and a major disadvantage. The advantage is that its focus on the forms of space and time gives it the chance, which the 'non-specific' line of interpretation sorely lacks, of corresponding to Kant's own arguments—and it thereby also can help to explain why, given Kant's overriding concern for idealism, he didn't focus on what I called earlier the general problem of knowledge as such. Anyone who studies the *Dissertation* and the genesis of Kant's idealism must concede that it is inappropriate to base that idealism on considerations that do not appeal, as Kant always does, to the special features of our forms of intuition. Allison's explanation of transcendental idealism properly stresses the essential role in Kant's arguments of these special 'forms of sensibility' and their relation to the specific problem of a priori knowledge. The disadvantage of his explanation is that it still adheres to an epistemic reading of Kant's idealism. On that reading there is still no reason to think that the non-ideal has a greater ontological status than the ideal. Here the ideality of the forms of space and time indicates simply their necessary structuring function in our experience, and it does not say that the non-spatio-temporal domain has any greater reality for Kant than does the spatio-temporal. To say that something is transcendentally ideal on this view is to say that it is relative to our sensible forms, but that is not necessarily to say that these forms are themselves relative.

Guyer and others have criticized such an interpretation. I have also objected to it because it does injustice to the fact that Kant clearly does believe in and speak of (which is not the same thing as making particular theoretical assertions about) the absolute reality of things in themselves with substantive non-spatio-temporal characteristics. The most obvious instance of this is perhaps Kant's 'transcendental theology', for which Allen Wood has provided an excellent commentary.[16] The epistemic interpretation, in understanding transcendental idealism as the claim that human knowledge is governed by certain sensible conditions, does not insist on Kant's own stronger conclusion, which is that there are objects which in themselves have *genuine* ultimate properties that do *not* conform to those conditions. However, despite this and other problems with the epistemic approach, something can and should be said for connecting epistemic and ontological considerations. This will not save either the epistemic interpretation or Kant's arguments, but it can do something to make them a little more understandable.

There is another complication though: sometimes Allison himself appears to use the non-specific rather than the specific version of the epistemic interpret-

---

[16] A. Wood, *Kant's Rational Theology* (Ithaca, NY, 1978).

ation, as when he says that '*behind* Kant's idealism...lies a principle...that whatever is necessary for the representation or experience of something as an object...must reflect the cognitive structure of the mind rather than the nature of an object as it is in itself'.[17] Such a principle could be made true by definition, but that would sadly trivialize Kant's work. On the other hand, if the principle is taken substantively, then it has the difficulties already noted for the non-specific interpretation of transcendental idealism. I therefore propose taking the passage rather as an abbreviation for a longer argument, the specific version argument. That is, I suspect that what Allison really meant to say is that, if the argument for the a prioricity and ubiquity of space and time goes through, then this is to be used somehow to reach the extra claim—which then surely is a conclusion rather than an underlying 'principle'—that these forms are *merely* subjective (in a transcendental sense, of course, which still allows their empirical objectivity).

Guyer, however, has claimed that here Allison is arguing 'that space and time cannot be properties of things in themselves *because* they are subjective forms of representation. But [Guyer adds] what Kant argues is exactly the opposite of this: namely, that space and time can only be *mere* forms of representation because they cannot be properties of things in themselves.'[18] Nonetheless, I believe Allison actually could accept Guyer's formulation, viz. that Kant's inference is *to* 'mere subjectivity' from transcendental non-reality, rather than vice versa. Note that in one sentence of the quote, but not the other, the word 'mere' appears, so the one sentence isn't quite 'exactly the opposite' of the other. There is a distinction to be made here between 'subjectivity' and 'mere subjectivity', a distinction that others have surely appreciated. Without the distinction, one could not even begin to understand a problem that Allison himself stresses, namely the old problem of the 'neglected alternative', the problem that, even if there is a subjective nature to the forms of space and time, in that they structure our knowing, this nature still might seem to be able to coexist with, rather than exclude, their transcendental reality.

This reconciling approach might seem to be undermined by Allison's own recent repudiation of Guyer's critique, but there again some presumed differences in the interpretations turn out to be verbal. Allison insists that Kant's argument is 'from the premise that space and time are forms [note, he does not say: "mere forms"] of sensibility to the conclusion that things in themselves are not spatial or temporal',[19] and this Allison *supposes* is the opposite of what Guyer means. Yet again it would seem that Guyer really could agree with this, since what Guyer is objecting to would be an argument that *begins* from what are called 'mere' (subjective) forms. The common issue that remains is how one gets in the first place *to* a conclusion about the non-spatio-temporality of things in themselves;

---

[17] H. Allison, *Kant's Transcendental Idealism* (New Haven, 1983), 27.
[18] Guyer, *Kant and the Claims of Knowledge*, 342; stress added by me in quotation.
[19] H. Allison, review of Guyer, *Journal of Philosophy*, 86 (1989), 220.

that is, how one arrives *not merely* at saying that space and time are forms of sensibility, but also at saying that they *are merely* forms of sensibility. (For simplicity I will bracket the proposal that 'form of sensibility' is a term that just *means* a 'form of appearance' which is 'merely subjective'.)

A problem here for any interpretation is that at first Kant does seem just to jump to the conclusion of the mere subjectivity of our forms of intuition by insisting on a supposed incompatibility of claiming both the transcendental reality and the a prioricity of such forms. (Note that what Kant presumes is that we must first consider giving up the former claim, which is just the opposite of what most of us would do today.) But then, if one recalls the problem of the neglected alternative, it would seem either that Kant's denial of transcendental reality for space and time amounts to a jump to an ontological assertion of non-spatio-temporal properties for things in themselves, and that this is, as Guyer suggests, a move that Kant really did make, though only on the basis of crude conflations; or that, as Allison suggests, the crudity of such an ontological inference forces us back to a more modest, epistemic, reading of idealism.

However, we are not really forced into such an absolute either/or. Instead, we can agree with Guyer that a merely epistemic reading is incompatible with Kant's position, which does involve a jump to an ontological conclusion; but we can also agree this much with Allison, that Kant's considerations here are not as crude as they may appear or have been alleged to be.

Part of the solution here is to say that, although transcendental idealism is asserted ultimately as an ontological and not just an epistemic doctrine, the initial argument of the Aesthetic can be naturally understood in terms of a more limited conclusion which does rest primarily on mere epistemic considerations. Recall that the immediate conclusion in Kant's Transcendental Exposition of Space is that transcendental idealism alone '*makes intelligible* the possibility of geometry' (B41; note that this phrase is also used when the 'Copernican' turn is introduced at B xvii). Such a conclusion by itself does not logically *exclude* the 'neglected alternative' of transcendentally real forms of sensibility, yet it does appear to warrant their neglect. For, if by some accidental harmony these forms also had such a real status, one could still ask how that alone would make our a priori knowledge of them any the more 'intelligible'. Of course, this point still does not entail Kant's idealistic conclusion; for, as Philip Kitcher has nicely argued,[20] one can also ask where Kant gets his confidence that we have a priori access even to 'merely subjective' *forms* of sensibility—for, as long as these are 'forms', they have an objectivity and necessity that transcends what we have a clearly intelligible immediate access to. Nonetheless, there are a variety of other reasons, sketched throughout the Aesthetic, why Kant could understandably believe that the avail-

---

[20] Philip Kitcher, 'Kant and the Foundations of Mathematics', *Philosophical Review*, 84 (1975), 23–50.

able 'objective' theories about such forms, notably Newton's and Leibniz's, each had specific deficiencies which made them especially unattractive; and this, along with the metaphysical economy of the 'merely subjective' option, would be sufficient to warrant a preference for transcendental idealism. This still would not amount to a logical exclusion of the 'neglected alternative', but that is just as well, for it could help to explain both why Kant felt it important to stress the Antinomies (which, it should be recalled, are what he says first led him into idealism)—because these supposedly would ground a definitive exclusion of realism—and also why Kant could have left the impression that his idealism was an appropriate position even without the Antinomies argument.

It thus becomes necessary to consider how these current interpretations see the relation between the Antinomies and Kantian idealism.[21] These commentaries involve a consideration that nicely connects problems of the Aesthetic and the Antinomies, albeit in a way unintended by their authors. This consideration is the distinction between conditional and absolute necessity, the conflation of which is, according to Guyer, at the heart of Kant's 'crude' error in the Aesthetic.[22] Allegedly Kant's main, and invalid, argument to idealism confuses

{CN = 'the principle of conditional necessity'}: necessarily [(x is an object and we perceive x) → (x is spatial and Euclidean)]

with

{AN = 'the principle of absolute necessity'}: (x is an object and we perceive x) → necessarily [(x is spatial and Euclidean)].

The argument scheme {CN} is said to express a mere conditional necessity, whereas {AN} asserts an absolute necessity. Moreover, {AN} is said to represent Kant's argument at the end of the Aesthetic (A48-9/B65-6), and to involve the only conclusion that would require a 'merely' subjective reading of space and time. This is because of the principle cited earlier, that we can't have a priori certainty of necessary noumenal properties. (So, once the properties are alleged to be necessary here, they cannot be noumenal.) Guyer's critique is that argument {CN} is the most that Kant is entitled to, whereas argument {AN}, the one Kant is supposed to need for his idealism, rests simply on an elementary modal confusion, viz. precisely the conflation of conditional and absolute necessity.

There are some incidental problems here. For example, even argument {CN} needs to be reformulated in terms of 'outer' objects, not objects in general. But there are also non-incidental problems. In particular, argument {AN} ascribes to Kant a conclusion about absolute necessity that seems all too clearly incompatible

---

[21] For more on the antinomies, see Arthur Melnick, *Space, Time, and Thought in Kant* (Dordrecht, 1989), and Carl Posy, 'Dancing to the Antinomy: A Proposal for Transcendental Idealism', *American Philosophical Quarterly*, 20 (1983), 81–94.

[22] Guyer, *Kant and the Claims of Knowledge*, 366.

with, rather than uniquely explainable by, transcendental idealism. Kant repeatedly claims that we cannot make absolute modality claims about phenomenal features; thus, the Fourth Antinomy indicates we need to be agnostic about saying that the world is absolutely necessary, or saying that it is absolutely contingent. (Guyer himself notes other similar passages, but he takes this just to show that Kant is inconsistent.) Above all, given that even on Guyer's reading Kant's idealism implies that objects which we perceive spatio-temporally, e.g. ourselves, really are non-spatio-temporal in themselves, it becomes quite extraordinarily uncharitable to ascribe to Kant the idea that spatiality, for example, attaches to objects with absolute necessity.

How then would anyone ever have come to think that argument {AN} fits Kant's view? One reason might be that it does nicely fit one kind of idealism—though this would be not Kantian idealism, but rather a kind of archetypal idealism, one that makes spatiality a necessary aspect of outer objects because those objects are then *nothing but* the products of a spatiality imposing subject, so that they could not exist at all without the spatiality we have put into their essence. But this would be tantamount to saying that we are, contrary to what Kant says, literally creative subjects.

Another reason for introducing {AN}—indeed, the main ground for Guyer—would be Kant's talk of relations of geometry as being not subjectively necessary but rather belonging of necessity, e.g. 'to the triangle itself' (A48/B65). However, there are *non*-absolute ways to understand the contrast here with what is being called 'subjective'. In this case the 'subjectively necessary' can signify a merely individual, or even a general but merely psychological, constitution, one that contrasts with the specific necessity (which is still not absolute) involved in our objective *knowledge*. Note that this would perfectly fit the passages cited earlier concerning Kant's rejection of pre-formation theories of knowledge. As long as we have relations that are not arbitrarily or mechanically arranged, but are genuinely even though conditionally necessary for any knowledge of objects we can have, then there is all the necessity that Kant is typically asserting.

Of course, with only such conditional necessity, it still can remain unclear how we can be said to *require* transcendental idealism rather than realism. But a plausible argument can be built up, one that inverts part of Guyer's interpretation and in so doing even provides a better account of the Antinomies.

The argument Guyer regarded as underlying Kant's reasoning can be outlined this way:

{PG} (i) There are a priori phenomenal features that are known as absolutely, not conditionally necessary (the triangle example);
(ii) but absolute necessity in things isn't knowable by us;
(iii) hence these features must apply to mere appearances, not to things in themselves.

Guyer believes that the first step here (PGi) is a very weak premise, but still he insists on ascribing it to Kant himself. We have just questioned this ascription, and others have as well, e.g. Allison in his review.

But another argument scheme to consider, one that Kant suggests in the Preface (B xx), is this:

{KA} (i) If something is a thing in itself, then it has absolute ('unconditioned') properties;
(ii) phenomena (using this term 'neutrally' to designate just something that does appear, without prejudging its transcendental ideality or reality), as spatio-temporal, do not have such properties, since ascribing them leads to antinomies;
(iii) therefore, these phenomena, as such, are mere appearances.

So, roughly speaking, Guyer's suggested argument goes: 'since space is (supposedly, in its necessity) absolute, it is therefore only ideal.' Our argument, in contrast, goes: 'since space (in the size of the world) is not absolute, it is therefore only ideal.'

This argument also has a very controversial first premise, (KAi), but Kant does appear to endorse it, and although this may seem dogmatic, it, unlike Guyer's first premise (PGi), does not require *knowledge* of any particular real absolute necessities: it just speaks of what things in themselves would be like if they could be known.

Admittedly, this 'argument' is presented so briefly in the Preface that it is hardly recognizable. Yet, it can naturally be understood, I believe, as an abbreviation for the overall argument that Kant means to give in the Antinomies. The argument there has been understandably criticized by many, including Guyer, as being manifestly question-begging against realism. But there is a way of unpacking the disputed steps (the ones behind (KAii)) so that the Antinomies can at least be saved from that objection.

One way—but not an adequate one—of trying to express the arguments of the first Antinomy is this: we can't experience the spatio-temporal world as finite, and we cannot experience it as infinite; but a thing in itself must be either finite or infinite, so the spatio-temporal world can't as such be a thing in itself. The standard general objection to such an argument is that what we can or cannot experience should not be relevant—unless we are already, illicitly, assuming idealism. Thus, the argument can't work precisely against the dogmatists it is aimed at.

However, there is another more accurate and promising way to formulate the Antinomies which would shift the blame to dogmatism. If we take the arguments *within* the Antinomies to be an attempt by dogmatists to determine the world's absolute magnitude, as finite or infinite, then Kant's overall reductio of their reasoning can be expressed this way:

(i) We can't experience the spatio-temporal world as (absolutely) infinite, so it is (absolutely) finite;
(ii) we can't experience the spatio-temporal world as (absolutely) finite, so it is (absolutely) infinite;
(iii) but a thing in itself can't be finite and infinite, so the spatio-temporal world isn't a thing in itself.

This may still look like question-begging, but one should ask: *who* is it that is claiming, to take a version of its second step, that 'since we cannot experience an end to the spatial world, therefore it has no end'? What is all too often forgotten here is that generally the arguments within the Antinomies are not Kant's own but are rather dogmatic ones that he is citing (and, of course, reformulating a bit). Once this point is appreciated, it is possible to see that the overall argument form here is not only non-question-begging but also quite relevant to helping out transcendental idealism. For, note what the common implicit presumption is of the first steps of this argument: namely, experience is an adequate measure of absolute dimensions. This might seem to be an idealist premise, but it is really used as a dogmatic instrument of transcendental realism, for it is required in leaping to positive claims about things in themselves, e.g. in saying that, since there is no experience of an end to the spatial world, therefore the spatial world is an infinite thing in itself. Rather than making such a leap, the non-dogmatist can observe that we can avoid the contradictory conclusion of the general argument by not presuming that our experience is an absolute measure. Then, for example, from the lack of an experiential end to space, nothing yet about the world's absolute magnitude follows. Of course, Kant could still be charged with having argued improperly when going on to make *other* claims, such as 'we surely can always extend our experience of the spatial world', and 'such a guaranteed extension isn't tantamount to a claim of infinite size', but these specific questionable claims are not the same thing as being caught in a manifestly question-begging and inappropriate argument.

There is a final irony here: namely, that this kind of defense of the Antinomies as non-question-begging parallels much of what is found in Allison rather than Guyer—and yet, it still can be understood as validating what Guyer rather than Allison says about what Kant *means* by his idealism.[23] It's just that, on my

---

[23] Another irony should be noted: the denial of an ontological reading can be seen as itself involving a kind of conflation of absolute and conditional necessity, this time in Allison. For his interpretation (given the principle 'behind' idealism that he alleges), is, as I understand it, that to think of something as a thing in itself is to think of it as *something which necessarily has no relation, i.e. no common properties, with an appearance*. But all Kant means, I believe, is that to think of something as a thing in itself is just to think of it *not as something that has (such) a necessary relation to an appearance.* The latter claim is a 'conditional negative'. It says not that there necessarily is no relation, but that, merely on the condition of this perspective, there is not necessarily any relation. Whereas Allison's absolute claim here rules out the

reading, Kant is here, as in the Aesthetic, innocent of some of the cruder conflations that have been ascribed to him—even if he also does hold on to something that many would regard as just as bad: namely, an ontological version of transcendental idealism.

'neglected alternative' of the transcendental reality of phenomenal properties all too quickly by definition, Kant's own view still leaves room for the possibility of an overlap of properties of things in themselves and appearances—an overlap that can be, and is, challenged only in the specific arguments about spatio-temporality.

– 4 –

The Critique of Metaphysics: Kant and Traditional Ontology

Kant's attitude toward metaphysics and ontology is ambiguous in his Critical work. On the standard view of the *Critique of Pure Reason*, the positive and negative aspects of this attitude map neatly onto the two major sections of that work. After that first section presents a 'Transcendental Analytic' of the understanding, or a 'metaphysics of experience', which legitimates the use of certain pure concepts necessary for structuring our spatio-temporal knowledge, a Transcendental Dialectic is provided to expose fallacies that theoretical reason entangles itself in when it extends itself beyond experience. Just prior to that Dialectic, Kant also inserts an 'Appendix' on 'concepts of reflection', which sketches how the restriction of our use of pure concepts to the domain of experience limits the general claims of the traditional ontology of the Leibnizian system. These attacks would appear to complement each other. Whereas the specific errors of rational psychology, rational cosmology, and rational theology are exposed in the core of the Dialectic, the critique of ontology and the general discussions of the operations of 'reflection' and 'reason' suggest a principle of closure for dismissing all claims of our theoretical reason that would stray beyond a merely immanent spatio-temporal field.

On this view, there is little positive theoretical doctrine in the latter half of the *Critique;* at the most, it is noted that Kant's discussion of the antinomies in cosmology can be seen as offering support for the doctrine of transcendental idealism. And even this discussion can be seen as making a negative point about a negative doctrine—that is, as showing merely that we run into contradictions if we take our spatio-temporal knowledge to apply to things in themselves. But, while the treatment of transcendental idealism is a high point of the Dialectic, by itself it is not sufficient for explaining Kant's entire mature attitude to the tradition. In the *Dissertation* (1770) he had already claimed the ideality of space and time, but this hardly stopped him from making numerous specific positive

Special thanks for assistance on this essay are due to Steven Naragon, Paul Guyer, Alison Laywine, and Eric Watkins.

assertions about the 'intelligible form' of things in themselves. In the *Critique of Pure Reason*, he reversed himself by challenging such assertions—and with such effectiveness that the general notion of a rejection of transcendent metaphysics met with more approval than Kant's own attempt to resuscitate pure philosophy in the form of a metaphysics of experience. However, this approval has rarely rested on a close scrutiny of Kant's own discussion, and often it has left unconsidered the possibility (which will be emphasized in what follows) that even in his late work there are significant limits to Kant's criticism of the tradition.

A proper understanding of Kant's criticism requires recalling the general outline of his new account of the dialectic of reason, but to evaluate that criticism it is also important to compare this account with the whole range of particular claims that Kant as well as the tradition had made previously. To determine how far the criticism really goes, one needs to look beyond the surface structure of the Dialectic and back to all the specific ontological issues of the traditional discussion. Hence, after an introductory outline of the Dialectic of the first *Critique* (readers familiar with Kant may skip over this and move directly to Section II), I will turn in more detail to a few less familiar texts where some neglected aspects of the contrast between Kant and his Leibnizian predecessors can be explored most directly.

I

The Dialectic proposes a general pattern for the errors of transcendent metaphysics. The pattern is not exactly, as one might first expect, the error of simply employing categories apart from their specific spatio-temporal schematization, for example by making claims about substance without considerations of permanence. This is an error, but by itself it is accidental in the double sense of being neither fully systematic nor imposed by any special force. For Kant, the dialectical errors of reason are anything but accidental. They involve special representations, called Ideas of reason, which are systematically organized and give rise to inferences with a special 'unavoidable' force, as if they were a 'natural and inevitable illusion' (A298/B355).[1]

The content of the Ideas is determined by ordered variations of the idea of something unconditioned, an idea that comes from making the general 'logical maxim' of reason, namely to seek the condition of any particular conditioned judgment, into a 'real principle' so that 'a unity [of reason] is brought to

---

[1] The following translations of Kant's writings are employed in these pages: *Inaugural Dissertation*, by G. B. Kerferd and D. E. Walford, in *Selected Pre-Critical Writings and Correspondence with Beck* (Manchester, 1968); the *Nova Dilucidatio*, by John Reuscher, in *Kant's Latin Writings*, ed. Lewis White Beck (New York, 1986); *Lectures on Philosophical Theology*, by Allen Wood and Gertrude Clark (Ithaca, NY, 1978); *What Real Progress Has Metaphysics Made in Germany since the Time of Leibniz and Wolff?*, by Ted Humphrey (New York, 1983); and *Critique of Pure Reason*, by Norman Kemp Smith (London, 1929). Page references in the text with short title, e.g., *Progress*, give the *Akademie* edition volume and page number.

completion'. One thereby assumes that 'if the conditioned is given, the whole series of conditions ... which is therefore itself unconditioned, is likewise given, that is, contained in the object and its connection' (A308/B364). This is a fallacy because the analytic connection of a given concept to its logical ground is not the same as the synthetic connection of a given thing and its real ground.[2] Yet there is a force allegedly making this assumption 'inevitable', namely the naturalness of taking 'the subjective necessity of a connection of our concepts, which is an advantage of the understanding, for an objective necessity in the determination of things in themselves' (A297/B353).

The 'connection of concepts' Kant has in mind here comes from what he takes to be the peculiar office of reason to connect representations in chains of syllogisms. Thus: 'We may presume that the form of syllogisms [*Vernunftschluss*] ... will contain the origin of special a priori concepts which we may call pure concepts of reason, or *transcendental ideas*, and which will determine according to principles how understanding is to be employed in dealing with experience in its totality' (A321/B378). The 'determination of things in themselves' that he has in mind here amounts to the thought of an unconditioned item, or set of items, corresponding to each of the syllogistic 'forms', viz. an unconditioned, i.e. unpredicable, subject of categorical syllogisms, an unconditioned, i.e. first, object for 'the hypothetical synthesis of the members of a series', and an unconditioned, i.e. exhaustive, source for 'the disjunctive synthesis of the parts in a system' (A323/B379).

To this ambitious scheme Kant immediately adds a further systematic proposal. He holds that the 'unconditioned subject' corresponds to the absolute 'unity of the thinking subject', that the unconditioned first item of the series of hypothetical syllogisms corresponds to the 'absolute unity [i.e. either an absolutely first item or a total series] of the series of appearance', and that the unconditioned ground of the disjunctive syntheses is 'the absolute unity of the condition of all objects of thought in general' (A334/B391). Even more specifically, the thought of an unconditioned subject is taken to lead to the Idea of an immortal self; that of the unconditioned appearance is taken to lead to the contradictory Idea of a completely given whole of appearances (and thereby the notion of the mere phenomenality of the natural world, which allows the Idea of transcendental freedom); and the notion of an unconditioned source for thought is taken to lead to the Idea of 'a being of all beings', God (A336/B393; cf. B395 n.).

These proposed connections are just the first layers of Kant's ingenious architectonic. The Ideas are determined further by the table of categories, so that the

---

[2] However, sometimes Kant seems not to challenge that the principle that the conditioned requires the unconditioned *is* valid for things in themselves, but rather argues that, precisely for that reason, since an unconditioned item cannot be found in the domain of spatio-temporal appearances, this shows they must be mere appearances rather than things in themselves (*Progress*, 20: 290; cf. n. 40 below).

subject is considered as unconditioned qua substance, quality, quantity, and modality (hence there are four paralogisms of rational psychology), and the whole of appearances as unconditioned qua quantity, quality, causality, and modality (hence there are four antinomies of rational cosmology).

More specifically, in the Paralogisms Kant challenges rationalist arguments from the mere representation of the I to a priori claims that the self is substantial, simple, identical over time, and independent of other beings. Kant's ultimate concern is with showing that the unique and ever available character of the representation of the I, which is central to his own philosophy as an indication of the transcendental power of apperception, should not mislead us into claims that it demonstrates a special spiritual object, necessarily independent of whatever underlies other things. But although Kant properly stresses that our theoretical self-representation does not provide an intuition of the soul as a special phenomenal or noumenal object, his exposure of certain fallacies does not directly undermine all traditional rationalist claims about the self.[3]

In the attack on rational cosmology in the Antinomies, Kant 'skeptically' contrasts pairs of a priori claims about the composition, division, origination, and relation of dependence of existence 'of the alterable in the field of appearance' (A415/B443). Roughly, the theses are:

The set of appearances is finite in age and spatial extent, composed of simples, containing uncaused causality and a necessary being.

The antitheses are:

It is given as infinite in age and extent, divisible without end, and without uncaused causality or a necessary being impinging on it.

Kant challenges these particular assertions by pointing out ways in which the indirect arguments for them fail, since the denial of the opposite claim does not entail the assertion of the original claim. Thus one can escape the antinomies by avoiding the general assumption that either, because no endless series is given, there must be an end in composition, division, generation, and so forth; or, because no end can be given as unconditioned, there must be an unconditioned series given without end. This solution is clearest for the last two antinomies, where Kant treats the causal and modal status of an appearance in general just as he does the phenomenal characterization of the self: it is an a priori truth that we can go on without end in seeking empirical acts of causality impinging on it, and empirical beings upon which it is dependent, and yet this does not yield a given unconditioned series because it always leaves open a possible involvement with some (non-given) non-empirical causality and non-dependent being. But although Kant can distinguish this result from dogmatic claims that there must be, or that there cannot be, a first causality and a non-dependent being, he still

---

[3] See my *Kant's Theory of Mind* (Oxford, 1982).

leaves open (for grounding elsewhere) both the assertion that there must be a priori laws governing phenomena and the idea that there is some ground for assuming something beyond phenomena. His discussions still presume, as Leibniz would want, that all items within the spatio-temporal field are thoroughly governed by a principle of sufficient reason, and also, as Newton would want, that they are located in irreducible (although not absolutely real) forms of space and time.

Just as one should not be wholly taken in by the anti-rationalist tone of the Dialectic, one also should not assume that its architectonic has an entirely rigid structure. Like much of the *Critique*, it was the product of a series of hasty rearrangements,[4] and the final product contains some surprising oddities. The discussion of the Idea of God largely ignores the table of categories, while the treatments of the self and of the world often seem to pick arbitrarily from that table, each using just four of the six main headings (quantity, quality, substance, cause, community, and modality). Thus the issue of the agency of the self, which was considered a proper categorial topic in notes prior to the *Critique*, disappears from the discussion of rational psychology, while the question of the substantiality of phenomena in general is not posed directly (see A414/B441). Furthermore, it is unclear why the notion of an unconditioned starting point for categorical syllogisms should lead to an ultimate subject considered only psychologically—that is, specifically as thinking, just as it is unclear why the nature of the thinking subject should not be considered (as it was by many rationalists) as just a part of the general theory of the world. The discussion of rational cosmology supposedly is to consider the world only as appearance (which is not the same as already assuming that it is only appearance), while the discussion of the subject can, and does, shift between regarding it as a phenomenon and regarding it as something beyond appearances. This distinction is not cleanly maintained, however, because sometimes (e.g. in the consideration of the simplicity of the components of the world) arguments about cosmology introduce non-phenomenal considerations (albeit in a way to be criticized—but the same is true in the Paralogisms), and sometimes (in the second and third Antinomies; cf. A463/B491) they focus on psychological examples after all.

These oddities do not present such a severe problem if it is not assumed that the three Ideas need to be approached in fully parallel ways. And in fact this is not a fair assumption, since Kant makes clear that he has very different views about the Ideas. Whereas he argues that rationalist claims about the self are fallaciously inflated, he does not do much within the *Critique* to rule out the idea of a consistent, albeit very formal and negative, pure theory of the ultimate nature of the self, for example as necessarily immaterial and rational. Cosmological claims,

---

[4] Cf. ibid. and Paul Guyer, 'The Unity of Reason: Pure Reason as Practical Reason in Kant's Early Concept of the Transcendental Dialectic', *Monist*, 72 (1989), 139–67.

on the other hand, get us into contradictory theses that are resolvable only by transcendental idealism, because we supposedly cannot say that the world is either of finite or of given infinite magnitude.⁵ Here the problem is not one of a lack of knowledge or detail: rather, for certain questions (e.g. 'How old is the world in itself?') there is simply no sensible answer about an ultimate nature (because there is no quantity of this sort 'in itself'). But this pattern of argument applies at best to only the first antinomy; for most cosmological issues, a fairly extensive rational doctrine (of phenomenal laws and noumenal possibilities) is allowed and is outlined in part in the *Metaphysical Foundations of Natural Science*.⁶ Finally, the theological Idea is like the psychological one in not leading to contradictions, but also is somewhat like the cosmology in providing a relatively full doctrine of attributes, although for Kant their instantiation is left without support until one shifts from theoretical to moral–practical considerations. We thus gain from rational theology the 'transcendental ideal' of a perfect and necessary being, even if speculative arguments all fail to establish its existence.⁷

II

In view of all these reservations, one can expect some remnants of the tradition to elude Kant's attack, even if it is unclear where one might best seek them. Two clues will be pursued here. First, in order to gain a fuller sense of Kant's view on the range of issues at stake in the tradition, I will refer briefly to his direct comments on Leibniz in the *Critique*'s 'Amphiboly of Concepts of Reflection' (A260–92/B316–49) and in the late draft on *What Real Progress Has Metaphysics Made in Germany since the Time of Leibniz and Wolff?* (1804). Second, in order to treat one of these issues in some detail and from a new perspective, I will focus on a

---

⁵ More specifically, Kant's strategy is to say that the transcendental realist presumes that the world has either an unconditioned, i.e. determinately given, finite magnitude or an unconditioned, i.e. determinately given, infinite one. Then it is argued indirectly that, because it cannot have such a finite magnitude, it must be said to have the infinite one, and similarly that, because it cannot have such an infinite magnitude, it must have the finite one. Kant's solution is to reject the realist's presumption, and hence the conclusions of the indirect arguments, so that, instead of a contradiction, viz. that the world is both determinately infinite and determinately finite, we rather get the result that it is just a continuing series of appearances neither determinately finite nor determinately infinite (cf. A518/B546 n.). It is questionable whether Kant's notion of a 'determinate infinite' is more than a straw man; therefore, it is not clear that his solution (that we can go on without end in experience) must be incompatible with traditional realism and can fit only (let alone provide an independent basis for) his own idealism; cf. nn. 12 and 15. But whatever Kant's problems are here, it is improper to assume, as all too often happens, that he is himself espousing all the various and peculiar arguments reported in the Antinomies. They are rather arguments which he takes to be tempting but dogmatic fallacies (cf. A521/B549 n.). This creates another problem, though; for if the arguments are not accepted in every regard except their last step (drawn on the basis of the original illicit transcendental realist presumption), then there may be other ways, short of transcendental idealism, for escaping contradiction.

⁶ The metaphysics of this doctrine is developed further in Kant's *Opus postumum*.

⁷ Cf. Allen Wood, 'Rational Theology, Moral Faith, and Religion', in *The Cambridge Companion to Kant*, ed. P. Guyer (Cambridge, 1992), 394–416, as well as his *Kant's Rational Theology* (Ithaca, NY, 1978).

central theme from Kant's extensive lectures on Baumgarten's Leibnizian metaphysics.

In the Amphiboly, Kant organizes his remarks in terms of four major Leibnizian doctrines: (*a*) the principle of the identity of indiscernibles; (*b*) the principle of sufficient reason; (*c*) the monadology and doctrine of pre-established harmony; and (*d*) the doctrine of the ideality of space and time. The last issue applies to all the rest. For Kant, even though Leibniz holds spatio-temporal determinations to be derivative, he is a transcendental realist about space and time: 'Leibniz conceived space as a certain order in the community of substances, and time as the dynamic sequence of their states' (A275/B331). Once Kant rejects this conception, as he does in the Transcendental Aesthetic, he can argue against (*a*) that otherwise indiscernible substances can differ simply with respect to space and time. The same point holds against (*b*), although initially Kant expresses it not explicitly in terms of the notion of sufficient reason, but rather in terms of the general idea that logical and real opposition are not to be equated, and that this cannot be appreciated when things are considered simply through the understanding (A264 f./B320 f.; A273/B329; but cf. *Progress*, 20:282). Finally, against (*c*), Kant presents not so much a counter-argument as an hypothesis, namely that Leibniz was led to the monadology because he could not conceive the inner states of substances in spatio-temporal terms but only in terms of simple founding properties, which we are supposedly aware of as representative states. This last conception is attacked, of course, in Kant's doctrine that even our inner sensibility is an appearance—not a self-illuminating intuition, but a datum requiring for its determination relational and even physical knowledge.

There is a remarkable confirmation of the continuity of Kant's late thought in the fact that almost exactly this same four-part framework recurs in Kant's discussion of Leibniz in his draft of the *Progress* essay. The major change is that the doctrine of space and time is not listed as just one issue among the others. Rather, it is taken out and appropriately mentioned first as a prior condition for approaching the whole framework; then at the end the doctrines of pre-established harmony and monadology are separated, so that a four-part structure is still maintained (*Progress*, 20:281–5). Kant's substantive critical points are almost precisely the same as before; there is just a slight change in the tone and focus. The object of criticism is now the whole school of Leibniz and Wolff, and a special theme, now stressed in each of the four points, is that this school violates 'common sense', losing itself in the 'whimsical' and the 'enchanted'. The school is also put into an historical context: its four doctrines constitute the 'theoretical–dogmatic departure' of metaphysics, which precedes the stage of 'skeptical deadlock' uncovered in the Antinomies, and the final stage of 'the practically dogmatic completion' (*Progress*, 20:281) of metaphysics in Kant's moral system. Here again, despite his restriction of the principles of general ontology, and his use of antinomies against the tradition, Kant continues to endorse a 'rational doctrine of nature', including a priori physics and psychology (*Progress*, 20:285–6). His aim is not to eliminate these, but to show what form they can take when they are based on the implications of the doctrine of pure forms of intuition rather than on mere concepts. But all this does not yet show that a doctrine such as pre-established harmony is false. In the *Critique*, Kant suggests that it is dependent on the monadology (A275/B331), but he must have known that this cannot settle the issue, for a monadology is compatible with doctrines other than harmony, namely occasionalism, and harmony does not require monadology. (Wolff and others had drastically revised the notion of monads, while still holding that at least in some contexts nothing better can be found than the doctrine of harmony.)

To put Kant's attitude to such traditional alternatives in their fullest context, one should turn to his treatment of Baumgarten's metaphysics. Kant continued to rely on Baumgarten's dogmatic textbook for organizing his own annual lectures[8] even when he had ample opportunity to reorganize his teaching fully in terms of his new Critical philosophy, especially after 1784 when Johann Schultz's Kantian handbook was available. With the recent availability of new data from these lectures, Kant's detailed treatment of Baumgarten can no longer be ignored as a

---

[8] Much of the material in these lectures was made accessible for the first time with *Akademie* 28 (1968) and 29 (1983). A large selection from them will be found in *Lectures on Metaphysics/Immanuel Kant*, ed. and tr. Karl Ameriks and Steve Naragon (Cambridge, 1997). In this essay, references to the lecture notes will use the following abbreviations, to which I here add the corresponding dates: *MH* = Metaphysik Herder (1762–4); *L1* = Metaphysik L1 (1770s); *MM* = Metaphysik Mrongovius (1782–3); *V* = Metaphysik Volckmann (1784–5); *vS* = Metaphysik von Schön (late 1780s); *L2* = Metaphysik L2 (1790–1); *D* = Metaphysik Dohna (1792–3); *K2* = Königsberg 2 (1793–4); *K3* = Königsberg 3 (1794–5). All of Baumgarten's *Metaphysica* (4th edn, Halle, 1757) is reprinted in Kant's *Akademie* edition at 17:5–226, except for the Empirical Psychology, which is at 15:5–53. (There is also a useful abridged German translation of Baumgarten by G. F. Meier (Halle, 2d edn, 1783).) I refer to the *Metaphysica* throughout by using *Bg*. Capitalization of 'Ontology', etc., refers to a subsection of the *Metaphysica*, just as capitalization of 'Paralogisms' etc. refers to a section of the *Critique*. The quite recent discovery of the *MM* and *K3* manuscripts (vol. 29) is particularly significant because they provide considerable independent confirmation for what is found in the other lecture notes. Although no individual note can be trusted by itself, the striking amount of overlap over the years demonstrates, I believe, that these student notes are in general a very good indication of what Kant taught. But they must be used with caution, especially because there are problems with their presentation even in the *Akademie* edition. See the articles by Werner Stark in *Kant-Forschungen*, vol. I (Hamburg, 1987).

Here is a brief outline of Baumgarten's *Metaphysica*: I. Prolegomena (§§1–3); II. Ontology (§§4–350), A. Internal Universal Predicates: 1. possibility, 2. connection, 3. thing (including essence and determination), 4. unity, 5. truth, 6. perfection, B. Internal Disjunctive Predicates: 1. necessary, 2. mutable, 3. real, 4. particular, 5. whole, 6. substance, 7. simple, 8. finite—and each of their opposites, C. External and Relational Predicates: 1. identity and diversity, 2. simultaneity and succession, 3. types of causes, 4. sign and signified; III. Cosmology (§§351–500), A. Concepts of World: 1. affirmative, 2. negative, B. Parts of World: 1. simples: in general, and qua spirits, 2. composites: their genesis and nature, C. Perfection of World: 1*a*. the idea of the best and *b*. the community of substances; 2. the means: natural and supernatural; IV. Psychology, A. Empirical (§§504–739): 1. existence of soul, 2. faculties, *a*. cognitive (lower and higher), *b*. appetitive (in general and qua spontaneous and free), 3. mind–body interaction, B. Rational (§§740–99): 1. soul's nature, 2. interaction with body, 3. origin, 4. immortality, 5. afterlife, 6. comparison of human and nonhuman souls; V. Theology (§§800–1000), A. Concept of God: existence, intellect, will, B. Divine Action: creation, its end, providence, decrees, revelation.

major indication of his own metaphysical views. It can even be argued that the new 'system' that Kant calls for in the *Critique* (A13/B27), but never published, is laid out precisely in these lectures, where the categories and their predicables are exposited in some detail.[9]

Although I have been attempting to abstract as much as possible from strictly psychological and theological issues, no treatment of Kant's critique of traditional ontology can wholly ignore substantive views about the mind and God, for it is distinctive of this era that often these impinge very heavily on general ontological issues. This is especially true of the several major discussions of causality in Baumgarten's *Metaphysica* that express the central doctrines of monadology and pre-established harmony. They color the more formal discussions (*Bg* §§19–33, 307 f.; cf. *L2*, 28:572), which treat the general notion of a ground and the standard distinctions between primary and secondary causes, concurring and occasional causes, and so forth, and they obviously determine the more substantive claims made in the scattered discussions of state and action, succession, and systems concerning substantial interaction (*Bg* §§205 f., 297 f., 448 f., 733 f., 761 f.).

Given all this, it might appear that a short and tempting account of Kant's critique of the tradition could say simply that, given his Paralogisms and Critique of Speculative Theology, the ground under rationalist ontology has been knocked away, and so all the 'explanations' of its metaphysics should be dismissed without further ado. Or, similarly, one could contend that the more general epistemological arguments of the Transcendental Analytic already show that all the non-trivial claims of the *Metaphysica* must be hopelessly dogmatic. Kant's own repeated treatments of Baumgarten fortunately did not always take such a quick and high-handed approach—and for good reason. If one looks closely at the *Critique*, it is not easy to show precisely how, even on its own terms, it has definitely undermined all claims of traditional metaphysics; indeed, from the *Critique* alone it is difficult to find out what all those claims are. To say simply that such claims are illegitimately 'transcendent' is to beg a lot of questions about what that means, and it is surely not easy to hold that all of the *Critique*'s own major claims, for example about the eternity of substance, are non-transcendent in an evident sense.[10] Until a specific flaw is exposed in a rationalist argument, it cannot be rejected just on the basis of an unappealing 'transcendent' conclusion; as long as there is no other objection, that conclusion could also be taken precisely as a disproof of claims that such conclusions are in general illegitimate. Moreover, there remain a host of specific topics and arguments within traditional metaphysics that deserve individual attention and that are not directly covered by the Transcendental Dialectic's taxonomy of fallacies.

[9] See Max Heinze, *Vorlesungen Kants über Metaphysik aus drei Semestern* (Leipzig, 1894), 599.
[10] This point was stressed by J. A. Ulrich as early as 1785; see Frederick Beiser, *The Fate of Reason* (Cambridge, Mass, 1987), 205.

These difficulties for Critical philosophy are compounded by the fact that Kant's own written work hardly presents a thorough treatment of 'immanent' ontology. The exact nature of substance, cause, matter, and so forth remains unsettled on Kant's own admission. Furthermore, we know that Kant was deeply attached to the truth of many traditional metaphysical beliefs (e.g. immaterialism, teleology) even if generally he shifted his views on their manner of justification in favor of only 'regulative' or 'pure practical' arguments. In the face of these complications, the fact that the Critical Kant did not simply ignore Baumgarten's arguments, but rather discussed them year after year, gains significance. It becomes important to determine what specific flaws Kant stressed here and what options, on balance, he came to favor with respect to the classical issues of ontology. This is a larger task than can be completed in this context, but in what follows I will sketch Kant's lecture treatment of traditional ontology in general and then focus on his discussion of one of its central doctrines, namely pre-established harmony.

In Kant's later lectures, the Critical perspective is laid out primarily in a long modification of the Prolegomena (only three paragraphs in Baumgarten) and the beginning of the Ontology section focusing on 'the idea of transcendental philosophy'. Unfortunately, from the 1770s we have few samples from that part of the lectures, except for fragments about one notion that is frequently reiterated later—the proposal that metaphysics begin not with the bare concept of a thing in general (*L*1, 28: 172; cf. *L*2, 28: 543, 552, 555; *MM*, 29: 811) but with a consideration of the possibility of knowledge of things, and thus the distinction between merely analytic and 'real' or synthetic knowledge. Baumgarten was already known for incorporating epistemological considerations into his metaphysics,[11] but Kant's point was that Baumgarten's work was largely vitiated by a failure to appreciate the distinction between analytic and synthetic propositions. Kant then moved very quickly from asserting that we need synthetic propositions based on sensible intuition (pure and empirical) to concluding that a study of the conditions of that intuition must be a study of our subjective nature rather than things in themselves—and that such a study is possible prior to any study of things (*L*1, 28: 180).

The standard format for all the later ontology lectures (e.g. *MM*, 29: 793 f.; *L*2, 28: 546 f.; *K*3, 29: 967 f.) thus inserts, in order, preliminary discussions of the distinctions analytic/synthetic, intuition/concept, transcendentally ideal/real (space–time). This leads into a discussion of judgments and categories, and the contention that the determination of 'real possibility' ('possibility' being the first concept of the old Ontology) and other fundamental concepts[12] rests on

---

[11] See Max Wundt, *Die deutsche Schulphilosophie im Zeitalter der Aufklärung* (Tübingen, 1945), 221. Cf. Lewis White Beck, *Early German Philosophy* (Cambridge, Mass., 1969), 285.

[12] Kant takes the same line on the 'internal universal predicates'. Thus, the proof of the principle of sufficient reason is rejected as making an unprovable universal claim, and it is denied that we have a priori

what is required by the conditions for our making synthetic assertions by applying categories to a spatio-temporal context, conditions that are supposedly accessible as part of our pure subjective nature.

By the 1780s Kant thus prefers to say that metaphysics is not about objects but rather about reason—that is, about the structure of human cognition (*V*, 28: 359, 364; cf. *MM*, 29: 786; *Pure Reason*, A xiv). Hence one should investigate first not the concept of cause, but rather the faculty by which it is possible for us to have a priori causal knowledge (*MM*, 29: 784). One might well ask why such 'subjective' investigations are thought to be easier. Kant sometimes indicates that they are so because they involve 'self-knowledge' (*MM*, 29: 756; cf. *V*, 28: 392), but this is a casual and misleading way of expressing his view. That is, this expression involves the unfortunate suggestion that self-knowledge in some ordinary psychological sense comes first or is more certain; but that is precisely not Kant's Critical view.[13] It becomes clear that Kant really must mean the term 'self' here just to be a shorthand reference to 'reason', and not the other way around. 'Subjective' investigations are privileged for him just insofar as they signify investigations of the elements of 'pure thought', such as the forms of judgment. The privilege arises from the fact that Kant believes a complete survey of these forms is accessible (*K3*, 29: 988; *vS*, 28: 479), whereas a survey of things would have no closure. One can wonder why these forms are thought to be so easily accessible. Kant suggested that they are implicit in our 'common language'; to the question as to how certain these are, he notes that they are 'as' certain as experience in general—this is all the certainty he demands (*MM*, 29: 804). Elsewhere he also argued that the 'limits of

---

access to a real essence that would provide the explanation of all of a particular thing's actual properties. No argument is allowed from the mere possibility of a thing, i.e. its concept, to the existence of that thing, and unity (in the sense of order), truth, and perfection, are held to apply only to the structure of knowledge rather than directly to things. The 'disjunctive' predicates receive a similar treatment. For example, a priori knowledge of necessity and contingency (vs. *Bg* §101) in any absolute sense is denied, and the mutable and immutable are treated (vs. *Bg* §124) as sheerly phenomenal predicates with no relation to absolute necessity. In discussing wholes and parts (vs. *Bg* §155), Kant introduces his distinction between 'real' and 'ideal' composites, where in the first case the parts are given prior to the whole, but in the second the whole, as with space and time, is given prior to the parts (as ideal because mathematically infinite). Baumgarten had already distinguished the determinate (maximal, total) metaphysical infinity of the most real thing ('*omnitudo*'), and the mere mathematical infinite of that which is unbounded (*Bg* §248), and he had argued not only that there is an absolute and unalterable infinite thing, but also that any alterable thing must be metaphysically contingent (*Bg* §§257, 131) and finite, even if in various quantitative ways it is mathematically infinite. Kant rejected these arguments, and his theory of space and time also affects his view of the first of external relational predicates: identity (*Bg* §265), simultaneity (*Bg* §280), and succession (*Bg* §297). Unlike the Leibnizians, Kant makes no absolutely necessary connection between simultaneity and extension; instead, he argues for the conditional necessity that, for beings like us, things can be *known* as being at the same time only via a consideration of things that are next to each other. Similarly, in the domain of our knowledge, spatio-temporal differentiation is what settles claims of identity and diversity, rather than vice versa (vs. *Bg* §407). Succession and the other relational predicates all involve causal notions (*Bg* §§307-50) and the remaining 'internal disjunctive predicates', which are discussed below.

[13] See the Paralogisms and P. Guyer, 'Psychology in the Transcendental Deduction', in *Kant's Transcendental Deductions*, ed. Eckart Förster (Stanford, Calif., 1989), 47–68.

reason', that is of items knowable by us, in contrast to things simpliciter, are determinable a priori because they are tied to the forms of our intuition, which are themselves determinable a priori (*MM*, 28: 781, 831).

All these views exemplify a broadly rationalist perspective. In the lectures, Kant's own metaphysics is repeatedly characterized as 'rationalist' or 'critical rationalist' (*K2*, 28: 992; *D*, 28: 619; *K3*, 29: 953), for he insists that philosophy must and can rest on a priori knowledge. The new aspect of his thought lies in his claiming to establish the order and limits of this knowledge. The main metaphysical argument that our knowledge must be limited to mere appearance arises from the 'dialectical' or 'antinomic' character that (he claims) assertions must take on as soon as they transcend the conditions of our sensible intuition and make claims about it as something unconditioned (e.g. *D*, 28: 620, 658; *L1*, 28: 187). However, the *Critique*'s Antinomies are notorious for appearing to be question-begging, and even in the later lectures there is remarkably little explanation of the crucial antinomic arguments.[14] An adequate consideration of the defense of transcendental idealism would require a closer study of the first two Antinomies, which are supposed to show that it is necessary and not just possible that the spatio-temporal domain is merely phenomenal. For ontology, the Second Antinomy plays an especially crucial and neglected role.[15] On the one hand, it belongs to the first pair of the four Antinomies, for which the 'both/and' solution (which says the theses and the antitheses, properly construed, are jointly possible—the first holding noumenally, the second phenomenally) proposed for the second pair is supposedly ruled out. Yet the argument of the text suggests that in fact the Kantian response is to hold both that simple substances are required (A434/B462f.; *V*, 28: 436; *vS*, 28: 517–8; *D*, 28: 663; *K2*, 28: 731; *MM*, 29: 850, 859), although they cannot exist as ultimately spatio-temporal, *and* that all spatio-temporal phenomena are divisible without end, but not absolutely substantial or real.

This result is obscured since the text is set up to shift the topic from the general ontological question of whether there are simple substances to the cosmological issue of whether beings 'in the world' *consist* of simple parts. Kant's view on the explicit thesis and antithesis is actually quite close to that of Baumgarten (*Bg* §428), who had asserted both that there must be simple substances and that, for any matter that we *perceive*, that matter can be further divided. Kant's crucial shift (cf. *L1*, 28: 209; *MM*, 29: 827), which is easily missed in reading the *Critique*, was not categorically to deny this, but rather to stress (vs. *Bg* §§419–21) that simple beings are not literally *parts* of bodies, not even what Baumgarten called 'absolute

---

[14] Cf. n. 5. The Third Antinomy, which is not fundamental ontologically, is what is stressed at *L2* and *K2*; see Heinze, *Kants Vorlesungen*, 572.

[15] For many more details on the first Antinomies, see Arthur Melnick, *Space, Time, and Thought in Kant* (Dordrecht, 1989); J. Bennett, *Kant's Dialectic* (Cambridge, 1974); and Carl Posy, 'Dancing to the Antinomy: A Proposal for Transcendental Idealism', *American Philosophical Quarterly*, 20 (1983), 81–94.

first' parts. The departure from traditional ontology comes not in a denial of simple beings, but in a refusal to allow them to be understood as directly spatio-temporal or as such that spatio-temporal properties can be considered as in principle derivable from the concept of those beings. Given the conclusion of the First Antinomy that the spatio-temporal domain is merely phenomenal, this means not that simple beings are to be dismissed ontologically, but rather that they are saved—even if their individual determination is ruled out for us.

Because it is impossible to clarify this issue fully without also going through all of Kant's complex view of substantiality and sensibility, here it will be treated further only insofar as it impinges on the concept of interaction, which is at the center of most of the rest of the *Metaphysica* (*Bg* §§19 f., 210 f., 297 f., 307 f., 448 f., 733 f., 761 f.), and provides the best access to Kant's attitude to the options of traditional ontology.

To appreciate Kant's Critical views on this concept, it is important to see their relation to his earliest work and its context. The issue of action in finite substances had been a major controversy in the Leibnizian schools. Bilfinger set the stage for mid-eighteenth-century German discussions by arguing that there are only three basic possibilities here: influx, occasionalism, and harmony.[16] The first system affirms intrasubstantial and intersubstantial action; the second denies both, and the last allows only intrasubstantial action. Baumgarten repeats this taxonomy (*Bg* §450), and by characterizing the influx theory in terms of an absurd 'real' transfer of properties he limits the discussion in effect to the latter two theories. Occasionalism is then faulted for allegedly also having to rely on an absurd real influx in explaining the action of infinite substance on finite substance (which is crucial because here the infinite substance is the constant source of all action), and, above all, for denying powers within ordinary finite things (*Bg* §452).

Kant was quite sympathetic to both these points. However, whereas Baumgarten stopped at presenting a version of the pre-established harmony theory (at *Bg* §§212, 329 ff., he tries to show that it is equivalent to a harmless 'ideal' version of the influx theory that dispenses with literal infusion), Kant clearly was trying to open up some kind of fourth option. At the end of his *Nova Dilucidatio*, (1755; see Proposition XIII, 'The Principle of Coexistence'), Kant briefly but systematically goes through the traditional three options. The 'crude' influx theory is dismissed by being tied to the (here disproven) bad presumption that the 'very origin of the mutual connection of things [need not be] sought outside the principle of substances considered in

---

[16] Georg Bernhard Bilfinger, *De Harmonia animae et corporis humani maximi praestabilita, Commentatio hypothetica* (1723). See Benno Erdmann, *Martin Knutzen und seine Zeit* (Leipzig, 1876). The trichotomy goes back at least to Pierre Bayle's 'Rorarius' discussion in his *Dictionnaire historique et critique* (1697). Cf. *Pure Reason*, A390.

isolation'.[17] The pre-established harmony and occasionalist views are criticized as both giving only an 'agreement' (on the first view, 'conspired' 'before', on the second, 'adapted' 'during' mundane action) among things, and not genuine dependence.[18] Kant proposes a fourth alternative: the idea of a unifying God who makes things interactive in the very act that makes them what they are.[19] He stresses that on this view the 'external' changes of a thing, its interactions with other things, are *just as* immediately attributable to it as any internal changes,[20] and hence there is no extra 'artificial' condition, no 'occasion' or 'pre-establishment', that needs to be referred to in explaining action: the interaction of things is revealed directly upon seeing what they are as lawful items based on one creator. This difficult argument foreshadows many themes of Kant's later Critical work: the idea that 'inner' attributions are not privileged can be seen as one germ of the Refutation of Idealism, and the centrality of the notion of lawfulness anticipates the Second Analogy.

In the early lectures these views are developed somewhat further. Like Baumgarten, Kant wants to argue from the start that action is always a mixture of spontaneity and reaction,[21] and that in any real action there are always several concurring causes (*MH*, 28:37). For example, when we listen with attention, outer things are a true ground of the experience; but, in attending, we are also playing a role, so we are active and passive at once (*MH*, 28: 26, 53; cf. *vS*, 28: 513; *V*, 28: 433; and *Pure Reason*, B157). In particular, Kant stresses that, even for God to put a thought into us, there must be a ground within us, a capacity to receive and have the thought; otherwise, there would be no point in saying that it is we rather than God who have the thought.[22]

This is a very significant claim—I will call it the 'Restraint Argument' because of how it restrains us from ascribing *all* activity and reality to God—and it balances Kant's early insistence on ascribing the *ultimate* source of all interaction, all true community, to God (*MH*, 28: 51; *L1*, 28: 212–4; *Dissertation* §19, 2: 408).

---

[17] *Nova Dilucidatio*, 1:416; cf. the argument at 414. This argument is also noted at Guyer, *Kant and the Claims of Knowledge* (Cambridge, 1987), 308.
[18] *Nova Dilucidatio*, 1:415. The Reuscher translation of the passage at lines 32–7 (in *Kant's Latin Writings*, 104) can give a misleading impression here.
[19] *Nova Dilucidatio*, 1:415: 'there is a real action of substances that occurs among them, or interaction through truly efficient causes, because the same principle that set up the existence of things shows them to be bound by this law.' Cf. *MH*, 28:887, for another early reference to law.
[20] *Nova Dilucidatio*, 1:415: 'By the same right, therefore, external changes can be said to be produced by efficient causes just as changes that happen internally are attributed to the internal force of a substance.'
[21] *MH*, 28:96; cf. *MH*, 28:51–2. Thus, judging and sensing aren't opposed as action to inaction; rather, the first is just a 'greater' action than the other (*MH*, 28:27). This general ideal may go back to Leibniz's *Specimen Dynamicum* (1695), which claimed that even passion is spontaneous and involves self-activity. Cf. *MM*, 29:723, 823; *MH*, 28:26; *V*, 28:433.
[22] *MH*, 28: 52. This argument is nicely complemented by one at *R* 3581, 17:71, which says that, while the patient must contribute something, he cannot contribute everything to an action. That is, if everything in us were active, there would be no nature in us for God to act on, i.e. nothing with an enduring identity that goes beyond the different states generated (by 'us') at each moment.

By the Restraint Argument, God *cannot* be solely responsible for that which we know is going on just in us and which is, at least in some significant part, due to us; if that were possible, the admission of God as the unifier of the world could be turned into a Spinozistic monism that makes all apparently distinct individuals into mere aspects of one substance.[23]

At first Kant follows Baumgarten's unusual terminology here in calling influence of this 'mixed' kind 'ideal' (and also by considering it a kind of pre-established harmony view[24]); 'real' influx would be a kind of 'miraculous' forcing whereby the patient makes no contribution to the effect[25] and just receives a 'transference' of properties from the agent via a kind of literal infusion, an idea already mocked by Wolff.[26] The common presumption here is that neither such transference nor such sheer passivity (given the Restraint Argument) makes any sense.

To try to nail down the absurdity of the vulgar 'real' influx theory, Baumgarten added an argument that, since the theory treats each patient in causation as sheerly passive, then supposedly all patients, all beings in the world, would be only passive, even the originally presumed 'agents', and so there would be nothing active in the world to get action started—that is, ultimately explained.[27] Kant did not repeat this questionable extra argument, and he also soon rejected Baumgarten's terminology. Since it is only 'real' causation of a 'vulgar' and nonsensical sort that is being excluded, Kant proposed that his system now be called one of 'real' or physical influence[28] because in all *other* ways, the only ways that make sense, it does allow interaction. From the beginning, he presumes that, although we can't claim to know or directly perceive how causality takes place, we should affirm that it exists rather than fall back into either of the non-interactive and non-commonsensical positions of Malebranche and Leibniz, positions that Kant says have no advantage over sheer idealism.[29]

In his *Inaugural Dissertation* (1770), Kant again rejects the vulgar version of the doctrine of real influence for giving the impression that action can be made

---

[23] On Spinoza, see nn. 43 and 44. On finite agency, cf. Leibniz, *Theodicy*, §32. Leibniz argued against occasionalism that it did away with the natures of individuals and so could lead to Spinozism.

[24] *MH*, 28:26, 52, 888. Cf. *Bg* §§212, 217. Erdmann, *Martin Knutzen*, 66, notes that similar language is used by G. F. Meier, who translated Baumgarten into German and on whom Kant also lectured.

[25] *MH*, 28:53: 'If we want to conceive that one power simply suffers from the other, without its own power and thus without harmony, then that is called *influxus physicus* or *realis*.'

[26] See Wolff's *Rational Psychology*, §558, cited in Beck, *Kant's Latin Writings*, 109, n. 44. Cf. Kant's *Prolegomena*, §9, 4:282; *MM*, 29:823.

[27] *Bg* §451. Elsewhere Baumgarten also adds a very weak argument that there must be a plurality of finite substances (*Bg* §§339–91).

[28] See e.g. *Dissertation*, §17, 2:407: 'If we free this concept from that blemish, we have a kind of interaction which is the only one which deserves to be called real.' Cf. *K2*, 28:759.

[29] *MH*, 28:886–7; cf. *D*, 28:666, 684; *K3*, 29:1008. Here Kant already denies that the heterogeneity of cause and effect is a sufficient reason to deny interaction; thus, he was unattracted to the Wolffian compromise of falling back on pre-established harmony for mind–body relations while accepting the influx theory elsewhere.

intelligible simply by viewing things separately (*Dissertation*, §17, 2:407). In discussing the two other theories, he now calls them doctrines of 'specially established' harmony, in contrast to the 'generally established' harmony of his own theory (*Dissertation*, §22, 2:409). Despite the terminological changes, he claims the same superiority as before for his theory: it alone gives a 'primitive bond of substances necessary because [of] a common principle and so ... proceeding from their very subsistence, founded on their common cause ... according to common rules', rather than being due merely to individual 'states of a substance ... adapted to the state of another ... singularly' (*Dissertation*, §22, 2:409). Kant concedes that his view is somewhat like Malebranche's in holding that we get to other things only via God (*Dissertation*, §22, 2:410; cf. *MH*, 28:888),[30] but he says he is unlike Malebranche in not claiming to know this through any privileged vision. His doctrine is now put forth as just the best hypothesis by one who 'hugs the shore' of common sense in allowing genuine interaction of finite substances (*Dissertation*, §22, 2:410; cf. *Progress*, 20:282).

The lecture notes from the 1770s are still very much in accord with the *Dissertation*: The mere existence of separate substances is insufficient to make interaction explicable, so a third item must be sought as a ground (*L1*, 28:212). The immediate basis for his own view is the familiar indirect argument against the alternatives. 'Vulgar' influx theories[31] are dismissed as providing no explanation (the 'original' interaction they posit is simply 'blind' and inexplicable), while the 'hyperphysical' theories of occasionalism and pre-established harmony are faulted for providing mere agreement rather than genuine interaction.[32] Although Kant agrees with the 'derivative' theories in not presuming that finite substances can directly influence each other, he holds to calling his own view one of 'real' influence, although not in the vulgar sense.

What does the Kantian view have to offer positively? The crucial points are that, unlike the vulgar view, it involves 'laws' (*L1*, 28:213, 215), and, unlike the mere 'agreement' views, these are 'universal laws of nature', not mere 'universal determinations' of a transcendent being.[33] These are points that fit in well with the eventual Critical view, but one can still ask why a direct influence of mundane

---

[30] Malebranche, the main advocate of occasionalism (although Kant and others often also attached Descartes to this doctrine—see *L1*, 28:215; *D*, 28:665), was famous for holding that we 'intuit all things in God' (*De la Recherche de la Verité*, III, 2, vi).

[31] *L1*, 28:213, '*influxu physici originario in sensu crasiori*'.

[32] *L1*, 28:215. These theories are still categorized as theories of 'derivative' (as opposed to 'original') interaction because they do not presume that the finite substances can directly influence each other. Cf. Kant's argument (*MM*, 29:932; cf. *D*, 28:664) against Baumgarten's 'quite poor' claim (*Bg* §414) that substances (in this case, monads) 'next to each other' must be in contact qua 'touching', as well as the claim (*Bg* §410) that all action as such involves not just interaction but also reaction qua resistance.

[33] *L1*, 28:214: '*harmonia automatica* is when for every single case the highest cause has to arrange an agreement, thus where the agreement does not rest on universal laws, but rather on a primordial arrangement which God put in the machine of the world.' However, as Alison Laywine has reminded me, sometimes Kant spoke of Leibniz as stressing the role of universal laws (see A275/B331, but cf. B167).

beings upon each other, without any involvement of a third factor (a being upon whom the laws are based), is being wholly ruled out. Even if one allows Kant's idea that *necessary* beings must be isolated,[34] because any interdependence would have to be comprehensible a priori and this would undercut the self-sufficiency necessary to *their* substantiality, it would still seem that non-necessary beings could have a direct, contingent, and actual interdependence that one would have no reason to expect to be comprehensible a priori.

The hidden premise here appears to be a principle that goes back at least to the time of the Herder lectures: namely that 'no substance can contain the ground of the accident in the other, if it does not at the same time contain the ground of the substantial power and of the existence of the other' (*MH*, 28:32). Kant seems to understand this to mean that nothing can be the 'very origin' of a mode in something else unless it is the ground of existence of the faculty of this mode. Given the Restraint Argument,

the existence of the action of another does not depend simply on one action and one power. Thus all predicates must be produced [in part at least] by one's own power, but since externally an alien power is also required [otherwise interaction is not occurring], then [if the 'alien power' is not itself the source of one's being] a third [being] must have willed this harmony [if the 'harmony' is to be anything other than mere coincidence].[35]

Even if this background makes Kant's argument somewhat understandable, there remains the perplexing question of why (by the 1770s) he didn't move on to take the reference to laws to be by itself a sufficient distinguishing characteristic of his theory; that is, why did he continue to bring in a reference to God? The Restraint Argument and the rejection of mere harmony, along with implicit assumptions about the orderliness of the Newtonian world, lead naturally to a theory of interaction expressed in terms of lawfulness, a theory that does not immediately involve any reference to a transcendent being.[36]

---

[34] I.e., such that there cannot be a plurality of them constituting a 'world' (*L1*, 28:214). Cf. *Bg* §357, *L2*, 28:581, and *MH*, 28:865: 'For by its concept every substance exists for itself, therefore appears to be isolated, and has nothing to do with an other substance'. Here, as often in Kant, talk about the 'concept of' something is short for talk about what can be a priori determinable about it, i.e. what is determinable insofar as it is necessary. Cf. Burkhard Tuschling, '*Necessarium est idem simul esse et non esse*', in *Logik und Geschichte in Hegels System*, ed. H. C. Lucas and Guy Planty-Bonjour (Stuttgart, 1989), 210; and his 'Apperception and Ether: on the Idea of a Transcendental Deduction of Matter in Kant's "Opus postumum"', in *Kant's Transcendental Deductions*, 193–216.

[35] *MH*, 28:52–3. All bracketed interpolations are my own interpretive additions. Cf. *L1*, 28:213: 'no substance can influence another *originare* except of that of which it is itself a cause.'

[36] In another passage—arising perhaps from an earlier phase in Kant's work (since this section may be composed of at least two treatments of the topics, with the second starting at *L1*, 28:214$_{28}$), Kant's theory is characterized simply in terms of 'laws of nature, it may ground itself otherwise on whatever it wants' (*L1*, 28:213). By calling the hyperphysical theories ones that really do not have laws (*L1*, 28:215; see n. 39 below), Kant may have been moving toward a perception of how crucial the reference to lawfulness was to his own theory. J. B. Schneewind has explored a parallel moral dimension of Kant's early interest in a 'divine corporation', which gives finite beings a power of self-legislation. See his 'Autonomy, Obligation, and

Here one might respond that this would leave the great orderliness of interaction an inexplicable given,[37] and thus one would be in a situation just like that of the vulgar influx theory. Kant may well have accepted this response at the time, but if he continued to hold to it, it would have blocked any move to his eventual Critical theory. The crucial step in removing that block was to exploit an extra idea that was not yet developed, namely the idea of a transcendental account of 'interaction' which would provide an a priori explanation of the need for law-governed relations between physical states as a principle of experience—that is, spatio-temporal cognition. Once Kant believed he had such an explanation, he left out reference to an ultimate source of interaction and focused just on its immanent structure; his general strategy in the Analogies is to construct epistemological arguments concerning a priori conditions of time determination[38] that warrant empirical analogues for the metaphysical principles of interaction in traditional metaphysics. There is a hidden aspect to this story, however; for, when Kant developed this strategy in his writings, what he did for the most part was to shift the issues rather than to explain exactly his current views on the traditional questions. Here one finds a more detailed approach in the lectures.

In the newly available 'Mrongovius' lectures, the issue of interaction is introduced by noting, 'this investigation was brought to its height by Wolff...and Baumgarten. But now that one seeks mere popularity, and with that gladly abandons thoroughness, this proposition [about how interaction is possible at all] has also been left lying, although it is one of the most important in the whole of philosophy' (*MM*, 29:865). From this one gets a palpable impression of a kind of nostalgia on Kant's part for the controversies of his earlier years. There follows one of the best organized accounts of the traditional options, with Descartes' system presented as the prime instance of occasionalism, and as only trivially distinct from Leibniz's theory. The skeptical 'idealist' consequences of the theories are especially stressed: not only do they dispense with real interaction; they also make separate bodies, as opposed to mere representations of bodies, pointless (*MM*, 29:867).

As before, these theories are rejected because of their idealism, while literal influx is rejected as a non-starter. But what is put in their place? Once again it is argued that 'the world must also have only one cause. The *nexus* of substances is on that account to be thought possible only as derivative [i.e. only via God], but with

---

Virtue: An Overview of Kant's Moral Philosophy', in *The Cambridge Companion to Kant*, ed. P. Guyer (Cambridge, 1992), 309–41, and his 'The Divine Corporation and the History of Ethics', in *Philosophy in History*, ed. R. Rorty, J. B. Schneewind, and Q. Skinner (Cambridge, 1984), 173–92.

[37] For a contemporary view, cf. Ralph Walker, *Kant* (London, 1978), 175.
[38] This strategy is detailed in Guyer, *Kant and the Claims of Knowledge*. The concern with time determination already appears in the old notes, albeit in a traditional context; e.g. at *L1*, 28:215, 'the actual representation of the conjunction of substances among one another consists in this: that they all *perdure*, that they are all there through one.'

that not as ideal, but rather concurrently as real.' But it is immediately added: 'This proof holds, however, only for the *mundus noumenon*. In the *mundus phaenomenon* we do not need it, for it is nothing in itself. Here everything is in *commercium* in virtue of space' (*MM*, 29:868). This reference to space is somewhat misleading, since, as the Third Analogy argues, it is not mere space but rather the conditions for our knowledge of the determination of things in it that is crucial, a determination that in turn is tied to 'general laws', the feature that Kant eventually stresses as the crucial one lacking in the idealistic accounts that he rejects.[39]

But even if this is all granted, one surely should still ask about the traditional arguments concerning interaction (unless one is abandoning 'thoroughness' for 'popularity'), and in particular about the 'proof' that there is 'one cause'. It is said that this holds (1) 'only' (2) 'for the *mundus noumenon*'. The first part of the claim is easy enough when 'only' is taken to mean, 'not empirically', but the second part remains difficult; what is it to 'hold' at all 'for the *mundus noumenon*'? The most appealing answer in this particular situation (I do not mean this for all cases of the Kantian phenomenon/noumenon contrast) is that the proof is meant to hold simply for beings knowable by the pure understanding alone. In that realm of hypothetical beings Kant seems to accept the principle that dependent beings require a necessary being,[40] and so if such beings were linked in a world, they would be in connection through God. Hence what he could say here (but, unfortunately, we do not have proof that he does say it) is just that, although the 'proof' is valid, the instantiation of its crucial premise, the preceding principle, is questionable. What it appears he actually stressed (*MM*, 29:868), however, is an additional problem, namely that the 'idealistic' theories are inconsistent because they supposedly are meant for an empirical domain, and yet they lack an empirical warrant.

This objection does not resolve the original issue, but it is helpful in reminding us that Leibniz's successors (unlike Leibniz himself) ran into trouble precisely by trying to make their metaphysics 'sensible'. Just as we can't make empirical sense of decomposing bodies into monads, so also the occasionalist or harmony theorist can't sensibly account for the interaction of the empirical individuals we know. But the lecture text also suggests something that is to be said beyond the empirical level, namely that a dogmatic rejection (e.g. by Leibniz or Malebranche) of the possibility of genuine intersubstantial action would be wrong, and that *if* there is *such* interaction it would be comprehensible to us only with reference to God (and effective finite substances). Unlike before, here Kant cannot utilize a commonsense presumption of interaction, because after the Critical turn he reserves common sense for empirical rather than noumenal claims. Nonetheless, Kant

---

[39] *MM*, 29:868. 'The *influxus physicus* happens according to general laws, but the two systems of the *nexus idealis* do not.'

[40] *MM*, 29:925; cf. *Bg* §§308, 334.

surely continues to *believe* that there is non-empirical interaction (as is clear simply from the implications of his moral theory[41]), so it would be good to know how this belief fits in with his old 'derivative' influx theory as well as with the new Critical philosophy. Once again, the lecture notes give us the most thorough—and perplexing—evidence on the matter.

Notes from several lectures of the 1790s are now available. In *L2* (28:581), after a reiteration of the theme that interaction in the sensible world creates a whole that is 'real, not ideal', it is asserted that 'all substances are isolated for themselves', and 'the cause of their existence and also of their reciprocal connection is God'. But these assertions are unsupported and are preceded by the claim that 'The intelligible world remains unknown to us.' The assertions come closer to Kant's own earlier views than to Baumgarten's text, so it cannot be presumed that Kant was simply citing someone else's dogmatic views. It is also striking that no specific flaw in these views of substance is cited; the impression remains that, *if* we are to think in an a priori way about these matters, this is the most appropriate way for us to think about them.

The Dohna notes are slightly more detailed and contain the usual characterization of the occasionalist and harmony theories, as well as the rejection of the 'occult' influx theory, which leaves only Kant's old favorite, the 'derivative' influx theory.[42] At this point a somewhat remarkable transition occurs, for there is no direct criticism of this theory but just a note to the effect that, 'if we regard space as real, then we accept Spinoza's system. He believed [in] only one substance, and he took all substances in the world to be determinations inhering in the divine.'[43] This suggests a *reductio* behind Kant's reasonings: namely that, if one did accept the 'interaction' of appearing things as ultimate, as constitutive of a complete and absolutely real system, then this would seem to force one to a kind of monistic and absurd Spinozism. Therefore Kant thought he had to show somehow that the domain of things we take to be interacting, things considered spatio-temporally, is not ultimate but rather 'transcendentally ideal'. But this leaves unclear what should be said once we abstract from space and time; there Spinozistic monism would still seem to be a significant threat. However, more is in fact said; for, rather than simply ignoring the question of whether, absolutely speaking, there is more than one subject, Kant at other places reiterated a version of the Restraint Argument to show that *noumenally* there must be plurality. This argument contends that, since the self is given as a finite and separate but dependent subject, not equal to or inherent in any all-encompassing being (e.g. Spinoza's God), there must be something in addition

---

[41] See also *MM*, 29:856, 927–8: 'the immediate cause of the sensible world is the *mundus noumenon*'.
[42] *D*, 28:666, 'There must be a being there from which all derive. All substances have their ground in it.'
[43] *D*, 28:666. Cf. *K2*, 28:732, and *K3*, 29:1008–9. *K3*, 29:977–8 equates Spinozism with transcendental realism.

to it that exists.[44] However, this argument is conclusive only in a context where it is already conceded that we do know the ultimate extent of the subject we are acquainted with through experience—and after the Critical turn this concession is no longer theoretically grounded and even appears to conflict with the main thrust of the Paralogisms.

The last lecture discussion, *K3*, is very similar to the others, and it still concludes: 'If I assume all substances as absolutely necessary, then they cannot stand in the slightest community. But if I assume the substances as existing in a community, then I assume that they all exist through a causality [i.e. the causality of one being]' (*K3*, 29:1008; cf. ibid. 1007). In the way of an evaluation of this claim, all that is provided is the usual rejection of alternatives and the remark, 'This idea [of derivative influx] has something sublime', followed by the conclusion that 'Space itself is the form of the divine omnipresence, i.e. the omnipresence of God is expressed in the form of a phenomenon, and through this omnipresence of God, all substances are in harmony. But here our reason can comprehend nothing more' (*K3*, 29:1008). This is a baffling conclusion, for it would seem that 'more' is not really needed, that 'reason' has already 'comprehended' too much. In particular, here it has been 'comprehended' that noumenally there is neither an all-inclusive being nor a sheer plurality of beings, but instead a derivative relation such that ultimately there is a plurality of finite substances related through, and only through, being determined by an infinite being, a position that corresponds closely to the pre-Critical view of the *Nova Dilucidatio*, the *Dissertation*, and the early lectures of the 1770s!

Such a result may seem remarkable, but it corresponds to positions repeated in other lectures. Consider the specific issue of mind–body interaction, the major focus of the problem for many philosophers at that time, and one that Kant felt he could handle especially well. His views here only reinforce the 'rationalist' impression of his general discussion of interaction. Thus, at one point it is said that the action of body on soul need not be said to be 'ideal' because it is 'just as' genuine as the action of body on body:

The body as phenomenon is not in community with the soul, but rather the substance distinct from the soul, whose appearance is called body. This substrate of the body is an outer determining ground of the soul, but how this *commercium* is constituted we do not know. In body we cognize mere relations, but we do not cognize the inner (the substrate of matter). The extended *qua extensum* does not act upon the soul, otherwise both *correlata* would have to be in space, therefore the soul be a body. If we say the intelligible of the body acts upon the soul, then this means this outer body's noumenon determines

---

[44] 'For if only a single substance exists, then either I must be this substance, and consequently I must be God (but this contradicts my dependency); or else I am an accident (but this contradicts the concept of my ego, in which I think myself as an ultimate subject which is not the predicate of any other being)', from *Lectures on Philosophical Theology*, 86 (28:1052); cf. ibid. 74–5 (28:1041f.), and *V*, 28:458; *D*, 28:666; *K3*, 1008 f.

the soul, but it does not mean: a part of the soul (a noumenon) passes over as determining ground into the soul, it does not pour itself as power into the soul, but rather it determines merely the power which is in the soul, thus where the soul is active. This determination the author [Baumgarten] calls *influxus idealis*, but this is an *influxus realis*; for among bodies I can think only such an influence.[45]

At other places the special mind–body problem is resolved similarly by being embedded in a treatment of phenomenal interaction in general: 'How is the soul *in commercio* (in community) with the body? *Commercium* is a reciprocal influence among substances, however bodies are not substances, but rather only appearances. Thus no actual *commercium* takes place' (*L2*, 28:591; cf. *L1*, 28:204, 209; *D*, 28:682; *K2*, 739). Similarly, in the 'Metaphysik Mrongovius':

The primary difficulty that one runs up against in the explanation of the *commercium* with the body is that motion and thinking are so different that one cannot comprehend how the one is supposed to effect the other; but the body is a phenomenon and consequently its properties are as well. We are not acquainted with its substrate. Now how this could be in *commercium* with the soul amounts to the question of how substances in general can be in *commercium*, and the difficulty due to heterogeneity falls away. That bodies are mere appearances follows quite clearly from this because all their properties and powers issue from the motive power.[46]

Thus, the elevating of mind–body interaction to a status 'just as' real as body–body interaction goes hand in hand with a debasing of a body–body interaction to a mere phenomenal status, a relation of states. The ultimate explanation of interaction is put off to the noumenal level, where, instead of a positive statement, one gets only the reassurance that there need not be an insuperable problem about 'heterogeneity' or any commitment to a literal transfer of properties. But what does it mean to say that there are 'connections' of 'mere' phenomena[47] that nonetheless do not amount to an 'actual *commercium*'?

One explanation here would be to employ a distinction stressed by Kant since the 1760s, namely the idea that we have access only to hypothetical necessities,

---

[45] *K2*, 28:758–9; cf. B427–8. For such passages it is worth recalling that in German the term for 'influence' (*Einfluss*) can be broken down into 'pours' or 'flows in' (*fliesst ein*). Cf. *L1*, 28:279–80: 'But we can no more comprehend the *commercium* between bodies among themselves than that between the soul and the body.'

[46] *MM*, 29:908. Cf. *K3*, 29:1029, 'An unknown something, which is not appearance, is what influences the soul, and so we obtain in us a homogeneity with things. In this lies the representation that not the phenomenon itself of the body but rather the substratum of matter, the noumenon, produces in us. The *influxus* on one another thought materially between soul and body, and yet so that both would be outside themselves, and each for itself, is something in itself impossible: and if one assumes it ideally, then this would be nothing but the *harmonia praestabilita*, and would no longer be *influxus*. It must thus be thought as immaterial effect of the noumenon of both, whereupon this means nothing more than that something influences the soul, and then no heterogeneity remains which might raise doubts here...' Cf. *D*, 28:684–5, *MH*, 28:886–7. An anticipation of the view that the mind–body relation is not a special problem can be found in Knutzen: see Erdmann, *Martin Knutzen*, 104.

[47] Such connections are also stressed in the lectures: *V*, 28:408, 522–4; *MM*, 29:788, 806–9, 813–18.

which provide grounds not of things but of our knowledge (*MH*, 28:37; cf. also 844). This would mean that the synthetic connections of empirical knowledge are distinguishable from mere logical relations but still quite unlike causal connections in an absolute ontological sense. On this view, the causality we speak of in knowledge claims is a relation used just for connecting accidents (representations) but not substances (*D*, 28:647). The obvious problem for this view is then what to make of the *Critique's* Analogies, especially the Third, which surely does appear to assert reciprocal causal relations between worldly substances—indeed, all of them. There Kant concludes that, if 'the subjective community (*communio*) of appearances in our mind' is to 'rest on an objective ground... objects may be represented as coexisting. But this is a reciprocal influence, that is, a real community (*commercium*) of substances' (A214/B261). In the lectures, on the other hand, appearances and substances in themselves are repeatedly distinguished; e.g. '*compositio* is the relation of substances insofar as they are in community; but this does not take place with *compositio phaenomenon*' (*MM*, 29:828).

In the end one must decide either that for Kant phenomenal substances truly are ultimate subjects, genuine substances in interaction, as the *Critique* often indicates (but not always: 'matter, therefore, does not mean a kind of substance ... but only the distinctive nature of those appearances'[48]), or that they are not, as the lectures generally say. On balance, I do believe that in this instance the lectures give the most accurate indication of Kant's own deeply ambiguous view. The most recent evidence confirms that Kant was unwilling to break away fully from traditional ontology. It is no accident that at one point transcendental idealism was defined as the view that phenomena are not substances but require a noumenal substrate (*D*, 28:682). While Kant had his differences with his dogmatic predecessors, the appealing epistemological and empirical aspects of the *Critique* should not blind us to the fact that to accept a wholly non-rationalist metaphysics would also have involved giving up on the ontological implications of transcendental idealism, something Kant was not ready to do.

---

[48] A385. For more references, see my *Kant's Theory*, 299, n. 79.

– 5 –

Kant and Short Arguments to Humility

I

There is an unusual relationship between Kant's own arguments for transcendental idealism and the way that his position has been presented by later philosophers. In our own time, many important *systematic* philosophers who are not very concerned with the details of Kant's texts have presented his position as a kind of 'global' idealism, that is, an idealism that immediately makes ideal *everything* that human beings can sense, or think about, or at least know in any way. Sometimes this kind of interpretation is accompanied by a *sympathetic* attitude, a desire to present Kant as merely rejecting a kind of transcendental realism that is committed to an allegedly *absurd* positing of entities that are in principle wholly beyond rational comprehension. (Critiques of 'metaphysical' realism by Hilary Putnam and Richard Rorty are examples of this tendency in contemporary theoretical philosophy; in practical philosophy the work of John Rawls and his students often appears to promote such an interpretation in its preference for 'Kantian constructivism' over moral realism.[1]) At other times, this kind of interpretation is presented by philosophers who are *suspicious* of idealism of any kind, and who aim to tar Kant with the brush of making everything much too ideal, as if he believed, for example, that our concepts and the properties they refer to are *nothing but* human constructions. (Nicholas Wolterstorff and Roderick Chisholm have suggested versions of this view.[2])

These kinds of tendencies can also be found in Kant's *first* readers. It is well known that Garve, Feder, and other early critics used the 'tar brush' approach and presented Kant's philosophy as a *bad* version of a global idealism of a 'subjective' Berkeleyan variety.[3] A lesser known but even more influential development in Kant's time involved an opposite tendency: followers such as Reinhold and the

---

[1] On Kant and contemporary metaphysical anti-realism, see my 'Hegel and Idealism', *Monist*, 74 (1991), 394–6. On Kantian moral constructivism, see my 'On Schneewind and Kant's Method in Ethics', *Ideas y Valores*, 102 (1996), 28–53.

[2] On Wolterstorff, see 'Hegel and Idealism', 394; on Chisholm, see my 'Chisholm's Paralogisms', *Idealistic Studies*, 11 (1981), 100–8.

[3] See the materials contained in Johann Schultz, *Exposition of Kant's 'Critique of Pure Reason'*, tr. and ed. J. C. Morrison (Ottawa, 1995).

early Fichte sought to 'save' Kant by presenting or slightly modifying his position in such a way that it would clearly assert what they took to be an *attractive* global form of idealism that would leave no significant room at all for a metaphysical 'thing in itself', i.e. a reality wholly beyond the posits of transcendental subjectivity.[4] A somewhat (but only somewhat) similar division of interpretive tendencies can be found in the work of current scholars—e.g. Paul Guyer, who has criticized Kant for holding onto untenable substantive claims of ideality, and Henry E. Allison, who has aimed to 'save' Kant by proposing that transcendental ideality has no immediate negative ontological meaning, and is primarily just a methodological instrument for reminding us of the importance of focusing on conditions of human knowledge as such.[5]

An interpretive approach that *differs* significantly from the 'global' reading of idealism noted above can be found in several of my own earlier treatments of this issue, which called for paying closer attention to the specific *basis* from which Kant actually argues for his idealist claims. This interpretation was presented under the heading of a critique of what I called 'the short argument for idealism'; the terminology derives from a passage in Reinhold, who thought such an argument was a very good thing systematically even while he allowed that it did not follow the 'letter' of Kant's work.[6] I use the phrase 'short argument' to designate any of a variety of 'global' arguments that, like Reinhold's, attempt to establish transcendental idealism (or at least what is alleged to be its true 'spirit') without going through the actual long and complex steps that Kant lays out in the Transcendental Aesthetic, Transcendental Analytic, and Transcendental Dialectic of the *Critique of Pure Reason*. The crucial feature of these steps is that they all involve starting from reference to *specific* aspects of our forms of intuition, space, and time (e.g., their involving particular synthetic a priori claims). The metaphysical and epistemological arguments in the Aesthetic, as well as the central arguments of the Dialectic in the First Antinomy, focus directly on the features of space and time. The strategy of the Analytic is more indirect; its arguments all center on an investigation of our non-intuitive faculty of cognition, namely, the understanding; but they conclude that, for all our theoretical purposes, the use of this faculty is tied down to a reference to space and time, and hence the claims of our understanding, as well, are essentially restricted by the ideality of these forms

---

[4] See my 'Reinhold and the Short Argument to Idealism', in *Proceedings: Sixth International Kant Congress* 1985, ed. G. Funke and T. Seebohm (Washington, 1989), vol. 2, pt 2, 441–53; 'Kant, Fichte, and Short Arguments to Idealism', *Archiv für Geschichte der Philosophie*, 72 (1990), 63–85; and *Kant and the Fate of Autonomy* (Cambridge, 2000), ch. 2; cf. Kant's eventual rejection of Reinhold and Fichte in his letter to Tieftrunk, Oct. 13, 1797 (12:207–8) and his public declaration, Aug. 7, 1799 (12:370–1).

[5] See my 'Kantian Idealism Today', *History of Philosophy Quarterly*, 9 (1992), 329–42.

[6] 'Thus one can begin to understand in a shorter way the impossibility that Kant established of knowing the thing in itself. The thing in itself is not representable, so how could if be knowable?'; K. L. Reinhold, *Versuch einer neuen Theorie des menschlichen Vorstellungsvermögens* (Jena, 1789), 255 (cited in my 'Reinhold and the Short Argument to Idealism', 442).

of intuition. On this approach, the arguments for transcendental idealism are necessarily 'long', complex, and in part indirect—whereas a 'short' argument moves to idealism relatively quickly and directly by beginning not with our specific forms of sensibility, but with some much more general or 'global' feature of human cognition.

The paradigmatic version of the short argument approach can be found in Reinhold, who began his *Elementarphilosophie* with the bare notion of representation, and claimed that reflection on this notion alone can reveal that all that we can think and know must be ideal, must be only what is 'for us' and not 'in itself'. Other possible starting points for a short argument emphasize the 'global' fact that in knowing we are, in part at least, essentially 'receptive'; or, in contrast, that we are, in part at least, also essentially 'active'. Similar short arguments can start simply from the fact that we use sensibility at all—or, in contrast, from the fact that we use concepts at all. The first fact might seem to imply that what we are given does not come to us as it is 'in itself' but only in a limited and filtered way. The second fact might seem to imply that what we know is in part molded by our own creative ways of organizing data, and so is not left as given 'in itself'. (Hegel discussed these contrasting options right at the start of the Introduction to his *Phenomenology* and suggested that they were the most natural ways of moving toward what *he* took to be Kantian idealism—a form of idealism that he still found much too subjective.[7]) There are, of course, many different ways in which arguments need to be, and have been, filled in from these starting points, and there is no reason to assume that in the end they must always turn out to be literally 'shorter' than Kant's own text. The key point here, however, has nothing to do with the terms 'short' or 'long' taken literally. The main issue, as Reinhold already saw, is simply whether Kant's *specific* views about space and time, and all of their complexities, play a *necessary* initial role in the argument, or, rather, whether there is a way to try to get to something appealing and at least very much like Kant's idealist conclusions by abstracting from these specific views from the very *beginning*, and by focusing on something supposedly simpler and more basic, such as representation as such.

Although the distinction between what I am calling 'short' and 'long' arguments is based fundamentally on a distinction that concerns the argument's premise, it naturally has implications for how the conclusion of the argument for idealism is to be understood. Sometimes, however, the conclusions need not look very different, and one has to do some work to keep in view the underlying structure of the argument. On a long argument, it is simply space and time—and all and only all that is (epistemically) dependent on them—that turn out to be ideal. On a short argument, on the other hand, the conclusion asserting ideality

---

[7] See my analysis in 'Hegel's Critique of Kant's Theoretical Philosophy', *Philosophy and Phenomenological Research*, 48 (1985), 1–35.

concerns a realm defined more globally, such as the whole realm of the representable—or the sensible, or the conceivable, or the knowable. One might thus be tempted to assume that long arguments concern only spatio-temporal things, whereas short arguments always concern much more. For many philosophers who use these arguments, however, matters are not this simple, because on some versions it can turn out that there are not, and perhaps cannot be, any more things (or ontological 'aspects') that are known, or sensed, or even 'clearly' conceived or represented, than the things that are spatio-temporal. In that case, the actual scope of what is ideal can turn out to be coextensive for the two kinds of arguments. Nonetheless, there is still a huge difference in methodology, if not in ontology, if someone says that what we represent is ideal *because* it is spatio-temporal, while someone else, such as Reinhold (and other German idealists) says that, on the contrary, what is spatio-temporal is ideal *because* it is represented. (Reinhold—and he was not alone—went so far as to argue that not only the ideality but also the specific nature of space and of time can be derived from what is required by a form of representation as such.[8])

II

Although attempts to find a short argument in Kant, or to construct an improved version of this kind for oneself, can be highly interesting and have a long and ever growing popularity, they remain very questionable for both historical and systematic reasons. Historically, they ignore and make strangely pointless large sections—indeed, the obvious central sections—of Kant's own work. And yet, whatever its interpretive oddities, the move to a 'short' approach is understandable, and it is no doubt motivated by more than simply the notorious difficulty of Kant's own writing. There appears to be a systematic payoff that attracts philosophers to the short argument, a hope of connecting Kant's work in a more direct and appealing way with traditional idealist doctrines and debates on skepticism, representationalism, and realism. Nonetheless, precisely because the claims of the short argument are so global, it is hard to see how they could be any easier to establish than conclusions like Kant's own more restricted claims—unless bold global claims such as 'all that is represented must be ideal' are meant to be understood in terms of a Pickwickian sense of 'ideal' (e.g. as meaning 'all that we represent must be representable by us') that leaves only a straw man to oppose them.

New light on this old issue may arise in the afternath of a very recent and challenging metaphysical study by Rae Langton, *Kantian Humility: Our Ignorance of Things in Themselves*.[9] It is a striking fact that, from the time of Kant's first readers to our own era, most of the advocates of the short argument approach have

---

[8] See my 'Kant, Fichte, and Short Arguments to Idealism'.
[9] Rae Langton, *Kantian Humility* (henceforth *KH*), (Oxford, 1998).

had an historical and systematic attitude that is highly *unsympathetic* to mainstream work in classical metaphysics. Working from a presumption that Kant (as the 'Critical' philosopher, or, as Mendelssohn called him, '*der Alleszermalmende*', the 'all-destroying') had a similar attitude, they have presented their short arguments precisely as an efficient way of moving to a wholesale dismissal of any outdated or 'pre-Critical' metaphysics of 'ultimate reality'. Langton, however, has a very different background and motivation. She is a student of David Lewis and a very able practitioner of contemporary metaphysics. This alone is rare for a Kantian. Until recently, the last half-century of English work on Kant was dominated by philosophers who were uninterested in, and not only unsympathetic to, traditional metaphysics as such—and the top contemporary metaphysicians returned the compliment by generally being equally uninterested in Kant. To be sure, Strawson's elegant work generated an important (indeed, dominant) and extensive wave of literature on Kant that might seem to be an exception to this trend. In fact, though, this work kept its focus primarily on epistemological issues (e.g. analogs of the private language argument) and was most influential because of its discussion of empiricism, skepticism, and themes close to positivist doctrines such as the verification principle. It is typical of this work that it provides little discussion of the main issues of Kant's Dialectic ('rational', i.e. philosophical, psychology, cosmology, and theology), or of the central issues in current metaphysics that can be found in more recent 'textbooks' by figures such as Chisholm, Armstrong, Lewis, or Loux.[10]

Langton opposes this trend by arguing vigorously that Kant can be understood and defended best when he is taken to be a classical metaphysician of contemporary relevance. She claims that the 'acid test' for this approach lies in finding a way to make sense of Kant's doctrine of 'our ignorance of things in themselves'. This doctrine is usually called transcendental idealism, but it is no accident that Langton does not use this terminology explicitly in her title. She aims to save Kant's doctrine by taking it to be simply a kind of quasi-Lockean claim about the unknowability of the *intrinsic* qualities of objects. Since, on her version of Kant, this kind of unknowability goes hand in hand with an assertion that there *are* such qualities 'out there', it has little to do with idealism as that term is often understood in English, namely, as a globally negative or skeptical notion. Hence she prefers to say that Kant's position is a combination of some *realist* metaphysical views (about intrinsic properties of external things) and various sensible *epistemological* doctrines that entail a fundamental 'humility' on our part, i.e. a resistance to traditional claims that there is nothing significant at all beyond what we can determine, at least indistinctly, through our own representations. Realism and humility go together. Precisely because one is such a realist

---

[10] A very clear and typical review of this approach is provided in Michael J. Loux, *Metaphysics: A Contemporary Introduction* (New York, 1998), 7–10.

about something 'out there', it is only proper not to be overconfident about what we can *know* about it. Nonetheless, this Kantian humility and ignorance is not simply a matter of realism; it also involves the metaphysical claim that certain features are such that we cannot know them as inhering in things precisely *because* they cannot ever belong to things in themselves as such. Hence they must be 'merely phenomenal' or 'ideal', even if they may always appear 'real' in an intersubjective experiential sense. Kantian arguments for humility are thus, at least in part, arguments for ideality as well, and so I will sometimes speak interchangeably about arguments for humility and for ideality, with the understanding that neither term by itself entails a rejection of all realism.

I must confess to finding Langton's notion of Kantian humility to be of considerable interest, not least because several years ago I stressed a similar (but only similar) point, namely, that 'transcendental idealism can be expressed as not so much a metaphysical extravagance as rather a principle of modesty, as a reminder that things in their intrinsic character need not be the way that our specific modes of knowing must take them to be'.[11] I backed this approach by extensive reference to Kant's earliest metaphysical remarks (and especially passages concerning our ignorance of the 'intrinsic'), a strategy that Langton also adopts. She provides helpful citations of many neglected metaphysical passages that overlap with or correspond to ones that I too thought worthy of emphasis, and so it might appear that her work could be welcomed as fundamentally a reinforcement for those committed to bringing out the metaphysical dimension of Kant's philosophy.[12] Nonetheless, despite several points in common, and the similarity of key terms such as 'modesty' and 'humility', there remain significant differences between Langton's reading and my own. A consideration of these differences may help to make clearer the main options that remain for those who would pursue a metaphysical approach to Kantian idealism. Only after an analysis of the main claims of her study will it become clear how much is at stake—how

---

[11] See my *Kant's Theory of Mind* (henceforth *KTM*) (Oxford, 1982; 2nd edn 2000), 7. It should be noted that, in saying that transcendental idealism 'can be expressed' in this modest way, I was not endorsing the view that this was the most accurate way to define it, and in fact I went on to argue that Kant himself seems committed to the bolder claim that certain features (of 'our specific modes of knowing') not only 'need not' be, but also cannot be, ascribed to things in themselves.

[12] Langton has independent reasons for focusing on many of the surprisingly neglected Kantian metaphysical doctrines that I have stressed in my earlier work. See e.g. her treatment of 'phenomenal substance' and matter as not substance in the pure Kantian sense (*KH*, ch. 3; cf. *KTM*, ch. 1, 299, n. 79, and *passim*; this issue is also discussed in James Van Cleve, *Problems from Kant* (New York, 1999), 120); her stress on the importance of the doctrine of the irreducibility of relations in Kant (*KH*, ch. 5; cf. *KTM*, 36, 65–7, 267–77); and her stress on the contrast between Kant's 'scientific' notion of experience and phenomenalist definitions of it, a contrast based on what Kant says about how things of experience are known 'through' representations (and are not equivalent to collections of them) as well as on his insistence that unobservable items, known through laws and not sensations, can be paradigms of 'empirical reality' (*KH*, 159, 143; cf. *KTM*, 113).

close and yet how far her valuable reading comes to what I take to be the truly Kantian approach.

III

A first and very crucial feature of Langton's approach concerns what she calls the fact of 'receptivity'. What she means by this fact, first of all, is simply Kant's insistence that we actually are affected by particular external things that we claim to know theoretically. Unlike philosophers (e.g. Berkeley, Leibniz, Malebranche) who allow that something external exists but then deny that it really affects us, and those (skeptics, strict phenomenalists) who deny that there is anything external at all (so that there is nothing that is even in a position to affect us), Kant stresses that we are sensible beings, and that this means that metaphysically and epistemologically we are dependent on how things affect us. The attempt to move immediately from this fact to idealism involves a strategy that I once called 'the passivity argument'. I explored this strategy as a popular and understandable way of at first approaching Kant, but concluded that it was so obviously deficient historically and systematically that it could not seriously be ascribed to him (*KTM*, 255–9). Langton, however, still seems to have a sympathy for something like the passivity argument, since she follows Strawson in regarding the claim that receptivity entails ignorance of things in themselves to be a 'fundamental unargued for premise of the *Critique*'.[13] In her own words, 'Kant believes that humility follows from this fact of receptivity.... If this is correct, then our ignorance of things in themselves is not supposed to be a special [NB] consequence of the arguments about space, time, or the categories; it is to be a general consequence of the fact that human knowledge is receptive' (*KH*, 3).

This passage reveals the fundamental nature of Langton's interpretation, and the fact that she is one more reader who remains very much in the grip of key features of the 'short argument' approach to Kant. What is new and interesting about her interpretation is her refusal to be content with a 'very short' argument, and her ability to spell it out very clearly in terms of a host of neglected metaphysical details. She sees that a move *directly* from receptivity to ignorance and ideality is hardly self-evident, and so she sets out to find extra premises that could be added to the fact of receptivity in order to give a plausible warrant for the conclusion of what she calls Kantian humility.

An alternative approach, of course, would be simply to resist Strawson's unsupported statement about Kant's so-called 'fundamental premise', and to deny that the crucial aspect of Kant's argument rests at all on an argument

---

[13] *KH*, 4, referring to P. F. Strawson, *The Bounds of Sense* (London, 1966), 252.

basically from mere receptivity.[14] It is striking, for example, that receptivity considerations would seem to tie ideality to specifically *empirical* features of knowledge, whereas the arguments of the *Critique* that Kant emphasizes (e.g. the 'geometry argument' of the Aesthetic, or the Analogies in the Analytic) proceed by laboriously establishing controversial a priori features of knowledge, and then asserting always that it is these unusual features that require ideality. This point is quite compatible with his arguing later that all our empirical representations involving space and time—and thus all our sensible representations—are also ideal, since this is precisely because they are determined by the ideal pure representations. Kant's famous letter to Herz, and his discussion in the *Critique* about the need for a Transcendental Deduction, make clear that the issue of the ideality of representations emerges for him from questions specifically about concepts that carry with them necessity and apriority (viz. the non-sensible representations that are the categories), and these are not a matter of our mere receptivity.[15] All this is ignored by Langton's starting point, and this reinforces the usual suspicions about any version of the short argument approach.[16]

Langton's analysis is, nonetheless, unusually intriguing, even if its most general form follows an old and disputed pattern. Unlike other advocates of a short argument, she believes that Kant has a substantive and understandable notion of something beyond our theoretical knowledge. In this way she is much closer, at least in her conclusions, to 'long' interpretations that stress the non-ideality of properties not tied to our specific forms of space and time. For her, the Kantian 'in

---

[14] Langton cites from the *Critique of Pure Reason* one passage that is apparently meant to support Strawson's claim: 'Properties that belong to things in themselves cannot be given to us through the senses' (A36/B52, cited in *KH*, 23). Note that this passage does not say that we cannot know things in themselves simply *because* we use sensible representations. It thus does not show that the unknowability in itself of what is given in our receptivity is a 'fundamental premise' rather than a conclusion in Kant's sequence of argument.

[15] See Kant's letter to Herz, Feb. 21, 1772 (10:131–2): 'Thus the passive or sensuous representations have an understandable relation to objects.... However, the pure concepts of the understanding must not be abstracted from sense perceptions... if such intellectual representations depend on our inner activity, whence comes the agreement that they are supposed to have with objects?' (tr. from *Correspondence/Immanuel Kant*, , ed. and tr. A. Zweig (Cambridge, 1999), 133). Cf. A85/B117 f. For more on interpretations of Kant's letter, see Predrag Cicovacki, 'An Aporia of A priori Knowledge: On Carl's and Beck's Interpretation of Kant's Letter to Markus Herz', *Kant-Studien* 82 (1991), 349–60.

[16] A major difficulty of Langton's approach—as with short arguments in general—is that it almost totally ignores Kant's considerations about space, spatial knowledge, geometry, and the antinomies, which on most traditional accounts are clearly central to the systematic and historical development of Kant's transcendental idealism and the development of his Critical philosophy. See e.g. typical studies by Ted Humphrey, 'The Historical and Conceptual Relations between Kant's Metaphysics of Space and Philosophy of Geometry', *Journal of the History of Philosophy* 11 (1973), 485–512; Günter Zöller, *Theoretische Gegenstandsbeziehung bei Kant* (Berlin, 1984); and Henry E. Allison, *Kant's Transcendental Idealism* (New Haven, 1983). It is easy to understand how Langton fell into this approach if she was taken by Kant's very earliest writings, which do not contain anything like the Critical account of space. Harder to understand is her response to this problem at the end of her book, where she seems to shift course and to tie the arguments for ideality only to space and matter rather than to force, and to speak of bodies as if they had a privileged reality. Her final sentence is: 'The ideality of space does not, in his [Kant's] own opinion, undermine the

itself' is not a mere analytic or methodological notion, not something that we cannot reach simply because it *is nothing* at all, let alone something that has *no meaning* at all. It is rather something that we *properly* 'yearn to know', something that Kant speaks of as being involved with real features such as affection, and for which he reserves 'distinctive and inner predicates' that he does not allow in the realm of appearances.[17] Unless we hold that Kant believes things can exist without 'inner predicates'—something he resists in all periods of his writings and lectures—there is no reason to *deny* a substantive metaphysical content for (what Kant meant by) the 'in itself', even if we cannot affirm positive (theoretical) *epistemological* claims about what it is like.[18]

This strategy raises an old and obvious problem that Langton confronts right from the start. Since Kant expressly denies *knowledge* of things in themselves, how can he consistently allow an affirmation of the 'inner predicates' and casual relations that have just been noted? Langton's answer is a variant of a strategy that is itself old and obvious—and still perfectly respectable, even if strangely neglected. The strategy is simply to say that Kant does not mean to block *all* kinds of knowledge of things in themselves, but only certain types. This strategy seems forced on us by minimal charity; for without anything like it, Kant would be talking wild nonsense in his many general discussions of things in themselves, in his many positive characterizations of them from a practical perspective, and in his many slightly more specific remarks about them as having 'distinctive and inner predicates'. As long as we do not claim to know positively the 'inner predicates' of specific things, it is not clear that Kant's general concern with humility and idealism is done any serious harm; there is still quite a lot left to be 'humble' about, and also a lot that can be called 'ideal' in a specifiable and significant sense. Langton's proposal is that Kant is concerned simply with denying our knowledge of the *intrinsic* properties of things, and thus with denying the 'transcendental reality' of relational claims. When he says that things in themselves affect us, or that we have detailed knowledge about the domain of experience, all we have are

---

reality of what is presented in space, namely bodies, constituted by forces that are mind-independent properties of absolutely independent substances, things in themselves' (p. 218). Unless this passage is meant only to reassert the 'empirical reality' of bodies in Kant—which no one would deny—it appears to suggest a notion of 'body' independent of space that is very hard to understand and has no place in Kant's final Critical work. By the time of the *Metaphysical Foundations of Natural Science* (1786, 4:503–8, and 520–21; cf. *KTM*, 40), Kant had explicitly completed the argument for the ideality of not only space but also all the matter and the bodies that fill space. This leaves room for the empirical—and only empirical—reality of bodies as such, but it implies that bodies are metaphysically ideal and that there is a non-empirical reality of the non-material thing in itself that underlies matter and bodies (cf. n. 42 below). From the *Critique* on, there is no non-equivocal sense in which space is merely ideal while bodies are real.

[17] A565/B593, cited in *KH*, 12.
[18] Langton (*KH*, 27–30; cf. *KTM*, 82 n. 100, and 269) makes good points here against suggestions (by J. Bennett) that Kant may have confusedly thought that the unknowability of the 'inner' was a matter of our not being able to know a 'bare' substrate. There is considerable material on this and related topics in *Lectures on Metaphysics/ Immanuel Kant*, ed. and tr. K. Ameriks and S. Naragon (Cambridge, 1997).

many bits of *relational* knowledge, and thus precisely not illegitimate (for a Critical philosophy) knowledge of things 'in themselves', i.e. things in their *intrinsic* nature.

This interpretive strategy suggests an interesting way in which Kant can be taken to make a claim about our necessary ignorance that is at least meaningful and can seem, on a sympathetic reading, to have some chance of being consistent with the rest of his philosophy. Moreover, it reveals how Kant's position contrasts very dramatically with that of his main opponent, Leibniz. *If* Kant held, as Leibniz generally was taken to hold, that relational claims are in principle *reducible* to intrinsic claims about individual substances, then he (Kant) would be caught, after all, with a dogmatic commitment to strong knowledge claims—and ones clearly inconsistent with the rest of his philosophy—about the natures of particular things in themselves. The relational knowledge that we possess about phenomena *would entail* (albeit in a way that we need not be able to see clearly) intrinsic truths about things in themselves. The crucial antecedent of the conditional claim cannot be asserted, however, because Kant clearly emphasizes that on his view there is precisely *no such reducibility* of relations.[19] And it is precisely this insistence that Langton uses as the essential supplement for the receptivity argument. Her argument is that the relational nature that characterizes our knowledge as receptive, combined with Kant's doctrine of the non-reducibility of these relations, is what implies humility: all we can know is relational, but the relational does not reveal the intrinsic (given the non-reducibility doctrine), so what we know is, in this sense, 'mere phenomena', not things in themselves. Or, to be more precise, Kant holds that what there is in itself must have *some* intrinsic nature, so we do have that kind of indeterminate knowledge *about* things in themselves, but this is still not any kind of illicit theoretical knowledge *of particular* things, or even of the *determinate* nature of things in general (*KH*, 13). This reading has some obvious advantages. It can easily supply an understandable and modest meaning for Kant's doctrine that our standard knowledge claims have 'mere phenomenality' as well as 'empirical reality', and it has no problem applying to the claims that involve the essentially relational attributions that occur within the framework of modern theoretical science and that are of special significance for Kant.[20]

IV

Langton finds grounds supporting her approach in considerations about interaction that go back to Kant's very earliest texts. In his 1747 essay on *Living Forces*, Kant defended the claim that 'substances can [NB] exist and nevertheless have no

---

[19] See the references above in n. 12.   [20] See the references above in n. 12.

external relation toward others at all'.[21] And from his 1756 *Physical Monadology* onwards, Kant argued that matter (as a play of forces) is not strictly speaking substance, but only *substantia phenomenon*, something treated *as if* substance,[22] and that, 'besides external presence, i.e. relational properties, there are other intrinsic properties without which the relational properties [forces] would not exist, because [otherwise] there could be no subject in which they inhered'.[23] As Langton notes, Lewis White Beck and others have thought that these claims are still basically Leibnizian, and were written to express a view (of Kant's at that time, supposedly) that relational properties such as force and space are *fully grounded* in substance in a Leibnizian way, as a *phenomenon bene fundatum*.[24] In fact, however, all that Kant borrows from Leibniz here are the ideas that a substance is something that ultimately exists on its own, i.e. is a subject or bearer and in no way an accident, and that 'substances in general must have an intrinsic nature which is therefore free of [i.e. not dependent on] all external relations'.[25] *Unlike* Leibniz, Kant holds that the relational properties of finite substances *cannot* be reduced to, or 'fully grounded' on (i.e. be shown to supervene on), their intrinsic properties. Moreover, although for Kant a substance is independent, it need not be absolutely independent in being *or* determination. That is, not only does Kant say a substance does not have to be responsible for its own existence (contrary to Spinoza), but he also allows—*unlike* Leibniz—that there is real interaction of finite substances, and he affirms that the properties of mundane substances are in part due to causal effects of other substances. In an early argument (in the *Nova dilucidatio*, 1755) for his 'Principle of Coexistence', Kant contends that substances do not exist together ('in the same world') unless they are in some causal interrelation.[26] He adds to this a 'Principle of Succession' that goes even further (and was eventually given up), and asserts that *no* change, not even in thought, can happen within a particular (finite) substance without some cause from *outside* that substance.[27]

---

[21] *KH*, 121, citing 1:21.
[22] On the claim that matter is phenomenal, see A277/B333 and the references above in n. 12, and especially *KH*, 50–63.
[23] *KH*, 101, citing 1:481.
[24] *KH*, 102; cf. above, n. 12. See L.W. Beck, 'Introduction', in *Kant's Latin Writings: Translations, Commentaries and Notes*, ed. L.W. Beck *et al.* (New York, 1986), 12.
[25] A274/B333, cited at *KH*, 32.
[26] *KH*, 107–8; 1:412–15.
[27] *KH*, 104–6; 1:410. Cf. my 'The Critique of Metaphysics: Kant and Traditional Ontology', in *The Cambridge Companion to Kant*, ed. P. Guyer (Cambridge, 1992), 249–79; as well as Eric Watkins, 'Kant's Theory of Physical Influx', *Archiv für Geschichte der Philosophy*, 77 (1995), 285–324; and his 'The Development of Physical Influx in Early 18th Century Germany: Gottsched, Knutzen, and Crusius', *Review of Metaphysics* 49 (1995), 295–339; and Alison Laywine, *Kant's Early Metaphysics and the Origins of the Critical Philosophy* (Atascadero, Calif., 1983). A point that needs to be stressed here is that Kant does not accept the Principle of Succession later (although he offers an epistemological analog for it in the empirical domain in his 'Refutation of Idealism'), no doubt because for his Critical philosophy it is too metaphysically dogmatic and would cause problems for his own theory of transcendental freedom.

All these considerations point to a fundamental and enduring Kantian distinction between intrinsic and relational properties. Intrinsic properties characterize what the substance is 'in itself', and a substance could not exist without *some* of these. Relational properties, on the other hand, are such that at least some substances *could* exist without any of them, and also such that, although they represent the actual relational truth about substances, they do not logically, let alone epistemically, entail (through reduction or supervenience) what is true about the substances intrinsically. Since the relational properties exhaust Kantian 'experience', or what we know about the phenomena, i.e. the items that we can actually empirically determine,[28] and since the intrinsic properties seem to be in principle beyond our access (since any candidate we offer for them appears to be replaceable by a set of relational properties that we can determine empirically, and there remains a posited 'substrate' that is always beyond whatever determinations we make, since these always turn out to be relational), it can seem understandable and attractive to equate the relational with what is phenomenal, and the intrinsic with what is in itself. The claim of our ignorance of the 'in itself' then appears fairly innocent and compatible with all sorts of causal or 'affection' claims about things in themselves. Whereas previously it might have seemed dogmatic to speak of any causal relations of things in themselves, now, on Langton's interpretation, we can say easily enough that, precisely by speaking of causality in terms of relations, we are not at all speaking illegitimately about what things are like 'in themselves', and yet, at the same time, we need not say that our causal knowledge is sheer error or illusion. On the contrary, it is a completely proper representation of the relational—but merely relational—truths about what there is.

V

All this can seem to leave us with an appealing dissolution of some old mysteries, and a nice metaphysical version of a short argument for Kantian idealism. But can it be all that simple? Can these early texts already reveal the essence of the transcendental idealism that Kant was to argue for much later and in a more complicated but (supposedly) substantially unrevised way?

Although these texts do involve some important characterizations of the notions of substance and the 'in itself' that Kant showed no signs of retreating from in his later works, they also seem to me to be in some very significant ways *unlike* his views later in his Critical period. It is striking that, unlike the *Critique*, the early works move directly to strong metaphysical claims, rather than starting from

---

[28] Langton properly emphasizes that, while Kant's notion of 'experience' corresponds to relational properties defining our modern scientific image of the world, it contrasts sharply with standard phenomenalist notions of immediate 'experience' as well as with arcane suppositions of certain physicists—including Newton—that supposedly have no empirical explanatory power. See above, n. 12.

epistemological or 'merely experiential' ones, and that at the start they concern mere sensible rather than a priori and necessary relations. Langton may think that it is a good thing (part of what she regards as Kant's 'empiricist' background) if little more than our mere receptivity points to a line of thought that seems only a short step from making intelligible a strong distinction between knowable phenomenal items and unknowable things in themselves; for her, 'humility does follow from receptivity, given irreducibility' (*KH*, 126). But this step still seems to me too short and easy to be valid, especially since it leaves key changes in Kant's doctrines through the 1760s and 1770s, as well as nearly all the details of his main arguments in the Critical period of the 1780s and after, without any clear relevance for his most important doctrine, the thesis of transcendental idealism.

But if something has gone wrong here, what is it? I would be the last to counsel against giving more attention to Kant's metaphysical statements and early works. Nonetheless, it is fair to ask exactly how far one can go with only these works and the kinds of statements to which Langton limits herself. The doctrine of transcendental idealism is so difficult that one should not turn away from considering any serious hypothesis that might shed light on it.

In this spirit I once examined, under the heading of an argument called 'the essence theory' (*KTM*, 267–70), a hypothesis somewhat similar to Langton's. This theory involves equating phenomena with contingent properties, and the unknowable aspect of things in themselves with essential properties. Given Kant's unqualified rejection of any Leibnizian notion that we can come to a (theoretical) determination of the substantive essences of particular things, the essence theory offers at least one relatively simple way of explaining why Kant might have thought that *we cannot* know things 'in themselves'. Nonetheless, I noted (as I have here with regard to Langton's interpretation) that such a theory does not seem to correspond to the complex epistemological considerations that Kant in fact emphasized in the course of the development of his idealist doctrines. Moreover, there seems to be no reason to deny that (even for Kant) there could be contingent (and unknown) rather than essential properties that could also belong to a thing in itself. Given the apparent possibility of contingent properties of things in themselves, mere essentiality cannot be assumed to be a clear necessary condition of nonphenomenality.

A similar problem can be pressed in the end against Langton's approach, even if that approach has features that keep it free from some problems that defeat the essence theory. She stresses tying the thing in itself to intrinsic properties, and tying the phenomena that contrast with the thing in itself to non-intrinsic, i.e. irreducibly relational, properties. This strategy has implications that *partially overlap* with the essence theory insofar as essential properties *can* be possessed as intrinsic and non-phenomenal, and (for Kant) there are specific relational properties that obviously *cannot* be essential for a thing in itself as such. Nonetheless, although it is essential that a thing in itself has *some* intrinsic properties, it is not clearly the case that all the intrinsic properties that it has (or perhaps any of its distinctive properties) are essential to it. This leaves the essence theory with a problem that Langton's approach does not have to worry about. The contingent but still non-phenomenal properties that give that theory trouble can be ascribed to things in themselves without any problem, in her view.[29]

Despite this advantage, there remains a difficulty for Langton's view. The view appears to entail two controversial theses: (1) that there can be no intrinsic but merely phenomenal properties; and (2) that there can be no relational but non-phenomenal properties. Against the first point, one might try to argue by supposing, in a way common to some views in contemporary debates, that 'sense data' as such, or 'qualia' of some sort, could be counted as both intrinsic and manifestly phenomenal. A contemporary advocate of qualia might stress precisely that they have a simple, immediate, and not essentially relational character, and that they have a presence that remains certain however things might go with the development of our ordinary relational and scientific knowledge. This is an interesting objection, but I would concede that it is not one that *Kant* himself would press very far. The immediacy that 'qualia' advocates emphasize is something that Kant (for better or worse) probably would not regard as having any *cognitive* character as such. And, insofar as we can move on to know what qualia are, Kant seems to presume that they should fit into a general and relational theory about the properties of the space–time (and hence, on Kant's view, merely phenomenal) domain.[30] Hence, if qualia are completely non-relational, then they are not knowable, and so they are not an instance of the Kantian phenomenal domain, which is exhausted by what can in principle be known through (what are at least in part) empirical means. And if they are relational and knowable after all, then they lose their character as sheer intrinsic qualities.

Even if objections to thesis (1) could be turned back in this way, thesis (2) remains vulnerable to a more serious and genuinely Kantian objection. The key issue here is whether there could be relational properties that ever attach to Kantian things in themselves as such. This might seem to be ruled out by definition; once a property is relational, then one might say it just is what Langton thinks Kant means by 'not in itself'. But this strategy threatens to appear like the 'analytic' and 'anodyne' high road that Langton criticizes in others. Why should

---

[29] I have argued that these contingent properties could be easily lost sight of by an advocate of the essence theory, since all the contingent properties to which we have access are, according to Kant, filtered through the forms of space and time, and thus (supposedly) inherit their ideality (*KTM*, 271). Thus, the intrinsic but *contingent* characterization of things, including ourselves, is an especially opaque realm—whereas we can easily enough, through the pure categories, at least imagine some non-theoretical but thinkable *necessary* features of things, things in their non-phenomenal essence as pure substance, cause, etc.

[30] See *KTM*, 293. It is no accident that Kant does not work out a separate science of psychological knowledge.

we think that Kant holds to the stipulative definitional route of making relations contrary to the very meaning of what can be possessed by any thing in itself *as such*? There is, after all, at least one possible property of things in themselves that seems relational and of great concern to Kant, namely, freedom. He clearly wants to be able to say, with at least possible truth (whatever the warrant may be—nothing here rests on our being able *theoretically* to know that we *actually* have the exercise of such freedom) that a subject is free, absolutely and 'in itself'. This freedom must be more than an intrinsic feature entirely within a subject; it must be an actual relational capacity, even if it is also said to be within the subject 'in itself' because there is no room for it as such (given Kant's empirical determinism) in the subject as phenomenon. That is, it must be a capacity of the subject really to affect something other than it, to be an uncaused cause of phenomenal events and some kinds of effects on other substances, especially other people. Otherwise, Kantian notions of morality and freedom are toothless beyond belief, no better than the fantasy of pre-established harmony.

Freedom is not an odd or atypical example of a possible property of a thing in itself; it is clearly the very kind of property for which Kant designed his theory. Hence, making room for it must override the benefits of a merely definitional strategy that would keep a clean division of relational properties and properties of things in themselves. The fact that, on Kant's mature theory, this property is one that in principle cannot be theoretically known in no way disqualifies it from being a property of a thing in itself as such. (Such unknowability is a feature that belongs in any case to all the properties of the subject in itself on Langton's theory as well.) Langton herself emphasizes that the relationality of a property possessed by a substance can be 'conceptual' and need not depend on the actual existence or state of another substance (*KH*, 38). Thus, regardless of whether there exists something else that a subject's freedom affects, it still can be the case that the subject in itself has the (relational) property of being a free being, of having a nature that *would* allow it to act freely and effectively in particular ways in an actual situation with distinct substances. The fact that this property in turn might require some more basic intrinsic properties does not mean that the property cannot be relational and possessed by the thing itself as such.

The example of freedom is only one of a group of similar properties that are highly relevant to Kant's system. Even though Langton makes extensive use of Kant's earliest work, she, like most interpreters, has little to say about Kant's views in the 1770s, after he had already introduced a doctrine of transcendental ideality in his *Inaugural Dissertation*. In the *Dissertation* Kant makes his initial argument for the transcendental ideality of space and time (as 'forms of the sensible world'), but he still holds to the doctrine that there is a kind of non-ideal theoretical knowledge that we can have of the 'form of the intelligible world'. It is striking that this knowledge has as its prime example an argument concerning the interaction of substances and the unity of the world of finite beings (§19, 2:408). It is very clear from the text that Kant still regards this knowledge as at once relational and concerning things in themselves as such. In his later work, in the *Critique of Pure Reason* and after, he severely tightens his limitations on what we can know about things in themselves, and he argues that not only the spatio-temporal form of the objects of experiences, but also all the causal laws that we can know for them (which in the end also indirectly cover all the content in our theoretical determination of the self) are essentially mediated by the forms of space and time and thus turn out to be transcendentally ideal. Nonetheless, this change does not affect Kant's *definition* of transcendental idealism, but only his conclusions about some of the features of our faculties of knowing and the scope of claims about what it is that is merely ideal. He never indicates that he wants to go back on what he has argued in the *Dissertation* in such a way that it would become *immediately* entailed by the mere relationality of a property that it cannot belong to a thing in itself. It is true that all the items Kant claims to be ideal are also relational, but all the weight in the actual arguments that the *Critique* makes for the ideality of various relational features (such as space and time, or self-knowledge) rests on *specific* characteristics of the relations involved. In each case ideality is concluded only after a discussion of a particular spatial or temporal relation that is involved, and only after noting that there are specific reasons for saying that ideality is the best explanation for the spatio-temporal dimensions of the things of experience, or of our a priori knowledge of their spatio-temporal form.

Matters are complicated somewhat by an unusual argument in the *Critique* that includes the statement that 'a thing in itself cannot be known through mere relations' (B67). Note, however, that this is a statement about *knowledge*, not about the properties of a thing as such, and it is compatible with, and probably aimed primarily at expressing, the innocent point that a thing cannot *have mere* relational properties without any intrinsic properties at all. The statement by itself does not rule out the possibility of a relational property possessed by a thing in itself, or even of a whole set of such properties had by things composing an 'intelligible world'.[31]

This is not to play down in any way the argument beginning at B67, for it is one of the most important and least understood passages in the *Critique*.[32] The argument is one of many instances where Kant added a point in the second

---

[31] Langton (*KH*, 97) argues that a substance cannot 'essentially have relational properties', since this would undermine Kant's belief in the independence of substances. But note that this is still compatible with allowing that *in fact* things in themselves as such could have relational properties. Moreover, even if Kant's earliest work does seem to disallow the essentiality of relational properties for things in themselves (in order to safeguard the independence of substances in a system that still makes no use of notions such as transcendental freedom), my own guess is that all that the Critical Kant held, or needed to hold, is that things in themselves cannot consist *solely* of relational properties, essential or not.

[32] See *KTM*, 272 f., on 'the Relation Argument'.

edition in order to clarify his theory of self-knowledge and to meet the vehement objections that were made to his conclusion that we have only ideal theoretical knowledge about the self. This is a conclusion that went against Kant's own earlier claims in the 1770s, and he did not reach it without careful reflection. He surely understood that the strong claim in the *Critique* that all our determinate theoretical knowledge is merely ideal would have to meet the main challenges of his predecessors. The main challenge here went back to Leibniz and his claim that we do know at least our own self as a substance relatively directly through inner intuition. Kant set out an argument at B67 to meet this challenge head on, and to bring 'closure' to his idealism by asserting that even the last 'Cartesian' reserve of knowledge did not violate his doctrine about how our theoretical philosophy is limited to merely ideal determinations. Kant's discussion is quite complicated, and one can easily misunderstand its conclusion that the mind 'then intuits itself not as it would represent itself if immediately self-active, but as it is affected by itself, and therefore as it appears to itself, not as it is' (B69).

There are a number of 'red herrings' in this argument that our self-knowledge is ideal *because* it involves 'self-affection'. Read in isolation, one could imagine that this passage vindicates the passivity argument, or Langton's argument from the fact of receptivity. But the slightest reflection reveals that it is crucial to ask precisely what it might be about 'affection' that leads Kant to link it with ideality. A number of suggestions arise immediately from this text and related passages. Our self-knowledge is 'affected' insofar as it is in general passive and sensible, and also insofar as (as Kant stresses) we have to exercise, and be subject to, a specific act of 'self-affection' that gathers our thoughts into a synthesis of apperception, and thereby raises them from mere inner sense to knowledge.[33] There is also a distinct kind of affection that Kant takes to be present in self-knowledge insofar as he holds that, at least sometimes, we need not only the judgmental aspect of apperception but also special acts of attention (see B157 n.) and reflection—acts that can be distinct from each other and insufficient for apperception. Kant stresses that these acts tend both to add distortions and to undermine the possibility of an introspective science of mind. Also, in contrasting our self-knowledge with that of a creative intellect, Kant seems to be suggesting that the limited activity of our finite mind testifies to another way in which our involvement with affection introduces a possible distorted character in what we know.[34] What is remarkable, however, is that all the different aspects of 'affection' that I have just mentioned clearly do not by themselves amount to a convincing reason

---

[33] On the distinction of inner sense and apperception, see *KTM*, 241–52.

[34] For a very helpful critical analysis of the 'myth of the giving', the thought that we somehow could know the self (or anything) simply through being active, rather than receptive, see Susan Hurley, *Consciousness in Action* (Cambridge, Mass., 1998), ch. I. 2, 'Self-Consciousness, Spontaneity, and the Myth of the Giving'.

for saying that we are *in principle* limited to knowing the self 'only' as it appears. Passivity and activity, reflection and attention, can all introduce incidental distortions, but they do not amount to a proof—and were never anywhere offered by Kant as a proof—that we *cannot* (theoretically) know the self in itself *at all*. People have been aware of these features for a long time without being led into anything like a doctrine of the ideality of all self-knowledge.

One cannot help but ask if Kant has some other line of argument in mind—and, in fact, he does, and the text makes the relevant line quite obvious. Right before the passage cited from B69, Kant says that '*the form of this intuition, which lies antecedently in the mind, determines, in the representation of time, the mode in which the manifold is together in the mind, since it then intuits itself not as it would represent itself if immediately self-active, but as it is affected by itself*' (B68–9).[35] The same general point is made earlier in the argument when Kant concludes 'that the subject can be represented through it [i.e. the "form of inner sense", time] only as appearance, not as it would judge itself if its intuition were self-activity only' (B68; cf. A37/B54 f.). In other words, the only way of giving any cogent sense to Kant's use of 'affection' here is to take it to stand for the specific kind of affection or limitation that we are subject to because we are subject to the specific *form of time*, a form whose ideality has been argued for earlier on a variety of specific epistemological grounds. Our being merely affected as such, even inwardly, in just any ordinary way, provides no ground at all for concluding that we *could not* know our self in itself as such, and it is no wonder that Kant never fell back on such a simple kind of argument.[36] This is not to say that we must regard as convincing or clear Kant's own complex argument, in either its claims about the ideality of the form of time or about the ideality of all our self-knowledge insofar as we are subject to being 'affected' by this form. But whatever the difficulties of Kant's long arguments for ideality, it is very clear that he made them, and made them repeatedly, and it is not clear why they should be ignored for the sake of arguments that have severe problems of validity and obvious problems of interpretive relevance.

VI

The problems with the short argument to humility are not limited to the difficult area of the self and self-knowledge. There are fundamental objections to accepting this argument *in general*. The specific passages on self-knowledge reveal the basic

---

[35] The passage is discussed in *KH*, 44–6. On affection, cf. *KTM*, 252–5.
[36] What can make matters confusing here is the fact that it is true both that all our spatio-temporal data are ideal and that they are 'affected' in the sense of being receptive—but this does not mean that they are ideal *because* they are affected by receptivity as such rather than by our form of spatio-temporality.

inability of the argument (as long as it does not resort to being stipulative) to address the claim that our knowledge must be ideal *in principle*. The fact of receptivity and some other elementary reflections can, to be sure, show that there is a distinction to be made between the qualities that we ascribe to things themselves and the qualities that we can happen to have in our own mind simply as the result of our contingent sensible situation. At any given moment it is always possible that our sensibility can give us only a distorted view of how things are in themselves. Moreover, if we accept the rejection of a reducibility relation between sensible properties and intrinsic ones, we can say, as Langton does against Leibniz, that we see through a 'broken mirror', and we cannot *assume* that even in an 'indistinct way the relational properties of our phenomenal knowledge reflect the inner natures of things' (*KH*, 127). Nonetheless, this does not by itself rule out the possibility of our making lucky true guesses, or even some kind of indirect arguments, from our sensible data, to those inner natures. Hence, insofar as the short argument approach relies only on considerations of receptivity and irreducibility, it is still far from presenting an argument that historically or systematically can begin to match the grounds that Kant had for blocking *in principle* our claims to know things in themselves, and it is very far from vindicating any claim to blocking even the possibility that we might have some true hypotheses about what those things are like.

In addition, there are general reasons for supposing (against what was called thesis (2) of the short argument) that Kant himself was committed to properties that are simultaneously inherent in things in themselves and in part relational. Langton focuses almost entirely on Kant's very early discussion of causality, in the 1740s and 1750s, but his interest in this issue came to its peak in his *Dissertation* of 1770. Throughout his early work, and despite numerous terminological complications, Kant sought to defend a modified version of a 'real influx' theory that would simultaneously respect the independence of finite substances and provide for a more than nominal (pre-established harmony) or wholly externally imposed (occasionalist) unity.[37] His *Dissertation* solution (given up later solely for epistemic reasons, not because of any noted metaphysical difficulties) was to propose that the unity of mundane substances can come about only from an underlying common cause, namely, God.[38] However, Kant stresses that even God cannot provide a true unity of such substances in just any way. He must respect a condition of what I have elsewhere called the 'Restraint Argument', namely, that there is something in the natures of particular things that distinguishes

---

[37] See the works cited above, n. 27.
[38] Langton notes (*KH*, 137) that 'Kant simply gives up on the problem, thus conceived. Abandoning the question of how a substance can be endowed with relations to form a world, Kant says that what is relevant as far as we are concerned is this: if we are to have experience of anything, then we must already be part of a world of causally interacting substances.'

them and makes it the case that the properties that God causes are not simply His own.[39] As Kant notes, if God causes a thought in me, for that thought to be mine and not His, there must be something in me that can receive the thought.[40] This point implies not only that I must have, as has been stressed so far, some simple intrinsic properties, but also that, given the way the world actually is, I must have some properties in myself that are fit to be acted upon by God and appropriate for fitting together with other substances in one world—in other words, properties with the right kind of relationality.

Langton does not explore this possibility for things in themselves, although she has an extremely useful discussion of the powers of substances. She notes that they do not directly entail particular effects on other substances because, given different laws of nature, the exercise of the powers will naturally have different effects, and perhaps no effects at all. A typical causal power thus has relationality built into its very *concept* (e.g. a power to bleach terrestrial things can be 'in' the sun, even if an obstacle such as clouds could keep the sun from ever actually bleaching such things), without this entailing a dependence of it, or the substance bearing it, on any other actual finite substance (*KH*, 116–18). After noting this point, however, Langton rejects the thought that we should therefore characterize Kantian powers as *intrinsic* properties. She points out that if the laws of nature were to change radically, then a thing that has the same intrinsic properties (properties it would have if it existed alone) as it has now (when it has, for example, the power of attraction in this world) could, in a different world, have a very different power instead. A causal power's properties thus seem to be 'extrinsic', because they are manifestly subject to the contingent laws of nature, which laws in turn, in Kant's philosophy, are subject to the infinite free power (and what might be called the 'superadding' habits) of God.[41]

This view leaves an enormous 'looseness' between intrinsic properties and causal powers, a looseness that Langton welcomes because it fits the sharp line she draws between things in themselves, defined by intrinsic properties, and merely phenomenal objects, which are understood in terms of powers, i.e. relational properties that (given the point just made about the laws of nature and the whims of God) do not 'reduce' to the intrinsic properties. Nonetheless, I do not see why a line has to be drawn *so* sharply in this way, nor why the non-reducibility of relations should lead to a dismissal of all possible (i.e. weaker than reductive) 'grounding' relations between relations and things in themselves. Given Kant's own Restraint Argument, it seems fair enough to say that changes

---

[39] 'The Critique of Metaphysics', 263.
[40] See *Metaphysik Herder*, 28:52; and *Reflexion* 3581, 17:71.
[41] See *KH*, 117, citing 1:415: 'A substance never has the power through its own intrinsic properties to determine others different from itself.... It has only the power in so far as substances are held together in a nexus through the idea of an infinite being.'

in the laws of nature, even by God, need not make *all* the difference.[42] Even if I am put into another world, so that I attract things in a different way than by Newton's laws, it seems possible to believe that there is something about me, even in that world, that has something to do with the power of attraction that I have taken on. Consider another example (inspired by the Restraint Argument): if the way that I think something is *simply* a matter of the laws of the world that God puts me into, then it seems that there is nothing relevant left to me as such, and I am a mere blank tablet on which absolutely anything can be drawn in a way in which I make no difference at all. A way out of this difficulty would be to allow that each thing has a set of relational properties already within it as a thing in itself. Very roughly speaking, these properties would allow for different powers to manifest themselves differently in some different contexts, so that if substance S is switched from world 1 to world 2, then it could take on form S2 rather than just any strange form, and this property S2 would be a *joint product* of its own complex nature and the world in which it is placed. In a similar way (only as an analogy, since the properties here are all phenomenal), we might say that, when a paper looks yellow in a certain light, this is of course very much the product of the light, but it is also to some extent a product of the paper 'in itself', for, with a different color 'in itself', it could have looked somewhat different in this light (even if in some other cases this would not make any difference). Similarly, for Kant a subject might have a good will in itself, as a relational disposition to the moral law and its implications, and yet how this will manifests itself—e.g. in extensive charity or mere justice—can be allowed to differ significantly depending on the world involved, even while the person 'in itself' remains an ineliminable source of the actions.[43] In other words, there may be a way of building relational properties into

---

[42] Cf. *KH*, 119: 'Intrinsic facts don't constrain relational facts in any way, else God would not be unconstrained', and 175: 'powers don't depend on intrinsic properties at all'. But why not 'at all'? Part of the problem here may be the fact that Langton may not realize that Kant, following Baumgarten and the scholastics, was quite aware of complex causal situations where a variety of different causal factors can 'concur' in an effect. (See *Lectures on Metaphysics*, 534–5, for references in the Concordance to many passages on concurrence and related topics.) Such situations leave room for not always tying the notion of causality to strict laws, and so it is no accident that Kant uses the language of concurrence in discussing instances where human freedom, along with other factors such as God, may play a role in something's coming to be. For a discussion of some typical passages, see my 'Kant on Spontaneity: Some New Data', *Proceedings of the VII International Kant-Kongress* 1990, ed. G. Funke (Berlin, 1991), 436–46.

[43] By sharply severing relations between things in themselves and phenomena (see above, n. 42), Langton leaves very mysterious the general relation between the physical (and phenomenal) world and things in themselves: 'If physical properties are the properties physics discusses [viz. relational ones "all the way down"], the conclusion is that there are non-physical intrinsic properties of which we can have no knowledge' (*KH*, 180). She notes, fairly enough, that Kant may still be in a better position than 'contemporary orthodoxy' here, since Kant at least (in insisting on a reference to underlying intrinsic properties) is 'not purporting to give an *explanation* of a physical phenomenon' (p. 176). This point is well taken; I have used very similar arguments to suggest that Kant's own position in philosophy of mind is at least no worse than Colin McGinn's 'transcendental noumenalism', which insists that there is an ultimate natural explanatory ground for all mental events but that it is in principle unknowable by us. (See my 'Kant and Mind: Mere Immaterialism', *Proceedings of the Eighth International Kant Congress* 1995, ed. H. Robinson

VII

A related and final difficulty for Langton concerns the well-known general problem of *transcendental* affection. A traditional objection to Kant's philosophy was that he could not consistently claim to be ignorant about things beyond experience and then also say (as he does) that such things affect us as receptive beings—for claims about this kind of affection would seem to imply knowledge about what is, in part, beyond experience after all. One traditional reply to this objection (and one to which I am still sympathetic) would make use of a general strategy that Langton also adopts in taking Kant's claim about ignorance as meant not really to rule out all kinds of claims beyond experience, but only those that involve some kind of relatively specific (theoretical) determinations. Along something like this line, one might argue that there is nothing wrong with positing simply that there is something 'underlying' experience—because the very notion of a 'mere phenomenon' in some way implies that there is something non-phenomenal.[44] Langton uses a variant of this argument that seems to rely not on a mere analytic implication (of 'mere phenomenon') but rather on a fundamental presumption that, for things to exist at all, there must be substances, and each substance must have some qualities that are intrinsic rather than merely relational. One might well ask where this presumption comes from, but Langton gives plenty of evidence that Kant never questions it (*KH*, 32); and Kant is hardly alone in holding on to the presumption.

This reply does not solve all problems, however, and there is a difficulty that arises precisely because of the main feature that Langton's approach relies on, namely, the sharp parallel distinctions between intrinsic and relational, and 'in itself' and 'merely phenomenal'. The difficulty has to do with the problem in principle of finding a systematic Kantian 'location' for transcendental affection. Kant clearly asserts, and Langton can hardly deny, that for him there is *transcen-*

---

a thing in itself without having to fall back into saying that all these properties involve a reducibility or mere phenomenality of relations.

(Milwaukee, 1995), vol. 1, 675–90.) Nonetheless, the fact that we cannot use features of things in themselves as reductive bases or sufficient 'explanations' (let alone physical explanations) for phenomena does not force us into the conclusion that they play no role at all. To use an analogy: on a traditional theistic view (spelled out in a Plantingian manner), God's freedom can put us into an endless variety of worlds, and in each of these His freedom may play the major role in determining the actual laws of nature and the shape that our evil actions take on; but that the actions are evil can still be due to us and our free essence (in a non-supervening way). It is perhaps no accident that Langton has been most influenced by very early works of Kant that still involve a deterministic perspective and do not express the main ideas motivating Kant's later turn to transcendental idealism.

[44] See B xxvii. A natural way to fill out this idea would be to argue that, once we learn that space and time cannot without contradiction be ascribed to things in themselves, then, unless all is 'mere illusion', there must be some things characterized in themselves in some non-spatio-temporal way.

dental affection, and not merely the kind of relations that occur within the causal context of phenomenal items. But this is to say that transcendental affection is at once non-phenomenal and relational—and Langton's short argument leaves no room for such a possibility. She can easily call ordinary relations (of matter, force, space, etc.) relational and merely phenomenal; and she can just as easily say that the intrinsic and non-relational characteristics of a thing in itself are non-phenomenal. But transcendental affection (which is simply a more indeterminate instance of the general structure underlying the property of absolute freedom discussed earlier) cannot be either simply phenomenal or simply non-relational.

In desperation, one might contend that Kant ought not to have spoken about this kind of affection, but his reasons for doing so are no stranger than those for the other principles that Langton allows. Moreover, accepting such affection still need not lead into an undermining of Kant's general Critical stance, at least as long as one has the charitable and relatively loose way of reading Kant's limits on knowledge that Langton also encourages. To allow the possibility or even the actuality of some transcendental affection is still not to claim to know illicit determinate facts about specific non-phenomenal things. It is not to violate the very bounds of sense. Someone might say that non-empirical causation of any type, for example of non-spatio-temporal items on spatio-temporal items, is immediate nonsense; but the fact is that such talk was allowed for centuries in rational discussions of broadly Platonic and theological contexts, and to claim now that it is dogmatic nonsense is to make a dogmatic metaphysical claim oneself. The main problem here is not with the *sense* of Kant's idealistic theory and its involvement with a doctrine of non-empirical affection. That theory can have sense even if it has obvious problems of vagueness and justification. The main problem is with a line of interpretation of the theory that cannot make clear room for even the possibility of this kind of affection (the 'acid test' of Kantian hermeneutics). For this reason, the difficulties of Langton's impressive efforts force us back once again to seeking an alternative to the whole short argument approach—an alternative that is alive to Kant's metaphysical roots but that stays closer to the central sections of Kant's Critical texts.

PART II

The Second *Critique* and Kant's Practical Philosophy

– 6 –

Kant's Deduction of Freedom and Morality

I

It has always been recognized that within Kant's philosophy the problem of a justification of freedom and the moral law has a central significance.[1] Moreover, for any philosopher interested in a defense of freedom and morality in a strict sense, Kant is no doubt still the figure to whom one would first turn. Yet even among Kant scholars there remains a fundamental unclarity about not only the validity but also the very meaning of Kant's major treatment of these issues in the *Foundations of the Metaphysics of Morals* and the *Critique of Practical Reason*.

In particular, there has been a lack of agreement about how to explain one apparent striking difference between these two texts. In the first work Kant seems to desire and develop a theoretical argument for freedom in a sense that is absolute and from which the objective validity of the moral law is to be deduced. In the second work, however, Kant appears directly to reverse himself and to replace this project of a strict deduction[2] with the idea that the moral law (i.e. its validity, not its entire exact formulation and implications) is simply given as an 'a priori fact of reason' (from which alone freedom can then be inferred).

Most commentators have admitted the appearance of a troublesome conflict here, but they have argued that there is a deeper 'reconciliationist' interpretation which shows that Kant has a position that is both consistent and defensible. Thus,

---

[1] Work on this article was made possible by a grant from the Alexander von Humboldt Foundation. I am also indebted to Professors Gerold Prauss and W. D. Solomon, and to a referee of the *Journal of the History of Philosophy*, in which this paper first appeared.

[2] By 'strict deduction' (or 'categorical proof') here I mean a 'linear' argument intended to be logically sound with premises that are all only theoretical as opposed to practical in any Kantian moral sense. I do not claim that this is generally what Kant must mean by a 'deduction'. (For details on Kant's notion of a 'transcendental deduction' see my 'Kant's Transcendental Deduction as a Regressive Argument', *Kant-Studien*, 69 (1978); and Dieter Henrich, 'Die Deduktion des Sittengesetzes', in *Denken im Schatten des Nihilismus*, ed. Alexander Schwan (Darmstadt, 1975).) My main claim is simply that both the need for something at least approximating a strict deduction of freedom and morality, and a clear attempt to provide one, can be found in Kant's *Foundations of the Metaphysics of Morals*, whereas in Kant's later work this is definitely not the case.

some (e.g. H. J. Paton and Dieter Henrich) have said that in fact the *Foundations* properly anticipates the *Critique* by *not* genuinely meaning to offer a strict deduction. Others (notably Lewis White Beck) have accepted that there *is* something like a strict deduction in the *Foundations* but have taken it to be continued and in effect well continued in the second *Critique*.

These lines of interpretation are obviously in conflict with one another, and I believe they are both unsatisfactory. I will argue not merely that Kant truly does change his position just as he appears to at first sight, but also that in each case he has a view that is intrinsically and Critically suspect. At the same time, I will attempt to vindicate Kant somewhat by showing that his views undergo what is at least an understandable development, and that often the weaknesses of these views are best appreciated on the basis of considerations suggested by Kant himself. Ultimately, however, there remains in Kant a central and insufficiently justified belief in an intrinsic connection between morality and absolute freedom. For other philosophers who still believe in such a connection, there is meant to be a challenge in my conclusion that a sympathetic but rigorous analysis of even Kant's view leaves it entangled in inconsistencies or very suspicious premises. In addition, at a strictly historical level my findings are meant to shed light on the central role of the notion of freedom in the development of Kant's entire system. Kant's attachment to absolute freedom can be shown to be rooted in a surprisingly dogmatic theoretical view of the mind that is held through even the first part of his Critical period. The dynamics of the latter part of that period can then be understood largely in terms of the replacement of inadequately developed theoretical arguments by new grounds for freedom that are practical but still too dogmatic.

In the analysis that follows I will begin with a study of the history of Kant's views (Section II). This will show how for a long time Kant had a very peculiar way of expressing himself which could leave the impression of a much less confident attitude than he really had then toward the possibility of our establishing human freedom. The implications of this study and of further information about Kant's development will then be applied directly to an interpretation of key passages from the *Foundations* and the *Critique* (Sections III and V). This interpretation in turn will be used as a basis for countering the alternative reconciliationist readings of Kant (Sections IV and VI).

II

In the metaphysics lectures of the 1770s, Kant appears to make nine basic points about freedom and morality which are then picked up in his later discussions. It is usually not the points themselves but only the specific support for them that is modified in the course of the discussions in the 'Reflections', the *Critique of Pure*

Reason (1781, 1787), the *Prolegomena* (1783), the 'Review of Schulz' (1783), the *Foundations* (1785), the *Critique of Practical Reason* (1788), and other later writings.[3] The nine points are these:

1. Practical (or comparative) freedom, that is, independence from mere sensual impulses, is to be distinguished from transcendental (or absolute) freedom, that is, independence from anything predetermining a being's action.[4]
2. We can justifiably assert that we have practical freedom.[5]
3. The assertion of practical freedom is sufficient for the needs of morality, that is, the acceptance of the categorical imperative.[6]
4. Compatibilism is unacceptable.[7]
5. Prima facie there are strong theoretical threats (God, science) to the possibility of our transcendental freedom.[8]
6. These threats can be dealt with.[9]
7. We can justifiably assert that we have transcendental freedom.[10]
8. Nonetheless, theoretical philosophy remains in some sense incomplete with respect to the issue of freedom.[11]
9. However, this incompleteness involves only a human 'subjective' difficulty and not the objective validity of practical philosophy.[12]

The most important matters here are the first points, and in particular the difficulty that would develop from the simultaneous assertion of points 1, 3, and 4. A compatibilist can easily accept that lack of or uncertainty about transcendental freedom is no problem for morality. However, in sharp contrast to his own early writings, in these lectures Kant already characterizes compatibilism as giving us nothing more than the freedom of a 'turnspit',[13] and therefore it is hard to believe he would say anything like point 3. What we would expect him to do is rather to say clearly that comparative freedom is precisely not sufficient for morality, that practical philosophy must also have a guarantee of our absolute freedom. Yet instead of doing this, Kant seems to repeat point 3 in his lectures and in a number of his mature publications.[14]

---

[3] Kant's works will be cited according to the following translations and abbreviations: A and/or B = *Critique of Pure Reason*, tr. Norman Kemp Smith (London, 1929); *Critique* = *Critique of Practical Reason*, tr. Lewis White Beck (New York, 1956); *Foundations* = *Foundations of the the Metaphysics of Morals*, tr. L. W. Beck (New York, 1959); *Prolegomena* = *Prolegomena to any Future Metaphysics*, tr. L. W. Beck (New York, 1959); 'Review of Schulz' = 'Rezension zu Johann Heinrich Schulz, "Versuch einer Anleitung zur Sittenlehre für alle Menschen, ohne Unterschied der Religionen"'; R = 'Reflexionen'; *Lectures* = 'Vorlesungen über Metaphysik' except for the 'Reflexionen', which are individually numbered; all citations from Kant will give volume and page numbers from *Kant's Gesammelte Schriften*, 28 vols. (Berlin, 1900–). It should be presumed that all emphases in quotations have been added by me.
[4] *Lectures*, 28: 255, 257. [5] Ibid. 255. [6] Ibid. 267, 269. [7] Ibid. 267.
[8] Ibid. 268. [9] Ibid. 268, 270. [10] Ibid. 267, 268. [11] Ibid. 270.
[12] Ibid. 271. [13] Ibid. 267; cf. B xxvii and *Critique*, 5:97.
[14] Cf. A803/831 and 'Review of Schulz', 8:13.

To make sense of Kant here I think we must introduce some hypotheses to correct the impression that his published work may first leave. First of all, Kant simply cannot have meant that comparative freedom in the absence of absolute freedom is *logically* sufficient for one to be able to accept the categorical imperative. Rather, I will suggest that a large part of what he meant is just that practical freedom is sufficient *in the sense that* any person committed to point 3 (and not himself necessarily in possession of a proof of point 7) would not be making any *material* error, for, given point 6 and other considerations, absolute freedom (i.e. its proof) is (supposedly) always clearly *within reach*, and so the foundation of morality is not really problematic. Thus, we should not understand Kant's statement at various points that it has been proven only that we are 'practically free' to mean that we do not at all need or cannot also have a proof of our absolute freedom. Secondly, I will argue not only that Kant could not and did not literally mean that practical freedom is sufficient for morality, but also that what he meant primarily was that the *proof* of absolute freedom, which we do need and have, has certain peculiarities that make *it* in a sense 'merely practically sufficient'. That is, Kant's main concern here was generally with the fact that we do not and can not have a theoretical proof of absolute freedom *in the sense* of an explanation of *how* such freedom works, that is, a speculative deduction or clarification of its noumenal operation. (Here points 8 and 9 become important.) Thus, we may have to settle with something less than a full theoretical account of freedom and so may be limited to a proof that in this sense is merely practically sufficient. I shall stress, however, that otherwise such a proof could be taken to be a straightforward theoretical deduction of our absolute freedom, and that this has great consequences for the interpretation of Kant's later and better-known texts.[15]

To justify these interpretive hypotheses, some details need to be given about how the points listed earlier are developed in Kant's works. In the lectures the distinction between absolute and comparative freedom is associated with a distinction between what rational and empirical psychology proves.[16] Our independence from mere sensory stimuli is taken to be an evident psychological fact, but one without the universal and absolute meaning that Kant thinks can be drawn out of the pure concept of the cogito. In the lectures he argues that one cannot say 'I think' without implying that one is an ultimate subject or substance, and to be such a thing is just to be independent of external determination, that is,

---

[15] Some have taken Kant rather to mean *simply* that practical freedom is sufficient for practical *philosophy* in that the rules it develops can be *exposited* without entering into the issue of transcendental freedom (see e.g. L. W. Beck, *A Commentary to Kant's 'Critique of Practical Reason'* (Chicago, 1960), 190). However, Kant makes his remarks about sufficiency not in the context of clearly defining branches of philosophy, but rather when speaking about what the common man needs in order to proceed properly (see esp. *Lectures*, 28:267, 269; 'Review of Schulz', 8:13), and so a more complex explanation is called for and can be justified.

[16] *Lectures*, 28:267, 269.

absolutely free.[17] As will be shown, arguments like this one are favored by Kant for a number of years, and I believe they are often what explain his loose talk about practical freedom as sufficient for morality: although our lack of awareness of external determination does not by itself prove the lack of such determination, this need not cause any worry, since a proof (though not an explanation) of the latter lack is always (supposedly) as close to us as our own thoughts.

This confidence can also explain Kant's attitude to points 5 and 6. The prima facie threat to freedom that first concerns him is the omnipotence of God. To this question and the problem of fatalism the notes give no direct solution, but only the observation that the fatalist case is not proved. However, given his concept of the cogito here,[18] Kant could (and later explicitly did) say that that case could not be proved, although this of course does not of itself tell us how we are to understand God's relation to us.[19] That is, to give a proof of our absolute spontaneity is not necessarily to give an explanation of how it operates. This fact constitutes point 8, which is emphasized not only in the lectures but also in nearly all of Kant's later discussions. The lectures also already give the main ground for point 9, namely, that it is only a natural and 'subjective' fact that we cannot 'explain' our freedom, for we happen to be beings who must always explain events by laws of experience, and these obviously are not to be found here.

Kant's use of points 8 and 9 in the lectures is very important because it helps explain why, even when he clearly felt himself in possession of what we would consider to be a straightforward theoretical proof of human freedom, he inclined toward seeing it as inadequate in some sense and hence to calling such a proof merely practical. What contrasts with 'merely practical' here is not proof that in fact we are free, but rather simply a complete theoretical explanation of how such an absolutely free causality works in relation to nature and God. The most revealing passage here is the statement that 'our concept of freedom is practically but not speculatively sufficient. If by reason we could explain our original free actions it would be sufficient.'[20] Kant also says that we 'go beyond the practical' when we ask *how* freedom is possible.[21]

All this confirms our earlier hypothesis that we need not take at face value Kant's suggestions that practical freedom (as in point 1) is sufficient for morality. We can avoid attributing a blatant inconsistency to him by saying that what he really believes is that transcendental freedom is needed (and provable), but that (for the reasons just given) our proof of this freedom is to be called 'merely practically' sufficient. (This belief may be called 3′ and could be used to replace point 3 in a more accurate formulation of Kant's position.) Another reason for

---

[17] Ibid. 268, 269.   [18] Ibid. 267.
[19] This is a problem that gives Kant considerable difficulty later. See *Critique*, 5:100 f.
[20] *Lectures*, 28:270.
[21] Ibid. 269.

Kant's terminology may be that the proof involves a claim about man as a practical being (i.e. one with a will), and in that sense it is not what Kant would call a strictly speculative proof from 'pure transcendental predicates'.[22] In these ways we can understand why the proof might be called merely practical, even though what it would establish is the existence of our absolute freedom, and its manner of proof is a set of straightforward factual (as opposed to deontological) propositions.

In the 'Reflections', there are no great shifts in Kant's position. R4220, R4336, R4723, R7440, and R7441 all support strong claims about proving freedom. If one turns to the *Critique of Pure Reason*, it is easy to find the same general pattern of points that characterized the lectures. In the first *Critique*'s Canon, Kant again distinguishes the transcendental and practical meaning of freedom (A801/B829, point 1). It is even said that practical freedom can be proven by experience (A802/B830, A803/B831). (This constitutes point 2 and also fits my explanation of the first part of R4724.) Kant also says that, although this does not establish transcendental freedom, this 'does not concern us' in 'the practical field' (A803/B831, point 3). Here it may be tempting to try to minimize this statement by ascribing it and the Canon in general to an earlier period than the rest of the first *Critique*, for in the Antinomies Kant clearly says that transcendental freedom is required (A534/B563, point 4).[23] However, the Canon also refers back to the Antinomies (A804/B832), and its formulations are similar to those found in other later texts. Once again, it seems best to assume that when Kant suggested that practical freedom was sufficient he meant that in a peculiar way, and he still felt confident that there was no bar to asserting transcendental freedom.

This confidence is admittedly not as clear in the first *Critique* as it is in Kant's other works closest in time to it. Whether we not only may but also should (on theoretical grounds) assert such freedom is difficult to determine from the section of the first *Critique* that gives the longest treatment of this issue, namely the Antinomies. Kant concludes his discussion there by saying he has not even argued for the possibility[24] of freedom (A558/B586; this page in effect offers points 8 and 9) but has tried only to show that it need not contradict the laws of nature (which now replace God—who is no longer a given in theoretical philosophy—as the backing for point 5). But there are stronger threads in Kant's discussion which can be taken to approach a repetition of point 7, and not merely an allowance that there may be transcendental freedom somewhere. Kant states that if transcenden-

---

[22] *Lectures*, 28:270.

[23] It should also be noted that the term 'practical freedom' is used with a new meaning here (see *Prolegomena*, 4:346), equivalent not, as in our definition, to a mere comparative freedom, but rather to a specific kind of absolute freedom, namely spontaneity in us as an intelligent agent. This point is distinct from but consistent with my observation that a so-called merely practical proof of freedom in Kant can involve a proof of transcendental freedom.

[24] Here one should keep in mind that often by the proof of the 'possibility' of something Kant means a determination of its 'real possibility', and this may be tantamount to requiring evidence of its actuality.

FREEDOM AND MORALITY

tal idealism is accepted, then transcendental freedom is not only a possibility but also a necessity: there must be some ground for appearances that is itself unconditional (e.g. A537/B565). He also obviously believes that independent arguments for the premise of transcendental idealism are available. He even suggests that otherwise nature itself would have to be rejected (A543/B571); that is, without his idealism the only objection to our freedom, namely the universal laws of nature and our apparent complete subjection to them, could not be justified (thus points 5 and 6 are covered; cf. R3855). Thus, the very item that raises the threat to the assertion of transcendental freedom ultimately points to the existence of things in themselves and so to the presence of transcendental freedom. This is consistent with the argument of the thesis in the third antinomy, in which it is claimed that without transcendental idealism we are led to a self-contradictory concept of nature (A446/B474). The argument is very questionable, but Kant never directly questioned it and rather seemed convinced by it.[25]

Thus, although at first sight it can appear that Kant's solution to the third antinomy is to say that both theses can be right in that there may be transcendental freedom although there is no such freedom in the world, his real position seems to be the stronger claim that there must be transcendental freedom outside the world although there can be no such freedom in the world.[26] The dogmatic Observation on the antithesis claims that this latter position is untenable (A451/B479), but the rest of Kant's discussion is aimed precisely at disproving this claim, at showing that transcendental freedom can act on the world without interfering with it (A538/B566 ff.; this supports point 6, but see n. 67 below).

There is still an important gap in the argument here, because, even if for the first *Critique* there must be some transcendental freedom, it is not clear that we must be transcendentally free. Kant tries to bridge this gap somewhat in the Antinomies by saying that in various contexts we all regard humans as transcendentally free (A547/B575), but he hardly builds his remarks into a philosophical proof. Such proof may still be said at least to have been believed in by Kant here, if it is recalled that all he needs are grounds for asserting that we are genuinely substances, that is, that the substrate which we already (supposedly) know must lie behind the phenomenal self is itself a (not numerically distinct) self. Such a belief may seem entirely pre-Critical, but it is striking that the first-edition discussion of the issue in the Paralogisms presents no argument against our mere substantiality. It argues only that this noumenal substantiality is of little use in that it does not prove a

---

[25] See e.g. *Critique*, 5:48.
[26] Only the latter formulation saves the exact formulation of the theses at A444/B472, A445/B473, but this is not so decisive, for Kant is often careless in such formulations. In the *Prolegomena*, for example, he restates the thesis as the claim that there are free causes in the world and the antithesis as the claim that there is absolutely no freedom (4:240)—in which case both statements would be obviously false rather than true. Perhaps Kant wanted to contrast improper dogmatic and proper Critical formulations here, but he hardly did this clearly.

phenomenally substantial, that is eternal, existence for our personality (A349–51). The 'sophisma figurae dictionis' in the first paralogism corresponds exactly to the one Kant attributes to the antinomies in general: from the transcendental premise that the conditioned requires the unconditioned (as our representations require an ultimate subject) and the minor premise that we are given something empirically conditioned (e.g. the predications of thought), it is falsely concluded that we are given something *empirically* unconditioned (e.g. a first mover, or absolute, i.e. eternal, empirical substance) (A500/B520). Kant here does not question the material validity of the premises, the claim that there must be some unconditional transcendental items, something underlying things in general as well as an ultimate subject underlying our thoughts and transcendentally free (see also A546).

Some years later Kant revised his Paralogisms, but in the meantime he consolidated rather than altered his position. In the *Prolegomena*, for example, the only positive addition to the topic of morality and freedom is a clear attempt to show that we do have a special reason to say that the transcendental freedom we know must exist somewhere in fact exists (at least) in ourselves. Kant stresses that not only do we feel a need to posit our transcendental freedom, but also when we do, then the natural way to conceive its influence—namely, according to moral laws—is such that it is particularly well adapted to give us a form of transcendental freedom that meets the difficulties presented by laws of nature. This is 'because [moral] grounds of reason give the rule universally to actions according to principles, without influence of the circumstances of either time or place'.[27] It is not clear whether here Kant means this to justify claiming that moral beings like us and only such beings are demonstrably free, but it is clear that he thinks at least a strong prima facie case has been built for this claim.

Kant was drawn to strengthen his case by the publication in 1783 of Johann Schulz's *Sittenlehre*, which tries to find a place for morality within a fatalistic metaphysics. In his brief 'Review of Schulz', Kant runs through the now familiar main points of his position: the distinction between transcendental and practical freedom, the rejection of compatibilism, and the perplexing suggestion that our practical freedom is evident and sufficient for morality.[28] These claims can be understood as usual if Kant has in the background a ready argument for asserting transcendental freedom, and in particular one that he understands to locate such freedom directly in us. In fact, Kant appears to present just the kind of argument that could be expected from the lectures and the 'Reflections'. He says that the mere claim to judge, that is to think objectively rather than simply submit to the mere casual 'play' of subjective data, implies a 'freedom to think', and that similarly when we undertake to act objectively, this involves a freedom to act.[29]

---

[27] *Prolegomena*, 4:345.   [28] 'Review of Schulz', 8:13.   [29] Ibid. 14.

Kant's argument here is not only brief and suspicious (conflating 'subjective' with 'merely subjective'), but also ambiguous and especially difficult to evaluate. At first Kant seems to be making an extremely strong claim, in the old style, about our (transcendental) freedom as derivable from features that are found in, or are closely analogous to, those found in the self's existence as a cogito. But Kant ends his review with a touch of hesitation: he says only that one must presuppose freedom if one will have morality and do one's duty. That man is absolutely free to act is not said to be directly proved. Rather, it is simply concluded that, if we cannot ever bring this 'practical presupposition' into harmony with speculative principles, 'not much is lost'.[30] It is possible to take this last phrase as but another way of making points 8 and 9, that is as a signal that we can never explain how our absolute freedom operates, especially in relation to God, even if we can be sure about its existence. But it is also possible rather to be struck by the lack of a distinct claim backing point 7 and by the introduction of a new hypothetical formulation: Kant says that 'as soon as' he is to 'do his duty', 'even the most hardened fatalist' must act 'as if' he were free.[31] This formulation is troublesome, for if we cannot have grounds for saying that we are really absolutely free, there is something odd (given Kant's anti-compatibilism) about acting as if we are; and if we could have such grounds, there is something odd about not appealing to or seeking them and instead resting content with an as-if attitude.[32]

The troublesome formulations in the 'Review of Schulz' have an influence on Kant's next work, the *Foundations*, which also adds several new complications. It would be nice to be able simply to assert that the *Foundations* attempts to improve upon the 'Review' by offering a clearer case against fatalism and for a categorical deduction of freedom. Unfortunately, although I believe this is the way the *Foundations* is ultimately to be understood, some complex exposition is needed here, especially in view of the famous contrast Kant makes in the *Foundations* between our being known to be free 'in a practical respect', that is, having to act 'under the idea of freedom', and our not being able to know we are free in a 'theoretical respect'.[33] I will now briefly suggest how this passage can be handled and explain what the general difficulties of the *Foundations* are; then, in the next section, I will give a detailed analysis of the text to clarify these difficulties and confirm my hypothesis that it culminates longstanding efforts on Kant's part categorically to establish our transcendental freedom.

In the passage just cited, we now can see the importance of the previous examination of what Kant means when saying that it is being shown 'only' that we are 'free in a practical respect'. It is tempting to understand this as meaning only that we are merely 'practically free' (as defined in point 1 above) or, as some

---

[30] Ibid. [31] Ibid.
[32] A similar point is made in W. D. Ross, *Kant's Ethical Theory* (Oxford, 1954), 73.
[33] *Foundations*, 4:448.

have thought (see n. 116 below), as meaning 'only' that we cannot help but do as if we are free but cannot say we are really free. However, although Kant does use the phrase 'as if' here, he does not mean thereby to question our transcendental freedom. What he says is that to know we are 'really free in a practical respect' *is* to know the *validity* of the law of a free will just 'as if its will were explained to be [*erklärt*] free by theoretical philosophy'.[34] This means that what a proof of our freedom 'in a theoretical respect' would add would be nothing about the truth of our freedom or its relevant practical consequences. We can presume that all it would add would be the 'theoretically sufficient' or 'strictly speculative' explanation (*Erklärung*) about how freedom operates that Kant spoke of earlier. Precisely this point is emphasized by Kant at the end of the *Foundations*, when he juxtaposes the claim that our freedom can be said to be 'unconditionally necessary' with the claim that 'how' this freedom is possible 'can never be discerned by any human reason'.[35] The problem in the latter case involves the opacity to us of noumenal mechanics, for example the difficulty of explaining how 'pure reason by mere Ideas' is able to 'instill a feeling of pleasure and satisfaction in the fulfillment of duty', that is, 'an effect which does lie in experience'.[36]

What makes matters especially complicated here is that, although Kant's ultimate statement on human freedom in the *Foundations* is categorical, when he originally speaks about showing our freedom 'in a practical respect', his discussion is not a proof but rather, as he says, a preparatory elucidation.[37] He means at first only to explain that, if it can be shown that because of some a priori quality beings must act 'under the Idea of freedom', then it can be asserted that they are free. Obviously, much still hinges on finding such a quality and determining that we have it, and it is in this context that the notorious problem arises of a vicious circle in Kant's discussion of freedom and morality. If the necessity that we act under the idea of freedom is just one placed on us insofar as we feel bound by morality, then we do not have the categorical foundation for freedom needed here if morality is to be strictly deduced. A circle can be escaped only if independent reasons (i.e. reasons that do not themselves appeal to the validity of the moral law) can be given for our having to act under the idea of freedom.

Matters would be much simpler if it could be assumed that this is the only circle that can threaten the *Foundations*. However, when Kant says that he is presenting a 'deduction' in the third section of the *Foundations*, he makes clear that it has two parts: to show (i) that we are transcendentally free (and so a necessary condition of Kantian morality is established) and (ii) that the validity of the categorical imperative follows from what we are 'directed to' by this fact (and so sufficient conditions are also established).[38] Circles could thus arise with respect to either of these two parts. A circle can arise directly for the second part (the argument 'from

---

[34] *Foundations*, 4:448 (amended translation).   [35] Ibid. 461.
[36] Ibid. 460; cf. 453.   [37] Ibid. 447.   [38] Ibid.

freedom') if one argues for morality on the basis of freedom and then is able to defend freedom only by appealing to morality. But there may also be a circle threatening the first part (the argument 'to freedom') of Kant's deduction, namely if one tried to establish this freedom by appealing to morality and then could justify the latter only by claiming one's freedom. I shall proceed now to analyze Kant's text in terms of this distinction between the part of the deduction that is an argument *to* freedom and the part that is an argument *from* freedom. Only in the full course of the analysis will the significance of the distinction and the consequences for other interpretations that have failed to pay adequate heed to it become clear.

III

It was just noted that, if the *Foundations* is to make a strict deduction, it should show in some non-question-begging fashion that we are beings who are under the necessity of acting under the idea of freedom. Yet instead of attending directly to this specific issue, Kant first argues that *any* rational being with a will stands under such a necessity. Kant's argument here is no surprise after what was said in his 'Review of Schulz':

> In such a being we think of a reason which is practical, i.e. a reason which has causality with respect to its objects. Now, we cannot conceive of a reason which consciously responds to a bidding from the outside with respect to its judgments, for then the subject would attribute the determination of its power of judgment not to reason but to an impulse.... [So] the will of a rational being can be a will of its own only under the idea of freedom.[39]

This argument brings thinking and willing even closer together than in Kant's earlier one, but at this point it remains as unclear and hypothetical. If a being, qua thinking, is to have a 'will of its own', then this can be taken to mean that its judging acts (like all others) must have their absolute source in him. But this still does not show that the idea of such a rational will is anything more than a 'mere phantom'. Kant may be right that if there were such a will then it would have to regard itself as having a 'will of its own', but it does not follow that anyone who regards himself as having a will of his own has such a will. A fortiori, it does not follow that we have such a will, even if we happen to regard ourselves as having one, for it is not clear that we have to regard ourselves in such a way.[40] This may be why Kant characterizes the discussion as a 'mere preparation' and immediately goes on to say, 'we could not prove freedom to be real in ourselves and in human

---

[39] Ibid. 448; cf. *Lectures*, 28:268, and 'Review of Schulz', 8:14.
[40] Cf. Henrich, 'Die Deduktion des Sittengesetzes'. 67; and Rüdiger Bittner, 'Kausalität als Freiheit und kategorischer Imperativ', *Zeitschrift für philosophische Forschung*, 32 (1978), 448.

nature. We saw only that we must presuppose it if we would think of a being as rational and conscious of his causality with respect to actions, that is, as endowed with a will.'[41]

Obviously, what still must be shown is an independent necessity for asserting that we have a rationality that requires absolute and not mere comparative freedom. Rather than turn directly to this problem, however, Kant goes on to the argument *from* freedom to morality. Here for the first time he suggests the problem of a circle, and he says it has to do with the difficulty of 'proving the reality and objective necessity' of the moral law 'by itself'.[42] This is rather striking, for it means that Kant sees the primary difficulty of his deduction as lying in its second part, the argument *from* rather than *to* freedom. Although, as Kant has just admitted, that first part has not yet been categorically established, what he wishes to discuss is rather 'what follows' from our freedom once it is posited. What Kant says 'follows' is 'the consciousness of a law of action', that is, that the maxims we choose should be able to serve as universal laws. What he focuses on then is the fact that this step is not yet clearly established; it is not evident why one should have to subject oneself to such a law. It is true that, if we *define* a rational will as a will of its own in the sense that it is to obey only self-legislated principles, principles which according to Kant can be only of a universalizable type, then subjection to morality can follow from freedom of will. But the entailment involves a kind of circle, for the free rational will that is the premise leads to morality only because its freedom is understood not as mere (negative) transcendental freedom, but as autonomy. Thus, Kant says that

> there is a kind of circle here from which it seems that there is no escape. We assume that we are free in the order of efficient causes so that we can conceive of ourselves as subject to moral laws in the order of ends. And then we think of ourselves as subject to these laws because we have ascribed freedom of the will to ourselves. This is circular because freedom and self-legislation of the will are both autonomy and thus are reciprocal concepts.[43]

Kant's self-analysis here is not easy to follow. Paton, for example, says that 'in plain fact the objection [of the above vicious circle] totally misrepresents [Kant's] argument. He never argued from the categorical imperative to freedom.'[44] On the face of it, this diagnosis seems correct although perplexing, for it is odd that Kant should be so unclear about his own argument. Here I believe it is helpful to keep in mind the two-part structure of the deduction. It is true that with respect to the first part, the argument to freedom, Kant here did not explicitly

---

[41] *Foundations*, 4:448–9. Cf. ibid. 450: 'That we ought to detach ourselves, i.e. regard ourselves as free in acting ... we still cannot see.'
[42] Ibid. 449.
[43] Ibid. 450.
[44] H. J. Paton, *The Categorical Imperative* (1947; reprinted New York, 1967), 225.

argue from the categorical imperative, but rather simply observed that if we are rational in a specific sense, then freedom follows. However, the main problem with this argument for Kant is not, as one might expect, that we have not yet established that we should ascribe rationality (in the appropriate sense) to ourselves. Rather, the problem seems to be with finding a ground for saying that our rationality must be regarded as independent of 'foreign influences' not only in the sense of not being sufficiently determined by 'impulses', but also in the sense of not being guided by any other than its own principles. That is, for the second part of the deduction we need (as a starting point) not mere transcendental or negative freedom but rather freedom in the positive sense that Kant calls autonomy (for it would seem that one could be negatively free and yet evil or indifferent, and so not positively free), and the argument presented by Kant from the nature of judging does not by itself have any good promise of getting us that far. To get that far we need a stronger premise, and the only one Kant mentions in his discussion here is 'the already assumed importance of moral laws'.[45]

We can now give some sense to Kant's diagnosis that in the first part of his deduction 'we assume that we are free in the order of efficient causes so that we can conceive of ourselves as subject to moral laws'. Although he did not explicitly argue first from a subjection to morality and then to our freedom (only later to argue to the validity of the moral law—which would make for a very small circle and not a 'hidden' one), it still seems that in effect this is the only way he could get to the positive and not merely negative kind of freedom that the second part of his argument needs. What disturbs Kant is thus the nature of the freedom argued for (so the argument from freedom can get going) and not a fear that no kind of transcendental freedom can be established (such that the argument to freedom cannot be concluded). However, if Kant could find a proof of an adequately strong freedom without antecedently appealing to morality, then he would not only have a chance for a non-circular argument from freedom, but also could have a more effective one to freedom. This fact is quite relevant to the discussion that follows[46] in which Kant claims to remove the suspicion of a 'hidden circle'. In particular, it can explain the odd fact that at the beginning and end of the discussion Kant speaks only of what follows when we think of ourselves as free, whereas in between what he discusses are new grounds for claiming that we are free in the first place. If, as I have suggested, what Kant was drawing attention to earlier was in effect the need for a better way of arguing to freedom, so that his argument from freedom would have a chance, then it is only natural that now Kant would go into the details of the former while emphasizing the latter in his preview and review.

[45] *Foundations*, 4:450. [46] Ibid. 450–53.

Kant's new discussion depends heavily on the development of a concept that previously had been only mysteriously alluded to as the 'third term' that would be needed to complete the deduction.[47] This third term is the concept of membership in an 'intelligible world'. The argument is not simply that if we are members of that world we are free, but rather that at one and the same time we can see that we are free and have such membership, and from such membership we finally can find the (supposedly non-circular) conditions for our subjection to the moral law. This argument can be persuasive only if what supposedly allows one to see all this is something more than Kant's earlier brief reference to the nature of judging. In fact, Kant's argument here becomes only much more complicated rather than convincing. At first Kant seems to concede that judging as such need not prove even mere transcendental freedom, for he says that the understanding is in a way bound to sensibility.[48] He therefore shifts to another aspect of rationality and also for the first time asserts that man does find rationality in himself.[49] Although everything would appear to hinge on this newly emphasized aspect of rationality, it is only briefly characterized as the 'pure spontaneity' exhibited in our having 'ideas' (a term that is apparently to be understood as designating the special concepts discussed in the Dialectic of the first *Critique*).[50] Moreover, in later summarizing his argument to freedom Kant makes no direct reference to ideas and seems rather to be saying little more than he did in his first formulation:

The title to freedom of the will claimed by common reason is based on the consciousness and the conceded presupposition of the independence of reason from merely subjectively determining causes.... the consciousness of itself as intelligence, i.e. as independent of sensuous impressions.[51]

In the end, although Kant feels that this 'presupposition' must be conceded and categorically affirms it himself, he does not clarify his grounds and rather says only that otherwise we would have to deny that man is a 'rational and rationally active cause, i.e. a cause acting in freedom'.[52] Here Kant never gives compatibilism a chance, never notes that, although what we intend when we use our understanding and reason may appear transcendently *intended*, our *intending* it nonetheless might be sufficiently explained by a natural process that involves nothing transcendent in *us*.

Instead of firmly shoring up the first part of his deduction, Kant seems to take it for granted and is fascinated rather by the belief, expressed clearly only in a later section, that now he has formulated its conclusion (viz. that we are free *intelligences*) in such a way that 'this thought certainly implies the idea of an order and legislation different from that of natural mechanism'.[53] This emphasis on an intelligible order is one-half of Kant's new strategy for completing his deduction.

---

[47] *Foundations*, 4:450, 447. [48] Ibid. 452. [49] Ibid. [50] Ibid. [51] Ibid. 457.
[52] Ibid. 458. [53] Ibid. Cf. *Critique*, 5:42.

To know that we are 'intelligible' in the sense of not being determined by sensuality is still not to know what our nature is; but if we know that our being intelligible makes us part of a distinct 'order', then that order must be positively defined and, presumably, by laws of autonomy. The second part of Kant's strategy is also elaborated only in another, later section of his discussion,[54] in which an argument is presented for saying that, given that we belong to an intelligible as well as sensible (natural) order, we should feel bound to serve the former. This argument rests on the claim that in general the intelligible world is the ground of the sensible one, and thus its rules should be preferred, and so in particular the rules of one's 'proper self' (as a member of the intelligible world legislating autonomous rules of conduct) should be given dominance over the rules of one's mere natural apparent self.[55]

In the original discussion that supposedly removes the suspicion of a hidden circle in Kant's argument, neither of these vital points is clearly set out. Instead, Kant emphasizes a peculiar argument (to be called the passivity argument) that the mere passivity of our sensible representations entails there being something in itself distinct from them and hence that even our own self, which we know through sensibility, has a distinct non-sensible nature in itself.[56] How Kant could even suggest an argument such as this is a mystery that eventually will have to be faced; first, it should be noted simply that by itself the argument is quite inadequate to do any real work in the deduction, and that hence it is only fair to appeal to the later remarks. Even if we granted that the argument shows that all things known by us have a sensible and an intelligible (noumenal) side, this by itself does not show our transcendental freedom, let alone our autonomy or subjection to morality. It needs to be shown that the intelligible side constitutes a realm of laws and that they relate to our will and should be given precedence by us—and whatever can show all this would seem to make the passivity argument dispensable. The real needs of the deduction are addressed (even if perhaps not met) not by the passivity argument but by the points later in Kant's discussion that were referred to above. Only they respond to the crucial need recognized by Kant in the end when he stresses that it is not enough to show, as he did in the first *Critique*, that transcendental freedom need not contradict nature:

> It must show not only that they [natural causality and transcendental freedom] can very well coexist but also that they must be thought of as necessarily united in one and the same subject; for otherwise no ground could be given why we should burden reason with an idea which, though it may without contradiction be united with another that is sufficiently established, nevertheless involves us in a perplexity which sorely embarrasses reason in its speculative use.[57]

---

[54] *Foundations*, 4:453–5.   [55] Ibid. 457, 461.   [56] Ibid. 451.   [57] Ibid. 456

IV

However one may judge its success, it is most significant that the *Foundations* at least sees what Kant's philosophy needs with respect to freedom and that it tries to meet that need. It does not rest content with the mere logical possibility of transcendental freedom, nor does it rest with saying that we can act as if we are free or as if there is some basis, but not a strong theoretical one, for saying that we are free. Kant sees that nothing less than transcendental as opposed to practical (in the sense of mere comparative) freedom will do *for him*, and also that *mere* transcendental freedom is not enough, that what must be shown is that this freedom is *in us*, and in such a way that it points to our subjection to morality. In Kant's later works these views are repeated except for one very important difference: he expressly no longer allows any theoretical argument to freedom. Kant continues to hold that freedom (in a positive sense in us) is certain, but now he says that this can be asserted only as a consequence of the 'a priori fact' that we see the moral law as binding.[58]

In effect, no strict deduction, let alone a non-circular one, of the moral law (i.e. of the validity in general of morality as opposed to the best formulation of its supreme principle) is offered, and no non-moral proof of freedom is given. (Thus, Kant uses the term 'fact' here precisely as a contrast to what is a mere consequence of a proof.[59]) Instead of a solution to the earlier charge of a circularity in the deduction, the original project of a deduction is in effect given up. Only freedom (now called 'the keystone of the whole architectonic of the system of pure reason'[60]) is argued for, and this on the basis of the ultimately un-argued-for premise of the validity of morality (and the unacceptability of compatibilism).

Instead of taking up the old problem of a vicious circle, Kant merely notes that there is no inconsistency in his present position, which takes freedom as the *ratio essendi* of the moral law and the latter as the (unique) *ratio cognoscendi* of freedom.[61] Strictly speaking, Kant is consistent here, but this does not compensate for the fact that the claim of transcendental freedom is not metaphysically secured, and that the matter that was originally primarily suspected of being only circularly grounded—namely, morality—is not grounded in a deduction. Similarly, the charge of circularity in arguing to freedom can be met, but this means little. Before, the assertion of our freedom seemed to be based on the assertion of morality, which in turn rested on an appeal to freedom. Now, instead of the last step, which does involve a circular grounding, no step at all and so no theoretical grounding is offered. In the place of ambitious but understandable attempts at a

---

[58] See *Critique*, 5:6, 31, 42, 43, 47, 55, 91, 104; *Lectures*, 28:582, 773; R7201, R7317, R7321, R8105; *Schriften*, 27:480; and for other references, Beck, *Commentary*, 166 n.
[59] *Critique*, 5:31.
[60] Ibid. 5.
[61] Ibid. 4.

strict deduction, Kant has fallen back into the invocation of an alleged a priori fact of practical reason.

The major interpreters have not been willing to accept at face value the enormous contrast between Kant's views here. Beck says that Kant's note in the second *Critique* (cited above) handles 'in a very concise and effective manner' the problem of a vicious circle.[62] Yet, as has just been shown, this note really is not directed to and cannot offer anything in the way of a solution to the difficulties that originally came under the heading of the problem of a circle. In another and more developed analysis, Beck contends that elsewhere in the body of the second *Critique* Kant presents considerations that in effect amount to a successful completion of the original deduction and thus a resolution of the circularity problem. Paton, on the other hand, argues instead that the circle is a 'side issue', and that what seemed like a deduction in the *Foundations* is best understood as a set of considerations that properly also do not go anywhere without moral premises and so are in (implicit if not explicit) harmony with the second *Critique*. I think both of these lines of interpretation distort Kant's texts and would not be even tempting were it not for the fact that rejection also leaves a very perplexing situation, namely, an apparent total reversal of positions by Kant on a central issue in the heart of his supposedly mature and settled Critical period.

The analysis presented so far may seem to increase this perplexity, for it implies that, if Kant offers no strict deduction of freedom and morality in the second *Critique*, this conflicts not only with what the *Foundations* attempts, but also with what it clearly and properly perceives as desirable. If one looks back at the *Foundations*, it is not hard to find fault with the specifics of Kant's attempt to carry out a deduction, but it is difficult to see anything very wrong with what he says about his need for one, and so it is very hard to see how later he could ignore that need. (Later Kant refers back to only the first two parts of the *Foundations*.[63]) I suggest that the only way to make sense of this situation is to face Kant's texts literally and to hypothesize that earlier Kant made such a point about a deduction only because (as before) he thought one could be easily provided; that meanwhile he discovered that *the* way he believed in was not a tenable or appropriate one for him; that thus out of necessity he had to renounce the attempt metaphysically to ground freedom or morality; and that, finally, it was only to make a virtue of necessity[64] that (given his deepest beliefs of longest standing) he felt it was proper

---

[62] *Commentary*, 59.

[63] See *Critique*, 5:8.

[64] Here I also differ with one of the few developed interpretations that does not carry out a reconciliationist line, namely Karl-Heinz Ilting's 'Der naturalistischer Fehlschluss bei Kant', in *Rehabilitierung der praktischen Philosophie*, ed. Manfred Riedel, 2 vols. (Freiburg, 1972), 1:126. Ilting says that Kant gave up the deduction not because he saw it was 'shattered', but because he had no 'need' for it, for he thought he could replace it with a reference to the willingness of people to sacrifice their lives on moral grounds (*Critique*, 5:30). Ilting puts an implausible weight on this reference and in any case does not explain why Kant does not

to announce that without the moral law 'we never could have been justified in assuming anything like freedom'.[65] I shall present the textual evidence for this complex hypothesis first and will come back at the end to deal with the opposing interpretations.

V

If now we look back to evaluate the deduction in the *Foundations*, we should recall that it involved three major steps. First, there is the argument to freedom in a negative transcendental sense. This step is originally based on the supposed implications of mere judging; later reference is made to a special faculty of ideas. The second step, which is filled out in the course of the reformulation of the backing for the first, is to characterize positively the transcendental self as subject to distinct rational laws (for action) of its own. Finally, it is argued these laws constitute morality and are to be obeyed because they represent one's 'proper self', one's being in itself, which is the foundation of one's mere appearance. All these steps can be severely criticized: the first, for not giving a fair chance to compatibilism and to a more sophisticated treatment of subjective causal grounds (which may do what 'mere impulse' can not to explain judgments or ideas); the second, for presuming too quickly that what is beyond nature must nonetheless be like nature in being a realm defined by a set of rational laws; and the third, for drawing normative consequences from what is at best an ontological truth, a truth that would in any case leave mysterious how it is that the supposedly 'grounding' intelligible self has at all allowed there to be an apparent self conflicting with it.[66] It cannot be said that these are the only objections possible here, but I believe that other familiar difficulties such as the mere comprehensibility of transcendental freedom (which is supposed to affect but not interfere with nature)[67] have been

---

make any use of the deduction. As I will show, the historical evidence gives us an answer here by indicating that Kant did see that his proof was shattered.

[65] *Critique*, 5:4 n.

[66] There are also other problems here. Kant argues, 'if I were a member of only that [intelligible] world, all my actions *would* always be in accordance with the autonomy of the will. But since I intuit myself at the same time as a member of the world of sense, my actions *ought* to conform to it' (*Foundations*, 4:454). But a naturalist might say similarly that if he were a member of only the world of sense, all his actions would be in accord with it, and so if he intuits himself at the same time as a member of another world, he still ought to do what he 'otherwise' (as a naturalist) always would have done.

[67] Here Jonathan Bennett's *Kant's Dialectic* (Cambridge, 1974) is typical. At times Bennett reads into some of Kant's ambiguous and early formulations the view that a second noumenal world would literally interfere in the course of the phenomenal one (pp. 199–200). Yet he generally sees that this is not Kant's view and objects then that freedom (in Kant's system) cannot 'act' on the world (p. 200; cf. Beck, *Commentary*, 92: 'If the possession of noumenal freedom makes a difference to the uniformity of nature, then there is no uniformity. If it does not, then to call it freedom is a vain pretension'). This is not a sound objection, for without any literal intervention, surely the noumenal can act on the phenomenal in the sense of being a (timeless) condition of it, in that, were the noumenal (e.g. one's character) different, the phenomenal would have been different. (Contrary to Beck, then, it is logically possible for there to be complete uniformity to

too strongly emphasized, and so these do represent in my view the major problems.

The mere fact that there are problems in Kant's argument is not itself that significant; for, although he appears to believe he has a strict deduction, he also properly indicates that all he must have are some good overriding reasons for our freedom in the strong sense that he understands it. Moreover, the weakness in the second step is not crucial for our purposes. Even in the second *Critique*, Kant held that autonomy and freedom are reciprocal concepts, although he no longer needed such an argument to autonomy (since this followed from the assumed fact of morality). That is, Kant argued that 'granted that a will is free', 'the law which alone is competent to determine it necessarily is a law of autonomy',[68] and he simply did not question that a free will must be 'determinable necessarily', that is that there must be some sort of laws analogous to nature fully governing it.[69] Kant's later distinction between *Wille* and *Willkür* in his book on religion implies a step beyond this presumption, but in fact it was never adequately developed by him.[70] Thus, if there is any rationale behind Kant's giving up the deduction of the *Foundations*, it must rest in a new attitude to the first and third steps, and in particular on a belief that these steps not only had not been convincingly carried out, but also cannot be carried out (without an antecedent appeal to morality) with any persuasiveness.

In what follows, the key claim that there is such a rationale will be backed by evidence of this new attitude in Kant quite soon after the *Foundations*. That this attitude replaces a view that was entrenched but only fully articulated shortly

our actions and yet for us to be absolutely responsible for them. For were we intelligibly different, we could have grounded another phenomenally uniform character, since obviously there is more than one possible way in which a being could have a 'uniform' phenomenal character. In defending this logical possibility I still of course do not mean to say that it, as opposed to a compatibilistic theory, points to a preferable concept of human freedom.) Bennett further complains that Kant's theory does not allow us a 'channel' to 'explain' and assess phenomenal occurrences by reference to the noumenal (*Kant's Dialectic*, p. 204), but this is precisely what Kant would regard as a virtue or at least an appropriate aspect of theory. The consequence is not, as Bennett fears (in citing Beck, *Kant's Dialectic*, 188), that we must say that my freedom operates 'if anywhere, then everywhere', that it may just as well be thought to be behind my heart's beating or digestion (pp. 189, 202). Kant simply does not require that our transcendental freedom be omnipotent. Such freedom can lie in an absolute choice with respect to a restricted range of alternatives and hence within the bounds of initial conditions laid down by God and not by us. A Kantian can say that the assertion of transcendental freedom (not to 'explain' anything but only to secure a supposedly necessary condition of genuine action) can be made only when (on Kant's later theory) relevant moral phenomena lead us to it, and that, at least in our own case (given the validity of morality and Kant's anti-compatibilism), such an assertion is fitting. Of course, as Kant himself notes, the ultimate evaluation of the scope and intention of this freedom can remain even in our own case beyond our ken, but this is no excuse for us to withhold ascribing any freedom or to pretend that the whole notion of transcendental freedom in a lawful world is incoherent. It still can remain certain and consistent within a Kantian framework to say that, to the extent that a particular matter is regarded as a moral phenomenon, to that extent one must regard it as founded in absolute freedom.

[68] *Critique*, 5:29; cf. 31.
[69] Cf. Ibid. 43.
[70] See *Schriften*, 6:226–7.

before is already evident from our analysis of Kant's earlier Critical writing. Although he had always definitely believed he had a strict proof of transcendental freedom 'in hand', Kant had never before so clearly emphasized it.

For example, it has been noted already that the Antinomies, which Kant himself designated as containing the key thought of his new Critical system, simply fails to make a clear statement on transcendental freedom in general. If one turns to the Paralogisms, the part of the *Critique of Pure Reason* that one would expect to lay down a doctrine about human freedom in particular, an even less clear picture emerges. This need not have been so, for if Kant had simply kept to the structure of his discussion of the soul in the lectures, he would have made freedom the topic of his fourth Paralogism.[71] What he did instead was rather inexplicably to substitute the topic of the external world. At first sight this shift might seem justified by the new desire to fit all discussions onto the table of categories, but as even Kant in effect concedes elsewhere, his new topic scarcely meets this desire any better. The shift might also be thought to be explained by saying that Kant simply lost faith in his earlier argument for freedom from the nature of the cogito. But texts, even after the first edition of the first *Critique*, such as the *Foundations*, hardly indicate any basic loss of faith here, and in any case such a loss would rather have been a justification for bringing the discussion of freedom into the Critical framework of the Paralogisms. Hence it is more likely that a major reason why Kant did not directly continue with this topic was that he did still believe that our freedom can be speculatively grounded (see A547/B575). It cannot be said that such a belief is so much out of line with the tenor of the first *Critique* that it could not have been held then; for, as was indicated earlier (and can be shown in more detail),[72] even the Paralogisms do not say much against similar basic rationalistic beliefs about the immateriality and simplicity of our being. It is true that systematic suspicions are raised against certain ways of arguing about the soul, and in particular about making too much out of the formal requirement of unity in apperception, but Kant clearly had not thought through all the ways these suspicions could be developed. If he had, a number of his later writings would be inexplicable, and the arguments to freedom in the *Foundations* would be totally mysterious. At the same time, it is understandable that Kant would not say too much in the first *Critique* to elaborate on his beliefs about the soul as a free immaterial being, for such elaboration would clearly complicate the proper Critical claims he wanted to make against rational psychology, and in any case it would have seemed to Kant that this could wait until the development of the practical philosophy he thought he would soon publish.

Given these considerations and the lack of convincing alternatives, I think it is possible and preferable to take the arguments of the *Foundations* at face value and

---

[71] See *Lectures*, 28:267.   [72] See my *Kant's Theory of Mind* (Oxford, 1982).

to see them merely as a slightly more self-conscious continuation of some relatively crude beliefs about freedom that Kant had held for some time and simply had not gotten around to submitting to a thorough critique. Moreover, it is only if we ascribe such a fundamentally lax attitude to Kant that any sense can be made of the odd passivity argument interjected in the *Foundations*. As has been noted, this argument does not serve an essential function in the primary task of the text—the *deduction* of freedom and morality. It rather serves to introduce a supposedly helpful *association* between the passive and merely phenomenal on the one hand and the active and noumenal on the other hand. Even in Kant's system this association cannot be let stand in this crude form. Although Kant seems to believe that something actively represented is necessarily seen in itself, it at no point is shown generally that something passively represented must be represented phenomenally and not as it is in itself.

Furthermore, taken literally, this association is not used in the rest of Kant's discussion, for what he goes on to argue is that there is an aspect of the self (spontaneity) known as it is in itself not specifically because it is actively represented, but rather because it (supposedly) involves an active represent*ing*.[73] Yet even though the passivity argument as such can play no valid essential role, Kant clearly needs something like it to set up the *suggestion* that, instead of speaking merely negatively about what is not merely sensible, we should think that there is a distinct order of non-sensible things that have their own way of being constituted, namely, by themselves rather than passively or heteronomously.

Only in view of this casually developed suggestive function can the passivity argument be understood. Contrary to what some have suggested, it cannot be taken as a short summary of the first *Critique* that is inadequate simply because of a lack of space, for in fact there is no way the argument as such *could* be filled out properly to represent the first *Critique*. If it were really the case that Kant held that the mere passivity of our representations makes them merely phenomenal, then there would have been no need for him to have made the extensive arguments that he did for transcendental idealism, and to have distinguished his idealism as he did from other kinds (see e.g. A36/B53). But although the passivity argument (as presented in the *Foundations*) can hardly be taken as a fair representation of the general argument of the first *Critique*, I believe it is understandable, given Kant's relatively undeveloped attitude toward the self, that he might have fallen into the idea that the passivity argument was permissible as a way of suggesting why the phenomenal–noumenal distinction can be made with respect to the self. Kant takes it as evident that we do passively perceive ourselves; and in the first edition of the *Critique* he gave no clear treatment of any other feature of self-knowledge in order to back his doctrine of the transcendental ideality of the (empirical) self,

[73] *Foundations*, 4:452.

even though he knew that analogs to the doctrine had already been sharply criticized.[74] It is true that originally Kant had formulated the doctrine with an emphasis on the temporality of our passive self-perception, but he never had said clearly what it is distinctly about temporal representations that entails their ideality. In particular, he did not and obviously could not argue that, just as physical knowledge is supposedly merely phenomenal because it rests on a synthetic a priori doctrine of space, so self-knowledge is merely phenomenal because it rests on a synthetic a priori doctrine of time. Were he to say this, Kant would have been led toward rather than away from a kind of rational psychology. The first *Critique* thus originally left unclear Kant's ground for the basic claim that we know ourselves only as phenomena and so made a focus on the passivity of self-perception (as a contrast to the dogmatic rationalists) tempting.

In the second *Critique*, Kant admits that the doctrine of transcendental idealism when applied to the self invites one of the two 'most weighty criticisms' of his system.[75] In having to face again the weighty criticisms on this issue in the reviews of his work, Kant naturally would have become acutely aware that he had hardly given a clear treatment of it. Once this occurred, I suggest that Kant must have realized that the passivity argument of the *Foundations* was especially inadequate and could give a wholly misleading picture of his doctrine of the phenomenality of physical knowledge. This realization in turn could have led Kant to see that, to the extent that he had developed any specific positive arguments for transcendental idealism, they depended heavily upon reference to presumed features of spatiality,[76] and so, if he were to hold to a similar idealistic position on the self, he ought to argue similarly. That is, he ought to argue explicitly that the phenomenality of our knowledge derives from the fact that for us all objective determinations are temporal, and that these, even with respect to the self, always involve an implicit spatial reference.

I am hardly endorsing this line of argument, but I am saying that it is the obvious one for Kant to have taken when pressed to reconsider his discussion of the self. Moreover, to see that this is just the line that Kant in fact emphasized right after publication of the *Foundations* (1785), one need only take a brief look at Kant's next two projects: the *Metaphysical Foundations of Natural Science* (1786) and the second-edition revisions of the first *Critique* (1787). In the former work, Kant digressed to explain why there was no distinct set of first principles for psychology and the realm of the inner to match the a priori principles for physics that he was developing. In revising the first *Critique*, he focused almost entirely on filling out this explanation by reorganizing the fourth Paralogism and related sections so as to make more prominent our dependence on spatial references in self-knowledge and to offer an explicit argument for its phenomenality because of

---

[74] A36/B53. Cf. *Schriften*, 10:128.   [75] *Critique*, 5:6.   [76] See e.g. ibid. 14, 54.

those references.[77] The tenor of these changes and the philosophical need for them have been noted by many interpreters, but no one has adequately accounted for their historical motivation. I now can present an adequate answer here: namely, that the changes were precisely what should be expected given the continued weak discussion of the self offered in the *Foundations* and the continued weighty criticisms that followed upon it.

The revising of the first *Critique* and the forsaking of the deduction of the *Foundations* take place simultaneously, and thus already in the second edition of that *Critique* there are a number of strong statements that freedom is to be argued for only *after* morality is accepted (B428 f., B xxviii, B xxxii). Kant decided explicitly to block any temptation to take as (theoretically) ascribable to our personal self the spontaneity and transcendental freedom known indeterminately to have to underlie our phenomenal self. This point is made most clearly in the 'general note' with which Kant concludes his revised section on the Paralogisms. Here he brings under critique the idea that dominates the arguments of all the moral texts we have analyzed, namely, the spontaneity of thought. Kant does not deny that thinking exhibits a 'pure spontaneity', but now he emphasizes that this represents merely a 'logical function' and that, although it 'does not exhibit the subject of consciousness as appearance', it also does not 'represent myself to myself as I am in myself' (B428). As Kant adds, this is not to say that there could not be other, non-theoretical means whereby there could be 'revealed a spontaneity through which our reality would be determinable' (B430), but since the only means Kant had in mind here are obviously moral ones, they could not be used in the deduction he originally attempted.

The clear insistence that the representation of spontaneity in our thought does not yield knowledge of the self in itself gives Kant for the first time a consistently Critical theory of self-knowledge and simultaneously undercuts the first and third steps of the *Foundations*'s deduction: now our rationality cannot get us to a free noumenal self, and whatever noumenal side the self is allowed to have, the restrictions on ascribing any personal character to it eliminate even the possibility of arguing from freedom to morality on the basis of what is (supposedly theoretically) known to be one's 'proper self'. Thus, by the time of his latest work, Kant had totally abandoned the distinctive points of the last section of the *Foundations*. However, in this abandonment Kant gave up not only some vulnerable points but also some valid ones. That is, Kant never gave any reason for ignoring his earlier idea that freedom should be argued for theoretically and that a mere absence of grounds against it is not adequate given the 'perplexity' our transcendental freedom presents for the system of speculative knowledge. Instead, at the very

---

[77] For details on these points, see Michael Washburn, 'Did Kant Have a Theory of Self-Knowledge?', *Archiv für Geschichte der Philosophie*, 58 (1976), 43, and 'The Second Edition of the *Critique*: Towards an Understanding of its Nature and Genesis', *Kant-Studien*, 66 (1975), 227–90.

end of his career Kant frankly acknowledged that his practical philosophy was 'dogmatic' and that only his theoretical philosophy was to be called Critical.[78]

Kant emphasized, of course, that his dogmatism was at least not mystical, that it rested on a given generally recognized cognition and not on a sheer feeling or ordinary intuition. Yet, although in intention his practical philosophy surely can be distinguished from the mystical excesses of the idealists who followed him, Kant must bear considerable responsibility for the latter. Only some technical peculiarities of his system prevent the labeling of his position as fundamentally intuitionistic; for, although the 'a priori fact' of the validity of the moral law is not a given particular, as a standard Kantian intuition should be, but is rather a kind of principle,[79] it shares the non-naturalistic ultimacy that is found explicitly and typically in intuitionistic systems. Moreover, this ultimacy is clearly taken by Kant to be a prime sign and proof of a special transcendent realm of being,[80] and to this extent he can be said to have licensed the return, at least in Germany, to a kind of dogmatic metaphysics—notwithstanding the fact that he repeatedly insisted on the limited content of any justified transcendent claims.[81]

The only thing that could appear as an attempt at a strict foundation of the moral law (i.e. its general validity, not its specific formulation) in Kant's last work is the 'credential' for it offered in the second *Critique* as a 'substitute' for a deduction.[82] The 'credential' Kant offers comes from the observation that the supposedly already established possibility of transcendental freedom in a negative sense is complemented by the 'positive definition' that the moral law can provide.[83] Kant then goes so far as to say that thereby there is an increase in the 'certitude' of theoretical reason's 'problematic concept of freedom', for now the 'empty place' that could not be positively characterized is given a determinable form.[84] Yet, however true it may be that the moral law gives us a way to think our freedom more concretely, strictly speaking, the idea of the law as such can add only to the content of that thought and not to its theoretical certainty. Even if, 'to fill one of its own needs', theoretical reason must assume some transcendental

---

[78] See *Schriften*, 10:297, 305, 309, 311; and Josef Schmucker, *Die Ursprünge der Ethik Kants* (Meisenheim, 1961), 373–93.
[79] See *Critique*, 5:42, 63–6.
[80] Ibid. 6; cf. R6343.
[81] Cf. Henrich, 'Die Deduktion', p. 97, n. 26; and Henrich, 'Zu Kants Begriff der Philosophie,' in *Kritik und Metaphysik*, ed. Friedrich Kaulbach and Joachim Ritter (Berlin, 1960), 53. A typical dogmatic development of Kant's thought can be found in Johann Henrich Abicht's 'Über die Freiheit des Willens' (1789) in *Materialen zu Kants Kritik der praktischen Vernunft*, ed. Rüdiger Bittner and Konrad Cramer (Frankfurt, 1973), 229–40. A short revealing attempt by Kant to respond to such developments can be found in his 'Von einem neuerdings erhobenen vornehmen Ton in der Philosophie', *Schriften*, 8:21.
[82] *Critique*, 5:47–48.
[83] Ibid. 47.
[84] Ibid. 49.

freedom, nothing (theoretical) has been said (in the later writings) to show that this must be met by something noumenal *in us*. Theoretically our freedom and morality still have only a hypothetical validity, and so Kant represents his (late) position most accurately when he simply says he feels that the moral law is 'fully established by itself'[85] and can draw no support at all (not even the slightest increase by probability) from theoretical reason other than the knowledge that freedom implies no 'internal contradiction'.[86] Thus, Kant's statement about an increase in our certainty can be taken only in this way: although it is the theoretical, that is absolute, concept of freedom that one becomes certain about when one accepts the 'a priori fact of reason', the ground of this certainty is still practical, not strictly theoretical.[87]

In saying that Kant definitely moved away from an attempt at a deduction, I again mean not to commend his move, but only to show how it was forced on him once he chose squarely to face both the full consequences of his theoretical philosophy with respect to the self and the implications of his deepest beliefs, his principles of practical philosophy. Although he could no longer believe he had a theoretical proof of our transcendental freedom close at hand, Kant still chose to reject compatibilism and to hold to the moral philosophy to which he had been committed longer and more intensely than he had to his theoretical system.[88] Without denying the temptation to wish that Kant had not taken these moves, my aim here has been to show that we must recognize that in fact he did take them, and that some familiarity with the history of his views can help to make the fact less surprising than most believe.

VI

We can now finally deal directly with the traditional interpretations that are contrary to ours and try to reconcile the earlier and later Critical texts on morality. First we will deal with a significant minority view, namely, L. W. Beck's attempt to reconcile Kant's texts by arguing that there is a Critical deduction of morality in

---

[85] Ibid. 77.
[86] Ibid. 4.
[87] This is my view as to how to understand the statement at *Critique*, 5:48: 'Denn das moralische Gesetz beweist seine Realität dadurch auch für die Kritik der spekulativen Verstand genugtuend'. Often for Kant the determination of something's 'reality' means not a theoretical proof of its existence but a positive specification of its nature. (Thus, without taking existence to be a predicate, Kant can speak of different degrees of 'reality', and even Beck can translate 'realisieren' as 'give content to', *Critique*, 5:49.) At the same time, it can turn out that a particular specification may amount to what would in one sense satisfy a demand of speculative reason—as in this case when we determine a *concept* of freedom that is the concept of something free in the absolute sense that speculative philosophy supposedly desires (see *Critique*, 5:3).
[88] See Henrich, 'Der Begriff der sittlichen Einsicht und Kants Lehre vom Faktum der Vernunft,' in *Kant: Zur Deutung seiner Theorie von Erkennen und Handeln*, ed. Gerold Prauss (Cologne, 1973), 238, on evidence of the categorical imperative in Kant's notes from 1765. See also Schmucker.

the second *Critique*.⁸⁹ Generally, instead of contrasting the *Foundations'* ambitious argument for freedom with other discussions, Beck holds that the *Foundations* has the 'same argument' as the 'Review of Schulz' and that it is only 'somewhat different' from that of the second *Critique*, which supposedly even offers 'more detail on freedom'.⁹⁰ In numerous places in his *Commentary* Beck insists that there is in effect a strict deduction of morality in the second *Critique*,⁹¹ and that in it an 'independent warrant' for freedom is provided that 'breaks out of the circle' suspected in the *Foundations*.⁹²

The 'independent warrant' that Beck finds turns out to be the 'need of theoretical reason' for some 'absolute beginning' outside the natural realm. But as was just noted, even if this need is granted, it hardly shows that *we* must be free, and yet only then could the beginning of a deduction from freedom to morality arise. Beck says Kant is arguing that 'the vacant place, into which the concept of natural causality cannot enter [apparently to answer the above "need"], is suited for only one kind of tenant'—the moral law.⁹³ Yet at no point in the second *Critique* can such a strong argument be found, and in fact there can be no such argument, for there is nothing in the mere idea of transcendental freedom that requires it to be understood in such a particular way. There simply is no unique relation to morality that can be discerned here. Moral freedom can be said to 'fill' the notion of transcendental freedom with appropriate content, but this does not at all show (or even make it theoretically more probable) that transcendental freedom is realized in us, let alone that it could be only so realized.

Furthermore, it should not be forgotten that this section of the *Critique* is not said by Kant to provide a deduction of morality, but rather is characterized as speaking only '*Of* the Deduction of the Principles of Pure Practical Reason'.⁹⁴ In speaking 'of' a deduction here Kant may mean simply to call attention to a significant possibility that he now thinks we cannot realize. And in fact this appears to be just what Kant is doing, for he goes on to claim that 'the objective reality of the moral law can be proved through no deduction'.⁹⁵ Beck is unwilling

---

⁸⁹ Implicit sympathy for a view like Beck's to the effect that Kant at least could have developed a successful deduction is suggested in Gerold Prauss, *Kant und das Problem der Dinge an Sich* (Bonn, 1974), 174, n. 100; and Warner Wick's introduction to Kant's *The Metaphysical Principles of Virtue*, tr. James Ellington (New York, 1964), xxxiv.
⁹⁰ *Commentary*, 16, 59 n.
⁹¹ Ibid. 52, 68–9, 111, 166–7, 172–5.
⁹² Ibid. 174; cf. 167, n. 12.
⁹³ Ibid 175. Cf. Henrich, 'Die Deduktion des Sittengesetzes', 73–4, 83, 87. Henrich takes Kant rather to be arguing in both the *Foundations* and the second *Critique* that these considerations show only that our transcendental freedom is not a 'wholly arbitrary assumption'—and that this is enough.
⁹⁴ *Critique*, 5:42. Beck somehow misses this, and in the same sentence in which he acknowledges that 'Kant denies . . . there can be a deduction of the principle of pure practical reason', he adds that Kant says this 'in spite of the title of the section' (*Commentary*, 171).
⁹⁵ *Critique*, 5:47.

to take this text as decisive, and in various places his translation makes Kant speak even less hypothetically about a deduction than he really does.[96]

Perhaps because of an awareness of the tenuousness of his interpretation and a cognizance that this is 'the most obscure part of Kant's ethical theory', Beck attempted a further explanation in an article published shortly after his *Commentary*.[97] This explanation develops a line of thought suggested already in the *Commentary* to the effect that 'in any willing there is a principle which is purely rational', and therefore pure reason is practical and the moral law is binding for us.[98] In his original discussion Beck admits that this line 'seems to be a rather tricky argument',[99] and in any case it is hardly fully developed. Beck quotes only Kant's statement in the *Foundations*: 'I say that every being which cannot act otherwise than under the idea of freedom is thereby really free in a practical respect.'[100] Then he says, 'But the Ideal of freedom is expressed in the moral law; hence to be conscious of moral constraint, i.e. of the law—this is the fact of pure reason—ipso facto validates the practical claim of the moral law.'[101] Beck's analysis here is questionable in a number of respects. First, it is notable that he does not directly support his interpretation of the second *Critique* with a passage from the body of that text. Second, the passage he does use does not clearly entail the strong conclusion Beck draws. Third, the passage happens to be one we have already analyzed at length, and we made sense of it in terms of an overall theory of Kant's development that is quite at odds with Beck's.

In his later article Beck tries to develop his interpretation with a lengthy discussion that confesses going beyond Kant's explicit doctrines. Beck's aim, though, is still to present a view that he takes to be the main implicit point of the second *Critique*, and which he thinks is an adequate counter to those who would call Kant an intuitionist. Part of Beck's counter rests on his overlooking Kant's admission that his practical philosophy is dogmatic. Beck claims that 'for Kant the metaphysics of the moral law is not Platonic; the moral law is a creation of reason'.[102] If this statement is stripped of metaphor, it may come to little more than the disputed assertion that there is a Critical theoretical foundation for

---

[96] Thus, Beck injects a too optimistic tone (about the possibility of a deduction here) by translating 'darf man nicht so gut fortzukommen hoffen' as 'we cannot hope to have *everything* as easy' (*Critique*, 47, l. 35). And on p. 48, l. 11 of the translation, he has Kant speak of 'our deduction' where the German clearly speaks only of 'the moral law'. (Beck's error here goes back to the use of 'it' on l. 6 of that page of his translation. The English reader might think—as Beck later clearly does—that here 'deduction' is the referent, but the gender of the German makes clear that 'moral law' must be the referent.)

[97] 'The Fact of Reason: An Essay on Justification in Ethics', in *Studies in the Philosophy of Kant* (Indianapolis, 1965), 212.

[98] *Commentary*, 169.

[99] Ibid.

[100] *Foundations*, 4:448.

[101] *Commentary*, 169.

[102] 'The Fact of Reason', 210.

morality in the later Kant. The remainder of Beck's counter rests on the claim that the moral law is 'a fact known reflexively and not intuitively'.[103] In particular, Beck argues, 'there is in willing a principle that is rational, whether the willing be moral or immoral, prudent or foolish. If volition appears to be independent of desires and to be morally unconditioned, then there must be an unconditionally rational principle for it.'[104] Beck believes that this amounts to a 'presupposition which is at least part of the answer to the external question of ethics', that is, the general question of why one should accept any morality as valid.[105]

Although Beck's discussion is more extensive here, there are still problems in its move from the mere appearance of a moral claim to the validity of an 'unconditional' principle. For us, however, the main issue is not this but rather what Beck's argument implies for interpreting Kant, and here it still seems clearly vulnerable on at least three key points. First, Beck's newly formulated argument still adds no direct evidence for being taken as a gloss of what the *Critique* really holds. (The only text he cites in his development of the deduction is again the passage from the *Foundations*.) Second, it is very unlikely that the argument could at all be accepted by even the later Kant, for the strategy of arguing for morality from features present in *all* willing is precisely what Kant rejects in the texts after the *Foundations* (recall, e.g., the revisions of the first *Critique*). Third, even if one could show that all willing presupposes an 'unconditionally rational principle', this would not of itself establish the categorical imperative, and even Beck admits that it is only 'part' of the answer to the external question. Hence even Beck's additional discussion has not been able to show how Kant offered what amounts to a deduction of morality in the second *Critique*. I conclude that, although my historical explanation of Kant's rejection of the *Foundations'* deduction is quite complicated and does not leave him with an intrinsically satisfactory position (given his own general system), the alternative of attempting to reconcile Kant's texts in Beck's way has at least these difficulties and has a much weaker textural grounding.

The other main traditional attempt to reconcile Kant's texts has involved a strategy that is the opposite of Beck's: namely, minimizing the theoretical deductive strain of the *Foundations* on the ground that in addition to its intrinsic difficulties it conflicts with the proper tendency of Kant's first two *Critiques*. The advocates of this interpretation could share my analysis (but not my evaluation) of the second *Critique* but for important reasons would reject that of the *Foundations*; for they say that there Kant did not seriously assert a need for deduction, and that, given his philosophy as a whole, he was right. On the first point my attack on this interpretation would rest not only on the key quotation from the *Foundations* (4:456) but also on all that our analysis has done so far to

---

[103] 'The Fact of Reason', 210.   [104] Ibid. 211.   [105] Ibid. 208.

show how systematically (though admittedly sketchily and probably invalidly) the (third section of the) *Foundations* is developed precisely as a response to the need for a strong theoretical deduction. The strategy of the opposing interpretation is simply to minimize the relevant passages bearing out this point. The motive for this interpretation is tied to its view on the second point, its idea that Kant's eventual declaration of morality as an 'a priori fact' is proper and unavoidable. This view, and a desire to recast all of Kant's work in what is supposedly its best light, makes the traditional attitude here on the first point more understandable but not more acceptable.

Two versions of this interpretation will be dealt with: the well-known commentary of H. J. Paton and the more recently developed analysis of Dieter Henrich.[106] Henrich's discussion is especially sophisticated and historically insightful, and it is difficult to find very much to question in it. Henrich does not deny that in the *Foundations* there is talk of a strict deduction, and he even puts this into a helpful context by comparing it with similar efforts in Kant's pre-Critical writings.[107] Nonetheless, Henrich is a reconciliationist in that he still insists that in effect the *Foundations* is to be understood as recognizing that freedom and morality are, strictly speaking, non-provable 'facts' of reason. Originally, Henrich apparently thought this was so because he falsely believed that it was implied by what Kant had to say about our inability to *explain* freedom.[108] More recently, Henrich's interpretation has been backed by a detailed analysis of the *weakness* of the *Foundations*' deduction, emphasizing that 'in effect' the deduction cannot validly reach its conclusion without reference to the experience of binding moral claims.[109] Given our previous analyses, we can now agree with Henrich that Kant's argument in the *Foundations*, even in its final filled out form, is not adequate as a proof.[110] Yet this is hardly sufficient to show that Kant did not

---

[106] Similar views can be found in Leonard Nelson, *Kritik der praktischen Vernunft*, in *Gesammelte Schriften*, 9 vols. (Hamburg, 1972), 4:44; Gerhard Krüger, *Philosophie und Moral in der kantischen Kritik*, 2nd edn (Tübingen, 1967), 198; and T. C. Williams, *The Concept of the Categorical Imperative* (Oxford, 1968), 100.

[107] Henrich, 'Über die Einheit der Subjektivität', *Philosophische Rundschau*, 3 (1955), 36; and Henrich, 'Der Begriff der sittlichen Einsicht', pp. 239–43.

[108] 'Das Prinzip der kantischen Ethik', *Philosophische Rundschau*, 1 (1953), 34; cf. Henrich, 'Der Begriff der sittlichen Einsicht', 253, n. 25.

[109] 'Die Vernunft erzeugt die Idee der sittlichen Freiheit allein in Beziehung auf einen Bezugspunkt, der selber schon die Überzeugung von der Realität der Energie des sittlichen Willens logisch impliziert. Die Deduktion muss notwendig auf das Bewusstsein Bezug nehmen, das ein vernünftiges Wesen von seinen Willen hat. ... Der Begründungsvorgang der *Grundlegung* bewegt sich damit zwar wirklich in einer Art von Zirkel' ('Die Deduktion des Sittengesetzes', 85–6). 'Da aber dieser zweiten Standpunkt in Blick auf eine intelligible Welt kein zureichender Grund fur die "Anmassung" sein kann, einen Willen zu besitzen, muss fur sie einen weiteren Grund geltend gemacht werden. Kein anderer könnte es sein als das Bewusstsein von Geltungsanspruch des Sittengesetzes' (ibid. 93; cf. 77, 86, 106, and 'Das Prinzip der kantischen Ethik', 36).

[110] See also Henrich, 'Die Deduktion des Sittengesetzes', 72, 93, 97; Henrich, 'Der Begriff der sittlichen Einsicht', 246–7; Paton, 211, 244; Ilting, 124; Nelson, 45; T. C. Williams, 211; Robert Paul Wolff, *The Autonomy of Reason* (New York, 1973), 211.

take his attempt at a deduction in the *Foundations* fully 'seriously', that he did not believe that a non-circular proof of freedom and morality was needed and possible. It is, after all, Kant himself who raises the question of a circle so as to claim that it has been fully resolved. Of course, on hindsight it is admittedly tempting to say that Kant still was (at the time) in a way aware of the weakness of his arguments, but the point of my analysis has been precisely to show that we need not fall prey to this temptation. Henrich claims that the awareness is implicit in Kant's remark at the end of the *Foundations*[111] that the deduction has been made for those who 'believe' themselves in possession of a will.[112] Henrich feels that this remark shows that Kant did not really think he was in possession of a categorical theoretical proof of freedom. However, I have shown that, although in the first formulation of his deduction Kant gives no grounds for adequately asserting that we have a will in the requisite sense, a central point in the rest of his discussion is precisely the insistence that we are beings who do 'find' in ourselves adequate theoretical grounds for making such an assertion.[113]

A similar point must be made against Paton's famous analysis in *The Categorical Imperative*. Although Paton generally prefers to use the *Foundations* as the model for expositing the fundamentals of Kant's entire ethical theory, it is remarkable that, with respect to the themes of the last section of the text, he suddenly interprets everything from the standpoint of the second *Critique*. Yet rather than simply replace (as Kant did) this section with what is said in the *Critique*, Paton dutifully records the *Foundations*' arguments while constantly insisting that one ought not to 'exaggerate the differences' between them and the *Critique*.[114] Paton can maintain this position only because he labors under the double belief that all the *Foundations* really can try to do is to 'defend' freedom, not justify it (i.e. it can show only that there is no contradiction in freedom, that 'dogmatic determinism' is untenable),[115] and that Kant is arguing not that we are free but 'only' that we must act under the idea of freedom.[116] The latter part of

---

[111] *Foundations*, 4:459.
[112] 'Die Idee der Freiheit gilt für einen Wesen, "das sich eines Willen bewusst zu sein glaubt". Damit ist in einer für den Text der *Grundlegung* eben noch erträglichen Weise eingeräumt dass das Freiheitsbewusstsein eine Voraussetzung in sittlichen Bewusstsein hat' ('Die Deduktion des Sittengesetzes', 93).
[113] *Foundations*, 4:452.
[114] *Categorical Imperative*, 203, 204, 221, 224, 252, 277. In all these pages Paton uses phrases such as Kant 'may seem' or 'does to some extent appear' to attempt a strict deduction. Yet no basis is given in the text for the qualifications. Instead, Paton says that 'if Kant really believes' he can make such a deduction, 'he is falling into fundamental error' (p. 226). The qualifications are thus surely based on Paton's hope to find in Kant what he himself considers to be the most tenable position. It is revealing that Paton says, 'whatever be his [Kant's] view' in the *Foundations*, we ought to follow what the second *Critique* says (ibid.), for this indicates, I believe, that here Paton is not up to explaining literally Kant's thought in the *Foundations*.
[115] Ibid. 271: 'all he [Kant] has to show is that there is no theoretical reason why we should not be entitled to act on the categorical imperative.'
[116] Ibid. 271. Cf. Wolff, 35; Ross, 6; A. R. C. Duncan, *Practical Reason and Morality* (Edinburgh, 1957), 139; L. W. Beck, translator's introduction to *Foundations*, v.

Paton's belief can be met directly by my earlier analysis of what Kant meant by a 'merely practical' proof of freedom. Paton sees the relevant point here—namely, that we cannot explain how freedom works—but he does not see that it is the relevant point, and so he falsely infers that this means that one can only defend freedom and not argue that it exists.[117] Paton's view also rests on ignoring the crucial passage from the *Foundations*[118] about the desirability of an argument establishing freedom, and on repeatedly simply asserting that Kant could not have taken seriously such steps as appealing to a 'proper' metaphysically primary self. Paton prefers to call this step a 'seemingly' new point and relegates it to an appendix as a mere 'additional' argument.[119]

In the end, Paton believes that the justification of the categorical imperative can be and is based solely on a kind of 'direct insight'.[120] The main problem with such a view is not that it turns the moralist as such into something of a dogmatist, for it may well be that the external question of the validity of morality, if it is accepted at all, can be answered only by an appeal to some kind of direct insight. The problem is rather that in Kant's case this answer involves an enormous consequence, a commitment to an instance of transcendental freedom that at one point on his own admission creates great 'perplexity' for his whole theoretical system.

Paton concludes his interpretation by saying that he argued 'above all' that 'Kant's ethics is independent of metaphysics'. Yet he immediately adds, 'Kant is...maintaining that there can be no morality, as it is understood, however obscurely, by ordinary men without the supposition of freedom.'[121] By 'freedom' Paton (like other Kantians such as Henrich, Beck, and Silber) means our transcendental freedom, freedom understood in a non-compatibilist way, and therefore he simply cannot get away with the claim that Kant's ethics is independent of a questionable kind of metaphysics that requires justification.[122] As various contemporary ethicists (e.g. Marcus Singer in America and Hans Reiner in Germany) have shown, there are still many Kantian insights that can be developed

---

[117] Paton, 272. A similar error is made in Duncan, 55: 'Kant repeatedly insists that freedom cannot be *proved*, that free causality must remain beyond the *comprehension* of the human intellect.' I have added the emphasis to make clear the contrast that Duncan and others have failed to observe adequately.

[118] See the passage cited above at n. 57.

[119] *Categorical Imperative*, 242, 250. Cf. Margot Fleischer's critique of Paton for playing down the latter part of the deduction ('Das Problem der Begründung des kategorischen Imperativs bei Kant', in *Sein und Ethos*, ed. Paulus Englehardt (Mainz, 1967), 387; and 'Die Formeln des kategorischen Imperatives', *Archiv für Geschichte der Philosophie*, 46 (1964), 201, 226), a point on which Henrich (e.g. 'Die Deduktion des Sittengesetzes', 90) could also be criticized.

[120] *Categorical Imperative*, 247. For a very interesting analysis of the notion of 'ethical insight', see Henrich, 'Der Begriff der sittlichen Einsicht'.

[121] *Categorical Imperative*, 277–8.

[122] The desperation of the situation of the Kantians here is indicated by the move made by Beck (*Commentary*, 194) and John Silber (introduction to Kant's *Religion Within the Bounds of Reason Alone*, tr. T. M. Greene and H. H. Hudson (New York, 1960), ci), namely, to deny that determinism (universally and not merely regulatively) applies to the phenomenal realm—a move that is absolutely incompatible with Kant's views at the time under discussion.

into a moral system without entering into such a metaphysical project; but, unfortunately for those like Paton, who profess to trying to take Kant whole and literally, only wishful thinking stands behind the idea that such a subject can be properly avoided. The same can be said, I believe, of the idea that Kant himself could and eventually did succeed in this project. We do the most justice to Kant when we face up to his dogmatism and use his own remarks to help show that it is unacceptable but ultimately historically understandable.

Furthermore, if, as Kant himself said, the idea of freedom is the 'keystone' of his system, there cannot fail to be important consequences if the backing for his belief in freedom varies as dramatically as we have argued that it does. It thus may be no accident that Kant was not able to fulfill his hope of developing a principle of the unity of theoretical and practical reason.[123] His critical epistemology eventually raised such powerful challenges to claims about the self's capacities that now we seem forced either to bracket part of his own conception of morality as being too infected with pre-Critical commitments, or instead to attempt somehow to save that conception by developing Kant's suggestion of a 'primacy of practical reason' in a more thorough and radical way than has been done so far.

[123] *Critique*, 5:91.

– 7 –

Kant on the Good Will

The first chapter of the *Grundlegung* begins with the famous claim that, 'It is impossible to conceive anything at all in the world, or even out of it, which can be taken as good without qualification, except a good will' (p. 393).* This claim has been sharply criticized, but in order to begin to evaluate these criticisms it is necessary to consider what Kant may mean by the term 'good will'. It turns out that there are a number of quite different ways this term can be taken, ways suggested by various Kantian texts and made use of in several current discussions.

I will distinguish three major interpretations of the term: (1) the 'particular intention' view; (2) the 'general capacity' view; and (3) the 'whole character' view. These views bear unevenly on the argument at the beginning of the *Grundlegung*, but I believe they all shed some light on how we might best understand the key term in Kant's claim. Kant and his critics do not explicitly formulate these specific views, and it is admittedly somewhat artificial to consider the views at first in abstraction from one another. Nonetheless, Kant's discussion in the *Grundlegung* is so brief, and the preconceptions of his critics are so various, that it is helpful for analytical purposes to introduce these simple models and then to flesh them out as needed. In stressing difficulties in all these models, my point is not that they undermine the basic principles of Kant's ethics, but only that one must be careful not to assume that the notion of the good will by itself is an unambiguous and unquestionable starting place. Like many other aspects of the first part of the text, it may have more of an heuristic than a foundational role within the system.

Before examining the three views, I will begin by noting very briefly some common but inadequate grounds for rejecting Kant's claim about the good will. The most popular and implausible attacks on Kant's claim usually rest on overlooking the fact that he is speaking strictly about only what is good 'without qualification'. As Paton repeatedly stressed, this restriction already indicates that Kant is hardly committing himself to such controversial views as that the will is the sole good (or even the highest good; see p. 396). Even if the will alone can be

---

* Unattributed page numbers in the text are to *Grundlegung der Metaphysik der Sitten*, vol. IV of *Kant's Gesammelte Schriften* (Berlin, 1900–); other works will be referred to as follows: *KpV* = *Critique of Practical Reason*, Rel. = *Religion Within the Boundaries of Mere Reason*, MS = *Metaphysics of Morals*.

good 'without qualification', there is no limit yet on what else can be good in some other way. Moreover, as Aune and Korsgaard have noted,[1] these other goods are not to be called mere 'instrumental' goods; for Kant is clear that happiness is good as an end and not as a mere means, although he insists this is not to say it is good 'without qualification'. (Confusion arises because he says the will is 'good, not as a means... but in itself' (p. 396).)

While Kant can meet popular objections by sensibly allowing a plurality of goods, this makes it no easier to see how he can pick out the will as alone good 'without qualification'. Sometimes Kant's discussions[2] seem to have the disturbing form of arguing that, since various items other than the will are good in a qualified way, therefore the will must be capable of unqualified goodness simply because there must be something that can be an unqualified good. This line of thought is suspicious because it ignores the possibility that all goods could be qualified in some sense, or that there might need to be only one unqualifiedly good will.[3] At the very least, one needs to determine precisely what kind of 'qualification' is at issue.[4]

Kant's own favorite explanation is with reference to context: 'unqualified' goods are good in all morally relevant contexts (cf. 'Moral Mrongovius II', XXIX: 599),[5] and so a good is 'qualified' when there is some possible context in which an 'impartial spectator' would not 'approve' of it (p. 393). Strictly speaking, this is most naturally taken as meaning not that the property of goodness as such is to be qualified, but that the *items* that can be good are to be called 'qualified goods' when they can be had in some circumstance without then being worthy of approval.

I

This 'natural' idea runs into difficulties when it is combined with what I designated as the first view on the meaning of Kant's claim about the good will. On the 'particular intention' interpretation, Kant's basic claim is that any apparently good objective property (any 'talent', 'temperament', or 'gift of fortune' such as prosperity) is such that it can occur in a context where its possession would not be approved, whereas a will (and it alone) which is characterized by a particular good intention would be approved in whatever context it might appear. The difficulty

---

[1] B. Aune, *Kant's Theory of Morals* (Princeton, 1979), 6; C. Korsgaard, 'Two Distinctions in Goodness', *Philosophical Review*, 92 (1983), 169–95 at 178.
[2] And those of his followers, e.g. C. Korsgaard, 'Kant's Formula of Humanity', *Kant-Studien*, 77 (1986), 183–202 at 186.
[3] Cf. H. Jones, *Kant's Principle of Personality* (Madison, Wis., 1971), 18.
[4] Cf. O. Höffe, *Immanuel Kant* (Munich, 1983; 2nd edn 1988), 176.
[5] These recently published notes must be used with care, but they are quite important, as they come from 1784–5, a time very close to Kant's work on the *Grundlegung*.

THE GOOD WILL

here is in understanding why there must be a clear asymmetry between the will and other value bearers. If prosperity turns out to be a 'qualified' good not because of any clear flaw in it as such, but just because there are circumstances in which its possession would not be approved, then it is unclear why a will with a particular good intention could not also be regarded as fully commendable as such, and yet of similarly qualified value in so far as there are circumstances in which its possession would not be approved.

Kant of course does not want to allow such circumstances, and his followers have agreed. Thus, Paton remarks without critique that, while 'the harm done by a stupid good man was due to his stupidity and not to his goodness . . . a good will as such cannot issue in wrong actions'.[6] Here it is being assumed that the man is good, while it is conceded that a 'good will' can occur in a context which *as a whole* need not be approved; that is precisely the point of saying that there is 'harm done'. To avoid the further concession that the possession of this will itself is in this instance only a qualified good, one must insist (as Paton does implicitly) on the idea that, although the context as a whole may not be approved, the 'good' will's presence in the whole is not the source of disapproval, for it is the other component of the context, the man's innate stupidity, that is responsible for the harm. But *if* something like stupidity is given such significance, there arises the difficulty that it seems only fair to introduce similar distinctions with regard to the 'objective' goods that are said to be only 'qualified'.

Consider, for example, Kant's statement that 'talents' and 'qualities of temperament' are 'without doubt good and desirable in many respects; but they can also be extremely bad and hurtful when the will is not good which has to make use of these . . .' (p. 393). Here, as in Paton's example of the stupid man, we have an instance where the context as a whole is bad, and yet the contribution of the item under investigation—in this case a gift of talent or temperament—is not what is responsible for the harm. On the contrary, it is expressly stipulated that it is the other component of the context, in this particular situation the orientation of the will, that is really responsible for the whole context being disapproved. Parity of reasoning forces the conclusion that, for all that has been said *so far*, there is no clear asymmetry between the good will and apparently good 'objective' items; each can be excused from being of qualified goodness because the badness of whatever bad contexts they enter into can be accounted for by the presence of other factors.

To attempt to avoid this difficulty, the Kantian might try insisting that when a natural gift is underdeveloped or misused it is not simply the whole context that has become bad: rather, the bad will has corrupted the value of the gift itself. The Kantian might add that what this implies is that even here it is the 'subjective'

[6] H. J. Paton, *The Categorical Imperative* (New York, 1967; first published 1947), 40.

factor that is ultimately responsible for the evaluation of the whole context. Thus, the claim would be that, while gifts can be good, they are so only while supported by a good will (hence they are only 'qualifiedly good'); and they turn bad (Kant does say, '*they* can be extremely bad and hurtful', (p. 393) as soon as the will that uses (i.e. fails to develop or restrict) them is bad. But do they themselves, as opposed to the context as a whole, really turn bad in such a context? And, if we do say this, why not also say, by parity of reasoning, that stupidity can turn a 'good' man's will into a bad thing?[7]

The Kantian surely resists this inference, but on what specific ground? Paton's reply here is simply that for the Kantian a good will has 'a unique and incomparable value which could not be outweighted by the evils resulting from his [a stupid person's] natural defects'.[8] This suggestion of 'weighing' different values is misleading at best. If the will can maintain its unqualified value by 'outweighing' the bad of the stupidity it may get involved with in a particular context, why can't a 'gift of nature' maintain its unqualified value by being said to 'outweigh' the evil of a will which may misuse it in a particular context? At this point, to avoid begging the question, it is no good to reject this 'outweighing' by pointing out that the context (with the misused gift) as a *whole* is not to be approved; for it has been allowed that a good will can 'outweigh' the stupidity it is involved with in a particular situation even when we also might not approve of the *whole* context of that particular situation. In essence, Paton's statement has little to do with 'weighing' as ordinarily understood; it can back a special status for the will only by resting on its claim that the will has 'unique and incomparable' value. But it provides this 'backing' in an unhelpful way, for the whole issue is what ground there is for giving the will such special status in the first place. This ground remains mysterious as long as the will is thought of as just one component among many in a particular situation of action.

An equally troublesome line of argument is suggested by that part of Paton's statement that mentions 'evils resulting' from 'natural defects'. This is misleading in so far as it is taken to imply that mere natural consequences could be (for the consistent Kantian) the source of unqualified evil. Kant unfortunately suggests a similar line of argument himself when he goes on to say that even a state of 'complete well being and contentment' is only a qualified good because without a good will it can 'produce' 'boldness' and 'overboldness' (p. 393). The problem here is that it would be very odd to hold that 'overboldness' is in itself an unqualified evil while not also allowing (as Kant does not) 'complete well being' to be an unqualified good. Hence, overboldness must be evil not simply in itself, but somehow because of its involvement in contexts which are to be disapproved

---

[7] Cf. R. P. Wolff, *The Autonomy of Reason* (New York, 1973), 59.
[8] Paton, *Categorical Imperative*, 41.

'without limitation'. But what would it be about such contexts that could make them bad in this way, given that the natural part of the context, the property of overboldness itself, is not simply bad?

The only answer here would be to say that the badness must be based ultimately on the way that the overboldness is related to the other component of the context, the will. But if, to be fair to the Kantian, we should grant him an absolute division between objective qualities of the self (such as stupidity and boldness) and the subjective orientation of the will, then we should also hold him to his view that these objective qualities cannot as such determine the will. But that implies in turn that a property such as overboldness cannot itself corrupt the will (and if '*overboldness*' is taken to *mean* a corruption of the will, then this only leaves the equally difficult question of how that overboldness could be the direct result of something such as mere boldness or contentment). And this means that the evil in a situation where a person is perfectly 'content' must be based entirely in the 'unique and incomparable' orientation of the will alone. All talk of natural 'results' and 'effects' only obscures this position—as Kant himself indicates (p. 394). But why should we believe that the will does have this 'incomparable' value?

Kant is fond of one answer to this question which says it is simply evident that what I have called 'objective' characteristics (Kant calls them the 'states', 'Zustände', of the person as opposed to the person himself: 'Moral Mrongovius II', XXIX: 607 and 631) cannot be of unqualified value because their value goes back to inclination (thus a talent seems valuable only because we are inclined to like it and its effects), and an impartial observer would prefer not to have inclinations at all (428, *KpV*, V: 118, 'Moral Mrongovius II', XXIX: 610).[9] This answer is mysterious, because by itself it does not explain exactly why an observer must judge this way, and it seems to add the unfortunate suggestion that inclinations as such are wholly without value (or even are disvalued).

This position is so stark that is becomes understandable that Aune, for example, has argued that Kant's argument at the beginning of the *Grundlegung* is really about how something can have *any* (positive) moral value if done only 'for duty', i.e. out of good will, and so the extra 'use of the term "unconditional"' is simply misleading'.[10] But Kant is not really going that far. It is true that if actions are to have moral value they must be done from duty, but Kant sees that there is more to value than moral value, and there is more to moral value than action. Hence, he does allow that properties such as talents and temperaments can have some moral

---

[9] Cf. C. Korsgaard, 'Aristotle and Kant on the Source of Value', *Ethics*, 96 (1986), 486–505 at 499. I abstract here from another sense in which Kant impugns inclination as 'qualified' because 'unreliable', namely his arguments that it cannot provide ends that give rules for action that are necessary and a priori; see P. Menzer, *Eine Vorlesung Kants über Ethik* (Berlin, 1924), 176; *Rel.*, VI: 24, 3; *Rel.*, VI: 35, 13 f.

[10] Aune, *Kant's Theory*, 21–2; cf. Wolff, *Autonomy*, 60: 'a good [!] will is the only thing which is morally estimable at all'.

value (a 'qualified' value, to be sure) as long as they are founded in a good will. What is still unclear, though, is what the original reason is for affirming this claim rather than saying that a will is good only when grounded in an 'objective' nature that is kind, not stupid, etc.

This all indicates that the question of what is good 'in all contexts' goes back to the question of what is good in an unconditioned rather than a conditioned way. *If* we could be sure that a good will has unconditioned value, then (accepting, in a Kantian way, that moral contexts are composed simply of the will and 'objective' factors) we could believe it is good in any relevant context— for, as a good will, it is assumed to be 'subjectively' good, and, as an unconditioned value, there is nothing that can take that goodness away. But similarly, if there were an objective unconditioned good, then even if somehow this grounded a will good in all contexts, the conditioned value of the will would block it from serving Kant's purposes. Thus, the crucial point that still needs backing is the claim that the will and the will alone, as a particular intention, can have unconditioned value.

Despite these difficulties in justification, there are understandable reasons why some have taken the 'particular intention' view of what Kant means in his claim about the good will. At first sight, it can seem most naturally to represent some of the more familiar examples of the text, e.g. the man 'overclouded by sorrows' who helps others in a particular 'action without any inclination' (p. 398). This fits the common idea, familiar since Hegel, that Kantian morality seems to emphasize the moral issues I confront in making the particular decision now before me and the purity of will I either display or fail to display in this act.[11] On this view, the notion of a good will serves at least as an understandable criterion for moral evaluation. The orientation of the will in a particular situation would always be the immediate locus of such evaluation, and, depending on whether that will is good or not, the nature of the agent (e.g. his temperament) and the effects of the will could be said to be good in a qualified way. There are, of course, still problems in determining what in principle makes such a will good, and in deciding when in fact it is exemplified, but at least there is something here that can, ideally, serve as the ultimate basis for dividing the moral domain into positive and negative segments. This function is not so easily served by other views of what Kant means by a 'good will', and yet we are forced to look into such views; for, whatever the advantages of the first view, it still has the fundamental defect of appearing to be question-begging when faced with having to defend its claim about the special status of the will.

---

[11] See Allen Wood's discussion of Hegel's understanding of the 'Emptiness of the Moral Will' in subsection 9.9 of his *Hegel's Ethical Thought* (Cambridge, 1990), pp. 167–9; cf. R. B. Louden, 'Kant's Virtue Ethics', *Philosophy*, 61 (1986), 473–89 at 480–1.

THE GOOD WILL

II

The second interpretation of the 'good will', the 'general capacity' view, provides an immediate and direct answer to the main problem with the first view. On this second view, the good will is not a mere component of a particular context of action. When it is looked at as merely such a component, it becomes unclear how Kant can give it such great priority over other components. When it is considered in general, however, as a capacity of persons to choose freely and in that way escape the natural determination that controls everything else, it becomes more understandable that it might be given special value. Indeed, Kant is quite clear that, without such a capacity for freedom, the whole notion of moral value would have to be rejected as a mere chimera or 'phantom of the brain'. On this view, then, the good will and it alone is of unqualified goodness, because it is simply the general ability to use our freedom properly, and morality is what results from the proper use of freedom.

This view is based not so much on the beginning of the *Grundlegung* as on Kant's well known remarks elsewhere that persons alone are of absolute worth and are 'ends in themselves'. It is obviously a general capacity of persons to will that must be meant as the source of this value, for otherwise agents who have a bad particular intention would then (absurdly) lack the status that grounds their being respected as absolute ends.[12] To this extent, the second, or 'general capacity' view does seem to have a clear advantage over the first, or 'particular intention' view. Yet this very focus on a general capacity as what is unconditionally valuable has led some interpreters to say that the term 'good will' is not really the appropriate one for it. Thus, Hardy Jones and Jeffrie Murphy have each criticized Paton's statement that, 'An end in itself must...be a self-existent end, not something to be produced by us. Since it has absolute worth, we know already what it must be—namely, a good will. This good or rational will Kant takes to be present in every rational agent ...'.[13]

The difficulty with this statement is that the term 'good will' strongly suggests a particular will that would contrast with the bad will of some other persons, and hence, if the absolute worth of a person required such a will, not everyone would be (contrary to Kant's clear intention) an end in itself. Therefore, although these interpreters want a general capacity for willing, in the sense of a free ability to 'set an end',[14] to be the locus of 'unqualified' value, they think it inappropriate to call this locus a 'good will'. Jones even goes so far as to say that, when Kant starts the *Grundlegung* by speaking of the unconditional value of the 'Wille' (p. 393), he

---

[12] Jones, 'Kant's Principle', 18; 56–7; J. Murphy, *Kant: The Philosophy of Right* (London, 1970), 79.
[13] Jones, 'Kant's Principle', 57; Murphy, *Kant*, 79; Paton, *Categorical Imperative*, 168–9.
[14] Korsgaard, 'Aristotle and Kant', 500.

really should have spoken of 'Willkür', the general faculty of choice.[15] The radicality of this proposal may serve as a clue to the fact that, although there is something odd about Paton's statement, those who reject it are also liable to severe difficulties.

The problem with Paton's critics is that they do not explain why a mere capacity to set an end should in itself be of special moral value. Indeed, Murphy goes so far as to say that, since this capacity does not, and cannot be allowed to, vary among moral agents, it is not, strictly speaking, a moral value.[16] It is something of 'absolute worth' but not of moral worth; is has a non-moral value that is the precondition of all moral value. This is an awkward position. Moreover, even if the capacity to set an end is allowed to have some kind of quasi-moral value (so that it can be as closely related as it must be to the 'qualified' moral values that presuppose it), and even if it is also granted that (as all these interpreters assume) the setting of an end involves an absolute freedom of choice, precisely why is that especially valuable?

Here Kantians have typically argued that it is because such a capacity 'depends on us' alone that it is of unqualified worth.[17] Kant himself suggests such an argument when he links unconditioned value and the unconditioned nature of free choice. (More specifically, he claims that the mere fact that something is caused, and in that sense conditioned, makes it ineligible for being of unconditioned value.) But this linkage seems to play on a mere equivocation, and there are several problems with making too much out of the sheer capacity for free choice. A small problem here is that, strictly speaking, it is really the effects or the exercise of the capacity, and not the possession of the capacity itself, that lies in our control—and yet it is the capacity as such that presumably has the 'absolute' value that grounds our respect. A more serious problem is that it is still not clear what is so good about simply having such a capacity. After all, there might be a being who could select among a variety of ends, and yet such that all of these ends are bad. (Some theologies have held that most humans are like this.) In such a case, the capacity to set an end freely would still be present; its existence is not by definition dependent upon a special description of the ends involved, and since it concerns mere freedom and not omnipotence, it surely does not have to be able to select among all possible ends. It is not yet evident that such an always wrong but still

---

[15] Jones, 'Kant's Principle', 173; cf. V. Rossvaer, 'Kant's Practical Philosophy', in G. Fløistad (ed.), *Contemporary Philosophy*, iii (The Hague, 1982), 187–217 at 203.

[16] Murphy, *Kant*, 80.

[17] See e.g. J. Atwell, 'The Uniqueness of the Good Will', *Akten des 4. Internationalen Kant-Kongresses*, ii (Berlin, 1974), 479–84; cf. 'Moral Mrongovius II', XXIX:640. In a similar argument, Korsgaard insists that, for conditioned values, 'we regard them as good whenever they are chosen with full rational autonomy; so full rational autonomy itself is the source of their value' ('Aristotle and Kant', 500). The emphasis on 'full' rationality may escape the counter-example I go on to offer, but only at the high cost of presuming that a 'fully' rational choice confers value of itself rather than through any perception of what is valuable apart from this choice.

'self-legislating' being would be morally valuable, let alone of absolute worth. Moreover, there is still nothing to prevent the same problem from arising even if one specifies that the being with this faculty of selection has considerable rational powers.

Precisely because of this problem, one can appreciate Kant's claim that it is the *good* will, and not just any kind of will, that has special value. But then what of the objection that not all agents seem to have a good will? It turns out that Kant can and does deny this, because, given one of the ways he uses the term, it can be said, as Paton noted, that all persons do have such a will; for having it requires not that they have a particular good intention, but only that they maintain the general capacity (the 'Wille') to set good ends. Kant insists that this capacity is not extinguished in us even while he stresses that there is 'radical evil' in man (*Rel.*, VI: 44).[18] And precisely because this is a capacity for goodness—indeed, the capacity for goodness, and not for the selection of just any ends—it becomes understandable how Kant might think that this capacity has a special moral value.

On the best version of the general capacity view, then, one can have a good will as long as one has the capacity for goodness; one need not have any particular good intentions. I have tried to show the advantages of this view, but it cannot be denied that by itself this view also has shortcomings. Like the first view, it can appear question-begging, since it presumes that the value in the capacity for selecting good ends cannot reside in the ends themselves (and it must concede that the capacity, precisely because it already exists, cannot be its own end). Furthermore, the view suffers from the debilitating feature of not serving to mark basic moral distinctions (e.g. between good and bad persons) and of having no specific relation to the concrete moral evaluation of individuals. Yet it is clearly this kind of evaluation that is at the very center of Kant's own discussion (e.g. of the shopkeeper and the 'friend of man', pp. 397–8) at the outset of the *Grundlegung*. So even if the second view can capture one important meaning of Kant's term, it cannot provide us with the true gloss of how 'good will' is functioning in the text at issue. It is necessary therefore to move on to a third view, one that can better incorporate some of the desiderata that have emerged so far, even if it may not turn out to be fully satisfactory either.

III

The third interpretation equates the good will with the proper and complete individual character, and thus it can be called the 'whole character' view. It picks up on the obvious and immediate connection that Kant draws in Chapter One of the *Grundlegung* between the good will and character. As the good will is stressed

---

[18] See also Menzer, *Eine Vorlesung Kants*, 249.

in the first sentence, so 'character' is emphasized in the second sentence. The term is not brought up explicitly for some time after that, but at the end of the second paragraph Kant does speak of 'the principles of a good will' (p. 394), and it seems fair to take commitment to such principles to be the essence of a proper Kantian character (cf. *Refl.* 7314, XIX: 310–11:[19] the good will 'is in a sense the person himself').

The third view is in a way a synthesis of the preceding views. Like the first view, and unlike the second, it has the benefit of offering an interpretation of 'good will' that can function as a basis for the moral evaluation of different individuals; and like the second view, and unlike the first, it offers something that is significant enough to be an immediately plausible candidate for being of special value.

More specifically, if we say that having a good will is equivalent to having a good character, then we can do better justice to the concern of the first view with Kant's idea that unconditional goodness is a matter of goodness in all contexts. The good will construed as good character meets this concern, because to have a good character for Kant is to have one's 'whole' character be good, and good in a way that, like the character itself, does not derive from anything else. It is not a matter of being good in one particular intention, or even through a series of events: it is a matter of being good in the free and overriding principle behind the more particular maxims that are behind all our even more particular and numerous actions. This point is not developed as much as it could be in the *Grundlegung*, but it surfaces in Kant's concern with our 'total worth' and the 'worth of character' (pp. 397, 399).[20]

This view of the will provides a quite different approach to the problem noted earlier about why the will should be the component that is given priority in every particular context. If the will is thought of as a mere particular intention, it surely can seem odd that it must always outrank such factors as one's lasting temperament, gifts, etc. On the other hand, once the will signifies one's *entire* character, then it becomes understandable why Kant might think the other components in a particular situation are morally relevant only relative to that character. This suggests that to have a good will is precisely to have the kind of principles that would be right for any situation one could be in (in his lectures 'Moral Mrongovius II', XXIX: 639, Kant speaks of our moral disposition as having 'infinite' consequences, for it implies what one would do in all similar circumstances); and, a fortiori, the right principle for each context one really is in. The main idea here is already indicated by Kant in one of his early remarks on his copy of

---

[19] See also Wolff, *Autonomy*, 59.
[20] This view is well supported by material in Louden and Harbison, but it can hold quite independently of Harbison's questionable proposal that 'The concept of a good character is precisely the concept that enables one to supply some content for that of a good will' (W. G. Harbison, 'The Good Will', *Kant-Studien*, 71 (1980), 47–59 at 48; cf. Louden, 'Kant's Virtue Ethics', 478–9). My proposal is just that character provides the locus, not the content, of a good will.

Observations on the Beautiful and the Sublime. There he notes that, since a proper will is one that harmoniously subordinates all its powers, the status of such a will must outrank that of any of its particular powers and effects (XX: 145, 17 ff.; cf. XX: 144, 17 f.).[21]

Despite these advantages, the third view has its opponents. It can easily seem that, if this is what Kant means when he speaks of acting from duty, then it is highly misleading for him to pretend to be discussing the moral worth of a particular act and the will which performs it.[22] The idea that seems to be behind this kind of objection is that an emphasis on one's entire disposition can appear to undercut the very drama that Kant himself seems to emphasize in examples such as that of the 'honest' shopkeeper (p. 397). If we think of the shopkeeper as someone without good will in this sense, as someone who would avoid cheating only because he fears its consequences, then it may appear that we must say he is bad 'in all contexts', i.e. the kind of person who just doesn't respect duty for duty's sake. But if that is his whole character, then there may seem to be no drama for him now, or in any particular situation; he can 'do no other' than be himself, *he* just can't be expected to take on a whole different attitude.

Such an objection is surely unfair to Kant's own intentions. Kant clearly thinks we are always free in such situations, and he explicitly countenances the possibility of moral 'revolution' in even what appear to be the worst souls. Indeed, Kant's examples at the beginning of the *Grundlegung* (e.g. the 'friend of man' who 'for the first time' acts from duty, p. 398) are designed precisely to remind us of instances of radical improvement. (This is the unrejected value of the view that, in the sense of a general capacity, there is good will in all of us.) Moreover, even if Kant were to say that someone is an all bad character, someone who (given that premise) would never act properly, this is on Kant's view only a consequence of his own free orientation and not an absolute necessity. The notion of a whole character as 'determining' one's moral value does not destroy the freedom of any particular action in accord with this free character, no matter how automatic that action may appear.

This response does not eliminate all problems. If having a Kantian good will requires a character that is 'good in all contexts' (and if a bad will means being 'bad in all contexts'), then it can seem that one must be all good in order to be good at all. However, there is an ambiguity in saying that the good will involves goodness in all contexts. Saying this could mean that one has the right maxim in *every*

---

[21] See also Menzer, *Eine Vorlesung Kants*, 21. This view is a bridge between a Leibnizian perfectionism and a clear insistence on an absolutely free but autonomous will. In addition, at times Kant seems to think it evident that, since such a will is good in all situations, its principle must be a principle of universalizability, just as he also seems to think that the 'unconditionedness' of being had by a will good in all contexts is enough to give the principle of such a will a categorical nature (cf. 'Moral Mrongovius II', XXIX: 609). Here I will have to abstract from such controversial further inferences.

[22] Cf. Wood, 'Hegel's Ethical Thought', 146–53.

situation that one is in; but it might rather mean just that one is a person who, because of a fundamental and unconditioned free attitude, has a proper character 'on the whole'. In the latter case it is still true that in each context one is in, one is a good person (because of one's character), and yet sometimes one might happen to have something other than the proper specific maxim in that context.

There has been considerable debate recently about this issue. Richard Henson has argued that a Kantian can say that moral worth (and presumably a good will) is present whenever one has a moral motive that is by itself sufficient to produce a dutiful action, even if it is the case that other (perhaps equally sufficient) non-moral motives of inclination are also present then.[23] A difficulty with this view is that it avoids the problem of seeming too antipathetic to inclination (as Schiller feared Kant was) only at the cost of making morality too cheap. That is, it seems that it could be enough for one to have worth on this view if one is in some single odd circumstance where one's moral motive is sufficient for dutiful action—perhaps just because in that sole circumstance there isn't very much to compete with it. On this view moral worth seems a matter of sheer luck, the luck of not being tested by anything like a really tough decision. Such a view seems contrary to common intuitions, as well as to Kant's remarks about the will as unqualifiedly good.

A diametrically opposed proposal, discussed by Barbara Herman, would be to say that one has moral worth in a situation only if one's moral motivation is so strong that, no matter how much of a challenge by conflicting motives one were to face, one would still act from duty. Herman herself believes that this proposal is too radical, for she says, 'failure in different circumstances does not require denial of moral worth to the original performance'.[24] Her own proposal is that moral worth requires only that the moral motive be the 'effective' one in the original circumstance, i.e. the sole actual cause (although other present motives may happen to be 'satisfied' by the act as well). This means that worth implies something more than just 'the presence of a moral motive sufficient to produce a dutiful action',[25] although it apparently does not imply so much as a motive that would produce a dutiful action in any more trying circumstances.

This proposal can appear in effect to differ little from the one by Henson, which Herman rejected because it turned moral worth back into a matter of luck. Herman notes that the problem of luck can seem to arise for her own view, but she

---

[23] R. Henson, 'What Kant Might Have Said: Moral Worth and the Overdetermination of Dutiful Action', *Philosophical Review*, 88 (1979), 39–54. Actually, Henson argues that Kant has two views on the matter, and that the liberal view discussed here is present only after the *Grundlegung*; but I agree with Herman's analysis, cited below, that Henson's analysis of the *Grundlegung* is wrong, and so I believe that Henson could have tried to apply this view to the *Grundlegung*.

[24] B. Herman, 'On the Value of Acting from the Motive of Duty', *Philosophical Review*, 90 (1981), 359–82 at 369; for an opposed view, see P. Benson, 'Moral Worth', *Philosophical Studies*, 51 (1987), 365–82 at 371.

[25] Ibid. 382.

insists that the issue is really one of the moral worth of actions, and not the moral virtue of agents. Her point is that, as long as an action has a motive that is proper in that situation and is in fact the cause of what duty requires, we can say that the action is a worthy one, and this judgment is not a matter of chance: 'although it may be a matter of luck *whose* actions have moral worth... it is not a matter of luck that the *action* has moral worth'.[26]

There is an obvious oddity here, one explored very recently by Sorell: namely, that this view does not fit very well with the fact that Kant introduces the notion of moral worth in the context of speaking of a *will* that is unqualifiedly good.[27] Herman's proposal suddenly separates the notion of worth from the will of the agent, and it makes the moral evaluation of the agent relative to chance. These consequences understandably drive Sorell back to proposing that the Kantian must say that a good will is one that acts such that a wrong '*could* not have been done in other circumstances'.[28] This means it is not enough if a wrong was not done in the actual circumstance, nor is it enough if a wrong would not have been done were there merely to have been various weak temptations in the situation. The good will, it appears, must be all good after all; it must be strong enough to persevere no matter how strongly it *might* be challenged by other motives.

Such a view may at least seem much more Kantian than the weaker alternatives that have been scouted, but the view still seems so severe and unattractive that it is worth considering whether Kant must be held to it. Fortunately, there seems to be a natural way out of these difficulties. We need only to return again to the 'total character' interpretation of the good will noted earlier, and to explore further the second of the two possible meanings proposed for it, namely the one that requires only that the person 'on the whole' have a proper character, rather than that he have 'the right maxim in every situation' possible.

On this proposal, a good will is one that does, and would, act from duty in the ordinary course of human events, but might fail in the face of extraordinary pressures.[29] It could still in a sense be called 'unqualifiedly good' because its goodness would be present in the character that it manifests in all contexts, and because its commitment to that character would not itself be a matter of circumstance, of external conditions. Even when a person with such a good will fails to act from duty in a trying circumstance, his goodness is there in the fact that it took such a circumstance to bring him down. The merits of this proposal lie first in its providing an intuitively satisfying compromise in the face of such overly lax or overly rigorous requirements as that a person with good will need not be able to

---

[26] Ibid. 371.
[27] Ibid. 362. Herman herself begins by taking note of this fact!
[28] T. Sorell, 'Kant's Good Will and our Good Nature', *Kant-Studien*, 78 (1987), 87–101 at 94.
[29] Benson, 'Moral Worth', 381, n. 7.

meet any significant temptations, or must be able to meet them all. This proposal, and it alone, simultaneously allows for a natural way of distinguishing morally between agents while preserving the connection Kant clearly wants to make between will and character. In contrast to proposals like Herman's, there are no free-floating maxims here; maxims are evaluated in the context of what they reveal about the person as a whole, just as one expects Kant would want.

The natural challenge to this proposal comes from the fact that Kant hardly speaks in these specific terms, and he often seems to use a higher, even if counter-intuitive, standard for a good will (e.g. p. 437). There is certainly a textual basis for this challenge, but there are also texts that push in another direction. There is, for example, the fact that Kant clearly distinguishes between a human and a (not really attainable by us) perfect will; and so, since he does indicate that people can have a good will, and that people can be subject to a range of moral comparisons, he should not be held to a theory that requires a good will to be all good and therefore tantamount to perfect. Furthermore, the mere fact that he is very clearly willing to speak of someone as having a good will in one sense, namely the general capacity sense discussed earlier, even when there can be nothing like perfection present, shows that he could not completely outlaw a non-perfectionist use of 'good will'. I believe that this leaves the interpreter with the license of finding or constructing a non-perfectionist sense of good will which does the most justice to the broadest range of Kantian language about the will. Because of the specific ways cited so far in which this criterion is satisfied better by the whole character view than by the proposed alternatives, I believe it is best designated as the Kantian view.

IV

Even if some version of this view is accepted as the best available interpretation of Kant on the good will, one can ask further about the internal viability of the view. I will conclude by briefly considering two problems that arise immediately when one considers aspects of the good will to which Kant's own discussion draws attention. One is the problem of making sense of the struggle with temptation within a successful good will; the other is the problem of making sense of the transition to a will that is good.

As Herman notes, 'temptation is an ordinary and natural part of moral life',[30] but it is not clear that Kant or Kantians like Herman have a simple and natural account of this phenomenon. One problem that complicates their discussions is the fact that, even when they show they know better elsewhere, they do not always heed the implications of Kant's theory of action. On that libertarian theory, inclinations can 'tempt' us not as forces that can overwhelm, but only as occasions

---

[30] Herman, 'On the Value', 360 n.

that can appear attractive to our free judgment. Similarly, the mere presence of a moral consideration cannot generate an action; the will of the agent must freely accept the consideration as the one on which he chooses to act. Hence, when a Kantian asks whether duty or inclination underlies a human action, these factors must be understood as formal rather than efficient causes. The person is always the efficient cause, as a will that chooses to act either for an end of duty, or an end of inclination, or perhaps, as Kant notes, rather for a neutral end, such as fish rather than meat ('Moral Mrongovius II': XXIX: 641). While such 'neutral' acts are possible, they still must be taken in the face of the limiting conditions of what duty permits, and, more generally, in the context of a whole character which manifests a basic disposition to give either the ends of duty or those of inclination overall precedence.[31]

Some of this is implicit in Herman's critique of Henson, especially where she stresses that he is wrong to speak only of 'present' and 'sufficient' motives, while begging off from any claim of an 'actual' cause.[32] As she notes, whatever epistemic difficulties there may be in determining the cause in particular cases, the Kantian must stress that in good acts there is a really effective agent cause, a cause that has 'a kind of independence from circumstance and need'.[33] Unfortunately, she does not stress how this must be true of acts in general, and sometimes she herself seems to revert to the suggestion that factors other than the free agent can cause action. Thus, she says action must involve not only formal or 'limiting' but also 'primary motives' (which, for the most part, are not moral), where 'a primary motive is one that can, by itself produce action'.[34] This sounds non-Kantian in so far as it implies that inclination can act 'by itself', bypassing our free will; perhaps this language is another consequence of her failure to bring out how all that a self does must be a affected by our whole free character.

Equally misleading suggestions about action can be found in analyses like that of Sorell, who properly stresses that the Kantian requires 'a good will behind a good nature'. The error here is the opposite one of claiming that 'inclination has no role to play in the motivation of an act'.[35] This claim is introduced in the course of criticizing Henson's idea that there is no reason why the 'presence' of a pleasure motive should deprive an act of rightness. The criticism consists in pointing to Kant's insistence that right acts have their 'sole sufficing motive' in our acting from duty (*MS*, vi. 220). Correct as this point is, it does not entail that pleasure cannot be 'present' (for consideration) then, albeit as a non-sufficient factor.

---

[31] See *Rel.*, VI: 20; and cf. p. 396, on the 'establishment' of a good will.
[32] See Herman, 'On the Value', 370.   [33] Ibid. 392.
[34] Ibid. 373 n.; cf. 377: 'he acts because he is, literally [!], moved by the others' distress'.
[35] Sorell, 'Kant's Good Will', 101, 91.

What is still needed is a truly Kantian account of how a good will can face the ends of inclination as genuine temptations that have some weight for it, although they can never really force themselves on the will, nor truly appear as properly overriding the equally non-coercive ends of duty. Clearly, for Kant the strength of a temptation cannot be a sheer product of natural forces, and yet some account must be given of how it appears that such forces can change the strength of the temptations before one.

To start with, we could say that these forces work not by making specific ends of inclination literally stronger, but rather by changing the moral situation, so that new ends become relevant, ends that have a greater appeal than the previous ones. For example, before a briber puts his money on the table, his talk may not do much to deflect us from our commitment to duty. Once the money is there, we have the struggle of facing the more tempting option of a bird in the hand rather than a nebulous shady proposition. As the money on the table piles up, more and more desired objects can appear to come within our reach, and the competition against doing the right thing can become truly powerful. But what is the source of this power? A Kantian must insist that it is internal; a person of weak character might be bought for pennies, while the rest of us may feel quite uninterested—unless the amount becomes considerable. Kant discusses this problem in terms of the phrase, 'every man has his price' (*Rel.*, VI: 38). What deserves emphasis again is the fact that for Kant this 'price' must be one set by the person himself. More specifically, what the person determines, in determining his whole character, is his degree of vulnerability. Different circumstances and different offers may play on this degree with different results, but morally these differences are secondary.

On this model, we would expect that the good man is one who feels relatively little temptation (although, given the differences just noted that may occur in actual circumstances, a nobler person might still by chance be tempted more often than a less noble one). And this is precisely what Kant often suggests, especially when he says that the more open we are to morality, the more it will seem 'irresistible' ('Moral Mrongovius II', XXIX: 617), so that, as we are trained properly, good action becomes 'easier' (XXIX: 639). Yet he also says that that will is better which succeeds in the face of a harder time (XXIX: 599), so that, while it might be said that a state ('Zustand') is better the more it 'gives' one, an act is better the more 'costly' it becomes (XXIX: 613).

One could explain away the tension here by saying that in each case the same degree of inner resistance to corruption is being honored; it's just that in some contexts this degree manifests itself in the fact of its arranging things so that it doesn't have to face much of a challenge (this implies a moral parallel to the Kantian paradoxes of self-affection: here we generate the very strength of what is to appear difficult for us to overcome), whereas in other contexts the same moral strength manifests itself in the fact of its 'coming through', even when challenges have been forced upon one. Thus, the noble man is one who tries to avoid battles but is also one who can handle them when they arise. This may be a proper explanation of the texts, but it is worth noting that it does not easily fit a common understanding of these situations in so far as it implies that, in contexts where the 'objective' temptations are the same, the more moral man is the one who feels less pressure in the first place.

Once we learn that for the man of good will temptation is easy to resist, we might feel that he has become considerably less admirable. This is hardly an insuperable objection, but it does show in one more way the radicality of Kant's conception of freedom: it is so radical that the very picture of inner moral struggle that many of us have, and most of us have associated with Kant, is precisely the improper one. This consequence also indirectly supports my earlier proposal that a good will be understood generally as a matter of being good 'on the whole', thus of having a high *degree* of resistance to temptation. If it literally requires being all good, so that one would never give any overriding weight to inclination's ends because one would never even allow that they have any attraction, then it becomes an inhuman standard.

This brings us to the last and most challenging problem for the Kantian story of the will: namely, how to explain the fact that Kant regards a good will as something freely pervading one's whole self, and yet also speaks of it as something to be 'established' (p. 396), apparently by a free 'revolution' which wholly reverses the overall ordering one gives to inclination and duty (*Rel.*, VI: 47). The paradoxes here are many. Right away one wonders what it is that is to do this 'establishing'. It cannot, of course, be any mere natural forces, or even any intellectual principles by themselves. It must be the person himself who freely brings about the good will. But what kind of person? Someone of bad character would have no such interest, and someone with good character would have no such need. The only chance for an escape from this dilemma is to recall Kant's stress that, in a sense, even the worst character still has an ever present capacity to affirm a good will. Suppose this happens; suppose that from now on a once miserly shopkeeper acts honestly out of duty. What then is to be said about his 'intelligible' character (A539/B568), which Kant must hold is something that covers one's entire being and that can be free precisely because it is the ground of one's whole temporal nature, and is not something within time and nature?

It seems that what must be said in such a situation is that the true character of the shopkeeper is a mixed one, and hence he was not fully bad to begin with. (Only by rephrasing matters this way can the initial dilemma be escaped.) He has a certain degree of inner goodness which appears in the temporal form of a segment of his life giving precedence to inclination and another segment giving precedence to duty. He has a good will but not a perfect one; the larger the segment is that gives precedence to duty, the better his character is to be judged. This fits with

Kant's discussion of long-term moral improvement as something that God can judge as a *sign* of sufficient inner goodness, as well as with my proposal that a Kantian will is to be conceived as a particular less-than-perfect whole character. The difficulty here is that once again even the best interpretation leaves a conception that does not fit smoothly with common language or even with Kant's own (taken literally). We seem forced to say that talk of moral 'change' is in one sense deeply misleading, for in some way outside of time the person is and must be what he is independent of the change. More precisely, the 'change'—which includes the states before, during, and after—must be but the effect of the person's inner character, not, as it is natural to think, the cause.

This conclusion may seem to be but one more instance of the strain that Kant's doctrine of the transcendental ideality of time puts on our beliefs. But I believe there is an extra problem here because of specific difficulties that arise for conceptualizing change in the sense of moral 'conversion' or 'revolution'. Even if we don't worry much about who does the change, or how or when it results, its 'why' remains mysterious. Why should a will which it is assumed in other contexts does not respect morality (this is just another way of expressing Kant's idea that for us the law is a burden, an imperative) 'suddenly' respect it in the context of the change?

On the Kantian view, the basic response must be that the person just sees what was all along compelling—compelling, of course, in a rational but not a natural sense. Yet this seeing is not a matter of attaining new intellectual insight; such a condition would only bring in again the very inequality and contingency that Kant wants to keep out of morality. As Kant stresses, neither sense nor understanding can be the source here; it must be the will ('Moral Mrongovius II', XXIX: 629). But if the will of a person is bad in some contexts, and there is nothing about different contexts that can force a difference in the will, why is it good in others? What is the difference here between saying that the will is free, and saying instead that as a matter of luck the will just takes things a certain way?

It is not enough to point to the fact that *what* the will takes, in the case of moral conversion, is free in the sense of what Kant at one point calls legislative autonomy (i.e. free in having a content determined by reason itself), for there remains the question of why the *taking* of a new position must be free in the 'efficient cause' sense of what Kant calls executive autarchy, i.e. self-caused rather than uncaused or externally caused ('Moral Mrongovius II', XXIX: 626).[36] The fact that legislative freedom is involved here does not by definition entail that executive freedom is involved. The link between the two is not that close, and conversion must be understandable independently of autonomy, for there might also have been a 'conversion' to immorality, and that would equally require explanation.

---

[36] Cf. Menzer, *Eine Vorlesung Kants*, 173 ff.

A final response would be to insist that, if one believes that all ordinary moral (i.e. pro or anti-moral) commitments involve freedom, then it is only consistent to think that even the unusual commitment involved in conversion should also be a free one. But the common reasons why most people think ordinary situations involve freedom have to do with a picture of a particular agency that knows little of the model of a total intelligible character independent of a thoroughly determined natural domain. Once one shifts to that model it is not so clear that absolute freedom is a common presupposition, as is indicated by centuries of theological debate over whether responsiblity for our total depravity (the analog to 'radical evil') does presume our independence. One cannot simply extrapolate from ordinary situations in which, given a particular character, one might seem to choose freely among various options, to the quite different level where one is speaking of the determination of character itself as some kind of choice among options made from no given perspective at all. This is not to say that the notion of such a radical choice at the heart of the good will is incoherent or demonstrably inadequate,[37] but it does indicate that the notion takes us some distance from common sense and even from the relatively concrete considerations present in the first two models of the good will. Thus, the very model of the good will that seems to save Kant from the severe shortcomings of most interpretations leaves us with some difficulties of its own.[38]

---

[37] *Pace* D. O'Connor, 'Good and Evil Disposition', *Kant-Studien*, 76 (1985), 288–302; and P. Stern, 'The Problem of History and Temporality in Kantian Ethics', *Review of Metaphysics*, 39 (1986), 504–45.

[38] For help on the issues of this paper I am very indebted to participants at the Sigriswil conference and colleagues at Notre Dame, and especially to Professors Otfried Höffe, Gerold Prauss, and Philip Quinn.

– 8 –

Kant and Hegel on Freedom: Two New Interpretations

The issue of freedom in the philosophies of Kant and Hegel has been illuminated by two very important new books: Henry Allison's *Kant's Theory of Freedom* and Allen Wood's *Hegel's Ethical Thought*.[1] On their respective topics, these works are surely the most significant studies now in English. They can be compared profitably on many issues, but the major question they provoke in common is the following: can Kant's theory of freedom be defended in contemporary 'incompatibilist' terms, as Allison believes, or is it vulnerable to Hegelian criticisms of the 'compatibilist' sort that Wood presents? I shall argue that the answer to *both* of these questions is negative, and that there is a third option: namely that Kant's real theory of freedom is not as well off as Allison contends, nor as weak as Wood claims.

To begin to understand these claims, one must first break the notion of freedom down into its *metaphysical* and *ethical* aspects. At the metaphysical level, Allison presents and defends Kant as an incompatibilist,[2] but in a way that allegedly does not involve what he calls the 'noumenal' metaphysics that traditional interpreters, such as Wood and myself, have claimed to be present—and present in a coherent fashion—within Kant's theory. As a Hegelian, though, Wood (unlike myself) finds this metaphysics deeply objectionable. But while Allison means to develop and defend a 'non-noumenal' version of incompatibilism on allegedly Kantian grounds, I will argue that, even if incompatibilism is not refutable (and it is not quite as bad as Wood implies), it is not especially attractive either, and that it is not even needed by most Kantians, despite the fact that Allison and Kant himself certainly are committed to it.

---

[1] Both books were published by Cambridge University Press in 1990. Page references in the text without further citation will be to Allison's book. Wood's book will be cited as *HET*.

[2] I will be understanding incompatibilism here as the denial of compatibilism, where compatibilism is taken to be the thesis that one could be said to be free even if one did not have any absolute power to do, or attempt to do, otherwise.

The ostensible need for incompatibilism comes largely from moral considerations. Allison does argue that Kant has good non-moral as well as moral reasons for insisting on incompatibilism, but I will counter that his arguments fall short, and that the only kind of freedom that we demonstrably need to assert is compatibilist freedom, freedom that has its locus in the empirical autonomy of ethical life—the kind of freedom that is the common core of Kant and Hegel's practical philosophy.

There are thus several relations between all these different philosophers which must be kept distinct. Allison is trying to save Kant's theory of freedom from both what he takes to be traditional and improper interpretations—notably including Hegel's and Wood's—of what that theory *means*, and from traditional and improper objections to its defensibility. I will be arguing in part with Wood (and Hegel) against Allison on the issue of the meaning of Kant's theory, and in part with Allison against Wood (and Hegel) on the issue of the defensibility of Kant's theory. Thus, in the end, although I will be defending an important part of what Allison and Wood say, I will also be concluding that in their major efforts here—Allison's defense of Kantian incompatibilism and Wood's attack on it—they both fail.

Before getting into the details of the crucial arguments, it is necessary first to have more of an overview of Allison's analysis.

Allison stresses the evolution of Kant's practical philosophy. He argues that in the first edition of the first *Critique*, Kant still had a 'semi-Critical' view. This view ascribes to the self an 'intelligible character', a general capacity to act independently of particular sensible stimulation. Allison contends that this capacity shows that Kant's position cannot be assimilated to compatibilism, and that it clearly reveals Kant already understood that our freedom is not limited to moral action.[3] But Allison stresses that at this point Kant still has not explained how the self is 'autonomous', i.e. capable of guiding itself specifically by a pure moral law that it gives to itself apart from sensibility altogether. And Allison argues that, even when this doctrine is developed in the *Groundwork*, it is inadequately justified, and that therefore, in what I have called the 'great reversal' (p. 201), Kant recasts the 'deduction' of freedom and morality in the second *Critique*. Rather than trying to argue from 'negative freedom' to 'positive freedom', Kant now begins with the notion of positive freedom implicit in the 'fact of reason', i.e. 'our common consciousness of the moral law as supremely authoritative' (p. 238). Instead of seeing this shift as a 'regression' to dogmatism—as I have charged[4]—or as a strategic retreat to a 'coherentist' approach to morality—as John Rawls has

---

[3] This theme is developed in another important recent work which complements Allison's nicely, viz. Onora O'Neill's *Constructions of Reason* (Cambridge, 1989). One should also compare these works with Gerold Prauss's *Kant über Freiheit als Autonomie* (Frankfurt, 1983).

[4] K. Ameriks, *Kant's Theory of Mind* (New York, 1982).

proposed—Allison ends by judging that, even if, as I have argued, Kant's effort here does not provide the 'independent warrant' for his theory that Lewis White Beck had claimed (p. 245), it is none the less 'a qualified success' (pp. 7, 248). Apparently this is because, although a skeptic might well raise the 'epistemic possibility' that the 'fact of reason' and the freedom it involves is an illusion, 'what is denied [by Kant] is ... the possibility of considering it as illusory from the practical point of view' (p. 247). The denial of this possibility is presumably significant in a compelling rather than dogmatic or pragmatic way, because to give up this 'point of view' would allegedly be to give up 'the whole, conception of ourselves as moral agents' (p. 247). At the center of this conception is the Kantian notion of the 'unique, pure character of the moral interest' where 'to take an interest in morality' is to 'recognize the moral law as providing reasons for and restrictions on action ... [that] do not reflect any of our needs as sensuous beings' (p. 247). At the very end, Allison concedes that, since he has not defended this notion in detail, this leaves 'a certain tentative character to the defense of the fact of reason' (p. 249). For this reason, contemporary non-Kantian ethical theorists of all kinds, and not just Hegelians, will hardly be converted by Allison's apologetics. Moreover, it remains unclear whether Kant's argument from morality for freedom has even the 'qualified success' that Allison claims. Here a lot hinges on the relation between the content of Kantian ethics and its supposed metaphysical preconditions.

In metaphysics, Allison aims to steer a middle course. He insists that Kant's transcendental idealism is crucial to understanding and defending Kant's theory of morality and freedom, but only because it can be given a non-'noumenalist' meaning. Here Allison builds on his earlier work, *Kant's Transcendental Idealism*,[5] which had claimed that the ideality of space and times rests just in their being epistemic conditions of our experience, and not in their being in any ontological contrast to some more fundamental set of noumenal things or properties.[6] Allison's interpretation of Kantian idealism has proven, quite understandably, to be a very popular strategy, especially since it is developed in a way that is much more historically sensitive than most approaches in English to Kant. There are, however, alternatives which should not be discounted.

Those who share Allison's distaste for the noumenal may argue against his insistence that Kant's 'incompatibilist' conception of rational agency is what is

[5] In reviewing that interpretation here, Allison says, 'epistemic conditions ... reflect the structure of the mind and therefore condition our representation of things rather than things themselves' (p. 4). I still do not see what grounds the 'therefore' and the 'rather' in Allison's remark, unless it is a matter of stipulation that would make the (theoretical) unknowability of things in themselves an uninteresting matter of definition.

[6] In his new work Allison appears to retreat from this a bit in saying that the transcendental distinction between appearances and things in themselves is 'not *primarily*, between two kinds of entity' (p. 3). However, the new book does not lend itself to developing this concession; for, by focusing on the human self, it happens to concentrate on the entity for which Kant was most interested in not asserting a radical duality of phenomenon and noumenon.

central and appealing in his practical philosophy. Allison does a good job of showing how Kant himself was attached to this conception, but this does not prove that Kantian ethics could not be developed more effectively (e.g. by Thomas Nagel)[7] without it. Alternatively, it can be argued that Kant's own idealism has stronger ontological commitments than Allison accepts—and ones that he might as well embrace.

These alternatives become significant when one sees that, like Kant, Allison is willing to grant that the law of causality governs all of the natural world.[8] If one then also insists on an incompatibilist conception of freedom, it seems hard not to place that freedom in our noumenal, i.e. non-spatio-temporal, capacities. Allison worries that this move would put our freedom in a 'timeless noumenal realm' which makes it 'virtually unintelligible and irrelevant' (p. 3). But if this move is rejected, what is to be made of Kant's talk of our 'intelligible character' and 'transcendental freedom'? Allison resists understanding this talk in terms of a literal causal relation between something non-empirical and something empirical. Rather, it is said to reflect what is simply a different perspective, a practical perspective on oneself as having a capacity to determine oneself by non-sensible norms. But, surely, any actual determining must itself be regarded ultimately as either caused naturally or not so caused. If nature is the closed system that Allison allows, then the latter option appears excluded, even if, as he claims, we 'can't help' but think ourselves free 'regulatively' in a practical respect. On a traditional 'noumenalist' reading, however, Kant's idealism easily leaves room for freedom by ensuring that we do not have to take nature to be a closed system. It is along this line that Wood, for example, has defended the coherence of the notion of intelligible character as a timeless causal ground of one's free choices,[9] but Allison rejects this notion because of unnamed 'notorious problems' (p. 51). Allison's alternative is that we are to think of reason not as an efficient ground or force, but just as the 'guiding rule' (p. 51) for our free adoption of maxims. But again, either this adoption is solely a temporal act, and then, with a non-noumenal metaphysics, it is absolutely determined after all; or else the Kantian must move back to a noumenal ground to save the claim of freedom. Allison claims that the spontaneous

---

[7] Allison remarks that his interpretation has similarities with Nagel's stress on the idea that 'nothing moves me to action without my agreeing to it', and that we have a capacity to 'stand back' from our motives and evaluate them (p. 82). But Nagel does not believe that these phenomena require an incompatibilist theory, and I agree with him that the burden of proof is on those who claim it does, especially if one appeals, as Kant often does, to what is presumed by common sense.

[8] Allison tries to detach Kant's claim that every event has some cause from the thesis that all occurrences must be subsumable under empirical laws (p. 34), but, as Michael Friedman has recently argued, in *Kant and the Exact Sciences* (Cambridge, Mass., 1992), these claims are necessarily connected for Kant. Allison himself argues against Beck's somewhat similar but desperate attempt to construe the Second Analogy as a mere regulative principle (p. 73). There Allison also nicely allays the old objection (recounted by Beck and Irwin) that Kantian transcendental freedom, if posited anywhere, has, absurdly, to be posited everywhere.

[9] A. Wood, 'Kant's Compatibilism', in *Self and Nature in Kant's Philosophy*, ed. A. Wood (Ithaca, NY, 1984), 73–101.

consciousness involved in the adoption of maxims is not an ordinary temporal act, but is rather a thought (p. 5) and not an 'experience' (a determined spatio-temporal occurrence)—but it would seem that this reduces either to a mere abstraction, or else to a kind of intellectual intuition after all. Allison repeatedly denies that this is what he intends, but he does speak of being 'directly aware' of free agency (p. 44). Moreover, although the traditional view of Kant that Wood articulates has been expressed in terms of 'two worlds' or 'two selves'—and this is a main reason it has been rejected—such talk is not really essential to it, for all that the view requires is a being that has at least two aspects, viz. spatio-temporal and (underlying) non-spatio-temporal powers.[10] Given traditional theology (i.e. at least that part which Kant accepted), there need be nothing clearly incoherent in the mere thought of such a being, and given Kant's other views, it seems most appropriate (for him) to posit that we are such a being.

In sum, if Allison insists on holding Kant to an incompatibilist metaphysics, it is unclear that he can get a good argument for the kind of freedom that this requires; and if in any case he insists on asserting that this kind of freedom does exist, then, if he wants to do metaphysics and remain in Kant's framework, it appears that he might as well also accept the traditional dual (phenomenal/ noumenal) ontology of Kantian idealism.

The traditional interpretation has a straightforward way to explain how Kant can insist that freedom somehow 'makes a difference' to us even if we can't 'intervene' in experience by literally changing the course of nature. Kant says, for example, that the 'resolution' to rise out of a chair can be a 'causally unconditioned beginning' (A451/B479). Now, surely the temporal aspect of this resolution, if it is not to (as it cannot, given the Second Analogy) disturb natural laws, must itself fit into those laws, and so accord with being in that respect causally conditioned. So, if there is absolute or 'transcendental freedom' here, it would seem to have to lie in there also being something not temporally conditioned, such as our timeless noumenal 'character' (*Gesinnung*). Allison grants that when Kant speaks this way he suggests a 'picture of reason functioning literally as a timeless causal power' (p. 48), but for Allison this is a hopelessly 'cryptic account' (p. 26) and not Kant's real meaning. But just what is it that is supposed to be especially 'cryptic' about this; why can't one's timeless character be the ultimate and free

---

[10] This is contra Allison's claim that 'actual timelessness must [!] be thought of as a property of a distinct noumenal self or agent and, therefore, not of one with an empirical character' (p. 52). (If Allison were right, it would seem to me that he would also have to say that even Leibnizian monads are 'distinct' beings from their empirical character.) Allison adds that the idea of a literally timeless character seems irreconcilable with the thought that our maxims involve 'sensuously affected' agents 'standing under imperatives' (p. 52). But the mere non-spatio-temporality of our intelligible character does not eliminate its finitude and susceptibility. A will can be flawed, or self-contaminated, internally, i.e. non-spatio-temporally, and this flaw can then have its appropriate 'expression' in a spatio-temporal character. Kant and traditional theology speak explicitly in such terms, and no matter how far-fetched it may seem to some, such talk appears at least conceptually coherent.

reason why one happens to be such that one is in the temporal situation where one must, *given* that situation, act in time as one does? That there is an *uncaused* cause (the choice of character) here should not be a special problem, since nearly all systems will end up with something that is uncaused. That the character itself is to be thought of as outside time, *qua* being *not time dependent* in its origin or nature, does, as Kant stresses, fit our own self-understanding in many ways. That something timeless in this sense can be the *ground* of something that is in time (such as moving up from a chair) is mysterious, to be sure (as all causality is ultimately mysterious)—and yet, given Kant's own stress, which Allison accepts, on the idea that causality is a 'dynamic' category linking 'heterogeneous' items, there is nothing incoherent in the notion. To say that an act took place *because* of the character then is to say that ultimately everything else provided the circumstances for that kind of character to operate as it did. Moreover, to say all this in the way Kant means is (I believe) just to add that an individual's being that kind of character is not itself a brute fact but something due to one's self, one's transcendental (and itself uncaused) power of choice, so that acts are imputable to one's self as their *real* ground.

In contrast, what Allison stresses is that here the transcendental idea of freedom is to be 'viewed as performing a modeling or regulative function with respect to the conception of ourselves as rational agents' (p. 26). That may also be true, but what is really cryptic is why he thinks Kant should be taken to mean this *rather than* that there is also a 'straightforwardly causal' (p. 32) relationship here.[11] Allison worries that such a relationship 'seems to foreclose the possibility of regarding the empirical character as itself an expression or instantiation rather than merely as a product of the causality of reason [i.e. the person's choice as a being with reason]' (p. 32). But it 'forecloses' no such possibility; the claim that there is noumenal causation (i.e. a noumenal cause with an empirical effect) does not entail the claim that there is 'merely' such causation, nor that a phenomenal 'expression' of reason is inappropriate, let alone impossible. And it does not have to 'raise the specter of ontologically distinct' (p. 32) beings; a noumenal character can underlie a phenomenal appearance of that very being, just as an empirical thing can underlie its appearance.[12] In other words, whatever story Allison wants to tell about the 'modeling' function of our idea of ourselves as free rational agents

---

[11] Cf. Allison's discussion at p. 44, where he rejects those who assume that 'being causally determined must be an ontological condition', because (Allison claims) 'for Kant, however, the concept of causality is merely an epistemic condition'. I would rather say that for Kant the theoretical and schematized concept of causality functions as an epistemic condition, but this leaves it free also to have a real and practical use apart from its sensible ('epistemic') schematization—where a 'practical' use is not simply a matter of some perspective we take, but rather reflects ultimate reality (ontology) as revealed to us by what our moral commitments seem to require.

[12] This is consistent with denying that in general we can assert a one-to-one correspondence of phenomena and noumena, for that would obviously threaten the thesis of the (theoretical) unknowability of things in themselves.

should be a perfectly acceptable addendum to Kant's noumenal metaphysics. The problem with that metaphysics is not what it excludes, but what it adds—and not because the addition is impossible or incoherent, but because its value is unclear: beyond satisfying a metaphysical desire to be able to regard oneself as an uncaused cause, it does no more work by itself.

Allison is quite successful in diagnosing various bad reasons that some interpreters may have ascribed to Kant as grounds for positing a noumenal causality of reason—but this diagnosis does not undercut the coherence of Kant's own ground. For example, Allison is right to counter those (including Wood)[13] who suggest that it was only to avoid mechanistic psychological hedonism that Kant spoke of reason as a noumenal cause (p. 35); but this point counts against only one bad way of thinking of our noumenal causality, not against the idea as such. We can agree with Allison that the suggestion runs clearly afoul of Kant's basic belief that, even if humans do universally seek pleasure, they are still rational and in some sense spontaneous agents who do so because of maxims that they have a ground for in a non-mechanistic sense. We can even agree, as Allison also stresses, that Kant believes these maxims have an expression in our empirical, temporal being, and that, as Kant says, this expression takes the form of 'laws of freedom' (A802/B830), e.g. about what ought to be done even for the sake of prudence. But we need *not* agree that the mere capacity to act according to such laws already defines us as having free agency in an *incompatibilist* sense.

Allison sees that there does appear to be a jump in such a conclusion, but he tries to make it plausible by pointing out that even in mere epistemic contexts, in acts of understanding that do not even involve the agency of something like getting out of a chair, Kant also speaks about ('intellectual') instances of synthesis or 'spontaneity' (p. 38). Just as the Kantian doctrine of apperception says that one's thoughts must always be able to be 'taken' as one's own, so, on the Kantian theory of agency, one's maxims must always be not sheer givens but 'taken' as one's own (p. 40). However, from all this Allison wants to conclude, 'the adoption of ... a rule cannot itself be regarded as the causal consequence ... of being in a state of desire' (p. 40). But, so far, I see no mature Kantian ground for this conclusion, apart from a dogmatic interest in an incompatibilist metaphysics that would underwrite moral imputations. And Allison himself concedes that these general considerations show not that 'we *really do* possess' a non-determined character, but rather just that we 'cannot *conceive*' (p. 41) of ourselves otherwise. But why not; why can't the compatibilist say that the fact that we don't *directly* see any desire necessitating a particular act still doesn't show that there is no desire in

---

[13] Cf. Allison's discussion of Wood at p. 49. I can agree with Allison against Wood here just on the point that it is misleading (though certainly encouraged by Kant) to speak of reason itself as the ultimate cause for action, rather than a particular person's power of choice (which then may agree to opt for rationality).

us at all which is ultimately behind it?[14] Allison goes to some lengths (in large part with the thought that he is refuting my interpretation of the 'Canon') to show that Kant does not mean to be *encouraging* a compatibilist position here (pp. 57–62),[15] but that does not show that, for all that has been said, the position has been *excluded* either.

Kant himself was extremely ambiguous about all this, and he suggested in many passages that freedom is involved in all sorts of simple experiences, including strictly logical judgments. But he also eventually stated that such experiences do not really settle the issue of freedom; they do not show that we are not very complicated 'turnspits' after all. Moreover, there is the obvious point that Kant easily could have made his incompatibilism quite clear, if he had wanted to, in the first edition of the Paralogisms, for if he had just stayed with the standard list of topics, he would have had immediately to address the question of whether there is a good proof of our absolute freedom.

All this reveals why Kant's discussion of autonomy is so important and why it culminated in his 'great reversal', which tries to show that our absolute freedom must be clear from (and solely from) our commitment to maxims that involve (either through acceptance or rejection) specifically moral ends. But here again another instance seems to appear of the weakness that plagued arguments from the general capacity to adopt maxims. That weakness lay in inferring from the *psychological* absence of a particular causal *content* in one's intentions (i.e. one doesn't see that one is acting as the 'mere' effect of a particular force) to the *metaphysical* absence of any natural cause as the *efficient* ground of the act which has that content. Similarly, in moral contexts, the fact that certain maxims involve a rule whose content makes no essential reference to human desires still does not show that the actual adoption of such maxims—and even the adoption of them for the reason that there is no such reference—is not in fact caused by desires.

---

[14] I have discussed a passage where just this point is made in Kant's recently available 'Moral Mrongovius II' lectures; see the Academy edition, vol. 29, p. 1022, and my 'Kant on Spontaneity: Some New Data', *Proceedings of the VII International Kant Kongress 1990* (Berlin, 1991). In that paper I did not have the space to develop the criticisms that I think can be made of the Kantian position, so it can appear there that I am closer to Allison's position than is really the case.

[15] Allison says my discussion 'seems based partly on the assumption that practical freedom amounts merely to a compatibilist conception' (p. 62). My point, however, is rather just that Kant does not say enough here to rule out compatibilism—and that he does need to say more if he is to be true to his own beliefs. (So I don't want to say that what Kant calls 'practical freedom', as opposed to transcendental freedom, *means* something compatibilistic, but just that it could be consistent with the truth of compatibilism.) Allison (in part) follows Beck in defending the Canon by saying that 'from the practical standpoint ... speculative questions about the transcendental status of our practically free acts simply do not arise' (p. 64). But if this 'practical standpoint' isn't simply a crude stance of willful ignorance, then it seems that, given Kant's own views, it must face up to the possibility that we are a 'turnspit'. It is Kant who says that, if metaphysics leaves us with no room for freedom, we should drop morality, no matter how much we are 'practically' committed to it (B xxix), and this seems to me to be the most consistent position for him to adopt, even if I also believe that he did not always take it seriously enough, and that we need not be as unsympathetic to compatibilism as he was.

Allison suggests that the causal theorist must be supposing that 'rules or principles function as efficient causes, which can produce or evoke a positive response ("pro-attitude") in an agent' (p. 51). But such a specific claim is not at all needed. The compatibilist hypothesis is not that 'rules' about sensible ends, or even beliefs about such rules, need be what cause our actions, but rather just that there can be desires present that in some, perhaps totally hidden, way are their ultimate efficient cause.

This hypothesis may seem similar to the 'anomalous monism' that Ralf Meerbote has ascribed to Kant, and that Allison rejects as 'fundamentally wrong-headed' (p. 81). For Meerbote, our rational agency is defined via our capacity for reasoned preference, which is said to be free just in so far as it involves apperception and deliberation. Allison is certainly right that this definition does not do justice to Kant's view that our reason has an 'intelligible character', an ultimate imputability, and a type of practical freedom (to adopt maxims even contrary to reason) not necessarily found in beings with all the capacities Meerbote outlines. But on the extra question of whether, apart from Kant's own beliefs, 'the conception of ourselves as a rational agent' with transcendental freedom is absolutely indispensable, Allison offers no extra defense but just applauds Kant for trying to 'come to grips' with the problem (p. 82), i.e. with trying to formulate an unrefuted version of incompatibilism. This attempt can be admired, but without our having to concede that it shows that Kant (or Allison) gives adequate attention to the possibility of a sophisticated compatibilism.

The most sophisticated challenge that Kant raised against this possibility was his claim, in the second *Critique* and after, that the 'fact' of our accepting moral demands requires that we think of ourselves as absolutely free. An obvious problem for this approach is that it makes it appear that in non-moral contexts we could have no assurance of our freedom. This problem explains why Allison puts such an emphasis in his book on many earlier passages where Kant spoke of freedom in non-moral contexts. We have seen the limitations of such passages, and surely the easiest way to understand Kant's 'great reversal' is to say that he also came to appreciate these limitations. Nonetheless, Kant's later theory gives some attention to the problem of non-moral contexts by developing (especially in the *Religion*) the notion of intelligible character in such a way that it concerns the entirety of one's life. That is, once it is admitted that every human action implicitly involves some maxim, and that each maxim must be implicitly judged with regard to its permissibility by the overall '*Gesinnung*' that defines the person, then it turns out that all action contexts have at least some relation to morality, and so can be seen as affected by whatever freedom that requires.

Allison does a superb job of explaining how this notion of *Gesinnung* is developed by Kant, but he does not get far with proving that whatever moral attitude it involves requires (as Kant assumed it did) an incompatibilist metaphysics. The 'phenomenal' fact that the maxims permeating our moral life appear as 'self-imposed' rules hardly settles the question of whether this imposition is free of natural determination. For Kant, the question of asserting our freedom ultimately comes down to the issue of whether there is moral autonomy in the sense of 'motivational independence' from all our needs as sensuous beings. (As Allison points out (p. 98), from just the idea that there is such an independence, one might still think that it could take a non-moral form, but in fact for Kant the only way we really can think of it is entirely in moral terms.) But how is such independence to be established? One line of argument that might seem very relevant here is the claim that moral demands have an unconditional form which cannot be grounded by any feature of our contingent 'natural constitution' (cf. p. 100). But even if this were allowed to show that the *justification* of 'categorical' imperatives cannot be based in anything 'material' and contingent, this still does not show that, if they are rather based in the legislative form of practical reason as such (which is 'autonomous' here as a principle, not as a property of a particular will), then they could have applicability only to beings who are autonomous in the specific sense of *efficiently* and freely determining themselves. Once again, from the content of a principle that is being followed, the causal history of the being that does the following (or even the generating of the principle) cannot be inferred. Moreover, it remains unclear that we can assert, in a non-question-begging way, that there are such 'categorical' imperatives, or that there must be unconditioned values.[16]

Like many other contemporary Kantians here, Allison tries to link the Copernican image of transcendental idealism to the specifics of Kant's practical philosophy, and in particular to its rejection of 'heteronomous' principles, of principles that locate value ultimately in some natural object independent of us. But even if the content of morality is determined by the structure of reason (rather than external contingent 'nature') itself, this does not make it 'ideal' in any significant ontological sense. Whatever reason requires, it requires absolutely of all beings. So the denial of transcendental realism is not requisite for the content of Kantian morality, and this fits nicely with the fact that its basic content was developed before Kant changed his metaphysics to idealism. The only reason Kant's practical philosophy calls for idealism is his supposing that that philosophy requires incompatibilism, and that the ideality of space and time—but not of moral principles—is the only way to keep incompatibilism from being precluded.

In sum, neither the content of Kantian morality, nor the idealism associated with its metaphysics proves that we are self-determining practical beings in an absolute sense. The independence of the issue of the content of morality from the question of the metaphysical nature of moral agents can be clarified further by

---

[16] Cf. the first part of my 'Kant on the Good Will', in *Grundlegung zur Metaphysik der Sitten: Ein Kooperativer Kommentar*, ed. O. Höffe (Frankfurt, 1989), 45–65.

means of a distinction that Allison himself stresses. Against those who suppose that Kant must believe, with a psychology that is hopelessly unrealistic, that people are always aiming at either just pleasure or just duty, Allison reminds us of the distinction between ends and grounds of action (p. 102). The ground of a sympathetic person's action may be that person's own pleasure, even though what the person aims at and has in mind are the pleasures of others, just as the ground of a good person's action can be duty, even if that person's immediate object is not the satisfaction of duty as such but rather the proper treatment of those who happen to be around the person. But this means that, whatever the ends are that make up the overt content of our intentions, our actions can also have hidden grounds of a different form. And whether or not these grounds are themselves also intentional in some sense (e.g. *qua* a principle of maximizing pleasure)—and they need not be—it seems clear that they could be or have causes that escape our knowledge. In fact, something like this is precisely Kant's own point, insofar as he is trying to suggest that, in addition to the evident natural history of one's actions, there can be (and, indeed, we are to think that there must be) hidden non-natural grounds as well. But this game works both ways, for metaphysically it is also open to the compatibilist to say that there can be ultimate natural grounds behind whatever ostensible free grounds we posit. Moreover, in his theory of 'incentives' and 'respect'. Kant goes to some length to show that even the actions of an ultimately free and moral agent will always have natural antecedents of a certain sort; all that he adds is that, metaphysically, these antecedent conditions can themselves be seen as relevant to a situation that we are in ultimately because of a cause that is non-sensible. Yet even if we allow that this is a metaphysical possibility, we need not say that it is a possibility that we 'cannot help' but affirm.

It is precisely this kind of objection that Wood has found at the heart of Hegel's critique of Kant. On Wood's interpretation, 'For Kant, whether or not one acts from duty is morally crucial because the autonomy or heteronomy of one's actions depends on how they are psychologically caused' (*HET*, p. 150). There may be some difficulties with the details of how Wood understands this causation in Kant (especially in suggesting a kind of intellectual determinism rather than libertarian incompatibilism), but his general point conforms closely with our analysis. What Wood likes about Hegel's ethics is that such causal questions are almost entirely ignored, and emphasis is placed instead on the content and actualization of the proper principles.

It was said that for Hegel causal questions are 'almost' ignored because, as I have noted elsewhere,[17] in some of his discussions of freedom Hegel, like Allison, also seems to desire an *in*compatibilist metaphysics that is not burdened by the noumenalism of traditional Kantian ontology. My objection then was that the

---

[17] K. Ameriks, 'Hegel's Critique of Kant's Theoretical Philosophy', *Philosophy and Phenomenological Research*, 48 (1985), 1–35.

grounds for asserting such freedom were even more obscure in Hegel than in Kant. But there are also reasons why this objection is not so pressing here. On the one hand, Hegel need not be as committed as Kant is to the universal rule of the principle of causality (and dropping that commitment immediately makes incompatibilism much easier to hold). The causal principle is the true keystone of Kant's theoretical philosophy, whereas it is not such a central feature of the Hegelian system. A certain causal 'looseness' in nature need not be such a basic embarrassment to the Hegelian, whereas it would cause a fundamental revision of Kant's transcendental account of experience. More importantly, there is present in Hegel a host of considerations for arguing that practical philosophy can get along well with a compatibilist notion of freedom. That philosophy spells out all sorts of ways in which specific modes of determination in the lives of human beings can warrant making sufficient distinctions within experience between basic levels of freedom.[18] Hegel does not always clearly or consistently develop this notion, but, precisely because his notion also stresses autonomy in its meaning, it could be profitably incorporated by revisionist—i.e. compatibilist—Kantians as well.

Although it is Hegel's philosophy that stresses that one might as well 'factor through' the admittedly indeterminable mysteries of the ultimate causal grounds of our action (and thus give compatibilism a chance), it should not be forgotten that, as we have just argued, Kant himself does not stress these causal factors when trying to determine the *principles* that are relevant for morality. Hegel needs extra grounds for specific objections against those principles, and yet, as Wood himself has argued, the Hegelian attack on the content of Kantian morality is not very persuasive when disengaged from the criticism of the Kantian theory of moral motivation. Indeed, for the most part, Hegel really wants to accept and amplify many of the Kantian principles. Hence as a theory of moral *action* there need not be much difference (except in detail) between Kant and Hegel. The crucial differences emerge rather when one looks at their accounts of the role of our intentions in morality.

It is here that Allison mounts an effective counter-attack on Wood, for Wood's Hegelian theory of moral motivation is extraordinarily liberal in its content and extraordinarily harsh in its dismissal of the Kantian alternative. His Hegelian claim is not only that action 'from duty alone' is difficult to discern, especially when it is presumed to require a non-natural, absolutely free cause; the claim is that such action is practically 'incoherent', and that, whatever moral intentions

---

[18] Richard Schacht has nicely documented Hegel's treatment of freedom along this line as consisting in 'self-conscious rational self-determination', such that 'true freedom becomes possible only with the emergence of the properly organized state as an existing reality'. R. Schacht, 'Hegel on Freedom', in *Hegel: A Collection of Critical Essays*, ed. A. MacIntyre (New York, 1972), 300, 326. Schacht can be criticized only for overlooking incompatibilist passages in Hegel, and for not attending enough to the metaphysical dimensions of the issue; cf. *HET*, pp. 150-1.

one might have, these need be only one factor in the action, not 'the' determining one (cf. p. 186; *HET*, pp. 152–3).[19] All our action, supposedly, involves our particular interests, and if the moral goodness of, for example, a policy of honesty is just *one* of the factors behind an otherwise selfish grocer's action, that can make it enough, on this view, to warrant approval as worthy.[20]

From this Hegelian perspective, one simply dismisses questions about whether there was a free 'inner' decision to go against morality or not. As Wood says, Hegel's theory is in general 'strikingly compatibilist':

> For Hegel I am responsible for doing a certain deed under a certain description if I in fact did the deed, knew what I was doing under that description, and intended to do it under that description. In principle these conditions could all be satisfied even if there were no possibility that I could have done otherwise. (*HET*, p. 151)

While I have been arguing that Kantians shouldn't prematurely exclude this kind of theory (and also that Kantians and Hegelians should be able to agree on combining it with at least the basic principles of 'abstract right'), it should also be noted that the theory is not without its faults, and its advantages can be exaggerated. At the metaphysical level, it has hardly refuted the possibility of Kantian incompatibilism, even on its 'rich' traditional formulation. Moreover, even at the empirical level, the idea that personal interests are always a factor in human action is hardly a strong objection to Kant, for he stresses that very fact as well. What Kant adds is just the thought that we can believe that a wholly disinterested factor can also be the relevant cause of an action. So, even if, as we have stressed, any such presumably 'pure' factor might still turn out to have an interest behind it after all; and even if, as Wood stresses, we can never in principle settle this question even on Kant's own account, still none of this shows that we should totally dismiss our causal hypotheses. If in fact the best view we have of a particular situation is that it seems that the ultimate intention of the action was completely disinterested, why should that conclusion not be the one affirmed, at least tentatively? (And if that goes against deterministic psychology, then that may just be all the worse for such a psychology.)

Such a possibility is of more than incidental and metaphysical interest. As Allison notes, there is something morally dissatisfying about the Hegelian's idea that merely taking some account of moral considerations is enough to gain moral worth for oneself. If we are in the business of assessing such worth, and we take it as a predicate of the person or character involved, and not just of the outer action and its form or consequences, then why not be concerned with what the causally overriding intention really was? Thus, why not say that a grocer of 'good will' is someone who truly does act 'from duty', at least to the extent that such motivation

---

[19] Cf., also, Wood, 'The Emptiness of the Moral Will', *Monist*, 73 (1989), 454–83.
[20] Allison reconstructs Wood's view this way: 'an action has moral worth if its moral goodness is one of the reasons why the agent performs it' (p. 190).

appears accessible to us? That is, why not say that the action is 'worthy' when and only when it at least has the appearance of a dominant orientation toward that end? Whether that orientation is one that ultimately requires a compatibilist or incompatibilist account is another issue—one that current theorists, like Kant and Hegel as well, have presumed is easier to settle than it really is. We ought not believe, for all that Allison has said, that Kant has vindicated incompatibilism, but we also do not have to believe, for all that Wood has said, that Hegel has buried it. What we can believe is that it is worth getting on with constructing a social theory that can be acceptable to both Kantians and Hegelians, despite the irreconcilable and perhaps unresolvable metaphysical differences that remain.

– 9 –

Kant's *Groundwork* III Argument Reconsidered

'as will is a kind of causality of living beings so far as they are rational...'

1. The Riddle

While most of the main works of classical modern philosophy recede more and more into 'mere historical' significance, Kant's *Groundwork of the Metaphysics of Morals* continues to have a unique impact on both the Anglo-American and continental traditions, where its systematic influence on current thought has increased dramatically in recent decades.[1] Nonetheless, the culminating argument of the text remains a riddle wrapped within an enigma—and all this covered by a shroud for good measure.[2] The riddle is the argument itself, the enigma is Kant's attitude to it before and after its composition, and the shroud is the story of its evaluation, which continues to be surprisingly favorable despite the appearance of several fundamental difficulties.

Many of the difficulties of the *Groundwork* have been stressed in my own earlier work on its third and final section, which begins with the subheading: 'The concept of freedom is the key to the explanation of the autonomy of the will' (IV: 445).[3] These difficulties were forced on my attention in part because of the

---

[1] The work of John Rawls is a major reason for this development. See especially his 'Themes in Kant's Moral Philosophy', in *Kant's Transcendental Deductions: The Three 'Critiques' and the Opus Postumum*, ed. Eckart Förster (Stanford, Calif., 1989), 81–113. See also the collections *Grundlegung zur Metaphysik der Sitten*, ed. Otfried Höffe (Frankfurt, 1989), and *Kant's Groundwork of the Metaphysics of Morals: Critical Essays*, ed. Paul Guyer (Lanham, Md., 1998); as well as Berndt Kraft and Dieter Schönecker, 'Einleitung', in Immanuel Kant, *Grundlegung zur Metaphysik der Sitten*, ed. Berndt Kraft and Dieter Schönecker (Hamburg, 1999); and Christine Korsgaard, 'Introduction', in *Kant: Groundwork of the Metaphysics of Morals*, ed. and tr. Mary J. Gregor (Cambridge, 1998).

[2] Cf. Winston Churchill, Oct. 1, 1939: 'Russia... is a riddle wrapped in an enigma'.

[3] See above, Ch. 6, which was originally published as 'Kant's Deduction of Freedom and Morality', *Journal of the History of Philosophy*, 19 (1981), 53–79. Unless otherwise indicated, quotations in English are from *Foundations of the Metaphysics of Morals*, tr. Lewis White Beck, (Indianapolis, 1959), and all references simply with volume and page numbers are to the Academy edition version in *Kant's Gesammelte Schriften* (Berlin, 1900–).

insightful work of others[4] on the central role of spontaneity throughout Kant's philosophy, and in part because of specific findings in my own research on the development of Kant's Critical epistemology and philosophy of mind, especially as revealed in his newly edited lectures on metaphysics.[5] While most current readings of Kant continue to try to develop a version of Kant's ethics—for both exegetical and systematic purposes—that 'leaves behind' ontological and metaphysical doctrines, it still seems to me that the *Groundwork*'s ultimate claims about freedom and autonomy preclude such a reading, and that they do so in a fairly obvious and understandable, even if complicated, way.

On my reading, the most remarkable—and inadequately appreciated—features of Kant's thought on freedom can be summed up initially in three basic points, points that are in an obvious tension with one another:

1. For a long time, that is, until shortly before publishing the *Critique of Pure Reason*, Kant *accepts* a 'direct' argument to *our absolute spontaneity* based simply on a premise expressing the power of the I to think or judge. (Kant tends to use these terms interchangeably.)
2. The distinctive doctrines of Kant's own Critical philosophy, and in particular the criticisms it makes of dogmatic theories of mind, have a fundamental tendency that is directed *against* the assertion of any such absolute power on theoretical premises.
3. And yet, in the 1780s, rather than coming forth with one clear position, Kant *wavers* in an astounding way in discussing—or, just as often, not directly discussing—the key points of his own position on the issue of freedom.

Kant's 'wavering' can itself be broken down into at least three distinct stages, stages that are also in an obvious tension with one another:

3a. In the *Critique of Pure Reason*, in both the first and the second editions, Kant takes remarkable care to *avoid* presenting a direct argument on our absolute spontaneity, one with a clear conclusion about whether or not we should say that we actually have it. Although spontaneity is a topic that explicitly has a central place in the canon of metaphysical issues that determines the main structure of the *Critique*, and although for years Kant lectured approvingly on our spontaneity, as demonstrated in the power of judgment, as precisely the initial and fundamental

---

[4] See especially Gerold Prauss, *Kant über Freiheit als Autonomie* (Frankfurt, 1983), and my review, *Review of Metaphysics*, 38 (1984), 136–9. Cf. also Wilfrid Sellars, '"This I or He or It (the Thing) Which Thinks"', *Proceedings of the American Philosophical Association*, 44 (1970–1), 5–31; and Dieter Henrich, 'Die Deduktion des Sittengesetzes', in *Denken im Schatten des Nihilismus*, ed. Alexander Schwan (Darmstadt, 1975), 55–112.

[5] See above n. 3, and *Lectures on Metaphysics/Immanuel Kant*, ed. and tr. Karl Ameriks and Steve Naragon (Cambridge, 1997); and my 'Kant on Spontaneity: Some New Data', *Proceedings of the VII International Kant-Kongress 1990*, ed. G. Funke (Berlin, 1991), 436–46.

claim of rational psychology, in the *Critique* itself Kant *silently* refashions the topic list of his discussion of rational psychology in such a way that the traditional arguments from the power of judgment to the assertion of absolute spontaneity are *neither* directly endorsed nor explicitly criticized in the manner of other paralogistic inferences. (Nor is the question of 'our' genuine agency resolved within the Antinomies, although at least one precondition for a resolution is established there: namely, that the doctrine of transcendental idealism precludes any inference to absolute determinism merely from the presence of a thoroughgoing chain of temporal causes.[6])

3b. At the same time—that is to say, in the course of the composition of the *Groundwork* (1785) right *in between* the writing of the first and second editions of the first *Critique* (1781, 1787)—Kant ventures nevertheless to construct an argument toward spontaneity that is still based on a supposed implication of the phenomenon of judgment: if, for example, I judge that S is P and thereby perform the cognitive 'act of synthesis' of combining these terms, then, I must believe that my I is an *absolutely free* source of this act (see Section 9, below).

3c. And yet, after the *Groundwork*, in all his other writings Kant *never* repeats or directly criticizes this pivotal argument; he simply switches to a very different way of expressing his commitment to freedom, namely, by referring to it as based *solely* on a 'fact of reason' (see below, Chapter 10), that is, a consciousness specifically of the moral law. (This is a switch because, however that perplexing 'fact' is interpreted, one thing that is clear about it is that it is *not* simply an act of judgment, considered generally as such.)

Despite these manifest difficulties, attempts to rehabilitate Kant's ultimate *Groundwork* argument, and to divest it entirely of its metaphysical dimension, persist in the latest work of leading philosophers. These attempts are not simply efforts of charitable historical reconstruction. They appear to be motivated by a deep and serious belief that Kant was on to something very important here, a philosophical truth of central systematic significance, notwithstanding the difficulties that appear to surround the text. Hence, there is ample reason now to reexamine Kant's argument, to find hidden strengths in it (or at least in considerations that bear a fruitful family resemblance to what Kant wrote)—or, if this fails, to try at least to understand somewhat more clearly what the deeper fallacies or attractions of the argument may be, and how anyone could get involved in such a strange line of deliberations, a line that (especially on my reading) appears to be in so much tension with some of the most important insights of Kant's Critical work.

---

[6] For a review of some of these points, see the Preface to the 2nd edn. of my *Kant's Theory of Mind* (Oxford, 2000). I stress in particular the way in which criticisms of dogmatic claims about the mind turn out to be the obviously dominant topic of the changes in the 2nd edn of the *Critique*, even though Kant still does not explicitly position this edition in relation to the claims made in between in the *Groundwork*.

2. The Context

The specific problems of the argument for freedom in *Groundwork* III are best approached only after an appreciation of the structure of the work as a whole and of the way that it fits into the general strategy of the Critical approach. The two earlier sections of the *Groundwork* lay out the main themes of Kant's moral theory, but they come only to the brink of the issue of freedom. In the first section, as in the first stage of most of his Critical deliberations, Kant starts from an analysis of common experience—in this case, 'common rational knowledge of morals', or what might be called the proper 'popular' standpoint on morals. On the basis of this analysis, it is claimed that our attachment to morality must be understood, above all, in terms of respect for duty and moral law.

In the second section of the *Groundwork* Kant proceeds, just as he usually does in the second stage of his Critical arguments, to isolate and philosophically expound (in effect, transcendentally deduce) a 'pure' component that must underlie the experience that has been characterized in the first stage. In Kant's language, this involves a move from 'popular moral philosophy' to a 'metaphysics of morals', and in particular from popular notions such as duty, respect, and law to underlying technical philosophical notions such as the 'categorical imperative' and the claim that this imperative is grounded in a 'principle of autonomy', whereas all other philosophical explanations of morality falsely rely on principles of 'heteronomy'. Very roughly, one might make a parallel between the relation of these sections of the *Groundwork* and Kant's transition in the Transcendental Aesthetic of the first *Critique* from an exposition of common mathematical judgment to a transcendental argument for pure intuition.[7] According to this exposition, ordinary people have supposedly always been making common mathematical judgments that have synthetic and non-conceptual features on their face, but it is a second and original step to realize this fact explicitly, and to go on to try to explain these features philosophically by arguing, as Kant does, that they must be rooted in a unique human capacity for 'pure intuition'.

The third step of Kant's Critical arguments involves moving beyond the initial characterization of a specific type of experience, as well as the transcendental isolation of an allegedly pure factor (a content, or 'principle') within this experience, to providing a final 'grounding', a culminating metaphysical account of the source of this factor. In the case of mathematics and the Transcendental Aesthetic, Kant emphasizes that the exposition of the relevant ground, namely, pure intuition, does *not* bring with it any *new first-level content*; rather, mathematicians themselves provide all the content there is, and philosophers simply offer an explanation of how that content can be a priori (A11/B25), first by explicitly

---

[7] *Critique of Pure Reason*, B40–1; cf. above, Introduction and Ch. 1.

introducing the notion of pure intuition, and then by moving, in the third main step of Critical philosophy, to argue that this intuition in turn can be explained through, and only through, the metaphysics of transcendental idealism. Sometimes, however, a significant *new* content can be added *before* the third step of a portion of the Critical philosophy. For example, at the beginning of the Transcendental Analytic of the first *Critique*, Kant argues that there are pure concepts (of the understanding) rooted in the forms of judgment; and then later in the Analytic he argues for a content of pure principles that philosophers, and philosophers alone, can justify. (The Transcendental Deduction in the Analytic of Concepts shows *that* there must be such a content, in some way connected with the forms of judgment; and the Analytic of Principles specifies and justifies the 'principles' of that content.) Afterwards, just as in the Aesthetic, the Analytic then incorporates the third main step of the Critical approach: after having argued that there is a kind of pure content—this time in the faculty of understanding rather than of intuition—Kant goes on to insist that this content is possible, that is, intelligible to us, only on the basis of a specific kind of metaphysics, the metaphysics of transcendental idealism (B41 f.).

Kant employs a similar three-part procedure in his moral philosophy; hence there is an obvious task left for the third section of the *Groundwork*. After having isolated and analyzed a basic form of experience in the *Groundwork*'s first section, and after having introduced various pure principles as transcendentally underlying this experience (the categorical imperative, autonomy) in its second section, Kant again insists in offering, in a third section, a metaphysical account of the very possibility of these principles—and, not surprisingly, this account also culminates in an invocation of transcendental idealism. One complication that arises here is the question of whether the second section of the *Groundwork* is to be understood simply as a meta-theory, somewhat like the Transcendental Aesthetic of the first *Critique*, or as itself introducing for morality a new philosophical content, just as the Transcendental Analytic introduces new philosophical principles of causality that go beyond the ordinary claims of everyday theoretical experience. That is, are notions such as the categorical imperative and autonomy supposed to be 'news' that are meant to add substantively to the content of our moral life, or are they merely theoretical tools, aimed simply at warding off exotic philosophical attacks or providing abstract materials to help with special calls for higher-level explanations?[8] Here we cannot go very far at all into the exploration of this central issue—one that brings with it the whole problem of the relation of 'popular' and 'philosophical' thought in the *Groundwork*—but it is important to be aware of the issue from the beginning, because it turns out that central concepts such as 'autonomy' appear to have a significant double life throughout Kant's writing,

[8] This theme is developed in an interesting essay in progress by Samuel Fleischacker, 'Kantian Morality as Soulcraft: Rereading the *Groundwork*'.

3. The Task: Establishing our Absolute Freedom

In whatever way one understands the second section of the *Groundwork*, it is clear that in its third section the invocation of transcendental idealism and an ultimate metaphysical perspective is a well prepared systematic move, and it occurs only after an intervening step that introduces at least one significant new content: the pure concept of *absolute* freedom. The very first step of the section is to argue explicitly that autonomy, the principle that incorporates all that has been argued for in the earlier sections, is necessarily connected with absolute freedom.[10] The question then becomes one of finding a ground for being able to assert that we really do have such a remarkable kind of freedom; and it is at this point that the consideration of the nature of judgment and, eventually, of the metaphysics of transcendental idealism becomes crucial. Hence, there is no escaping the fact that the central point of the culminating argument of the *Groundwork* rests for Kant precisely on the metaphysical relation of the concepts of autonomy and of freedom; this alone can resolve the issue of whether the autonomy that morality is said to require is anything more than a 'chimera' or 'phantom'. (This is the fundamental question raised in the last paragraph of the second section of the *Groundwork*, IV: 445.) But as soon as one looks at how Kant directly addresses that relation right at the beginning of the third section, it turns out that there is much more involved with these concepts than one might think at first sight.

---

[9] There is a related but less significant terminological issue that arises with respect to how 'purely philosophical' the second section of the *Groundwork* is to be understood, an issue that has to do simply with the twofold way in which the term 'metaphysics' is used by Kant. Sometimes, as in the 'metaphysical deduction' of the *Critique*, and also here in the second section of the *Groundwork*, Kant employs the word 'metaphysics' to stand for the *specification* of a set of *pure* principles, and so it might be said that the second step of the Critical approach is already fully metaphysical. But the term 'metaphysics' can also be used (and this tends to be its primary meaning for Kant) to indicate the highest level of philosophy, the one that seeks to provide the *ultimate grounds* for such principles, i.e. that moves to a doctrine such as idealism. This move occurs only in the third step of the Critical approach, and it takes place in the *Groundwork* with the assertion of the 'real efficacy' of 'pure practical reason'. These complexities are reflected in the title of Section 3, 'Transition from the metaphysics of morals to the critical examination of pure practical reason'. In one sense this is a move from 'metaphysics' to a 'groundwork of metaphysics'—hence the *Groundwork's* title—but one could just as easily say that only now is a quintessentially metaphysical level reached, i.e. an ultimate groundwork for the phenomenon under investigation.

[10] To be sure, Kant does not here use the expression 'absolute' freedom, but he speaks immediately of a causality effective 'independently of foreign causes determining it' (IV: 445), and that is the basic feature of what I mean by 'absolute' freedom, namely, causality that is real and itself uncaused (period) by anything outside it. Later in the *Groundwork* Kant connects this notion with his idea of 'things in themselves' and an 'intelligible world', but even without getting into these complications it is clear right at the outset that Kant's notion of freedom must be metaphysical in that it cannot be like 'the case of physical causes, or the nature of the sensuous world (where the concept of something as cause brings with it the relation to *something else* as effect)' (IV: 447; Kant's emphasis, my translation).

Kant begins with a sentence that defines 'will' as a form of causation in beings 'so far as they are rational' and that defines 'freedom' in this context at first negatively as a causation 'independent of foreign causes' (IV: 445–6). (I take it that this is meant as an independence of the specific effect from *all* such causes, and not only from some, although the mere existence of the effect and of the agent may ultimately depend on something external, e.g. a creator; cf. note 10 above.) These definitions are meant to contrast the extremes of rational freedom and natural necessity, but they also indirectly suggest (I say 'suggest' because Kant himself does not explore these possibilities here) a second pair of contrasting concepts: causation that is 'psychologically natural', that is, defined *simply as not* operating through an 'inner' or separate higher faculty of rationality; and 'non-free causation', that is, causation defined *simply as not* operating independently of foreign causes. Note that these two possibilities could coincide but they do not amount to exactly the same thing: 'natural' and 'non-free' differ in intension, and they could also differ in extension. That is, for all we know, 'psychologically natural' or 'non-rational' beings (here, and throughout, I amend Beck's translation, which has 'irrational' for *vernunftlose*) *might* operate always in a way that is entirely dependent on foreign causes; but another possibility is that there is a way (that we do not know) that these beings could operate at least in part *independent* of such causes (in which case, to be sure, they could not have what Kant calls a free 'will', since by definition they would lack rationality and so would not be a will at all, but they still could be free 'agents' in a significant sense).[11] This complex possibility is obscured when Kant himself moves on immediately to use only the notion of 'natural necessity' and to say that it 'is the property of all non-rational beings by which they are determined by the activity of foreign causes' (IV: 446). In other words, he is interested only in the 'worst case scenario' for 'natural' beings, and not in the possibility of beings that are 'psychologically natural' simply in the sense of being non-rational but such that they might operate in some sense *freely* rather than simply with necessity.

The exclusion of this possibility might seem to be explained by the strong contrast Kant often makes between the realms of nature and freedom. Given this contrast, one might think that natural beings must be defined simply as beings that operate by determined laws *rather than* by being free. But, in fact, even for Kant the mere notion of a 'natural being', *either* in the 'psychological' sense of a non-rational being (e.g. an ant not operating inwardly 'through' the psychological processes of reason, however 'rational' its 'actions' may look from outside), or in

---

[11] On the general Kantian notion of 'action' (*Handlung*) as present even in 'merely physical' contexts, see Volker Gerhardt, 'Handlung als Verhältnis von Ursache und Wirkung: Zur Entwicklung des Handlungsbegriffs bei Kant', in *Handlungstheorie und Transzendentalphilosophie*, ed. Gerold Prauss (Frankfurt, 1986), 98–131. For a more critical treatment of Kant in the same volume, cf. Rüdiger Bittner, 'Handlungen und Wirkungen', 13–26.

the 'systematic' sense of a being operating according to a structure of laws, does *not mean* that the being can in no way be free. Even if a being operates entirely non-rationally and *according to* natural laws, it does not follow that 'in its causality' or 'in itself' the being could not also be a spontaneous ground of its states. This possibility of a being that is in some sense both free and natural is one lesson left over from Kant's Third Antinomy and doctrine of transcendental idealism. It is a reminder that, for all that has been said so far, nothing has been established against the well-known quasi-Leibnizian thought that an entity could act in a way that is 'covered' by natural laws even while it is in a sense absolutely spontaneous in itself.[12]

In addition to this neglected possibility of *natural* and *non-rational* but in one sense 'free' beings, there is the equally neglected and even more relevant possibility of *rational* (and in that way alone, in one sense already more than 'merely natural') but *non-free* beings. Hence, although it is tempting to think simply in terms of Kant's initial sharply contrasting possibilities of (1) being both rational (and in that sense 'non-natural') and free vs. (2) being both non-rational and non-free (i.e. 'naturally necessary'), there is another set of contrasting possibilities that also should be kept in mind: namely, (3) being both non-rational and free vs. (4) being both rational and non-free. One would think that (4) is a possibility that Kant cannot neglect for long. For him the issue of morality leads to the question of freedom, and the question of our absolute freedom is precisely the question of whether in fact our rationality, which is the core of our morality, *must* bring this kind of freedom along with it. Nonetheless, Kant does not move at first to an explicit reflection on the *direct* relation of *rationality* to freedom, but instead moves immediately from what he calls a 'negative' 'definition of freedom' (as the property of not being externally determined) to a 'positive concept' of it (IV: 446). This positive concept is to be used for completing the characterization of a free *will*, something that (to recapitulate) has so far been characterized as operating not only as (a) a cause and (b) something free in at least an absolute negative sense, but also as (c) something that is a cause precisely 'so far as' it is rational (IV: 445–6).

4. Connecting the Concept of a Free Will and the Concept of Autonomy

Up to this point Kant has offered what might be taken to be merely a series of innocuous terminological stipulations. After steps (a)–(c), however, he suddenly

---

[12] Cf. *Critique of Pure Reason*, A538/B566. Kant may be uninterested in the thought of such an entity (which is spontaneous but subrational) in the *Groundwork* because, although 'free', it would not technically meet his definition of a free 'will', nor would it be 'entirely natural' since, unlike beings of 'natural necessity', it would not be determined in its very 'activity'. Although this may explain Kant's neglect of this thought here, it does not justify it, and the remainder of my argument will fill out the case that it is worthwhile to consider such thoughts in greater detail.

introduces some very substantive and controversial claims. A first such claim is his insistence that in general a cause must operate according to laws, and hence, insofar as a free will, as a will, is a cause, it also 'must be a causality according to immutable laws' (IV: 446). This is a fateful and questionable step, but I will not focus on it here.[13] An equally remarkable step, and the main one to be focused on here, occurs when Kant moves on to fill out the positive concept of the freedom of the will by asking, 'what else' can it be but 'autonomy, i.e. the property of the will to be a law to itself' (IV: 447)? It is understandable, of course, that at this point Kant would want to connect his discussion of freedom to the notion of autonomy that had been the endpoint of his discussion in the previous sections of the *Groundwork*. Nonetheless, the new notion of something being a 'law to itself', just like the notion of autonomy, is hardly transparent, and it requires more explanation than it is given directly in the text, for there are several distinct meanings that could be relevant for it.

Instead of focusing directly on the notion of being a 'law to itself', Kant himself seems most concerned with moving on to the further claim that this notion, as a principle of autonomy, gives us 'just the formula of the categorical imperative and the principle of morality' (IV: 447). This remarkable claim immediately becomes the prime object of Kant's discussion, but it is important not to be distracted by it too soon, and not to skip over his prior quick move in connecting a positive concept of freedom with autonomy in the first place. The justification that he states for this move appears to be simply that 'natural necessity is, as we have seen, a heteronomy of efficient causes, for every effect [in a domain of natural necessity] is possible only according to the law that something else determines the efficient cause to its causality. What else, then, can the freedom of the will be but autonomy . . . ?' (IV: 447).

One way of representing Kant's argument in this section is to reconstruct it in the following steps:

(A) *Positively* characterized, the freedom of the *will*, in accord with the essence of anything that is a cause, must involve acting according to some *law* (presumed at IV: 446).
(B) A *free* will, simply as a free entity, must have at least the negative freedom of not being determined in its action by foreign causes (from IV: 446).

---

[13] Although it is put forth here as if it were self-evident, this is a very controversial claim even for Kant. In much earlier work, rather than immediately rejecting, as he does here, the thought that freedom is 'lawless', Kant had in fact endorsed the thought and opposed freedom and law. One still can find a sediment of this position in a passage in the *Critique* (A447/B475). Since the passage occurs in an opening argument of an Antinomy, I am not assuming, as some commentators do, that it represents Kant's own position, rather than that of someone under the sway of dogmatism. All that matters is that the thought is presented as at least one to which a serious philosopher might feel committed. For reminders of the importance of this topic in Kant's early *Reflexionen* on freedom, I am indebted to the teaching of Gerold Prauss.

(C) Hence the law of a free will, and *its* positive freedom, must involve its acting according to some law that does not express or allow determination by foreign causes (from (A) and (B)).
(D) But a law for action must express determination by something, that is, either by foreign causes or by oneself (from definitions and excluded middle).
(E) Hence, the law of a free will expresses the will's causally determining itself, that is, its self-determination (from (C) and (D)).
(F) Hence the positive freedom of the will consists in its self-determination, that is, autonomy just in this sense (from (A) and (E)).

This reconstruction appears sufficient to capture the core of Kant's argument for an equivalence of free will and autonomy although, amazingly enough, it does not directly invoke the terms 'natural necessity', 'heteronomy', 'rationality', or 'law to itself'. One might well wonder, then, how anyone could expect to get from steps like (A)–(F), steps that are so general and innocuous (the least 'innocuous' step here is probably (A), but in fact, even without this step and all the references to 'law', an argument could still be put through that would have a conclusion about self-determination, and in that way a kind of autonomy), to anything like Kant's own conclusion, which is supposed to be tantamount to substantive claims as specific and controversial as the categorical imperative (IV: 447). Clearly, the answer must involve many more controversial steps, and here only a few of the most obvious problems in the first steps can be discussed.

5. Objections: A Being 'not Determined by Foreign Causes' Need not be a Will, and a 'Phenomenologically' Characterized 'Will' Need not be a Cause

In order to point out some of the difficulties of connecting Kant's argument immediately with a notion of autonomy that we can usefully connect with our own situation (which is a precondition for our being able to use it to provide a foundation for moral concerns), I will begin by indicating the relevance of some of the neglected ambiguities mentioned earlier. Recall that Kant's argument speaks of beings that are determined by foreign causes as having 'natural necessity' and operating under a 'heteronomy of efficient causes' (IV: 446, right before 447). Such language is clearly a reminder of his earlier sentence about 'non-rational beings' that, *insofar as* they are *also* said to operate by 'natural necessity', are 'determined ... by ... foreign causes' (IV: 446). As was noted earlier, however, it is important to keep in mind that 'non-rational beings' need not *by definition* be subject to what Kant means by 'natural necessity' here, or (to fill in the ellipses from the above quotation) be 'determined *in their activity*' (IV: 446). All that is required here by the definition of a non-rational being as such is that it is something that is not a cause in virtue of rationality; and from this it does *not follow* (especially on Kant's own view) that it is something *absolutely* determined—not even if it fits a pattern 'according' to which, for each temporal effect that it is involved in, there is a preceding temporal cause. This means that, from the mere discussion here of the concept of beings subject to what Kant calls 'natural necessity' and 'heteronomy', there is still *no* ground for saying that beings that are *not* like that; that is, that are not absolutely externally determined, must even have rationality or be anything specifically like us. Of course, *if* we add a stipulation that we are concerned only with the concept of those non-externally determined beings that are *also* said to have a 'will', then, by Kant's definition of will, we will have a concept of beings that are thought to operate in *some* sense from reason, and that therefore will seem to resemble us to that extent—but in this case we still do not know what the exact relation is between their being in fact not externally determined and their having rationality in the way that we are familiar with from our own case.

This becomes a significant problem when we consider that all we are directly familiar with in our own case is rationality that appears at first in the form of the 'psychological' complexity of our *taking*[14] ourselves to operate 'through' reasons rather than, for example, explicitly at the mere behest of forces. In this way we are 'phenomenologically' distinguished from what we take to be non-rational beings, 'mere animals' or less. For Kant, however, the will is defined as a *causal* faculty within a being whose rationality has actual efficacy, and in this case rationality implies a 'real' and not merely a phenomenological property. This means that, even before we get into the specific question of '*free* will' and consider whether this requires some kind of special empirical or non-empirical power (so that it is not determined by *anything* 'foreign' to it), there is a sense in which we can wonder if in fact 'reason is real' at all. That is, even if it is agreed that the *concept* of a will is the concept of a genuinely effective rational cause, it still does not follow that anything that we actually 'take' to be rational beings and wills—including our own selves—are ever causes in anything more than a loose 'phenomenological' sense. To use ideas discussed in much more detail in Kant's third *Critique*, there remains the significant possibility that, for all we know, there might be something like mechanism 'all the way down'. Not only the apparent 'teleology' of organic systems in general, but also all our own overt intentional experience might have nothing more than brute natural laws 'actually working' in it (note that the main point here holds even if it turns out that for Kant a 'noumenal substrate' can, or

---

[14] The importance, especially in Kantian contexts, of what we 'take' ourselves to be has been emphasized in the interpretations of Robert Pippin, 'Kant on the Spontaneity of Mind', *Canadian Journal of Philosophy*, 17 (1987), 449–75; and Henry E. Allison, *Kant's Theory of Freedom* (Cambridge, 1990), as well as in the earlier work of Gerold Prauss.

even must, also be posited—since, whatever this substrate may be, no reasons have been given yet for holding that it operates intentionally). Thus, despite our operating often 'through' reason in a phenomenological sense—that is, simply with explicit thoughts (or later 'rationalizations') of rational grounds for what we are doing—it might be the case that the real power that makes the events that are those thoughts 'effective' is nothing more than nature (and/or a 'foreign' noumenal ground of that nature) in its *sub*rational power. In that case, we might be said to be working 'through' the appearance of reason but not 'really by' it, and our whole everyday intentional life would be little more than a mere 'stance', an epiphenomenon at best.

Of course, this is not a situation that I am at all suggesting Kant believes is the case. On the contrary, my point is that he very much does *not* believe in it—and yet he is passing over it very quickly, and that makes all the more urgent the question of what reason, if any, he has for dismissing it. That is to say, even before Kant gets into special worries about the relations of free will, morality, and pure practical reason, we can ask, why does he think, or believe, that we have a good ground for holding that his general concept of will as genuinely efficacious rationality has *any* instantiation or relevance to us (so that it would be even possible for it eventually to help ground our moral attitudes)?[15]

6. A Further Objection: Restricting the Discussion to a Will that is Really Effective and not 'Determined by Foreign Causes' can Make Every Will Autonomous

So far, I have not focused *directly* on how the notion of autonomy may figure in Kant's argument, and it is natural to hope that this notion may help in answering the question of the real efficacy (and thus the reality) of our will. In fact, the way that the notion is explicitly introduced in the argument here does not help very much at first. The notion of autonomy arises in III at first as only the opposite of heteronomy, and, as has just been noted, at this point the feature of heteronomy is employed only in terms of the notion of a 'heteronomy of efficient causes' (IV: 446). Hence, to be merely the opposite of *this* kind of heteronomy, all that is needed is what Kant calls negative freedom—and so, *if* autonomy were taken to be merely the opposite of heteronomy in this sense, then there would be no immediate necessary connection between autonomy and rationality or will at all. The term 'autonomy', as simply the opposite of a 'heteronomy of efficient causes', would signify the property had by anything that is not completely externally determined. This may not be as unhelpful as the phenomenological property of merely seeming to be something that is a cause, but it is not much better.

---

[15] Since Kant cut his teeth on problems of the occasionalist tradition, this issue could hardly have struck him as exotic. See above, Ch. 4.

Fortunately, although all that Kant's sentence says explicitly about heteronomy concerns the property of natural necessity, the full context of his discussion indicates that his sentence is not simply about just anything that might have this particular property or its contradictory, but rather is implicitly about something that can be a *will*, and in particular a will premised to have at least negative freedom. In that case the issue is not about autonomy in just any causal sense, but is rather about an autonomous *will*—and the concept of such an autonomous will can obviously contain more than simply the negative property of being not heteronomous in an 'efficient' sense. Since the concept of a will is introduced as the positive concept of a rationally efficacious will, it follows that, in being a will at all, there are clear positive features that must attach to anything that might be considered as a possible autonomous will.

Note, however, that for all that has been said so far, it now can suddenly seem that the mere definition of a will, given the efficacy that it must have as a rational cause, *already* by itself entails *a kind* of 'autonomy': each will that is a will at all must be something that acts 'through its own' property of reason. Moreover, given what Kant presumes about action as always presuming lawful causality, this would imply that each will, simply by being a will, acts from a law 'of its own', namely, reason—for if it did not do that, there would be no point in saying that the will is a *particular* kind of causality, namely rational causality. Hence, *even before* any consideration of *free* will as such, it seems that we must already say that in a sense each will is self-determined, that it is in this sense autonomous, and autonomous in a way that even explicitly involves its own laws. In that case, though, the concept of freedom, i.e. the need to add that we are dealing with a 'free' (i.e. not externally determined) will, can seem to be irrelevant, and not, as Kant promises, 'the key to the explanation of the autonomy of the will'. Moreover, autonomy would take on such a general meaning (signifying any action of a being insofar as it is rational at all) that it would be especially hard to see how it must express anything as specific as the 'principle of morality'.

7. A Further Objection: Not Putting Autonomy into the Concept of the Will as such can Leave only a 'Phenomenologically' and not Really Effective Will, or a Real Effectiveness that is not Free

There are various options at this point. One could embrace this situation, and explore the value of a very broad notion of autonomy that goes beyond Kant's own specific and primarily moral ultimate objectives. Another alternative, one that lingers more over Kant's own apparently more narrow objectives, would be to try to escape a premature assertion of autonomy in a broad sense by giving a more modest reading of the initial steps in the definition of the will as rational causality.

I have already mentioned one kind of modest reading of the role of rationality in the notion of a will. This would involve giving it a merely 'phenomenological' sense, and saying that no more is *meant* by the notion of will as rational causality than the idea that one is aware of reasons 'in oneself' before action (or at least that one can make them available, in retrospect) in some kind of way that goes naturally with *taking* them to be the causes of the action—but that does *not* have to be a matter of making any claim to have insight into the existence of an actual causal efficacy of the will as such. This modest strategy has the advantage of keeping the mere claim of the presence of a will to involve some kind of sense of self-determination by reason without working either the real efficacy or the absolute freedom of the will already into the definition of a will as such. And yet, despite this advantage, it is hard to accept this reading as good exegesis, for it should be obvious that it does not do full justice to Kant's own explicit desire for the concept of a will to bring with it a real causal efficacy of reason (IV: 445–6), and not merely a phenomenological close substitute for this.

While it therefore seems necessary to go beyond a merely phenomenological reading of autonomy, it also seems that, as soon as we do so, we are immediately brought back to an earlier problem: namely, that a will, if it is said to be a real and not merely an apparent cause, would seem already to have a kind of autonomy that makes a further inquiry about freedom in some further sense seem unnecessary, for it would by definition be a will that actually operates precisely through itself, through reason 'instead of' through 'foreign causes'. There is a traditional way to try to respond this problem: namely, by emphasizing a distinction between saying simply that our reason is *a proximate* cause of something, and saying, *in addition*, that it may or may not have the negative freedom that occurs when this efficacy itself is not determined by anything outside it. In this way, something might be said to be a will in a real and not merely a phenomenological sense insofar as it has an effect that actually (and not only 'psychologically') goes through its rationality—but there would still be room for saying the will is *not* a *free* will if that rationality in turn has a foreign cause of its effectiveness.

Although this approach has obvious advantages in contrast to the other approaches just discussed, it is also makes other problems all the more vivid. In particular, as soon as it is allowed that there can be a real rational causality that is effective but, for all we know, could be 'rooted' in foreign causes, then it becomes immediately possible to suspect that this 'real' causality of reason could ultimately be regarded as a mere superficial causality, something that would still allow us to regard our rationality as a mere 'phantom', and our agency as a mere 'turnspit' (*Bratenwender*) or instrument of foreign powers—precisely the problem that Kant raises at the end of the second section of the *Groundwork*, with the clear suggestion that it would be solved in the next section. As long as a will's being a 'real cause' does not by itself exclude the possibility that the effect is ultimately determined by a foreign cause (a cause that causes us to do our causing), then mere 'real causation' by the will as a rational will may not (especially for typical Kantians) look like it is worth much more than the pseudo-causation that occurs when the will is said to be autonomous in a merely phenomenological sense. What is troublesome here is that this is a situation that seems fully compatible with the full *positive* meaning that so far has been attached to autonomy (as rational causation) in this discussion—for if the distinctive *meaning* of autonomy (insofar as, on *this* reading, it is precisely *not defined* as simply the opposite of a 'heteronomy of efficient causes') is a positive mark that is simply a matter of some kind of proximate 'self-determination' by reason, then all this still seems compatible with a 'turnspit' situation.

On this liberal (i.e. compatibilist) reading of autonomy, it follows that, even if one's reason has a 'real causal role' (as well as perhaps even a phenomenological sense of its being efficacious), one could still possibly be the 'mere conduit' of foreign causes. The disturbing consequence here is that, if one does not mind allowing self-determination to mean simply determination that in fact *goes through* one's reason, then—even when there may be foreign sources beyond one's self that ultimately cause one's self (and its reason) to be what it is—there could be wills that, simply by being wills, are *in a sense* autonomous and genuine wills but might not need to be called free at all, or at least not really free 'all the way down'.[16] They would have autonomy in one clear sense of 'the property of the will to be a law to itself', insofar as they are (and take themselves to be) real rational and lawful causes of action—and yet all the while they might not be an ultimate cause of action at all, but rather the 'mere tool' of necessary and sufficient grounds in 'foreign causes'.

If this approach is not satisfactory, if it still seems to leave us with a much too weak sense of autonomy, there remains only the option of insisting that being 'self-determined by reason' in a genuinely autonomous sense must be a matter of being a 'law to oneself' in a way that goes *beyond* both the phenomenological and liberal (compatibilist) readings. To specify this stronger reading, one could make use of a Kant's argument at IV: 446–7, where he concludes that autonomy is a matter of being a 'law to oneself'; and one could understandably propose that what he basically meant to say is that in such a situation there must be 'freedom of the will' in the sense of an effect that is ultimately through oneself *rather* than (as on the heteronomy of efficient causes) at all 'according to the law that *something*

---

[16] This problem was a commonplace in Kant's time in discussions of reactions to Leibnizians. The recently edited and translated (in part) lectures on ethics provide some new and especially clear expressions of Kant's explicit position on this problem in his later period. For example: 'So the fact that a man is determined to action on the grounds of reason and understanding does not yet release him from all mechanism of nature', from 'Moral Vigilantius', Fall 1793, in *Lectures on Ethics/ Immanuel Kant*, ed. Peter Heath and J. B. Schneewind, tr. Peter Heath (Cambridge, 1997), 270 (XXVII: 504).

else determines'.[17] On this reading, what becomes crucial is the presence in the will of negative freedom in an absolute sense. Here it is no longer the phenomenological presence of reason, nor even the mere efficacy of reason, that matters. What matters is the fact that the *ultimate* source of the action is one's own reason *alone*. Being a 'law to oneself' now *means* being an *absolutely free* will, that is, being an uncaused rational cause of one's state, rather than being simply an apparent or proximate cause. At this point the meaning of autonomy has been so strengthened by putting all its possibly relevant components together that it is finally easy to see how it can be said, after all, to be equivalent to 'freedom of the will' (IV: 447)—in such a way that this freedom is itself understood to contain strong negative as well as positive meanings.

8. Kantian Autonomy Thus Requires Absolute Freedom—which is not Yet Established

While this reading of 'law to itself', with its explicit equation of strong senses of autonomy and free will, seems closest to what Kant was trying to say and overcomes several problems that plague the other readings, it has difficulties of its own. One difficulty is that this reading trivializes the relation between freedom and autonomy—neither is being argued to from the other in terms of any meaning that does not already include the other by definition.[18] Another problem is that, despite the very 'strong' components of its definitions, there is still nothing in the reading that explains Kant's next claim: his insistence that holding that the will is a 'law to itself' is tantamount to expressing the principle of morality (IV: 447).[19] Yet another problem, and one that will be my final concern here, is that, precisely by relying on a strong sense of autonomy that goes beyond both the phenomenological and liberal readings, this reading takes away the ladder needed for anyone to have an adequate reason for saying that we are in fact wills in this strong sense. (I mean this as a systematic problem for Kant and the whole Kantian approach inspired by the *Groundwork*, and not as an exegetical objection to the

---

[17] An unfortunate complication is that the text itself has not 'at all according to the law' but 'only according to the law....' Hence it suggests a 'weaker' reading, for if autonomy is merely the opposite of being determined '*only* by something else', then this autonomy could exist in a situation in which something is still fundamentally determined by something else, say as a machine is determined by its governor, as long as the machine *also* engages in some actions that are in part determined by it. But this kind of merely relative 'negative freedom' obviously does not amount to anything that could be meant to meet the 'turnspit' objection, and it is fair to presume that it is not what Kant meant.

[18] Kant may be showing awareness of this difficulty in going on to suggest that he was arguing 'in a circle' (IV: 450). See above, Ch. 6, and cf. Dieter Schönecker, *Kant: Grundlegung III. Interpretationen zur Deduktion des kategorischen Imperativs* (Freiburg, 1999).

[19] It is impossible to do justice to this complex issue here. What I have been stressing is that before one can even begin to ask how being a 'law to oneself' is tantamount to morality, one needs to fix what might be meant by 'law to oneself'.

reading itself.) That is, if autonomy *means* being not merely an apparent and/or proximate cause by one's own reason, but also something that is not ultimately determined in its causality by anything foreign at all, where can the ground come for ever saying that we have such a remarkable property? Most of the reasons that people actually offer for claiming autonomy seem to rely precisely on the popular and weaker meanings of being 'a law to itself' that we have just examined and that Kant himself now does *not* appear to regard as sufficient. But once Kant builds so much into his concept of autonomy, how can he imagine that it can be insisted that this concept is any more than a 'phantom' of reason, and is something that we have a clear justification for asserting? In particular, how can he hold that absolute freedom, the difficult core of the difficult strong sense of autonomy that he insists on, can be, of all things, a helpful 'key' to 'explaining' autonomy itself?

9. The 'Presupposition' Attempt to Establish our Absolute Freedom—and its Vulnerability to the Earlier Objections

Kant seems quite sensitive to precisely these problems because he immediately presents a new way that the concept of absolute freedom supposedly makes itself evident as instantiated in us after all, one that does not derive from morality but rather can help provide an independent foundation for morality's principle. Kant's new argument dominates the remainder of the *Groundwork*, and its main idea is set out in a new subsection with the appropriate but astonishingly bold heading, 'Freedom must be presupposed as the property of the will of all rational beings' (IV: 447). Kant begins with an incidental observation that he wants to work *forward* to an argument that would derive the validity of morality for us *from* a premise of freedom ('morality... must be derived exclusively from the property of freedom', IV: 447), and for this he thinks he needs to present an independent argument that would first allow us to get *to* freedom. The remarkable fact is that here he suggests that such an argument can be derived simply from the notion of a rational will—the very notion that by now must seem manifestly inadequate, in the light of our review of Kant's own earlier discussion in the *Groundwork* as well as our observations about the whole character of his other Critical texts. Kant seems to have become interested in an argument from the feature of rationality because, as he recounts, he believes that morality applies to all beings insofar as they are rational wills, and so, *if* there is a relevant argument to morality from freedom, it must be an argument from what is involved in being a rational will at all (IV: 448). However, at this point Kant does not seem to appreciate that from this hypothetical fact it does not follow that there *has to be* an independent argument 'to' or 'from' freedom. It could be true that morality applies to all rational beings as such, and that any rational being to whom morality applies necessarily has freedom, even if it turns out that there is no good argument (independent of already presupposing morality) *to* freedom from mere rationality.[20] And not only is such an argument to freedom not clearly needed: it is not at all clear how it might be carried out, given that, according to the account that Kant himself has just offered, our freedom as rational wills would have to involve nothing less than the extraordinarily difficult to establish feature of being completely free from the 'influence of foreign causes'.

Despite these difficulties, Kant proceeds by beginning with the claim that 'every rational being who has a will also has the idea of freedom and acts only under this idea' (IV: 448).[21] The immediate justification offered for this claim is simply the statement that 'in such a being [i.e. a rational being with a will] we think of a reason that is practical, i.e. a reason that has a causality with respect to its objects' (IV: 448). This statement, however, merely recapitulates the definition of will examined earlier; and, for the reasons just gone through in considerable detail, it should be clear that it does not by itself entail anything at all specifically about freedom. Being a 'real' will is not by definition being a 'free' will. It is therefore only proper that Kant immediately adds an extra step that appears to begin to build some bridge between the notion of a rational will and the notion of freedom: 'we cannot conceive of a reason that consciously responds to a bidding from outside with respect to its judgments, for then the subject would attribute the determination of its power of judgment not to reason but to an impulse' (IV: 448). (Note that this argument focuses on precisely the basic power of judgment, the very phenomenon that is at once the core of Kant's early sympathetic discussions of rational psychology, the unique positive doctrines of his Critical epistemology, and also his Critical strictures in the Paralogisms against drawing any 'personal' metaphysical inferences from our mere epistemic capacities.)

It is not easy to determine exactly how to understand the *key point* here that our reason as such cannot 'consciously respond to a bidding from outside'. One way to take this point is as suggesting a partial definition: a rational will just is a will that, at the least, *thinks* of its own reasons, rather than anything else *by itself*, as the ground, that is *justification*, of its judgments. This reading, however, does not explain why a rational will could not *allow* that in each case in which a justified judgment is made, there might *also* be, at the level of causes, a real determination of our mind by natural factors such as hidden impulses. (Spinozists would naturally press such a consideration.) Such a will would not, in the very act of judgment, *think* of itself in terms of simply 'responding' to something 'from

---

[20] One way of explaining Kant's different approach in the *Critique of Practical Reason* would be to say that Kant came to appreciate this point. But there are many other aspects to the story; see above, n. 3, and below, Ch. 10.

[21] Note that, even if this argument could be successful, it would not by itself give a reason for saying *we* are free; to make such a claim, it would have to be shown that we have 'a will' in the special sense that is meant here; I believe Kant fully realizes this point, and this is one reason why the third section goes on to take up as much length as it does; cf. above, n. 3.

outside', but it might still allow, on a moment's reflection, that what is 'outside' has a significant (indeed, actually determining) causal role with respect to what the will actually thinks.

Given this difficulty, it would seem that Kant's 'key point' must be meant to make a stronger claim. One stronger way to interpret it would be to read it as making, in addition, an *explicit claim about causes*: namely, that a rational will must be one that 'takes' its reasons to be real causes (and not merely justifications) of its acts of judgments and related actions. So understood, the point becomes tantamount to no more than what I called the mere 'phenomenological sense' of the idea that the will, as practical reason, is a 'law to itself.' As was stressed earlier, however, this point by itself still does not say anything specifically about *freedom*, so it remains unclear why anyone should think that it does anything to *establish* the claim at issue, namely, that someone who merely 'has a will also has the idea of freedom and ... acts only under this idea' (IV: 448).

The best I can do to construct an explicit connection of freedom with what I have called Kant's 'key point' is to note that

(*a*) Kant's 'key point' does seem connected with the phenomenological notion of taking one's will to be a 'law to itself'; and
(*b*) this notion can be equated, understandably enough, with one sense of 'autonomy'; and
(*c*) Kant has just equated 'autonomy' and 'freedom of the will' (IV: 446–7);
(*d*) hence, it might be argued, by substitution, that the original 'key point' is equivalent to a claim about freedom.

Unfortunately, this argument is invalidated by an equivocation on the pair of meanings we have just distinguished: 'autonomy' in step (*b*) involves only what might be called 'mere phenomenological autonomy', whereas 'autonomy' in step (*c*) goes beyond this in explicitly involving a causal claim of absolute negative freedom.

These problems come to a head in Kant's next sentence, which begins, 'Reason must regard itself as the author of its principles...' (IV: 448). Aside from an unexplained shift from speaking about mere judgment to speaking about the special kind of judgment called a 'principle', the most obvious feature of this phrase is the fact that it again appears to be basically a formulation of what I have been calling the merely phenomenological notion of will and autonomy, the notion that one 'takes' oneself to be the rational determiner of something. Such 'taking' does not even establish real efficacy, and even if it did coincide with such efficacy it would not demonstrate any claim of negative freedom. But precisely this claim is added in the remainder of the sentence: '... independent of foreign influences' (IV: 448). With this assertion there is finally a direct connection between the idea of being a will and the idea of being free: to be a will is supposedly to take oneself to be able to judge and, in that sense, be a will 'of its own'; *and* to regard oneself this way is supposedly to believe not simply that one *is* a rational cause but also precisely that *nothing other* than one's own reason is the cause of one's judgments. But why would one ever think that a rational will as such has to make this extraordinarily strong final claim? Leaving aside the difficulty of *proving* that as a rational will one is actually negatively free, why claim that every such will would even *have to* think, or believe, or 'presuppose' that it is free in this sense?

At this point one might retreat one more time to a stipulative approach and read Kant as saying simply that what he *means* by a rational will is one that includes commitment to the specific claim that one 'cannot act otherwise than under an idea of freedom'. But this is no help if someone else happens to use some other notion of rational will that does not clearly involve this kind of necessary commitment to an idea of freedom and that still fits the core definition of a rational will (i.e. is rational, and is a will). Moreover, such a use is not merely an abstract possibility but is rather a very familiar occurrence in many popular as well as philosophical traditions. Thus it remains wholly unclear how we can even begin to decide *which* notion of rational will should be accepted, or whether *any* strong notion has actual reference to us.

10. The Footnote Attempt to Establish our Absolute Freedom— and its Vulnerability to the Earlier Objections

It is as this point that Kant adds a very famous footnote which many contemporary readers appear to think provides some kind of solution or alleviation of all these problems (IV: 448 n.).[22] He says that in some sense he is not claiming to 'prove freedom in its theoretical aspect' (I have given my own interpretation of this peculiar phrase elsewhere—this is not Kant's only use of it[23]), but this by itself hardly proves or indicates what it is that he is trying to prove. The one positive claim that he does add is simply 'that it is sufficient for our purpose that rational beings take merely the idea of freedom as basic to their actions' (IV: 448 n.). Given that the title of this subsection announces that Kant's 'purpose' here is to establish that 'freedom *must* be presupposed' in rational beings, we obviously must ask how his claim that such beings 'take merely the idea of freedom as basic' could really be 'sufficient' for this purpose. One way in which the claim obviously would be 'sufficient'—and in which it often seems to be read—would be if the claim of the subsection title were read to mean no more than what is said in the footnote; in that case, to say that freedom 'must be presupposed' just is to say that rational

---

[22] See e.g. Henry E. Allison, *Idealism and Freedom: Essays on Kant's Theoretical and Practical Philosophy* (Cambridge, 1996), 126–8, 133–4, 141–2; Christine Korsgaard, *Creating the Kingdom of Ends* (Cambridge, 1996), 172–80; Allen Wood, *Kant's Ethical Thought* (Cambridge, 2000), 175–80.

[23] See my *Kant's Theory of Mind*, 196.

beings *as such* 'take the idea of freedom to be basic'. But this only brings us back to the initial problem: since it now obviously will not do to say merely that some wills sometimes happen to use this idea, we must ask, *why* believe that rational beings, as wills, *must* 'take . . . the idea of freedom as basic' (IV: 448 n.), that is, as a property of rational wills as such?

Heavy weather is often made here of the fact that Kant ends his argument by saying that he is speaking of what is said 'from a practical point of view' (IV: 448). This sounds exciting, but I believe it may mean little more than that his discussion *concerns* what are in part practical issues, and that he is not committed to any theoretical *explanation of how* freedom actually works (since often for Kant taking a 'theoretical' rather than 'practical' point of view is precisely giving such an 'explanation'—which is not simply a philosophical account, but a quasi-mechanical story of how something actually works, even for 'practical' matters). Contemporary interpreters are often eager to read the phrase 'practical point of view' as already *meaning* the perspective of someone who is specifically committed to or interested in making practical decisions in some moral sense.[24] But Kant clearly cannot be saying *here* that his argument rests on practical *premises* in such a relatively narrow sense, involving controversial or specifically moral ideas; for the explicit aim of this section is rather to construct an argument *to* morality based simply on the idea of 'rational wills' as such. Furthermore, even if it is insisted that the argument itself is nonetheless to be read as being *made* only 'from' a *particular* 'point of view' (rather than only *applying* to one), it is still true that, no matter how much issues are contextualized for any such 'point of view', the key question always remains of what the backing can be for saying that something *must* be the case, or must be taken to be the case, even from that point of view—and then of why that view should be relevant to us simply as rational beings. Obviously, the more any particular controversial thought is built in as necessary to a 'point of view', the harder it becomes to argue that the view is of general relevance, something necessary for 'all rational beings'.

The issue here also cannot be decided by a pragmatic turn or an appeal to something like a mere personal existential stance. When Kant claims here that a rational being must 'act under' the 'idea of freedom', he surely does not mean that it does so in 'blind' action or a leap of 'practical faith'. What Kant means is that, in any situation in which it takes itself really to be acting—and that means even in its simplest act of judgment—it must also *take*, i.e. understand and believe, the 'idea of freedom' 'as basic'. There need no longer be any mystery about what the terms 'idea' and 'basic' mean here. From the context that has just been analyzed, the

---

[24] See above, n. 22, and also *The Sources of Normativity*, ed. Christine Korsgaard *et al.* (Cambridge, 1996). A significant issue of freedom entirely within the context of Kantian morality is whether, given Kant's talk of 'self-legislation', values are themselves to be understood as 'constructed' in a way that contrasts with moral realism. For some first thoughts on this issue, see below, Ch. 11.

most natural way to understand the use of the term 'idea' is to see it as standing for nothing other than the concept of absolute freedom, including its strong negative component—since this is clearly a relevant 'idea' in Kant's specific sense (i.e. a concept of something non-sensible), and is the meaning with which the term 'freedom' directly entered the discussion in these pages of the *Groundwork*. Kant is thus claiming nothing less than that, whenever rational wills (whether or not they are on some other ground absolutely free) engage in and properly consider a simple act of judgment, they *must think* of their judgment as free in this strong sense. But in what sense of 'must' must they do this?

There are only so many relevant modalities to consider here—logical, metaphysical, epistemological, deontological, natural. Straightforward logical and metaphysical claims of necessity appear obviously unpromising. A naturalistic account of 'must' is worse than hard to establish. Here it would be self-defeating, for it would be absurd for Kant, of all philosophers, to insist that wills as such are naturally *forced* to think of themselves in a particular way. A deontological reading also must obviously fail here. As has already been established, at this point Kant cannot mean that one 'must think' of freedom simply because otherwise one could not think oneself as a practical being in the sense of a *moral* being—because he has just indicated that he is seeking an argument that precisely does not already have a moral premise but instead can help provide an independent foundation for morality. Nor would it be relevant to say one 'must think' of freedom, because otherwise one could not think of oneself as a practical being merely in the sense of a *real* agent—because, as also has been repeatedly emphasized, it is quite possible to think of an agent that is actually a cause even if it lacks (absolute negative) freedom.

This leaves only an epistemological reading of the 'must', namely, that wills 'must think' of themselves in terms of absolute freedom because the evidence for such a claim makes it the appropriate thought for a rational being. But then we are left with the question of what evidence there can be that makes the idea of freedom one that a rational agent as such 'must' affirm. I see no answer to this question, but I think that ultimately this is an embarrassment not for Kant but for contemporary apologists for his *Groundwork* argument.[25] Kant himself went on to argue quite differently elsewhere, and this is itself a kind of evidence that ultimately he would agree with the weakness of this particular argument. One easily imagines that he came to see the frog smiling at the bottom of the mug precisely at the same time that he was working on the project of developing an even more Critical discussion of claims of our spontaneity in the massive revisions of his discussion of

---

[25] Arguments of this type have nonetheless had an enormous influence on post-Kantian thought and its reception by current philosophy. I have argued against these tendencies in other works; see e.g., ch. 5 of my *Kant and the Fate of Autonomy: Problems in the Appropriation of the Critical Philosophy* (Cambridge, 2000).

mind in the second edition of the first *Critique*. This development liberates us for the tasks of pursuing, as Kant did later, only arguments about freedom that already presume morality—or of looking more closely into a sense of autonomy and freedom that is free of his specific absolute and moral presuppositions.

– 10 –

'Pure Reason of Itself Alone Suffices to Determine the Will'

1. Context and Structure of the Text*

The main problem of the *Critique of Practical Reason* is to determine whether 'pure reason is really practical' (p. 3), that is, 'whether pure reason of itself alone suffices to determine the will' (p. 16). This problem receives its best known treatment in an appeal to what Kant calls the 'fact of reason', *das Faktum der Vernunft* (pp. 6, 31, 42, 43, 47, 55, 91, 104). I will refer to the discussion of this issue in sections I (pp. 42–50) and II (pp. 50–7) of *KpV* as the 'Faktum Text'.

Whereas section I focuses on the fundamental claim that pure reason really is practical, section II plays the secondary but essential role of responding to the objection that such an assertion can appear to transcend the bounds of what is permissible to say within the Critical philosophy itself. More specifically, it is clear that for Kant the key problem for the very possibility of morality is the special kind of absolute or 'transcendental freedom' (pp. 3, 99) that he believes is obviously required if the authority of pure practical reason is not to be challenged as a mere 'chimera'. In providing, with the 'fact of reason', a way of 'showing' that pure practical reason in fact, or in deed (*in der Tat*, p. 42)[1] is real, and therefore possible, Kant takes himself to have 'deduced' the actuality of absolute freedom, and this claim raises the problem of whether an improper 'extension' has been made in our use of reason.

Since Kant characterizes the concept of freedom as the 'keystone' (p. 5) of the 'whole structure' of reason, it is only fitting that the Faktum Text's discussion of the *possibility* of freedom and morality has a central position in the main part of *KpV*, right before chapter II of the Analytic. Whereas the earlier part of chapter I

---

*Unattributed page numbers in the text are to the *Kritik der praktischen Vernunft* (*KpV*,) vol. V of *Kant's Gesammelte Schriften* (Berlin, 1900–).

[1] This 'proto-Fichtean' expression is stressed in O. Schwemmer, 'Das "Faktum der Vernunft"', in *Philosophie der Praxis* (Frankfurt, 1986), 271–302; and M. Willaschek, *Praktische Vernunft: Handlungstheorie und Moralbegründung bei Kant* (Stuttgart, 1992).

fills out the 'principles' of morality, and thus gives its *content* an initial specification by arguing for various analytic relations between basic concepts of morality and freedom, chapter II elaborates the 'concept' of the 'object' of freedom, namely good and evil, and chapter III addresses the *motivational* issue of the 'incentives' of pure practical reason.

Kant's ordering of these issues is different only a few years earlier in 1785 in the *Groundwork* (*Grundlegung der Metaphysik der Sitten, GMS*). Section I *begins* with questions about the proper motive of moral action (acting 'from' duty), section II offers a formulation of morality's pure 'principle', and then section III concludes the book with an account of morality's key 'concept', freedom (which is invoked to fill out a more detailed account of moral incentives). The argument of *GMS* thus goes in a direction that is precisely the reverse of the sequence of terms in its title—from 'morals' to 'metaphysics' and then to a 'groundwork'. The end of *GMS* provides the foundation for morality by presenting an argument for our freedom and autonomy from the mere notion of our having an 'intelligible' will, and by grounding this 'possibility' (IV: 453) ultimately in the Critical doctrine of transcendental idealism.

In *KpV*, Kant does not comment on this shift in detail but instead notes that his new work borrows from only the first two sections of *GMS* ('the principle of duty and ... a determinate formula', (p. 8)—as if section III had suddenly become irrelevant or superseded. Rather than dwelling directly on this surprising development, Kant prefers to explain how he has adopted an order for the presentation of his main issues that contrasts with that of the *Critique of Pure Reason (KrV)* rather than *GMS*. Whereas *KrV* 'ascends' from our specific kind of sensibility to general concepts and principles, and then to dialectical questions emphasizing the inescapability of the metaphysics of transcendental idealism, *KrV* proceeds in a reverse 'downward' order, for it 'shall begin with principles [chapter I] and proceed to concepts [chapter II], and only then, where possible, from them to the senses [chapter III]' (p. 16). There is nothing inaccurate in this contrast, but, as we will see, it does draw attention away from the way in which *KpV* appears to have relocated—and perhaps fundamentally reconfigured—a key argument from a text that is much closer to it in time and topic than *KrV*, namely *GMS*.

2. The Argument of Section I

The main section of the Faktum Text has sixteen paragraphs and can be divided into two main parts (paragraphs 2–12 and 12–15), plus a preliminary and a concluding paragraph. After paragraph 1 gives a brief introduction of the fact of reason, paragraphs 2–12 lay out an extensive comparison of theoretical and practical reason. The turning point of the text is paragraph 12, which begins with the declaration that 'the *exposition* of the supreme principle of practical reason is now finished', and moves on by elaborating the point that practical reason 'cannot hope' to have a '*deduction*' like theoretical reason has of the 'objective validity' of *its* basic principle (p. 46). The second main part of the section continues through paragraph 15 with an explanation of how, even though 'the moral law cannot be proved by any deduction', it is given in a consciousness that is 'a priori' and 'apodictically certain', and such that, *given* this consciousness, a deduction of freedom can be given *from* practical reason (i.e. from the moral law) and can provide an 'objective reality' for *this* concept, something that theoretical reason was not able to do (p. 47; cf. 93).

To understand the first part of section I in more detail, it is essential to keep in mind the initial contrast of theoretical and practical reason drawn in paragraphs 2 and 3. Whereas theoretical reason starts with sensible *intuition* and works toward speculative principles determining our cognition of all the possible *objects* of such intuition, it can do little more for the domain beyond sensible intuition than 'preserve' a 'negative' (i.e. not filled in) concept of absolute freedom (p. 42). Practical reason, in contrast, begins with the *pure* moral 'fact of reason' that 'even determines' freedom 'positively and lets us *cognize* something of it, namely a *law*' (p. 43; my emphasis). This contrast is repeated in paragraphs 9–11. Whereas *KrV* shows how theoretical reason moves from 'intuited' 'objects' to determine a priori 'cognition' of them as merely 'sensible' (p. 45), *KpV* exhibits how pure practical reason starts with 'maxims', and considers them in an a priori way that applies 'laws' and 'concepts' (such as freedom) while abstracting from questions such as whether 'the causality of the will is adequate for the reality of the objects' (p. 45). This formulation is an elaboration of a distinction Kant makes in paragraph 8 between 'two very different problems', how we 'cognize' objects by theoretical reason and how we 'determine' the will by practical reason (pp. 44–5; cf. below Section 3). The remainder of the first part of this section, paragraphs 4–7, is devoted to the theme of the autonomy of practical reason. In paragraph 5, Kant simply declares that 'the most ordinary attention to oneself' discloses, through the moral law, a 'pattern for the determinations of our will' (p. 43). Fortunately, paragraph 6 adds some detail, with examples of how this 'pattern' involves use of the notion of 'universal law' to determine proper maxims (e.g. not to end one's life 'at will') in accord with 'the idea of a nature not given empirically and yet possible through freedom, hence a supersensible nature'. Practical reason thus reveals (paragraph 7) a 'nature which is subject to a [pure] will', in contrast to theoretical reason, which reveals 'laws of a nature to which the [empirical] will is subject' (p. 44).

3. Autonomy

The central topic throughout this section is obviously autonomy. At the very beginning of the Faktum Text (paragraph 1), Kant equates the 'fact' (*Faktum*) of reason with 'autonomy in the principle of morality by which reason determines the will to deeds [*zur Tat*]' (p. 42). This 'determination' has at least *two* aspects— 'formal' and 'efficient'—that need to be kept distinct, even though they are closely related. To say that reason provides a *formal* determination of the will for morality is to say that the *content* of morality is basically determined by pure rational considerations, 'form' not 'matter' (p. 39). To say that there is in this sense a *formal* determination of the will by reason is already to say that there is a kind of self-determination, or autonomy of reason, since for Kant the will is the faculty of practical reason. Hence, one sense in which Kantian autonomy is a principle 'by which reason determines the will to deeds' is just that, insofar as reason provides a proper standard or content, it can be said that the rational will in general can will itself, that is, affirm its own form as the object of proper intentions. With respect to *this* kind of autonomy, the question of whether 'pure reason can be practical' has already been settled prior to the Faktum Text: *pure* practical reason clearly *can* determine the will by determining *what* it should do. When Kant declares that practical reason gives us 'laws that are independent of any empirical condition and thus [N.B.] belong to the *autonomy* of pure reason' (p. 43), he is simply expressing this formal aspect of the contrast between autonomy and heteronomy, an aspect that is concerned not with the ultimate causes or actual effects of our intentions but solely with their content (p. 43).

There is a further distinction, however, that can be made *within* the formal dimension of practical reason. If we distinguish reason in general, as an abstract domain of principles, from reason in particular, as a concrete cognitive faculty in individuals recognizing these principles, then we can contrast two moments within the 'formal' aspect of practical reason: (a) the content of the principles themselves, which constitute reason's own ideal structures; and (b) the *discerning* of that content by rational beings who see what the right principles are and thus 'determine' them in an additional sense, namely epistemically. Thus, Kant's remark that morality 'transfers us into an intelligible order' (p. 42) is a reminder, among other things, of both the pure content that is cognized by our practical reason and the correlative pure act and faculty of cognition that we use in cognizing it. (A similar pure duality is found in Kant's notion of 'pure intuition'.)

Although Kant dwells on the formal aspects of autonomy (p. 43), there is a second and much more concrete kind of autonomy, or self-determination, that is his ultimate concern. This kind of autonomy has to do with the rational will's truly determining itself by being an *efficient* cause, and in particular by being an absolutely free cause. Given Kant's libertarianism, it is clear that only if reason 'determines the will to deeds' in this efficient sense is it reason in 'fact'. We might know what would be the right thing to do *according* to reason without our actually being able to do it *from* reason. And for Kant, in the context of morality, it is not enough for an action 'from reason' that reason be the immediate cause of the action: it would have to be the ultimate cause as well. This requires that the individual agent not only operate 'through' reason in some psychological or evaluative sense (that would be sufficient for a compatibilist), but also that, in its willing, it be literally an uncaused cause—hence Kant's frequent references (pp. 48–9, 54) back to the discussion of this general notion in the Third Antimony of *KrV*.

Unfortunately, the full complexity of this fundamental double nature of the practical self-determination of reason as both formal and efficient is somewhat obscured in the way that Kant immediately applies the key passage noted earlier (paragraph 8), which distinguishes 'how . . . pure [speculative] reason can cognize objects a priori and how . . . [as practical reason] it can be an immediate ground of the will' (pp. 44–5). The problem is that Kant goes on to discuss the 'cognition' issue here as if it arises only with respect to *theoretical* reason, while he discusses the 'determining ground' issue as if it has a single meaning with respect to *practical* reason. That is, Kant neglects to distinguish here two closely related and crucial points of this own theory, namely: (a) that practical reason itself is capable of a kind of a priori 'cognition' (p. 46: 'the moral law is not concerned with a cognition of the constitution of objects that may be given to reason from elsewhere but rather with a cognition that . . . '); and (b) that this is so because even the 'grounding' provided by practical reason alone has more than one meaning. Its 'determination' of the will to deeds involves not only a special kind of efficient causation (namely, free intentionality) but also a kind of formal specification that requires cognitive activity on our part. As pure practical and self-determining beings, we must be able both to do the right things and antecedently to know what these are.

That there is a kind of formal and cognitive self-determination within even practical reason is obvious enough from the story Kant has just given of the pure content of morality (pp. 35–41). He realizes, however, that on his view this content would not truly attach to anything unless there are agents who have the *free power* to will it from reason. Mere conceptual reflection can reveal the autonomy of morality's content, but, given Kant's libertarianism, it cannot by itself reveal that in fact this autonomy is anything more than a 'chimera' in our lives. If we do the right things, even with the right reasons before our mind, but in such a way that our minds are made to operate as they do by something outside of (and unknown to) them, then in doing them we do not have a moral character at all. Similarly, wrong actions, even with the worst of thoughts before one's mind, do not count as acts of an immoral being if the being is not absolutely free in its choice, and thus capable of having done the moral thing fully on its own accord. The requirement of absolute freedom of choice adds a crucial and very strong dimension of meaning to the efficient aspect of our autonomy.

Given Kant's notion of our place in a sensible world that is in principle thoroughly law-governed, some ground seems needed for the strong claim that in fact we are fully autonomous in his strong efficient sense. Nothing in the mere formal independence of reason warrants this claim. Moreover, as Kant himself indicates, a mere exploitation of a distinction between 'lower' and 'higher' faculties (pp. 22–3), is not enough. Even if we construct a distinct 'object' for our practical intentions that has a *form* that takes us beyond what our lower faculties could generate, this still shows only that there may be a faculty of reason that has an especially elevated *focus*, not that it has a genuinely pure *power*. The very fact that Kant can specify—as he does, before the Faktum Text—a fully rational set of maxim contents, and in *that* sense an autonomous style of life, without yet entering into issues of ultimate causation, can make one wonder why Kant thinks that he has to hold onto the insistence on our autonomy in a strong efficient sense.

Whatever advantages others might see in avoiding the whole issue of free causation, the fact is that Kant turned his back (after mid-career) on all non-libertarian theories and resolutely insisted on an autonomy of reason with a strong efficient as well as formal component. The argument of *GMS* recognizes the strong claims involved in this insistence, and it at least attempts to provide some kind of obviously inescapable warrant for this kind of strong autonomy. In *KpV*, however, Kant drops the suggestion of any argument *to* freedom (and then to morality *from* this kind of freedom) from the mere consideration of 'intelligence' or willing in general. He declares: 'this [moral] law [cannot be deduced from] consciousness of freedom, (since [N.B.] this is not antecedently given to us)' (p. 31). After this shift to a reliance on a specific moral 'fact of reason', it becomes unclear what the Faktum Text can do to provide any *support* for the claim of our strong autonomy with respect to its controversial efficient (i.e. absolutely free) component. Indeed, the question of support, or separate warrant, may not even seem appropriate anymore, once the term 'fact' has been introduced. Kant himself asserts that the 'moral law . . . itself has no need of justifying grounds' (p. 47). But if this is all that can be said, then his position can seem all too vulnerable to charges of dogmatism.

One alternative to sheer dogmatism would be to seek support in something that is given, if not antecedently, then at least *with* the 'fact of reason'. Some portions of the Faktum Text may suggest a kind of phenomenological approach along this line. When Kant speaks of the will being 'conscious of its existence as determinable in an intelligible order of things' (p. 42), his words could be taken to involve something more than the mere formal aspects of autonomy mentioned earlier. They could be taken to designate not a mere appreciation of an abstract rational standard, but a concrete, intense, and presumably effective belief that one is actually doing something aimed toward this 'order'.

The fact that such beliefs exist, and that they need not be taken to reflect the mere peculiarities of individual subjects, is certainly worth noting. Moreover, such beliefs have an interesting double role that combines formal and efficient aspects. Proper moral beliefs need to have the right form, and this very form also has to be central to the immediate causal nature of the agent's choice. Nonetheless, for non-Kantians it remains unclear whether, in addition to all this, agents need to have an absolutely free causality. It also remains unclear whether agents even 'have' to *believe* this *while* they are acting—and what difference it would make if they did not. (Perhaps all they need to believe is that they really can act rationally, and not also that their acts have an uncaused cause.) This is a problem, because Kant's notion of the fact of reason as 'identical' with 'consciousness of freedom of the will' (p. 42), cannot mean simply that there is a *later* philosophical reflection that eventually comes down on the side of libertarianism against its traditional philosophical opponents. Kant is claiming the general and already accepted 'fact' of an *immediate* belief in the 'presence' of the moral law, and in a kind of absolute freedom revealing itself through that law. The difficulty here is not only that, even in moral contexts, such a belief may not be as common as Kant supposes; a deeper problem arises from a point that Kant himself emphasizes, namely that many common beliefs with a source in reason itself can turn out to be highly unwarranted and improper, even if they are not dialectical and definitely false. Why shouldn't we worry about our belief in absolute freedom being similarly dispensable?[2]

It might seem that Kant is not worried about the problem of our free power, because when he mentions the 'causality of the will' here he says 'its power in execution may be as it may' (p. 45). But all he means is that proper moral intentions can fail to be *successful* in their effect on the world. However, if the 'causality of the will' is unable even freely to *choose* the proper maxims that it tries to implement, then this kind of 'inefficiency' of reason would make its formal self-determination an idle point, and leave us without what Kant regards as full autonomy. This is clear from the beginning of the Faktum Text, since as soon as Kant introduces the notion of our being 'transferred' to an 'intelligible order', he makes the crucial qualification that this happens '*if*' [and presumably only if] freedom is 'attributed to us' (p. 42). In sum, the problem is that *responsibly* asserting what Kant means by the pure practicality of reason still seems to require not only an appreciation of formal autonomy and a 'common' belief in strong autonomy, but also some reason for this belief, some reason to hold onto a rigorous morality and the thought that we actually do have the remarkable power of absolute freedom—especially in a context where it is conceded that all the causings we can know we know as caused causings.[3]

---

[2] See D. Owens, *Reason without Freedom: The Problem of Epistemic Normativity*, (London, 2000); S. Smilansky, *Free Will and Illusion* (Oxford, 2000).

[3] Cf. A. Rehberg, 'Rezension der *Kritik der praktischen Vernunft*' (first published 1788), in R. Bittner and K. Cramer (eds.), *Materialen zu Kants, 'Kritik der praktischen Vernunft'* (Frankfurt, 1975), 179–96.

4. The Faktum Text as a 'Reversal'

The deep systematic problems arising from the evaluation of Kant's position can raise questions about whether Kant's intentions have been properly interpreted. This is a controversial matter, but most recent readings[4] accept that the Faktum Text is not a slip on Kant's part but represents, for better or worse, a carefully thought out 'reversal' in his methodology, a retreat from the more 'foundational' approach that appears to be taken at the end of *GMS*. Whereas *GMS* proposes an argument to freedom and morality starting from the absolutely inescapable idea of a rational will as an 'intelligence' (IV: 452), *KpV* stresses from the start (4 n.)—and reiterates in the Faktum Text—that freedom (of the relevant absolute kind) can be *known only* on the presupposition of morality (in Kant's strict sense), rather than being derivable from any neutral common ground, such as the mere notion of oneself as a thinking, willing being (pp. 46, 93).

This interpretation is still consistent with talk 'of' a 'deduction' within *KpV* because an important kind of deduction remains possible in the move *from* morality 'to' freedom, even if an argument without substantive practical presuppositions is no longer to be encouraged *to* morality itself. Hence, the title of the section, 'On the Deduction of the Principles of Pure Practical Reason', which is two steps short of a direct assertion that there is a deduction of morality itself. First, the title states merely that it will comment 'on' a deduction, rather than saying that there literally is a deduction. Secondly, the deduction it speaks of here concerns specifically the 'principles' of pure practical reason. This is consistent with the thought that, even if an absolute foundation cannot be given for morality itself (e.g. involving a strict and 'independent', i.e. non-moral, proof that we have absolute freedom), a deduction could still be given of the *various* 'principles' or contents alone appropriate for morality *once* one posits the idea of a possible pure practical reason that determines necessary structures for the proper relations of wills. It is true that for this kind of account Kant usually uses the term 'exposition', (p. 46) in contrast to a 'deduction'; but these terms can overlap, since sometimes he calls his metaphysical expositions 'deductions' as well (e.g. in the Transcendental Aesthetic), and sometimes he uses the word 'deduction' in a context where it may seem he has a transcendental argument in mind when in fact he seems primarily to have a metaphysical exposition in view, as when he says that the 'concept of a cause … having arisen wholly from the pure understanding, also has … objective reality in respect to objects in general assured by the deduction

---

[4] K. Ameriks, *Kant's Theory of Mind* (Oxford, 2000; first published 1982); A. Reath, 'Introduction', in M. Gregor (ed.), *Critique of Practical Reason/Immanuel Kant* (Cambridge, 1997), vii–xxxi; J. Rawls, *Lectures on the History of Moral Philosophy* (Cambridge, Mass., 2000); for background, see D. Henrich, 'Die Deduktion des Sittengesetzes: Über die Gründe der Dunkelheit des letzen Abschnittes von Kants Grundlegung der Metaphysik der Sitten', in A. Schwan (ed.), *Denken im Schatten des Nihilismus* (Darmstadt, 1975), 55–112.

inasmuch as, being in its origin independent of all sensibility...' (p. 55; other aspects of this passage are discussed below). There is nothing wrong with this terminological overlap, since we can understand that a metaphysical 'exposition' is itself a kind of deduction insofar as, in showing that a particular representation has a meaning that requires an a priori origin, it also discloses the only possible source of the representation—although this is not yet to justify or explain the actual reference of the terms in question.

Such an exposition, or metaphysical deduction, is still something short of a standard transcendental deduction, which would show that the pure concepts in question do have determinate objective reference. This is not to say that a Kantian transcendental deduction ever has to be understood as an 'absolute' justification that would work against all kinds of skeptics.[5] Rather, it is an argument that shows how, *given* various premises, that is, steps that are not themselves deduced (viz. the general notion of 'experience' at the base of the transcendental deduction of the categories in *KrV*; cf. the summary of this procedure at p. 47: 'only experience can justify...'), the pure representations are justified. Such an argument is still 'transcendental' when the premises it relies on are ones that appear inescapable for experience 'at all'.

The argument of *GMS* exhibits a transcendental structure of this type, but *KpV* rejects its kind of neutral starting point as a ground for the moral law. The Faktum Text claims right from beginning to 'show that pure reason can be practical... *by* a fact ["Faktum"] in which pure reason proves itself actually practical, namely autonomy in the *principle* of morality by which reason determines the will to deeds' (p. 42; my emphasis). That is, *given* the actual autonomy of a moral being that determines acts formally and efficiently, it then can be 'shown' that the faculty of reason in that being is practical in a genuinely pure sense—and therefore free (presumably because, in Kant's view, no other position seems compatible with the unconditional meaning of moral imperatives). Kant immediately goes on to indicate that his reference to a 'fact' here signifies not an abstract possibility but an actual 'deed' (*zur Tat*) of a moral being—or at least the immediately and universally presumed capacity to carry out such a deed. Hence, our freedom, and the simultaneous truth that 'pure reason' truly is practical, can be said to be 'shown' in a double sense: it is *deducible* from the presupposed 'fact' of accepted moral claims, and it is *exhibited* in the very presence of such claims, in the 'consciousness' of them and the acts they generate.

At one point Kant says that this all amounts to a 'credential' for the moral law (p. 48), and in one English version the next sentence is translated as saying that this

---

[5] K. Ameriks, 'Kant's Transcendental Deduction as a Regressive Argument', *Kant-Studien*, 87 (1978), 273–87.

is 'fully sufficient in place of any a priori justification'.[6] This should not be understood as saying that a justifying deduction for the truth of morality itself is being presented. The German makes clear that Kant's point is merely that the Faktum is 'sufficient' for *freedom's* deduction *from* morality, and to fill the 'need' of speculative reason for *some* positive specification or 'supplementation'—*zur Ergänzung*—of its concept of unconditioned causality (a 'need' that does not have to be met in one specific way). The assertion of freedom on the basis of practical reason adds something that *fits in* with speculative reason's framework here, just as the assertion of pure spatio-temporal intuitions adds something that fits in and 'fills a space' for specifying our general speculative concepts (the categories), but these *specific* assertions do not derive from anything deducible from reason in general.

The feature of non-deducibility is central to Kant's notion of a 'fact' of reason. Kant introduces the term 'fact' not for the positive reason of indicating anything that is literally the object of a 'special intuition' (p. 42), but rather for the negative reason of indicating a contrast with anything that is itself *derived*. This is why, *as soon as* Kant makes the famous statement that 'the moral law is given, as it were, as a fact of pure reason', he adds, 'the moral law cannot be proven by any deduction' (p. 47); and elsewhere he says it 'may be called a fact because [N.B.] one cannot reason it out from antecedent data of reason' (p. 31).

This point implies that, if there are those who claim not to recognize such a fact, then there is no Archimedean lever, no 'neutral' ground, from which such skeptics can be defeated. Kant did not seem to think one would have to worry too much about running into sincere skeptics of this kind, but he was not oblivious to the limitations of his position here. This is one reason why he insists that the fact he is invoking here is 'of reason'; that is, it comes from and reveals a distinct higher faculty that is supposedly inescapable for all normal persons. In this way it is meant to contrast with all incidental needs (p. 5), and even the systematic interests of theoretical reason, which involve a drive to unification that is strong but does not have unconditional force. Indirect evidence for an awareness of the limitations in any argument that relies on something like a mere 'fact' of reason can be found in the existence of section III of *GMS*, which shows that Kant certainly knew how to attempt an argument starting from a general faculty of 'intelligence' that does not require a prior acknowledgment of any particular practical doctrine. He must have realized that *if* he could hold on to such an argument, then the step down to reliance on a 'fact' involving specifically moral considerations could be avoided, and so, it might seem, the systematic difficulties noted earlier could be escaped. However, the structure of such an argument is not only too ambitious

---

[6] A. Wood, 'Introduction', in M. Gregor (ed.), *Practical Philosophy by Immanuel Kant* (Cambridge, 1996), 178.

to remain convincing upon reflection (see above, Section 3); it also involves special dangers for the Critical system, difficulties that it appears Kant came to appreciate right at the time he was drafting *KpV*.

The main difficulty is that, if absolute freedom is taken to be demonstrable from general theoretical considerations, then the firewall claimed to be built in the Transcendental Dialectic (*KrV*) against all speculative metaphysics would seem to be directly endangered. There is considerable evidence now that Kant became very sensitive to this problem in the 1780s,[7] although this development is sometimes still neglected. For example, an introduction to a recent English edition remarks, 'In April 1787 [just before beginning *KpV*] Kant had completed his revisions [for the second edition of *KrV*], and his only [N.B.] extensive rewriting beyond the Transcendental Analytic was in the Dialectic's chapter on "The Paralogisms of Pure Reason", a part having no direct bearing on moral philosophy'.[8] This observation passes over the fact that, even if in some narrow sense the Paralogisms may not have a 'direct' bearing on 'moral philosophy', Kant's massive revisions of them and his new treatment of many closely related topics (e.g. the Refutation of Idealism and the clarification of apperception in the rewriting of the Deduction) in *KrV* B are clearly crucial for understanding the ultimate structure of his entire philosophy and especially the background of the Faktum Text. The detailed changes in the Paralogisms are an indication of Kant's deep preoccupation with refining his whole treatment of the self and the central property of freedom, the concept that he had called the 'key' to 'the explanation of the autonomy of the will' (*GMS* IV: 446), which is obviously the ultimate basis for his entire moral theory. Given the fact that Kant faced severe objections to his theory of the self in *KrV* A, and that he chose, in page after page of revisions in *KrV* B, to adopt the new tactic of stressing difficulties with any suggestion that the subject could gain knowledge of itself independent of spatial determinations, it is very hard to believe that he did not realize what he was doing here—that he was systematically blocking the door, once and for all, to even the suggestion of any kind of argument to absolute freedom starting merely from a consideration of the self's general capacity for 'intelligence'. What the Faktum Text shows, on this account, is not only that in 1788 Kant was turning to the concept of freedom to 'flesh out' the 'positive' meaning that the idea has in moral contexts. More fundamentally, it shows Kant's preoccupation with making as clear as he could what he now took to be the sole context for our saying that we truly do have a faculty of absolute freedom: not theoretical considerations, and not just any kind of 'practical' considerations, but moral ('pure practical') considerations alone are the *ratio cognoscendi* (4 n.) from which our freedom can be asserted.

---

[7] Ameriks, *Kant's Theory of Mind*.   [8] Wood, 'Introduction', 135.

5. 'On the Warrant of Pure Reason in its Practical Use to an Extension which is not possible in its Speculative Use' (p. 50)

Section II of the Faktum Text concerns what can seem to be a relatively secondary problem, an explanation of how the commitment to freedom asserted in morality can 'extend' reason in a non-dogmatic way. But the section is essential, and the title alone is a significant achievement. In introducing the term 'warrant', which has recently gained popularity in analytic epistemology as a basic term preferable to 'justification',[9] Kant signals his belief that claims about the actuality of freedom can have something less than an empirical or transcendental deduction behind them and yet still be quite proper for us (i.e. 'warranted'). Earlier I criticized the reliance on the 'fact of reason' for not being able to provide a basis for what it asserts, either from some prior transcendental ground for morality or from some feature that incontrovertibly comes along 'with' the belief in it. But even if we question the 'apodictically certain' (p. 47) status of 'moral experience' that Kant seems to assume, the mere fact that many readers have responded so positively to his characterization of it implies that there is 'something to be said for' the fact of reason. It reflects a standpoint that certainly appears widespread and highly significant in its implications, and even if it cannot be 'deduced', it is not thereby much worse off than most of what is asserted by philosophers—as long as the doctrine is at least consistent with the other main points of Kant's work.

Section II is aimed primarily at showing how the fact of reason is fully consistent with the Critical philosophy. After a brief introductory paragraph, paragraphs 2–6 and 9 lay out a contrast with Hume (pp. 50–3, 56) that consists in a recapitulation of the main claims of *KrV*. After characterizing Hume as a skeptic of reason, or 'pure' substantive claims in general, Kant presents it as a reductio ad absurdum that strict Humean empiricism would force us to dismiss not only traditional philosophy but also all significant mathematics and science (pp. 51–2). Kant then reminds his readers of how *KrV* had addressed the Humean challenge to the concept of causality in general. Agreeing with Hume that the concept has a component of necessity in its very meaning, that such necessity cannot be warranted by particular experiences, and that any theoretical ground that we can have for the application of the concept must not entirely transcend experience, Kant repeats his argument that the concept can be transcendentally warranted as a pure condition for our experience in general ('as appearances they must necessarily be connected in one experience in a certain way': p. 53).

Whatever the merits of the Second Analogy argument to which Kant is alluding here, his main objective is to remind his readers of the even more fundamental doctrine of *KrV*, that the very *origin* and *meaning* of a pure concept such as

---

[9] A. Plantinga, *Warrant: The Current Debate* (New York/Oxford, 1993).

causality has a general character that 'can be used even of noumena', since its 'seat in the pure understanding was secured' (p. 54). The underlying point here is simply the general claim of his metaphysical deduction that our pure concepts are based in the logical structure of judgment. Kant thus culminates his attack on empiricism by saying that not only could Hume not give a justification for the concept of cause, but even the pure and general meaning that Kant finds for it is something that 'would not be the case if, as Hume maintained, this concept of causality contained something in it that is always impossible to *think*' (p. 54; cf. p. 56: 'Had I, with Hume, deprived the concept... of all meaning...').

Kant notes that there may still seem to be a problem, because the *justification* of the *application* of the concept of causality in theoretical philosophy rests on the way the concept is needed in order to unify sensible appearances in one experience, and this kind of justification is evidently lacking for *practical* reason. This is a difficulty, however, only if Kant's defense of practical reason, in its use of causality, somehow had to involve trying to make a claim about its unifying sensible data or determining 'the constitution' (p. 56) of objects—but this is not what it is doing. Still, one can ask what *specific* meaning and warranted use practical reason can provide for the concept of causality if it does not employ that concept in the way theoretical reason does. Kant's answer is that, even without a context of *theoretical application,* practical reason can still borrow and build on the *general meaning* of the concept of causality laid out in *KrV*, since this meaning was presented from the start as having a source in a context that is independent of any specific sensible considerations (p. 55). Such a borrowing by practical reason is understandable and even inevitable, since 'in the concept of a will, the concept of causality is already contained' (p. 55). And to any objection that, outside of an empirical context, such a concept remains merely an empty logical form, Kant is well armed at this point to reply that his discussion of the moral law and the idea of freedom in that context has provided very specific and useful ways to determine a 'positive' meaning of causality.

A more serious difficulty arises when Kant backs off, in a final point, to say that we are only 'authorized' (p. 56) to make a 'practical use' of nonsensible concepts such as freedom, and that this is 'to be counted not as knowledge but only as a warrant to admit and presuppose them' (p. 57). The motivation for this qualification is understandable, but the options it leaves us with have to be thought through to the end. *If* by 'knowledge' one means (as Kant often does) only claims that have a strong basis in *general theoretical* considerations, then *KpV*'s use of practical reason obviously does not constitute 'knowledge', let alone transcendent knowledge, and so in that sense worries about being 'given encouragement to fly into the transcendent' (p. 57; the final words of the Section) can be dismissed. Nonetheless, a final and difficult dilemma remains. If one uses a looser and much more common conception of 'knowledge', as including whatever it is assumed that any rational being should properly assert as such, then *KpV* implies that the moral law and what it entails is something that can be said to be known after all. (Thus, it is no wonder that Kant often uses terms such as 'cognize', *erkennen* if not *wissen*, in describing our relation to it.) But if the claims of pure practical reason are meant that strongly, then there is all the more reason to ask again whether a 'fact of reason' is truly an adequate ground for them. Without a genuine deduction of morality being even attempted any more, these claims can seem no longer well-founded at all, and can appear to be a mere 'standpoint', albeit one that is in fact 'taken' by many readers. But then, if one retreats, as many contemporary 'Kantians' urge,[10] to a position in which pure practical reason is presented as simply such *a* standpoint—one that we supposedly 'have to' treat 'as if' it is true but also as such that we can no longer directly assert that it and its implications about absolute freedom say anything about what there actually is—it becomes unclear why we still must call this the standpoint of *reason*, especially if so many rational beings continue to dispute it, and no deduction is offered to defend it.

Thus, just as it appears that *GMS* tries to prove too much, it can be argued that *KpV* proves too little—and that contemporary Kantians still need to seek some better way 'in between', with an appreciation for both the appeal and the limitations of the Faktum Text.

[10] C. Korsgaard, *Creating the Kingdom of Ends* (Cambridge, 1996).

– 11 –

On Two Non-Realist Interpretations of Kant's Ethics

1. On Schneewind and Kant's Method in Ethics

In a number of recent studies, and in most detail in an important paper on 'Natural Law, Skepticism, and Methods of Ethics', J. B. Schneewind has developed a highly original way of interpreting Kant's ethics in its historical context.[1] Schneewind's interpretation is in line with the some of the strongest trends in current ethical theory, but his outstanding knowledge of the history of ethics allows him the special advantage of a broad view, of being able to present Kant in terms of his whole age and the major developments of modern moral thought. All too often we have been taught to look primarily at the *differences* between Kant and his forerunners, and especially his British predecessors. Schneewind shows quite convincingly that if we take a slightly longer historical perspective than is common, these predecessors reveal many deep and rarely appreciated *parallels* to (and possible influences on) Kant's thought. Schneewind also notes several specific features unique to Kant's theory. The question that naturally arises is whether these differences, or other significant points, still deserve more weight than the significant similarities that Schneewind has emphasized. It can be conceded that, if what one means by 'Kant's thought' is its popular and influential image, what might be called the broad phenomenon of traditional Kant*ian* theory, then Schneewind is right to stress the skeptical similarities to the British

---

[1] J. B. Schneewind, 'Natural Law, Skepticism, and Methods of Ethics', *Journal of the History of Ideas*, 52 (1991), 289–308. References with 'A' and/or 'B' are to the first and/or second edition of the *Critique of Pure Reason*, and references with roman volume number, followed by colon and page number, are to *Kant's Gesammelte Schriften* (Berlin, 1900–). Other especially relevant essays by Schneewind are 'Kant and Stoic Ethics', in *Aristotle, Kant, and the Stoics*, ed. Stephen Engstrom and Jennifer Whiting (Cambridge, 1996), 285–301; 'Kant and Natural Law Ethics', *Ethics*, 104 (1993), 53–74; 'Autonomy, Obligation, and Virtue', in *The Cambridge Companion to Kant*, ed. Paul Guyer (Cambridge, 1992), 309–41; 'The Use of Autonomy in Ethical Theory', in *Reconstructing Individualism*, ed. T. C. Heller, M. Sousa, and D. Wellbery (Stanford, Calif., 1986), 64–75; and 'The Divine Corporation and the History of Ethics', in *Philosophy in History*, ed. Richard Rorty, J. B. Schneewind, and Quentin Skinner (Cambridge, 1984), 173–91. See also below, n. 29, and *Lectures on Ethics/ Immanuel Kant*, ed. Peter Heath and J. B. Schneewind, tr. Peter Heath (Cambridge, 1997).

that he has found. However, if one means by 'Kant's thought' the full intricacies and genuine implications of that philosopher's system, then it seems to me that there are serious differences worth further exploration. Hence, after reviewing what I take to be the main points of Schneewind's interpretation, I will argue for an approach to Kant's ethics that still distances him significantly from the modern British method, and in ways that need not make his position any less plausible intrinsically.

Before approaching this controversial issue, I will offer a brief six-point review of highlights of Schneewind's analysis. First, Schneewind provides a general characterization of what he calls 'a skeptical method in ethics'. Second, he gives a number of examples of this method in modern moralists. Third, he sketches three advantages of this method, noting how these come out somewhat differently for his various examples. Fourth, he argues that Kant's theory meets the defining characteristics of the skeptical method, and thus benefits from its general advantages. Fifth, Schneewind explains how, primarily because of its libertarian conception of agency, Kant's ethics also differs from that of his British predecessors in a number of respects. Finally, Kant's ethics is compared with another modern theory that shares his basic conception of agency, namely that of Crusius, and the striking difference nonetheless between their moral views is emphasized. This is taken to indicate that there is a deep and substantive agreement about morality and not only method that leaves Kant closer to the British than to figures such as Crusius.

Some of the specifics of this outline need to be filled in a bit. Three central claims of the skeptical method are that: (1) there is a distinct, universal, and non-theoretical human moral faculty; (2) what it treats as morally basic are motivational states; and (3) our acts have rightness simply by being generated by such states. Three purported advantages of the method[2] are that: (1) it can meet moral skepticism without recourse to dogmatism; (2) it can fit us into a post-Newtonian world while still capturing our uniqueness through an account of our motivational states; and (3) it can explain morality as binding on us because it relies on grounds accessible to ordinary people and their concern for 'self-governance' rather than on esoteric or arbitrary commands.

Let it be granted that Schneewind is correct in showing that these features are exemplified in the thought of figures such as Shaftesbury, Hutcheson, and Hume, as well as in Kant's ethics. This alone is an important matter for Schneewind to have established, but I will focus on the fact that he also emphasizes a number of more specific claims that are not so immediately obvious. These claims develop out of a recognition that there are differences in importance among the various features of the skeptical method, as well as significant differences in the way the

---

[2] Schneewind, 'Natural Law, Skepticism, and Methods of Ethics', 300.

various examples of the method develop these features. The feature that gets the most attention is the response to modern skepticism about moral knowledge.

On Schneewind's analysis, there is a rather complex pattern in the responses to this skepticism. The skeptical method involves a cognitivist response in Shaftesbury; then it shifts to a non-cognitivist approach in Hutcheson and Hume; and finally it returns to a cognitivist approach in Kant, but in a form that is in several ways very unlike Shaftesbury's response. This last approach is closely connected with Kant's distinctive theory of agency. By means of a discussion of Crusius, who agrees mainly with just the metaphysics of Kant's theory, Schneewind suggests that overall it matters remarkably little whether one is a naturalist or a libertarian about agency: what matters most is not metaphysics but rather how much an agreement on the general features of the skeptical method can bring with it a common humanistic vision of what morality is all about. This is an appealing story, but I will be questioning whether it is compelling and really holds for a philosopher as metaphysical as Kant.

This issue will depend very much on how we are to regard the problem of skepticism that the skeptical method supposedly resolves. Schneewind understands the problem in terms of a worry that morality is in trouble when questions arise as to how we can know anything external, including the commands of God or natural laws of eternal 'fitness' in the cosmic order. In contrast, I would emphasize that this worry becomes acute precisely at that point at the beginning of the modern era, when it is insisted by some that such knowledge must and does ground morality, and when it is also realized more and more by others that such a claim seems insupportable by anything like the new paradigms of knowledge in natural science. Schneewind connects the rise of this problem more with the resurgence of interest in ancient skepticism of the Pyrrhonian form which has no 'beliefs about the way things are'.[3]

While this kind of skepticism is surely a familiar concern of modern philosophers, it is not obvious that it plays such a central role in the history of ethics. Note that the familiar story about science that I gave offers at least one sufficient alternative way to account for the rise of radical modern doubts about the foundations of morality, one that clearly abstracts from Pyrrhonian worries about having any certainty about 'how things are'. Moreover, one common way of looking at eighteenth-century developments is precisely to stress that, for those who believed that modern science did give a good account of the external world, the natural next step was to make moral qualities something of an analog to secondary qualities in general: in this way they could have a kind of 'objectivity' (viz. intersubjectivity) without having to make claims about the ultimate structure of external reality. Finally, note that this account would still be compatible with

[3] Ibid. 295.

the characteristics of the skeptical method that Schneewind stresses, and it can fit an appealing version of that method which makes moral perception relatively immediate and equally open to all.

Nonetheless, even if consideration of Pyrrhonian skepticism does not seem essential to motivate interest in the skeptical method, it is true that Shaftesbury, Hume, and others did occasionally present their approach as if it could meet even such a challenge. Thus, they provided the occasion to entangle themselves and their successors (and their interpreters) much more in the thickets of skepticism than I believe is necessary. The very formulation of such skepticism notoriously generates deep problems. Take, for example, the notion that the skeptical method is said to be helpful because it makes no claim 'about how things are'. Note that someone favoring the skeptical method might naturally claim still to have some certainty about how something really is, namely oneself and the mind in general, even without having any beliefs about the external world, strictly speaking. Indeed, this seems to have been precisely Shaftesbury's approach in his conception of our having a cognitive moral sense.

The natural response here is to claim that Shaftesbury's method was an inferior version of the skeptical method, one still dogmatically rooted in claimed perceptual certainties, albeit certainties about merely our affections. One could then argue (as Schneewind suggests[4]) that the breakthrough of Hutcheson and Hume was precisely to give up such claims, and to treat morality non-cognitively, as primarily a matter of reactions ('an inner disposition and an inner emotional response') in which one adjusts to the appearances of social life without any essential reliance on taking beliefs about what there is to be true. This treatment can extend to philosophical accounts of morality as well as to first-level affections: the function of a good account is to reinforce our original proper affections, not to ground them with certain beliefs. In that way even Pyrrhonian skepticism can be consistently met, for this method can eschew all cognitive claims.

Although this development is historically understandable, it is not evident to me that there is much of an advantage in this kind of a response to skepticism. The fundamental features of the skeptical method can still be maintained, after all, in an approach like Shaftesbury's. Moreover, the major faults with his specific approach seem to me to be independent of the issue of global skepticism. If we immediately object to his cognitivism, this is probably not because it cannot ensure certainty (since so much of what we commonly believe has that problem) but because it seems unlikely that moral sense cognizes the particular quality of 'harmony' that Shaftesbury selects, or because we wonder how a sense that is (what he calls) an 'affection of an affection' can provide trustworthy cognition. Note also that with none of these problems is there much help for Shaftesbury in the fact

---

[4] Schneewind, 'Natural Law, Skepticism, and Methods of Ethics', 300, 301.

that his focus is on what is internal; the same basic limitations of his kind of method could arise whether the focus is on the self or the world.

Similarly, one can question whether Hutcheson or Hume really benefits from their radical anti-skeptical strategy. A Kantian surely would not think so, for as Schneewind himself points out, 'On Kant's view, what happens when my moral faculty approves my acting on a specific maxim is not fully described by saying that a reflective motivating disposition reinforces a spontaneous disposition. It must also be said that I believe that action on my maxim is permitted.'[5] This point about a belief in what is absolutely *permitted* is one of several ways in which Kant is said to depart from the other practitioners of the skeptical method. A first difference is the basic point about agency noted earlier: Kant holds that what morality requires is not merely desire mediated by reflection, but rather a power of choice free from desire. Schneewind connects these two points by continuing, 'Only then [when I judge the maxim is permitted] will I freely allow my desire to set a goal.'[6] Since for Kant there is evidently a close connection between these points, one might think that the main issue between Kant and his predecessors comes back basically to the issue of agency. But that would be a mistake, for note that we can omit the controversial term 'freely' and still acknowledge the Kantian's fundamental point, namely, that only when I 'judge' that a maxim is permitted can I properly adopt the maxim suggested by the desire. This implies that the crucial thing to note is that there is a kind of cognition, or at least an unavoidable propositional state, that is at the heart of doing what is morally acceptable. Anyone who accepts this—and I find it very hard not to accept it—has already moved beyond the earlier view that morality is merely a matter of reactive dispositions or expressions. In this way we seem committed at least to 'taking' something as itself absolutely true after all, and we have given up the game of a 'pure' response to radical skepticism.

I do not mean to claim that any of this proves the superiority of Kantian over Humean ethics. A Humean might still argue that the judgment of permission essential to our self-understanding as moral agents is based on something more fundamental, and that ultimately it is somehow still the result of our affections. My own view is that such a strategy is implausible not so much because of moral considerations, but because of general Humean difficulties in explaining the general nature of judgment, its special structure and normativity. The relevant point, however, is that once again a dispute as to how one should develop a modern method in ethics might proceed independently of commitment to a kind of skepticism. Similarly, this dispute can even abstract for the moment from the question of whether it is the ends of desire or rather the ends of pure reason that are to be affirmed in moral judgment: the first thing to see is simply that the first

---

[5] Ibid. 304   [6] Ibid.

question about our moral activity is one of judgment. Whether or not one concedes that pure practical reason must be the formal cause of this activity, let alone its efficient cause, one can still accept Kant's second departure (the 'procedural' point about judgment, rather than the metaphysical claim about freedom) from his immediate predecessors in the tradition of the skeptical method. And this naturally leads to the thought that Kant's other departures may be so fundamental that ultimately they undermine the project of aligning Kant with these 'predecessors'.

Other departures are to found already in disagreements with Shaftesbury. Schneewind makes two points here: (*a*) that Kant alone 'gives us a formula which articulates the principle on which the moral faculty rests';[7] and (*b*) that Kant does not ascribe moral properties to our initial desires or maxims 'independent of their relation to the moral law ... [for Kant] moral goodness is not prior to [moral law], but is an outcome of its operation'.[8] I will concentrate on this last point, because it is closely connected with Schneewind's claim that Kant ought to be aligned with the skeptical method because, in accord with its general strategy of avoiding claims about that which worries the skeptics, on this view, morality (specifically, 'awareness of the categorical imperative') would not 'reflect some knowledge of an independently existing moral standard'.[9]

Such a claim naturally raises the fundamental question of whether Kant is best regarded as not being a 'strong realist' about the moral realm. Schneewind, like other Kantian 'constructivists' today,[10] does seem at least indirectly to be suggesting a kind of non-realist interpretation, no doubt because this fits the 'Copernican' imagery of Kant's philosophy in general, and because a kind of Copernican approach is obviously central to the skeptical method with which he wants to align Kant. ('With the British moralists, Kant holds that we can live in accordance with an order that we impose on ourselves as individuals.'[11]) But there is considerable ambiguity in all talk of denying 'independent moral standards'. The 'realist' alternatives to the Copernican approach that concern Schneewind appear to be traditional divine command and dogmatic teleological schools. Note however that a certain kind of divine command theory could be equally characterized as one that in a sense denies 'independently existing moral standards', for it may say that these standards rest on a rational will too—the will of God. This indicates that the main criterion of 'independence' for Schneewind is really an epistemic

---

[7] Schneewind, 'Natural Law, Skepticism, and Methods of Ethics', 301.
[8] Ibid. 305.
[9] Ibid. 303.
[10] This influential view has been inspired very much by John Rawls' approach to Kant. See especially his 'Kantian Constructivism in Moral Theory', *Journal of Philosophy*, 77 (1980), 515–72. For an important recent formulation of the view, cf. Christine Korsgaard, *Creating the Kingdom of Ends* (Cambridge, 1996); and C. Korsgaard *et al.*, *The Sources of Normativity* (Cambridge, 1996).
[11] Schneewind, 'Natural Law, Skepticism, and Methods of Ethics', 307.

rather than an ontological one: a dogmatic method would require us to *know* something outside the will of human beings (such as God or the world's general structure) before we can determine what is right. However, even if it is granted that Kant is non-dogmatic and believes that in a sense human knowledge must come first, if it turns out that the knowledge of human beings that is required by his theory remains *in crucial ways like* knowledge of independent things, then, I would argue, there still can be something misleading about lining Kant up with a method (the 'skeptical method') that claims to bypass such knowledge.

There are several ways in which the practical knowledge on which Kant bases his ethics is quite unlike what is usually understood by knowledge of human beings as such. This Kantian knowledge does not rest on a cognition of the harmony of human affections (as Shaftesbury's does), nor is it tied to a mere natural disposition of approval (as Humean morality is). Nonetheless, constructivists want to say that Kant teaches us how we can understand morality as a 'human creation'.[12] Such a claim is common to many other interpreters, but what is its precise warrant? Obviously, no one means the claim to be taken literally, since everyone would concede that Kantian moral law is not a literal product or a mere companion of 'human' taken as a biological species. Indeed, its validity is meant to be eternal and clearly independent of any natural actions. Moreover, unlike most modern philosophers, Kant is an astute critic (cf. the Paralogisms) of the 'Cartesian' approach that is the natural accompaniment of the original form of the skeptical method, the approach that presumes that claims about our inner world have some kind of automatic epistemic privilege over external claims.

One motive for an anti-realist interpretation of Kantian morality could be this. The skeptical method tells us to make do with appearances rather than worry about ultimate reality—and so it might be thought that this is simply another way of drawing the Kantian distinction between phenomena and noumena. But this would be a very misleading parallel; for, although in a sense Kant does teach us that theoretical philosophy does best by sticking to the appearances, he also insists that in practical philosophy we move beyond appearances, we have absolute truth, albeit without a 'speculative' ground. (Although Kant holds that we do at least require, as Schneewind also recognizes, theoretical knowledge which shows that the absolute truth claims made by morality, e.g. about our freedom, cannot be contradicted by speculation.) Another way to see this point is by noticing that, while Kant makes all (concrete) theoretical knowledge merely phenomenal in the sense that it is relative to beings restricted by a certain kind of contingent and limited epistemic equipment (viz. spatio-temporal intuition; which is not to make it relative to a particular individual or natural species), he also invokes pure concepts that are not so restricted. (This is precisely one of the main reasons

[12] Ibid.

why the deduction of the categories is so complicated.) Moreover, in his practical knowledge Kant is quite clear that these concepts have a use through the moral law that applies (though not necessarily as a 'command') to rational agents of all kinds: humans, God (whose goodness for Kant also necessarily fits the law and obviously cannot be determined by 'human creation'), and other possible types of being. Thus, he holds to the traditional view that 'the general rules of the good stretch over all rational beings, even God, for they apply to cognition'.[13]

This indicates that we might do better to try again to take the idea of a non-realist view here more in epistemic than metaphysical terms. Even if the moral law is not meant to apply only to appearances, or only to humans, perhaps the point is that we cannot make sense of it except from our distinctive human perspective. Again, what Schneewind stresses is that 'moral goodness or badness is not prior to [the moral law], but is an outcome of its operation'.[14] The question is whether this means that our access to it must depend, as morality does for the British, on something recognizably and merely human and internal.

The obvious text behind Schneewind's remark is the famous discussion in Kant's second *Critique* of how 'the concept of good and evil is not defined prior to the moral law'.[15] However, as far as I can see, in context this phrase supports connecting Kant with anti-realism or a fully skeptical method if and only if 'the moral law' can be tied simply to human beings, while the concept of good and evil prior to the law is tied to what is external to them. But it is not at all clear that this is how Kant's argument proceeds. The argument rather presumes the hypothesis of 'the possibility of practical laws a priori',[16] and then it argues indirectly that any beginning with an independently defined concept of good and evil would have to use pleasure as the ultimate moral criterion, and that this, contrary to the original hypothesis, would make determination of practical laws in an a priori and universal way impossible. There are several controversial steps here, but we can abstract from these and note simply that Kant's intentions appear to have little to do with cutting morality down to the human domain. The problem with the alternative that Kant rejects is, according to him, not that it rests on something too independent for us to determine or make sense of, but, on the contrary, that it is precisely too tied down to human nature to meet in any possible way certain assumed characteristics of morality. These are the familiar Kantian characteristics

---

[13] *Lectures on Metaphysics/ Immanuel Kant*, ed. and tr. Karl Ameriks and Steve Naragon (Cambridge, 1997), 260 (Metaphysik Mrongovius, XXIX: 892). (Roman volume nos. refer to *Kant's Gesammelte Schriften*, Berlin, 1900–.) This point occurs repeatedly in Kant's works, especially when he is contrasting ethical with aesthetic value. Many other references could be given on these points from Kant's ethics as well, but in this discussion I am not aiming at a comprehensive historical treatment. See below, n. 29.

[14] Schneewind, 'Natural Law, Skepticism, and Methods of Ethics', 305.

[15] *Critique of Practical Reason*, V: 62, cited at Schneewind, 'Natural Law, Skepticism, and Methods of Ethics', 305. For related uses of this text by Schneewind, see also his 'Kant and Stoic Ethics', and 'Autonomy, Obligation, and Virtue'. This passage is, of course, a favorite of Rawls'.

[16] *Critique of Practical Reason*, V: 63.

of a prioricity and necessity, features that, it will be noted, have no explicit place in the skeptical method—although they may well be implicit in the fact that Kant believes his principle provides a rule that each agent can always use in daily life.[17]

Once one sees that Kantian morality requires necessity and a prioricity, once one notes that in his practical philosophy Kant has none of the specific tools he uses in his theoretical philosophy for insisting that claims must be restricted to the merely human or phenomenal, once one recognizes that on the contrary his moral claims are meant to apply to all possible rational agents, it becomes very difficult here not to characterize Kant more as a traditional rationalist than as a subtle advocate of a kind of skepticism.

One last way in which one might try to defend treating Kantian moral philosophy as fully Copernican is by stressing that the claims of morality are still limited 'only' to rational agents, and indeed to the 'self-legislation' of such agents to our own rational demands.

Is there any anti-realism entailed by these ideas? The observation that certain claims are relative to rational beings surely is not sufficient. The deliverances of reason alone are precisely our prime examples of claims with no significant restrictions, of what must be real simpliciter and in no way a mere appearance or 'human all too human'. Thus, in a typical remark in the recently published Moral Mrongovius II lectures (1784–5), Kant speaks in a straightforwardly realist way about morality by saying (after rejecting divine command theories) that moral laws reside in the 'Natur der Dinge',[18] i.e. the 'nature of things', in the sense of a general and knowable essential structure.

What of the other idea here, the familiar theme of self-legislation—doesn't this show that Kantian ethics must part company with dogmatic rationalism? Taken in its proper context, this theme only further reinforces our reading: by 'self-legislation', Kant primarily means our determination by our own 'true being' in the sense of our rational as opposed to merely natural character. The rational self can in certain ways be spoken of as 'inner', while the natural is treated as 'outer', but these are superficial characterizations. In fact, determination by nature alone can be from either internal (psychological) or external (physical) sources. Similarly, moral self-determination may seem inner since it reveals freedom, which, as a capacity for choice, is necessarily an internal matter, but this executive freedom is not sufficient for what Kant means by self-determination. What is essential is that this freedom be bound by laws and rationality, and the experience of compulsion here is not itself exclusively internal, any more than the experience of the compellingness of laws of logic reveals something merely internal.

---

[17] Cf. Schneewind, 'Natural Law, Skepticism, and Methods of Ethics', 305.
[18] Kant, XXIX: 633; cf. 634, 'im Wesen der Dinge'.

These distinctions turn on two fundamental Kantian concepts, concepts that in the Moral Mrongovius II[19] receive the helpful labels of (1) 'legislative autonomy', the characteristic of a morality determined by the ends of reason rather than natural ends such as the ends of sense; and (2) 'executive autocracy', the characteristic of absolutely free choice (the ability to set and select among ends at all). Schneewind's final comparison of Kant and Crusius illustrates the independence of these characteristics. One can see Schneewind's use of the example of Crusius as revealing in effect how someone might endorse a kind of autocracy without appreciating full autonomy. Similar examples might be found in Kant's own early work. In arguments for the necessity of categorical ends of reason, he abstracts from a clear proof (indeed, he usually settles for an immediate commitment rather than an argument on this issue) that freedom of choice is also required by such ends; hence some of his immediate followers even developed the idea that our only options are to be determined either directly by reason or directly by sense. Kant also makes remarks that, like those of Crusius, indicate a commitment to autocracy without a clear understanding of the notion of autonomy.[20]

I thus can agree with Schneewind that, despite the importance of Kant's conception of our free executive power, it cannot determine our overall placement of his moral philosophy. Philosophers otherwise quite unlike him might happen to share his libertarianism. However, this does not mean that philosophers such as the British moralists, who reject that libertarianism while agreeing on some other points with Kant (such as the rejection of divine command views), are best regarded as members of a common movement and advocates of a common method. Until there is more of an explanation of how Kantian rationalism can be properly integrated into the skeptical method, it seems permissible to me to regard Kant himself as still far on the other side of the channel from his ultimately non-realist British predecessors.

This is not at all to say that Kant's method is dogmatic like that of Leibniz, Wolff, Baumgarten, let alone Crusius. In more recent work, Schneewind has rightly stressed some of the crucial differences between Kant and his German forerunners. However, Schneewind's interpretation still attempts to save Kant from commitment to an 'independent standard'. Kant is described as 'coming down on the side of the voluntarist'.[21] This does not mean that Kant accepts an arbitrary will as the source of value, but only that, in contrast to Leibniz, (*a*) the ontological 'equation of being and goodness' is not assumed, since nature as such is defined as 'indifferent' to human concerns; and (*b*) the epistemic model of our

---

[19] Kant, XXIX: 626; cf. XXIX: 900 (Metaphysik Mrongovius).
[20] These points are explored in the interpretations of Henry Allison, *Kant's Theory of Freedom* (Cambridge, 1990), and Josef Schmucker, *Die Ursprünge der Ethik Kants* (Meisenheim an Glan, 1961).
[21] Schneewind, 'Kant and the Stoics', 294.

access to value as being based on something like perception is to be rejected. The first claim is surely correct, but the second claim involves a significant problem.

What Schneewind emphasizes is that Kantian morality essentially requires the feeling of respect, and 'respect is not the perception of some good. It is a unique feeling caused by being humbled by a law that we know we must follow.'[22] Schneewind is right to stress that Kantian respect is not a Leibnizian perception of ontological perfection, but it would be wrong to think that the role of respect in Kant's theory is to supplant 'independent standards' rather than merely to supplement them with a story about motivation. Kant introduced respect because of his concern with the problem of what he believed required the 'philosopher's stone' in ethics: the fact that ethical insight of itself does not inevitably lead us to proper action. Human beings can know the right thing and still not do it, and so, in addition to seeing what is right, one has to be moved by the special feeling of respect that comes with freely accepting the moral law as an effective guide to one's action, i.e. not by simply willing, but by adding a commitment of the will to what is judged to be morally correct.[23] None of this takes back the point that, even in Schneewind's own words, 'there is a law that we first must *know* that we must follow'. That the rule for our action is 'relative' to the law of rational will in general, and that we can actually bring ourselves to act on this law only by a special exercise of our own will, and not merely our intellect, does not mean that in any restrictive sense the law itself is a product of human making. Kant can be a strong moral realist even while stressing the ontological and motivational inadequacy of traditional rationalism, i.e. even while allowing that there is more to good action than the necessary effects of 'clearing' up our perceptions and having our desires rearranged.

This kind of orthodox Kantian realism eschews the false dichotomy of 'either imposed by us or imposed by another'; it allows the standards of proper action to be beyond human making but necessarily in line with human reason, while leaving the following of those standards up to free agents. Like many current readers of Kant, Schneewind seems caught in a constructivist conclusion precisely because of not looking beyond this false dichotomy (or false trichotomy: either imposed by us, or imposed by another, or simply 'perceived' as a natural feature). After starting from the correct observation that Kant takes as basic the feeling of moral respect rather than slavish obedience to a 'superior authority', Schneewind concludes that Kant must mean that moral necessities are 'imposed' 'by us', by the activity of our 'noumenal self'[24]—for, supposedly, they have to have been made

---

[22] Ibid. 295.
[23] For some further references on the nature of Kantian respect, see my 'The Hegelian Critique of Kantian Morality', in *New Essays on Kant*, ed. B. den Ouden (New York, 1987), 179–212; now also in my *Kant and the Fate of Autonomy* (Cambridge, 2000), ch. 7.
[24] Schneewind, 'Kant and Natural Law Ethics', 71.

by somebody, and Kant does after all stress our activity in many ways. In this context, however, an ultimate stress on our activity makes little sense, and Kant explicitly realized this; for, as was noted earlier, it is not *our* noumenal self, but rationality in general that counts, for there is no way that something simply imposed by us can yield rules like those of morality which would necessarily hold even for a non-human will, a divine will. (Note that these considerations do not have to presume that such a being exists.) It is only our own limited sense of options, and not Kant's best and actual views, that impose an imposition theory of value on him.

Constructivism is so popular now that it may well seem that, if we go back to looking at Kant in a realist way, we will lose our best chance for drawing out what is most likely to be worthwhile in his moral theory. There is clearly a non-historical issue here, one that goes far beyond my brief remarks and points to a burden that needs to be assumed in further work. And there is also an historical burden. For, just as Schneewind has boldly proposed that, despite our common first thoughts, Kantian morality can be accommodated within a promising but skeptical humanist tradition, so anyone who has second thoughts against such an accommodation would do well to try to find some broader pre-skeptical tradition with which Kant can be more fruitfully aligned. Research like Schneewind's properly reminds us that great philosophical theories are likely to have very complex roots, and so even those who have objections to some of his specific hypotheses ought to feel obliged to build on his work and to develop their own 'genealogy of the method of morals'. But it should not be simply presupposed that, even from a Kantian perspective, such a genealogy will have to come out in favor of a skeptical humanism.[25]

2. On Larmore and Self-Legislation in Kant

In a recent discussion of my defense of a non-constructivist interpretation of Kant's ethics, Charles Larmore has argued from a perspective that exemplifies a significant position which is both like and unlike Schneewind's.[26] Like Schnee-

---

[25] For discussions on these issues, I am especially indebted to J. B. Schneewind, Philip Quinn, Patrick Kain, and an audience at Oberlin, where the original version of this paper was presented in a conference in 1986. Since then Schneewind's work has expanded considerably, most notably with the publication of his *The Invention of Autonomy* (Cambridge, 1997). Many new details are added in his discussion there, but for my purposes the main extra issues that need to be addressed now are treated in Section 2 of this chapter.

[26] Charles Larmore, 'Back to Kant? No Way', *Inquiry*, 46 (2003), 260–71. This sentence marks the point at which, after the material in Section 1 of this chapter, reprinted (unrevised except for adjusted references) from 'On Schneewind and Kant's Method in Ethics', *Ideas y Valores*, 102 (1996), 28–53, I have added, in Section 2, a significantly revised portion of my 'On Being Neither Post- nor Anti-Kantian: A Reply to Breazeale and Larmore Concerning "The Fate of Autonomy"', *Inquiry*, 46 (2003), 272–92. Larmore's essay was written primarily in response to the presentation of my position in *Kant and the Fate of Autonomy*, but also with explicit reference to my earlier discussion of Schneewind.

wind, this position presumes that in fact Kant is not a moral realist; but—unlike Schneewind—it takes this to be a weakness rather than a strength of Kant's approach. Larmore's contribution provides an appropriate occasion for expanding my earlier argument that in fact Kant is not an anti-realist—and that he therefore can be neither praised nor blamed for holding to a form of moral non-realism. In my original discussion of Schneewind, as well as in my more recent *Kant and the Fate of Autonomy*, a major motivation of my work has been precisely to introduce a reading of Kant that acknowledges the emphasis on the concept of autonomy in his philosophy while nonetheless indicating how genuine Kantian autonomy can be consistent with a sensible form of value realism. My main aim at this point is to show in more detail how, once it is clear what Kant really means by 'self-legislation', we need not be forced to make a choice between autonomy and realism, as Larmore and many others have presumed.

On my reading, Kant is a rationalist—but a *Critical* rationalist. On the one hand, he stresses difficulties in earlier 'dogmatic' views of reason, and, if he had only had the chance, no doubt he would also have stressed similar difficulties in later highly ambitious German Idealist claims about reason. On the other hand, Kant shares some of the systematic aims of rationalism in general, and the *Critique* stresses, for example, that reason properly demands a system 'on the basis of one principle' (A645/B673). Larmore takes this kind of remark to indicate that Kant is fairly closely linked to ambitious forms of idealist rationalism. I believe, however, that even in comments like this one, calling for a system based on 'one principle', Kant does not at all mean to be encouraging an ambitious rationalist system of theoretical determinations of reality in itself (or of the 'Unconditioned'), as in a monadology or phenomenology of spirit. Rather, he intends simply to remind us of the basic notion of judgment and its pure forms, which provides the categorial framework for all his Critical investigations (see A xx, on the 'common principle'). Another passage that Larmore himself cites says that 'reason . . . must itself show the way with principles of judgment' (B xiii), and this fits perfectly with other passages I have cited in reconstructing what I call Kant's 'modest' rationalist system.[27]

Matters are complicated here by the fact that there are different kinds of statements in the *Critique* about the 'demands of reason'. Sometimes this phrase can designate the legitimate demands of a modest or Critical form of reason that trims its projects to determining the general forms of particular kinds of experience. This is not what Kant has in view, however, when he speaks in the Dialectic about the 'demand' of 'reason' (A332/B389). In the context of his accounts of the dialectical side of reason, Kant is perfectly willing to stress that sometimes there are ambitious demands of Reason, in a 'capital R' sense, that a Critical thinker

---

[27] See my *Kant and the Fate of Autonomy*, 37, which cites *Lectures on Metaphysics/Immanuel Kant*, 111.

should precisely *not* expect to find satisfied (e.g. in the search for one 'root' of our faculties), and that it should instead regard as the unrealistic demands of an improperly regulated faculty.

In addition to the modest notion of reason's principle of judgment, and the immodest and fallacious notion that Reason can provide a theoretical determination of unconditioned aspects of reality, Kant also speaks of reason as a faculty of self-determination. For example, in the Preface to the second edition of the *Critique*, he says that we should follow 'reason's own devising' (B xiii). I see no ground to believe that here he has in mind Reason in the strong Idealist sense that would *contrast* sharply with the modest work of the pure understanding—and yet I would agree that here he is suggesting something that goes beyond the mere notion of a principle of forms of judgment. The reference to 'reason's own devising' broaches the further thought that the activity of reason in general, and therefore even the theoretical use of reason can in some appropriate way be characterized as a kind of self-legislation. Larmore does not directly pick up on this passage, but he argues that within his own Critical system Kant *should* have allowed theoretical claims of self-legislation, since 'in its theoretical activity too, reason is bound by categorical norms—by the rules of logic, for example'[28]—and, supposedly, the only possible Kantian account of categorical norms must be in terms of self-legislation. Larmore himself takes any such Kantian account to be doomed, however, because he believes that categorical norms cannot ever be explained as a matter of mere self-legislation, since this would undercut their authoritative claim over us. Larmore believes this because he understands self-legislation in terms of a fundamentally active capacity of human *creativity*, and so he thinks that any Kantian account of norms as self-legislated must fail because of the general limitations of any 'creative' account of categorical norms. (Similar highly influential objections to what is assumed to be Kant's position have been raised by philosophers such as Kierkegaard and Anscombe.)

There are a number of different issues to be sorted out here. I agree that in fact Kant is committed to an a priori claim that the faculty of reason in each of us has a special self-constituting causal power. But this individual causal power is not itself understood as a legislative power for creating normative authority; it is simply the *executive* power to be an absolutely free efficient cause of one's own agency as a moral being, and in that way to mold one's own actual self. The *ratio cognescendi*, but *not* the *ratio essendi*, of this executive power is the moral 'fact of reason'. This 'fact' reveals itself to us in the context of our particular selves appreciating—but not creating—the legitimacy of the demands of categorical practical reason in general, i.e. of appreciating that we should, and therefore really can, freely act for duty.

---

[28] Larmore, 'Back to Kant: No Way', 269.

NON-REALIST INTERPRETATIONS OF KANT'S ETHICS

The peculiar libertarian metaphysics involved in Kant's ideas here is of course very controversial. But whatever one thinks of Kant's notion of our absolute free agency, as supposedly revealed in our respect for the demands of pure practical reason, it is important to keep the notion of the literally individual and self-making or self 'creating' causal activity (which, properly speaking, is a matter of an 'executive' rather than literal legislative power) that is involved here distinct from the meaning that 'self-legislation' takes on at the level of Kant's theory of norms. This level has to do with what might be called the formal and final, as opposed to efficient, aspect of pure reason. To say that reason is a formal ground of action, and is self-legislative as such, is to say that the *standard* or basic general principle of what is right is determined by reason itself—as opposed, for example, to mere sensation or habit or authority. The determination in this case is not a matter of causation or mere knowledge, but of its essence as an end. The notion of reason as efficiently self-determining is therefore not at all the same as the notion of reason as formally self-determining. The first notion means that an appreciation of reason is *in fact* what moves (with the assistance of the consequent feeling of respect) a particular person to action; the second notion means that the form of reason itself, as opposed to the content of some 'external' factor such as sensation, is what defines what it is that we all *should* do. Kant has the basic belief that for us reason is self-determining in both the efficient and the formal sense, but others might hold that reason has only one of these powers at most.

Whether or not one goes along with Kant's basic belief here, it is very important to realize that there are these two different aspects of reason. One aspect is basically individual and literally involves a kind of self-making, but the other aspect is not basically individual, and it does not involve a literal 'making' of a self or its norms (since reason here is not an efficient power at all, but a kind of standard). A failure to appreciate this distinction often lies behind the charge that Kant's stress on our autonomy, or self-determination, makes us absurdly into beings that can literally create rather than appreciate what is right. Since the efficient sense of reason does involve a kind of creativity, it might be thought that Kant intends the formal sense of reason to be creative too, since it is, after all, also called a kind of 'self-determination'. But this additional characterization in terms of creativity is gratuitous and immediately turns Kant's position into a very questionable one. There is no need to insist on this additional step, and no need to believe that Kant himself was not quite aware of the distinctions that have just been made between creative but non-formal reason, and non-creative but formal reason.

Larmore's critique of Kant's doctrine of autonomy as too subjective is but one example of interpretations that assume that Kantian self-legislation must mean something like mere 'imposition', as in instances of arbitrary and efficient causality, where something is created as authoritative merely by the act of taking it to be authoritative for oneself. In the context of contemporary philosophy, this assumption has understandable grounds, since there are many strands of common language, and schools of so-called neo-Kantian thought, where autonomy is understood in this way as a matter of individual self-imposition (as if to be a Kantian is to make up norms for oneself like a teenager budgeting one's own life for the first time). Whatever its sources and influence, this perspective blocks the road to understanding Kant's own notion of self-legislation in its formal and most important (and non-absurd) sense. Kant repeatedly distinguishes the concepts of legislative and executive determination,[29] making it obvious that the Kantian 'self' that is 'acting' in the pure legislation of norms is nothing like the arbitrary imposing individual who is the villain or hero of countless contemporary tracts concerning the development of 'autonomy'.[30] The fact that Kant has a sense of norms of reason that are totally independent of any kind of literal self-imposition should be clear enough simply from the fact that he regards the principle of contradiction, for example (or the table of the forms of judgment), as involving a categorical principle of transcendental theoretical reason without in any way implying that its validity—as opposed to its application—is a matter of any of 'our' particular 'impositions'.

In other words, one can agree with Larmore that if 'autonomy means anything it means self-legislation',[31] and yet one need not believe that for Kant any of these terms has to be understood as a matter of giving principles *validity* simply by 'imposing' them on ourselves in any ordinary sense as an efficient cause. It is revealing that Larmore's way of speaking about autonomy uses paradigms such as voting procedures, which clearly are settled by individuals working together in particular and efficient self-legislative ways. His critical and anti-constructivist point is that this is 'an activity that takes place against a background of reasons that we must antecedently recognize'.[32] Suppose this point is granted. What follows, I think, is simply that self-legislation in a merely particular and efficient sense cannot account for categorical norms fully or 'all the way down'; it cannot be the 'source' of their normativity. This still leaves open the possibility of a kind of self-legislation of reason in a formal sense, where reason is the very essence of such norms—and it is precisely this kind of autonomy that I believe is Kant's prime concern (even if he is also very interested in autonomy in other senses in empirical,

---

[29] See Section 1 above, as well as John Hare, 'Review of Christine Korsgaard, *Creating the Kingdom of Ends*, and *The Sources of Normativity*', *Faith and Philosophy*, 17 (2000), 371–83; John Hare, 'Kant on Recognizing our Duties as God's Commands', *Faith and Philosophy*, 17 (2000), 459–78; and Patrick Kain, *Self-Legislation and Prudence in Kant's Moral Philosophy* (Ph. D. dissertation, Notre Dame University, 1999); and cf. Clemens Schwaiger, *Kategorische und andere Imperative: zur Entwicklung von Kants praktischer Philosophie bis 1785* (Stuttgart, 1999), and T. K. Seung, *Kant's Platonic Revolution in Moral and Political Philosophy* (Baltimore, 1994).

[30] This tendency is effectively criticized in several works by Larmore and also in Donald H. Regan, 'The Value of Rational Nature', *Ethics*, 112 (2002), 267–91.

[31] Larmore, 'Back to Kant: No Way', 270.

[32] Larmore, 'Back to Kant: No Way', 270.

e.g. political, dimensions). Just as, in general with Kant, we must distinguish the transcendental work of the necessary forms of judgmental representation (which determines the necessary conditions for all particular empirical cognitive claims) from an individual self's empirical theoretical acts, so, too, in Kantian practical philosophy, we must distinguish the legislative work of pure practical reason, and the necessary rules it reveals for proper willing, from questions about particular acts of will.

Following a distinction introduced by Schneewind, Larmore suggests that the most one might get along this line of interpretation is 'self-governance', which is not a matter of self-legislating authority as such, but simply a matter of seeing and doing what is right 'regardless of the threats and rewards' that others might offer. I agree that self-governance is a limited notion, but I also believe that Kant's position has more to offer.[33] I have proposed that we understand self-legislation for Kant as a matter of following 'the sheer rationality' in 'our essential nature'.[34] I take this to be a positive notion that goes beyond mere self-governance, since one might be self-governed, as defined so far, and simply go off on a whim.[35] The crucial point about Kant's notion of reason as self-*legislative* is that it involves *laws* in a *strong* sense. His moral rules are not simply any generalized intentions, but principles whose generalization is *supported by* and *aim at* reason in general; e.g., the principle 'respect rational agency' has an inherent positive ground that makes it unlike the general but pointless maxim 'don't anybody whistle while you eat'. This makes pure principles 'self'-legislated in the strong sense that for any rational being they are not merely in accord with rationality but are from and for its own 'true self', which is reason as such, in a positive universal sense. This is not a trivial claim, because, on other philosophical conceptions, reason might lead to the claim that the ends of sense have priority; or sense might lead to the claim that the ends of reason have priority; or, as in Hume, sense might lead to the claim that the ends of sense have priority. Kant has neither an empiricist nor a mixed view; he is a rationalist from start to finish.

The meaning of 'self' in Kantian self-legislation is thus obviously tied to the nature or structure of reason itself, not to the self in any mere empirical or psychological or physical sense. This 'nature' is not something completely abstract, because an empirical self can actually live—or not live—in fulfillment of the laws of pure practical reason, just as its theoretical epistemic 'acts' can properly

---

[33] Larmore, 'Back to Kant: No Way', 271, citing Schneewind, *Invention of Autonomy*, 4.
[34] Ameriks, *Kant and the Fate of Autonomy*, 14. See also Section 3.5 of the Introduction to this book, on Kant's 'Copernican turn'.
[35] Hence I agree with much of Regan's analysis, but not with his presumption that the Kantian 'agent must either choose on the basis of empirical desire . . . or else must launch herself arbitrarily' ('The Value of Rational Nature', 281). This perspective too quickly forecloses the possibility that a rational being can have an understandable attachment to its own rational nature that is neither arbitrary nor rooted in a prior empirical interest.

or improperly employ pure concepts that have a meaning that transcends merely empirical contexts. Underlying this whole process is reason's own pure practical self-legislation; the idea of the will's rational nature itself defines the goals that must be observed if reason is to be realized by concrete agents. This might sound like a mysterious hypostatization, but it need not be understood in any mystical way because in this case the determining is originally formal rather than efficient. The idea of self-legislation here is not that reason literally does something, as a person might cross a street. The idea is simply that the nature of reason itself primarily determines—as a matter of essence—what the basic goals are *for* reason. In theoretical contexts, this is no more mysterious than saying that consistency and the working out of implications is not only assisted but also demanded by reason itself—which of course leaves open the empirical issue of whether particular rational beings will assert consistent sentences. In practical contexts, Kant's notion does get more controversial because it involves the thought that pure practical reason can of itself (given, of course, that it has materials to consider) generate substantive action guiding norms that are categorical in fact, and not only in meaning. This thought might be a non-starter for a moral skeptic or radical empiricist, but it should be at least a possibility for Larmore and others like him who allow the notion of categorical practical norms.

Another way to express this interpretation is to say that it takes the autonomy issue to be literally what Kant says it fundamentally is: namely, a matter of the autonomy of *reason*. We might not immediately catch this simply because Kant calls it the autonomy of *Wille*,[36] but for Kant this term is equivalent to pure practical reason. This is nothing like the willful autonomy 'of me' in the 'me generation' sense of our times (a derogatory sense with predecessors even in Greece, where the Sophoclean chorus chastized Antigone for being 'autonomous'[37]). At the same time, Kant's libertarianism and other features of his thought insure that, unlike other universalistic theories such as utilitarianism, his theory from the start respects the common belief in the ultimate reality and significance of the individual human agent. Just as in his discussion of the transcendental features of theoretical knowledge, there is no need to presume that Kant's discussion of pure practical reason does not apply to concrete individuals and show how they are to be fulfilled—even if it is no way built up from an investigation of their mere natural and empirical peculiarities.

A remaining stumbling block for many interpreters here may be Kant's talk in the *Groundwork* about a moral being as 'subject only to a law given by himself'.[38] But Kant immediately makes clear that the self of this being is generic (he similarly speaks of the forms of judgment as coming from one's own 'self', A xiv), and its

---

[36] *Groundwork of the Metaphysics of Morals*, IV: 433.
[37] I am indebted to Ido Geiger for drawing my attention to the striking use of this term in the play.
[38] *Groundwork*, IV: 432.

'lawgiving' must be 'universal' in a transcendental rather than merely empirical sense, for it has to do with the 'reference of all action by which alone a kingdom of ends is possible'.[39] There is nothing in the notion of this kingdom that forces a contingent and arbitrary 'active', as opposed to realistic and 'appreciative', reading of moral rules, since these rules are dictated by the *general* conditions of what *necessarily* makes a *universal* harmony of wills possible. Insofar as they involve 'activity', it is in a harmless way, having to do with the fact that they entail principles that every rational will is supposed to approve and act from in order to fulfill rational activity in general. This approval and activity is important, but it is not a condition of the validity or authority of the rules themselves. Readers might be misled here by the fact that Kant speaks of 'maxims' as being 'imposed',[40] but this can be literally true at an individual level (since the 'incorporation' of a maxim in one's life *is* a matter of contingent self-imposition), even while the *laws* that proper maxims observe are not themselves 'imposed' in any troublesome particular sense.[41]

There obviously remain many questions here, such as whether the structure of pure practical reason is rich enough in detail to be norm generating in anything like the way that logic and mathematics may be. Also, once reason is understood, as it is here, as something more like a pure and general faculty than an individual act or orientation, one can wonder how particular sensible agents can come to have an interest, let alone a sense of overriding obligation, in respect to it. After all, an 'underground man' might say, 'yes, I understand now that that is what the faculty of reason (even the voice of reason in me) says—but I am not going to follow that voice, I am going to follow my own natural, egocentric voice!' Not surprisingly, this brings us back to some of the most basic problems of Kantian ethics—how can pure practical reason provide content, and how can it motivate?[42] These are challenging questions, but they are not the same as the question that has been our main topic, namely, whether there is a realistic and at least

---

[39] Ibid. 434.

[40] Ibid.

[41] For this reason and many other considerations given in the material cited in n. 29 above, I believe that even these passages fit a Kantian value theory that is consistent with taking moral ends to be fully real, although not in the absurd sense of stretching to a realm that is beyond reason altogether. Here again it is important to keep in mind the point that Kant's transcendental idealism is specifically a doctrine of what is ideal because of space and time, and in no way implies a non-realism about values. On Kantian value realism and 'respect' as the acknowledgement of 'objective value', cf. Allen Wood, *Kant's Ethical Thought* (Cambridge, 1999), 46 f. and 157 f.

[42] I believe Kant does have an answer here about how reason can appropriately provide an interest in acting morally, but I am not so sure he has a non-question-begging answer to the question of why we must choose always to let the voice of reason override that of nature. See above, Ch. 7, and *Kant and the Fate of Autonomy*, ch. 7. The deepest problem here may be that the general capacity to set ends may not be of clear moral worth (since all the ends that a free being might actually set could be evil and compatible with an externally harmonious world of agents), whereas the capacity to set good ends may turn out to have value only on question-begging grounds or insofar as something external to rational nature is given moral priority after all.

intelligible notion of autonomy that is truly close to Kant's own texts (especially his rejections of all empiricist ethics) and yet does not have the self-defeating characteristics that interpreters such as Larmore fear. To the extent that my considerations point to a way that such a notion can make sense after all, autonomy can have not only a fate but also a future.[43]

[43] There is obviously more that needs to be said about how a 'realistic' reading of Kant's idea that pure practical reason is self-legislative can be defended against and distinguished from subtle constructivist interpretations such as those found in the later work of John Rawls and his associates. For some arguments in this direction, see n. 29 above, and cf. Allen Wood, 'The Objectivity of Value', in *Unsettling Obligations* (Stanford, Calif., 2002), 159–85. In my work on the issues of Section 2 of this chapter I have been helped in many ways by challenging discussions with Fred Beiser, Daniel Breazeale, Paul Franks, Patrick Frierson, John Hare, Patrick Kain, Charles Larmore, Robert Pippin, and Marcelo Stamm.

Part III

The Third *Critique* and Kant's Aesthetics

– 12 –

How to Save Kant's Deduction of Taste as Objective

1. How to Save Kant's Deduction of Taste

Kant has been taken to argue in his deduction of taste that aesthetic response is grounded in a perception of form that engenders a feeling of proportion which is a 'subjective state' necessary for all cognition. He then seems caught in being able to preserve the necessity of taste only by holding the quite non-Kantian principle that *all* objects are beautiful.[1] Those who recognize this difficulty think that the only way out is to take aesthetic response rather to involve a special kind of sensitivity in particular people that would avoid making all objects beautiful only at the cost of not allowing a ground for the claim that aesthetic judgments are universal and necessary.[2] I shall argue that there is a better way to escape this difficulty, one that allows for Kant's claim of the universal validity of taste to be maintained. I shall also note that the price of saving Kant's argument here is to restrict its significance, but this is a fact that Kant can and does accept. In a second part of this chapter, I go on to explain how understanding Kant's conception of taste as *objective* (even though, for specific reasons that are explained, Kant himself did not want to use the term 'objective') makes it easiest to understand his own account of the *need* for a deduction of taste.

1.1 Locating Kant's deduction of taste is no easy matter, for the text contains two widely separated passages, viz. §21 and §38, which have been taken to be distinct and full arguments.[3] There are also earlier passages (Introduction, §6)

---

[1] Cf. Donald W. Crawford, *Kant's Aesthetic Theory* (Madison, Wis., 1974), 145 ff.; and R. K. Elliott, 'The Unity of Kant's Critique of Aesthetic Judgment', *British Journal of Aesthetics*, 8 (1968), 255. I think this view is well countered by Paul Guyer, *Kant and the Claims of Taste* (Cambridge, Mass., 1979), 351 ff.

[2] Cf. Guyer, *Kant and the Claims of Taste*, 67 and 325; and Konrad Marc-Wogau, 'Das Schöne', in *Materialen zu Kants 'Kritik der Urteilskraft'*, ed. Jens Kulenkampff (Frankfurt, 1974), 321.

[3] Citations like this will be to the section numbers of Kant's *Critique of Judgment*, tr. J. H. Bernard (New York, 1959), followed by the number of the paragraph within the section. Other citations preceded simply by 'A' and/or 'B' will be, as is customary, to the first and/or second edition of Kant's *Critique of Pure Reason*, tr. Norman Kemp Smith, (London, 1929).

that can be read as sketches of a deduction, as well as later passages (in the Dialectic) that appear to be presented as new essential stages of one. I will have to minimize this problem here and will focus on what all would agree at least looks like the first thorough (even if not quite complete) presentation of a deduction of taste, namely the discussion around §21. Kant's argument here can be reconstructed in the following steps:[4]

1. Cognitive judgments are communicable (sentence 1).
2. Each cognition has an accompanying subjective state (sentence 2).
3. If cognitions are communicable, then so are their accompanying subjective states (sentences 2 and 3).
4. These subjective states involve various proportions in the activities of our faculties, and there is some such proportion that is 'most beneficial' for the relation of imagination and understanding (sentences 2–5).
5. States with such a proportion are communicable (entailed by above).
6. They are aesthetic (from (4) and other remarks).
7. Therefore aesthetic judgment (as an expression of a specific kind of communicable state) is valid (from above).

Although I take this argument to be an acceptable one, its steps are obviously quite controversial. Paul Guyer, for example, thinks the first step infects this whole presentation of the deduction, for its supposedly commits Kant to dubious claims about communicability that conflict with the allegedly more proper and 'methodologically solipsistic' approach in the transcendental deduction of the first *Critique*.[5] There is a response to this objection. While one can grant that Kant need not begin by assuming that solipsism is in fact false, one can also say that he need not be tied to the project of defeating radical skepticism. Thus, it is unclear why we must accept as a fair model Guyer's specific conception of Kant's first deduction, namely that it is to prove the objectivity of concepts *tout court* from the 'Archimedian point' of the unity of consciousness.[6] This familiar view of the deduction has been challenged elsewhere.[7] Here it may suffice to point out two obvious problems for Guyer's view. First, it contrasts with Kant's explicit characterization of the goal and conclusion of the deduction as the justification of *pure* concepts. Secondly, it conflicts with Kant's qualifications about the premises to be employed here, that is, with his stress on beginning with the notion of experience, in the sense of empirical judgment (as opposed to mere awareness), as well as with

---

[4] In this reconstruction and elsewhere, I am indebted to Guyer's book. Cf. my review in *New Scholasticism*, 54 (1980), 241–9. It should be noted that for complex reasons Kant's full explanation of these steps goes far beyond §21 alone.
[5] Guyer, *Kant and the Claims of Taste*, 157.
[6] Ibid. 276, 290, 327.
[7] See above, Chs. 1 and 2.

his critique in the Paralogisms (cf. A352, B138 f.) of a priori inferences from the mere appearance of a unity of consciousness.[8]

I suspect that a major reason why Guyer was led to this extreme interpretation is that he has too narrow a conception of the alternatives. He may well believe that otherwise Kant's argument must (since it doesn't refute the *complete* skeptic) have a trivial form. This belief is common enough, but it dismisses much too quickly a broad range of significant philosophical arguments.[9] Another error, and one that appears to figure more prominently in Guyer's particular case, is the assumption that in working with objective judgments in his argument Kant is also asserting, or immediately inferring, their *actual* intersubjective validity. That this is Guyer's assumption is implied by his remarks that other formulations of the deduction seem preferable to this one because they 'at least' do not presuppose the existence of other persons or of our being in actual communication with them.[10] But we *need not* think that Kant is making such an objectionably strong presupposition here; for all the first step of his argument commits him to is a claim about the communic*ability* of judgments, not any claim that they are actually communicated, or even that the mere existence of a cognition in one person entails the real physical possibility of communication with others.

Guyer's implication that there is such a presupposition in Kant rests largely on various early and unpublished remarks such as that 'solitary eccentrics never have taste'.[11] But even such remarks can be taken simply to stress how little *attention* would likely be given to beauty in situations of solitude; they need not mean that society and actual communication are requirements for one to be in principle capable of responding to the beautiful. It is notable that at the same time Kant also says that 'our knowledge is nothing unless others know we know'.[12] Surely this is meant as a claim about the relative significance given to cognition in an asocial realm and not as a serious restriction on having any knowledge then. It seems only fair to argue by analogy that Kant's remarks about taste should be read the same way.

1.2 All this still does not tell us enough positively about how the terms 'cognition' and 'communicable' are functioning here, or at least how they should be taken in an ideal Kantian argument. Although Kant sometimes uses a rather

---

[8] See ibid., and also my *Kant's Theory of Mind* (Oxford, 1982); my 'Chisholm's Paralogisms', *Idealistic Studies*, 11 (1981), 100–8; and my 'Review of R. C. S. Walker's *Kant*', *Teaching Philosophy*, 3 (1980), 358–63. On the notion of 'experience' in Kant in particular see B161, B218, and *Kant's Gesammelte Schriften* (Berlin, 1900–), XI: 315, XX: 774.

[9] See e.g. R. Chisholm's methodological remarks in *Person and Object* (London, 1976), 15 ff. That Kant himself is not always going against an extreme skeptic is clear enough from such passages as B20 and A165/B206. See also n. 14 below.

[10] Guyer, *Kant and the Claims of Taste*, 315.

[11] Ibid. 25. See *Kant's Gesammelte Schriften*, XXIV: 45–6.

[12] Ibid.

narrow notion of cognition, I think it is best here simply to take a cognition to be an ordinary perception, that is, an experience that involves a claim to 'universal validity' because it is about what all should be able to see.[13] The meaning of 'communicability' is more difficult. What Kant says explicitly in the first sentence of §21 is that, if cognitions did not have an objective ground, they would not be communicable. What he is saying implicitly is that since, by definition, they have such a ground, they are universally communicable.[14] Now, if 'universal communicability' is given any meaning that requires the actual existence of others or of a special faculty in them, this last inference is obviously invalid. But if it simply means the sheer possibility of communicating about x, since x is an objective state of affairs, the inference makes perfect sense although it may sound trivial.

To move toward giving it a little more substance without endangering it too much, we can use some of Kant's own remarks, although only after some revision. Kant devotes §39 to a discussion 'Of the Communicability of Sensation', and he implies that smell, for example, cannot be said to be universally communicable because there are those who are 'deficient in the sense of smell (§39; cf. §17.1, A820/B848). Universal communicability would thus *seem* to require a sensory apparatus that is actually had in common. Yet Kant is obviously in trouble if he takes this requirement in too specific a manner. He surely believes in our ordinary cognitive judgments and takes them to be universally communicable, but he has not spelled out any specific sensory apparatus that we have in common to back them. It might be thought that his doctrine of space and time as universal forms of sensibility is the answer here, but they are obviously insufficient, for they alone do not justify the ordinary empirical judgments (e.g. of size or shape) that we make about particular things and take to be quite cognitive and universally communicable. I think we must conclude that whatever it is that warrants such judgments can also warrant saying that in principle even smells and sounds and so forth *are* universally communicable—although there might *in fact* be many deaf and impaired people who cannot directly confirm them.[15] For (even if we bracket Kant's controversial remarks about color) it is clear that for Kant certain common visually perceivable objects (e.g. flowers, seashells) are paradigms of beauty and therefore our experience of them is universally communicable, and yet if he were to carry through consistently his claim about smells, he also would have to deny

---

[13] See Section 2 below.

[14] Kant's first sentence in §21 is: 'Cognitions and judgments must, along with the conviction that accompanies them, admit of universal communicability for otherwise there could be no harmony between them and the object, and they would be collectively a mere subjective play of the representative powers, exactly as skepticism desires.'

[15] Thus, I think Kant cannot hold on to the view, expressed most recently by Mark Johnson, that 'only these formal element [figures in space, sensations in time] can be perceived in the same way by all subjects' ('Kant's Unified Theory of Beauty', *Journal of Aesthetics and Art Criticism*, 38 (1979), 273).

the beauty of these paradigmatic objects simply because there are in fact blind people.

The notion that the cognition of objects must be communicable thus should not be read as requiring that others actually do sense or are equipped to sense objects just as we do. Rather, I suggest it means that, given that an act is a cognition, we should believe it has an objective ground; and if it is a perceptual cognition, then we should believe that the objective ground involves an appearance that all should be able to see if only they are normal and in appropriate circumstances. All this may seem to make the mention of 'communicable' so stipulative as to add nothing to what is already obvious in the notions of cognition and objectivity. But there is at least one point that would be natural to make and that would give some significance to introducing the term 'communicable'. The point is that Kant probably holds the traditional theory that communication involves having matching subjective states. On this theory, I understand you when the (inner) ideas I have are appropriately like the ones you have. Moreover, if persons have ideas with the same objective ground (as is the case when they perceive the same object), or at least under normal conditions could have such a ground, then it is only natural to hold that their ideas are alike and in that sense communicable. Cognition thus implies communicability not trivially, but through the mediation of the premise that like causes yield like effects. Skeptics can of course challenge this premise, and much of the traditional problem of other minds goes back to this challenge; but it is notable that Kant is not at all tempted by such doubts (§21.1), and in any case it is not necessary to raise them here, for if Kant can give a justification of aesthetics that rests on grounds no *more* questionable than this, he still has accomplished something notable.

1.3 In explaining the first step of Kant's argument, we have in effect tackled the next two as well, for we have suggested that any good non-tautologous meaning that is to be given to the first step will involve what is stated in the third step. This simply amounts to the notion that, *if* we believe we experience objects in a 'universally valid' way, then we should believe that others can experience those objects similarly (thus with similar 'subjective states') if only they are appropriately placed.

The conditions that are specifically needed for aesthetic judgment still need to be isolated, though, and this is where the central fourth step comes in. This step is the one best served by the text of §21, for it is here alone that Kant states the crucial idea that each cognition 'has a different proportion [in the activity of the various cognitive faculties] according to the variety of the objects that are given', and that 'there must be *a* proportion [which is] genuinely the most beneficial for both faculties' (revised translations). The text makes two points: (i) every cognition involves subjective states in some proportion of faculties; and (ii) among these states, which from previous steps we know to be all communicable, some are to be singled out. These singled out states would not be states necessarily involved in the perception of *every* object, but rather would be states experienced *whenever* the particular object (or one like it) that produced them in an ordinary perception is again perceived in a normal way. These special states manifest what Kant calls a 'harmony of the faculties', and it can be said that only some objects and not others are able to generate (under normal conditions) this particular harmony—and yet when it does occur it occurs as simply a special species (namely as the most 'harmonic' one) of a proportion that must always exist in *some* form in any cognition (viz. as that *general* 'proportion' or agreement of faculties that is necessary in any coherent experience).

The main reason it may have appeared that there is a problem here is that, soon after speaking of the *special* proportion, Kant happens to say that he has found something that is 'the necessary condition of the communicability of our knowledge' (§21; cf. §39.4). It is important to see that this still need not be taken to mean that he has found that it is specifically the aesthetic harmony of the faculties that is the condition of all knowledge. Rather, Kant's statements are consistent with the mere conclusion that he has found *something* that is the necessary condition of all cognitions (viz. some general communicable inner proportion of faculties), and something else (viz. a special most harmonic proportion) that is the condition of certain acts and yet is communicable basically because of the same reasons that the ordinary accompaniments of any cognitive act are communicable.

There are two easy and basic ways to go wrong here, and I believe that two major recent interpreters of Kant, Crawford, and Guyer, have each taken one of them. One error would be to say, as Crawford has, that Kant is taking the aesthetic harmony of the faculties to be a condition of all cognition.[16] This would leave Kant in an evidently inconsistent and absurd position, and so it is fortunate that his text need not be taken as committed to that claim. The other error would be to say, as Guyer has, that Kant can escape the absurdity of calling every object beautiful only by saying that the harmony of the faculties is a state that does not always arise simply because its occurrence depends on a person's having special psychological capacities.[17] Guyer allows that this escape would mean the death of Kant's claim to necessity in aesthetic judgments, but he feels it is the best alternative.

The way to escape this last alternative is to say that it can be special objects or features, and not special people or faculties, that are primarily responsible for the fact that some experiences are harmonious and others are not. Guyer himself

---

[16] Crawford, *Kant's Aesthetic Beauty*, p. 66. Cf. Elliott, 'Unity of Kant's Critique', 245; and Guyer, *Kant and the Claims of Taste*, 114. See n. 19.

[17] Guyer, *Kant and the Claims of Taste*, 296.

offers a consideration that can be used indirectly to back this idea. He notes in passing that people vary in the facility with which they can apply ordinary empirical concepts.[18] On exposure to an object, it happens that people with the same background can vary considerably in the speed and accuracy with which they recognize and classify the object. But surely this variation does not show that the concepts applied to the object are subjective and such that we cannot say of any of them that *all should* use them to characterize the object. Similarly, the fact that the same object exposed to persons with similar backgrounds does not in fact always cause the same harmonic and aesthetic response is no sign that there is not a particular harmonic response that that object is apt to produce for normal persons. Hence it may be fairly designated as beautiful even if it is not actually experienced as beautiful by all.

1.4 The only step that still needs to be evaluated here is the sixth, which aims finally to resolve the distinctiveness of the aesthetic by tying it to a special harmony of faculties. This notion has a kind of invulnerability that is tied not coincidentally to its indefiniteness. It is worthwhile therefore to note that there are some specifiable virtues in Kant's notion of harmony. For example, although Kant does not stress this himself, the notion can quite naturally be conceived in such a way as to accommodate the important fact that there is a considerable range in the degrees to which we ascribe beauty.[19] Unlike 'all or nothing' criteria such as disinterest and non-cognitivity, harmony is immediately understandable as taking on various better or worse instantiations. Although Kant speaks only of 'the' proportion of faculties that is 'best', his language naturally suggests *a range* of proportions that manifest harmony within which there naturally could be some that do this better than others, and this would provide some explanation for our commonly making distinctions *within* the class of beauties.[20]

---

[18] Ibid.
[19] Donald Crawford has argued more recently that Kant must deny that there are degrees of beauty and hence cannot make comparative aesthetic judgments. But Crawford's claim rests on the view that for Kant 'the judgment of taste is based on the experience of pleasure, but a pleasure of a special kind—one resulting from the conditions for cognitions being satisfied in general *but only in general*' ('Comparative Aesthetic Judgments and Kant's Aesthetic Theory', *Journal of Aesthetics and Art Criticism*, 39 (1980), 291). Fortunately, this interpretation is not necessitated by Kant's own text, given our reading above of §21.
[20] Bringing out other virtues of this criterion similarly requires some slight modifications of Kant's own discussion. For example, Kant is especially taken by the idea that this harmony and the aesthetic go together because they can both be thought of as involving freedom. Yet this idea is grounded only in a series of specific claims, e.g. that here we are not 'bound down' to a concept in the way an *entirely* conceptual act is (§§5.2, 9.4, 16.6); that here we are not bound down to an 'immediate' cause in the way an entirely sensual reaction is (§§5.2, 9.2); and that here we are not bound to some struggle to maintain our state but instead are quite naturally led to continue it (§12.2). All these points are logically compatible with allowing aesthetic responses ultimately to be conditioned by empirical events just as other phenomenal occurrences are. On the other hand, although it is thus hardly established that aesthetic response must involve absolute freedom, it does seem to involve the specific kinds of independence that Kant discusses, and there is certainly a genuine sense in which people have taken experience of the beautiful to be especially liberating because of its harmony.

A further virtue of the harmony criterion is that it indicates that aesthetic response is to be thought of as a kind of higher order or reflective state, a response not so much to typical simple properties as to properties of properties. Surely it is likely that some states are caused by a relatively immediate stimulation of our faculties, whereas others involve a kind of extra interaction of the faculties themselves in addition to the act of stimulation. And it is likely that some such interactions are peculiarly satisfying (i.e. especially fulfilling for the relation of certain basic faculties), are not likely to be set going by our own arbitrary musings, and can have natural grounds in typical features of the objective environment.[21] These points are sufficient to indicate the possibility of a universal response bearing characteristics of what would be called aesthetic. Kant's theory of harmonic response thus remains a plausible hypothesis to account for the possibility of a particular type of valid experience that in various specifiable ways has ties to common conceptions of the aesthetic.

Admittedly, it would be nice to be able to spell out Kant's hypothesis more and to show that there can be no better transcendental account. But it is unfair to press too far here and to complain that Kant has not provided a list of the objective features that are sufficient to key the response he describes. A fair reply that Kant can and does make here is that this simply is not his task as a *philosopher*. He reminds us that on his theory there is no 'doctrine' of aesthetics as there may be of science or morals, and that, insofar as there is a 'science' as opposed to mere 'art' in this realm, it has to do solely with the transcendental task of explaining the possibility of this realm, i.e. the right to make judgments of an appropriate type (Preface and §34.2). For all Kant has said, it is still possible that there are few purely beautiful objects, and that actually achieving agreement on them may be very difficult. All this is and must be left just as open by his transcendental philosophy as the matter of how easily the nature that confronts us is in fact classifiable by us into specific kinds and laws. From a Kantian position, there comes a point where such matters must simply be left to the de facto situation of the practicing scientist or critic.

It should also be granted that the harmonic response Kant postulates could be a fairly insignificant kind of experience even where it does exist, and it may well be one that does not map smoothly onto much of what people have in mind today when they speak of 'beauty', the 'artistic', and the 'aesthetic'. Kant can concede all this, for he makes it quite clear that here he is providing a a deduction only of 'pure beauty'. Hence he is excluding a very large group of aesthetic experiences that he himself took to be most important (cf. §16.7, where Kant talks of aesthetic

---

[21] There are familiar difficulties with Kant's specific suggestion that these features are tied to an object's 'form', but I think there are some natural ways to extend his theory to help meet this objection. See e.g. David Carrier, 'Greenberg, Fried, and American Type Formalism', in *Aesthetics*, ed. G. Dickie and R. Sclafani (New York, 1977), 461–9.

experiences that go beyond pure beauty and are most important because they involve a 'gain' in 'all' our faculties), namely those of the sublime or of dependent beauty, that is, (roughly) experiences of beautiful forms that are appreciated for complex conceptual reasons and are usually generated artistically rather than naturally. The fact that significant parts of modern aesthetics and Kant's own third *Critique* may go well beyond his deduction of taste should not be allowed to obscure the valid and objective meaning that the deduction can have.[22]

2. The Need for a Deduction and the Objectivity of Taste in Kant's Aesthetics

Before beginning his deduction of the categories in the *Critique of Pure Reason*, Kant stresses that 'the reader must be convinced of the unavoidable necessity of such a transcendental deduction' (A88/B121). Unfortunately, in his *Critique of Judgment*, Kant does not so directly address the issue of why a *transcendental* deduction of taste is *needed*. It appears that his main ground for a separate deduction here rests largely on the claim that judgments of taste (i.e. judgments of pure beauty; this is what Kant's deduction focuses on, and it is all I will discuss here) are not only universally valid but also subjective in a distinctive and significant sense. There are a number of features of taste that Kant appeals to in his attempt to back his claim about the subjectivity of taste, but I will argue that none of his considerations are sufficient.

Many of the points I will make against Kant have already been raised by other interpreters, but for some reason they have neglected to pull these points together and to draw the radical conclusion that a Kantian ought to acknowledge the *objectivity* of taste (which, in this context, means that it rests on objectively beautiful and immediately perceivable natural forms). I aim to show (i) how this conclusion is the best accompaniment for the essential starting point of Kant's aesthetic theory, viz. the idea of universally valid aesthetic judgments; (ii) how some explanation can be given of Kant's failure to draw this conclusion explicitly himself; and (iii) how this all helps to illuminate the peculiar role that individual empirical judgments play in Kant's philosophy in general. My argument here that Kant's discussion is best understood in terms of a fundamentally objective understanding of taste is meant as a natural supplement for the reconstruction

---

[22] This point marks the division between the article published originally as 'How to Save Kant's Deduction of Taste', *Journal of Value Inquiry*, 16 (1982), 295–302, and reproduced here, with very slight amendments, as Section 1, and the article published originally as 'Kant and the Objectivity of Taste', *British Journal of Aesthetics*, 23 (1983), 3–17, and reproduced here, with very slight amendments, as Section 2. Except for a few new transitional sentences and some very minor corrections, I have not revised the content of the essays. For purposes of reference it is useful to have the articles in their original form, and related arguments are in any case carried further in the chapters that follow.

just given of the main steps of Kant's deduction of taste.[23] I do not mean to foreclose the possibility, however, that some readers may be able to make use of the reconstruction of the deduction while not employing the considerations offered here about objectivity—or vice versa.

2.1 The difficulties in understanding the need for a deduction of aesthetic judgment begin with Kant's prefatory analysis of such judgment. Kant breaks this analysis down into four moments: disinterestedness, universality, subjective purposiveness, and necessity. For my purposes, the second and fourth moments are practically indistinguishable; I take them to be of fundamental importance and will return to them in some detail. The third moment has significance because of the role of the notion of purpose within the project of the third *Critique* as a whole, but it is of secondary value within the analysis of taste itself, and especially with respect to the issue of the need for a deduction. As for the first moment, some have thought that it is of the greatest importance for aesthetic judgment, but I will argue that, if one attaches too much emphasis to the idea of disinterestedness, this only obscures the need and structure of the deduction of taste. In particular, it can cover up the fact that in Kant's theory the relation between aesthetic judgment and mere disinterest can be contingent.

This point can be made with practically any plausible candidate for the definition of 'disinterest' here, e.g. Kant's own simple remarks that a disinterested judgment is one indifferent to the object's existence (§2.1), or Paul Guyer's interpretation that it is primarily marked by indifference to the object's 'causal nexus'.[24] The main point is that Kant concludes to the feature of disinterest only via a quick argument by exclusion: he says that, since in fact the only types of interest we are familiar with are sensual and moral, and that since he believes he can show that aesthetic judgment cannot be based on either mere sensual or moral grounds, it follows that aesthetic judgment is disinterested (§§2.2, 8.7).

The cash value of Kant's discussion is thus simply the distinction between aesthetic as opposed to sensual and moral judgments. If it did turn out that in fact aesthetic judgments were in some other hidden way interested (i.e. really based in some non-sensual and non-moral interest), this in itself need not endanger the essence of Kant's position on aesthetic judgment. In particular, the key claims of universality and necessity could be maintained, for Kant's own analysis of moral judgment allows that these features can be compatible with judgment based on interest. Logically, there is no way that the mere interest involved in sensual or moral judgments is what makes them distinct from aesthetic judgment; rather, there are independent intrinsic distinctions between such judgments and aesthetic judgments, and it just happens that sensual and

---

[23] See Section 1 above.   [24] Guyer, *Kant and the Claims of Taste*, 195.

moral judgments share features that Kant thinks allow them to be grouped as 'interested'. The most Kant need believe is that, *given* the quick (and dubious) argument by exclusion, disinterest might be helpful, not logically but epistemologically, for distinguishing aesthetic judgments; a judgment's not appearing interested (in either of the two specified ways) to us may be *a* ground for considering that judgment genuinely aesthetic.

Ultimately, I will argue that for Kant not only does disinterest have at best this shaky epistemological attachment to aesthetics, but, moreover, even this attachment is dispensable. Many interpreters have denied this by suggesting that the primary Kantian *way to determine* if a judgment is aesthetic is in effect to check one's mental history to see if it is disinterested in origin.[25] But if it turns out (see below, at the end of Section 2.4) that really determining disinterestedness is impossible or insignificant without *first* determining certain features of the object to which the judgment is directed, then the establishment of disinterest as such can be really unnecessary (although attention to it, i.e. its appearance, sometimes might be handy as a kind of shortcut way of gaining a preliminary estimate of the nature of one's situation).[26]

If disinterest as such need not distinguish aesthetic from sensual and moral judgment, then the crucial question remains, what are the operative intrinsic differentia for Kant? Fortunately there is a ready, though rarely emphasized, answer here. The basic features that Kant always stresses in his arguments are what can be called the *universality* and the *non-conceptuality* of aesthetic judgments. Briefly, the pattern of his argument involving the first feature is this: an aesthetic judgment is meant to be valid for everyone; but, although an aesthetic judgment essentially involves pleasure, no judgment that asserts merely sensual pleasure can be valid for everyone; therefore an aesthetic judgment cannot rest on mere sensual grounds (e.g. §13.3). The argument about non-conceptuality generally has this pattern: when we determine that an object has (pure) beauty, we can do this without use of the concept of the object, i.e. without a notion of its perfection or what it ought to be; but to make a moral judgment is always to judge on the basis of concepts and what ought to be; therefore aesthetic judgment as such cannot rest on moral grounds (§§4.2, 15).

When combined, these two arguments present the fundamental problem of Kant's aesthetic theory: how can a judgment be valid when it is aesthetic and not

---

[25] The phrase 'one's mental history' comes from Guyer's interpretation, which I believe (despite some of the criticisms he makes of the notion of disinterest) generally encourages this view. See *Kant and the Claims of Taste*, 173, 205, and n. 39 below. Cf. also Harold Osborne, 'Some Theories of Aesthetic Judgement', *Journal of Aesthetics and Art Criticism*, 38 (1979), 138.

[26] Moreover, as others have argued recently on independent grounds, it is unclear that disinterest is in any case a concept essential to aesthetics (see e.g. George Dickie, 'All Aesthetics Attitude Theories Fail: The Myth of the Aesthetic Attitude', in Dickie and Sclafani, *Aesthetics*, 800–14.) Thus, it is unlikely that any substantive loss would be incurred by holding that the discussion of disinterest as such is tangential to the logic of Kant's argument, although accepting this fact no doubt would involve taking away much of what most people have thought especially distinctive about Kant's theory.

sensual or moral, and so apparently is meant as universal and yet is not resting on conceptual grounds (§31.1)? This problem *alone* generates all of Kant's attempts to legitimate taste, and it is notable that in its formulation and resolution no specific mention of disinterest is necessary. The case for the need of a deduction of taste thus rests on the arguments from universality and non-conceptuality, and it is to their evaluation that we now must turn.

2.2 The limitations of the non-conceptuality argument (= 'proposal one') are perhaps most familiar and evident. The argument simply does not show that in principle aesthetic judgments are independent of concepts; all it can show by itself is that they are independent of moral concepts (broadly speaking). Thus, even if it is granted that in judging that a sunset is beautiful one is not making any claim about the moral significance of the sun's setting, or the perfection of its being in that state, it still can be held that here one is necessarily applying concepts, e.g. the concepts 'sun', 'setting', 'colourful', etc.

Although Kant does not always link his claim about the non-conceptual nature of aesthetic judgment to an implicit premise that to use a concept is to consider something's perfection or how it ought to be, the only relevant specific arguments that do not follow this exact pattern follow others which are of no more help. For example, what Kant stresses sometimes is simply that the non-conceptuality of aesthetic judgment is apparent from the fact that we do not believe that a matter of taste can be *proved* by concepts alone. We believe a person 'must see for himself' if he is to decide by taste about something's beauty (§§8.6, 33). Obviously, this point still does not rule out *all* use of concepts in taste, and in fact recognizing this is alone compatible with Kant's own later remarks that aesthetic judgment involves an indeterminate concept (e.g. the supersensible, §57.4). This point also shows the limitations of another version of Kant's argument, where he notes that we can call a flower beautiful without knowing or applying the *botanist's* concept of it (§16.2, cf. §29.17). Even if this is not meant simply to tie the concept of a thing again to the full or 'perfect' concept of its species, its stress on what is only a very specific kind of notion of the concept of a thing (its complete scientific description) makes the argument quite similar to the others. Another technique Kant uses is simply to oppose 'aesthetic' to 'logical judgment' while defining the latter as involving mere conceptual *subsumption* (§38, Remark).[27] Here again, only a very special kind of terminology is behind the idea that taste is 'non-logical' or 'non-conceptual'.

What Kant's arguments show at most is that in taste the consideration of concepts, or at least of some types of concept in certain kinds of ways, is not

---

[27] Cf. Eva Schaper, who links the claim that beauty is not objective to the idea that there is no rule whereby it can be 'read off' and 'there is a marked absence of general principles' by which it can be determined (*Studies in Kant's Aesthetics* (Edinburgh, 1979), 50, 27)—facts that surely apply to many objective features and even, if Kuhnians are right, to many scientific features.

sufficient, not that it is not (in some ordinary sense) essential. Although this point may serve in Kant's system to distinguish aesthetic judgments from some moral ones, this is not much of a conclusion, for it is a fundamental fact of that system that *no* particular phenomenal features are determinable from concepts alone. From the clear fact that not only Kant but also his opponents would grant that beauty is a phenomenal as opposed to a deontological or noumenal feature, it follows that *of course* we cannot determine beauty by concepts alone. I suspect that Kant did not come clean about this primarily because of a lingering tendency to equate mere concepts with concepts of things *qua* Leibnizian noumena, or at least *qua* types fully determinable scientifically and/or a priori (either sheerly logically or morally; see §16.4). The remark that aesthetic properties are not found in the concepts of things in *this* sense is still compatible (in Kant's world) with judgments of beauty functioning just as objectively as ordinary particular empirical judgments.

Now that the limitations of the non-conceptuality argument are apparent, we can turn to Kant's other main consideration, his argument from universality. This feature is in fact the crucial one for aesthetic judgment, for without it the idea of a deduction would immediately have to be given up. But the feature is easily misunderstood, and, although Kant himself is quite clear about the first likely misunderstanding, he does not attend enough to a consequence of his own explanation. What he makes clear is that by calling aesthetic judgment universal he means not that it is logically universal, but only that it is 'universally valid'. That is, the judgment of beauty he is discussing is always meant as a judgment about some particular x, not as a universal judgment of the form, 'all x's are . . . ' (§8.5). What Kant does not explain, however, is how this point alone makes the need for a special deduction of taste appear problematic. Kant's transcendental deductions are paradigmatically deductions of a priori concepts (categories) and so they aim to show that these apply to a whole realm of possible experience (see e.g. A93/B 126, B168). But, as Kant himself stresses, in aesthetics we are not trying to prove anything like this, for, whereas we may try to show that all objects must fall under the categories, we are *not* out to show that all objects (of our experience) are beautiful. (Kant is also surely not even trying to show that all objects can or ought to be considered beautiful, in the sense in which all objects might be held to be at least surveyable in accord with various regulative ideas.)

One response to this difficulty is to contend that, although what the first *Critique* aims to deduce is a list of concepts that must apply to all the objects of experience, it does this by arguing that these concepts are essential to 'experience' and thus to various kinds of empirical judgments, such as of the form, 'the sun warms the stone'. Therefore, since the categories are deduced as necessary conditions of such judgments, the deduction argues not only that categories are needed, but also that such judgments are in need of them. Thus, there is something *about* logically non-universal judgments that needs to be deduced, and so the mere particularity of aesthetic judgments does not exclude the relevance of some kind of deduction for them. In addition, it can be replied that, although Kant also notes that all particular aesthetic judgments are *a posteriori*, i.e. known via experience (Introduction, VII: 4), this too need not make a deduction irrelevant, for the same can be said of other types of particular judgment.[28] But, while this counter-argument shows that there *could* be a relevant deduction bearing on aesthetic judgment, by itself it still does not show exactly why *aesthetic* judgments are to be approached *separately*, or precisely how they are to be explained. One might, of course, contend that the reason why aesthetic judgments require a distinct deduction is not to justify the assertion of any particular quality of any particular judgment—for Kant does not mean his original deduction of non-aesthetic judgments to do that either—but simply to justify aesthetic judgment itself in general as a distinct type. But here this is simply to beg the question, since the distinctiveness of aesthetic judgment is precisely what is to be established.

Nonetheless, Kant insists there is a universality in aesthetic judgment that calls for a special deduction, namely in the fact that a claim of beauty is meant as a claim that *all* other subjects (with our form of sensibility) *should* agree with. It is this feature (= 'proposal two') that Kant uses immediately to distinguish aesthetic judgment proper from sensual judgment (§8.2 f.): a sensual judgment (judgment 'of sense' rather than 'of taste') is supposedly meant as 'privately valid' (§9.2); the agreement of others is not at all relevant to it.

There clearly are some difficulties with the formulation of this point, for, as should be especially obvious to Kantians, there is something quite odd about the notion of a sensual judgment. Either an apparent judgment is a judgment, and so must be meant as valid for all, *or* it is not that, and is rather a mere act of sense or a sheer attitude. This point can be tested by considering a typical sensual judgment, e.g. the claim, 'the fragrance of this rose pleases me'. Here we can easily account for the example without introducing literally 'private validity'.[29] The judgment 'the fragrance of this rose pleases me' is still meant as universally valid, for everyone is to accept that that is how the rose strikes me. (I here abstract from the further analysis of this judgment, i.e. from whether the claim is best understood as simply 'it seems to me that the rose is fragrant',[30] or as 'this body has, i.e. is undergoing, a fragrant sensation'.[31]) The lack of universality has to do with not the validity but the content of the judgment.[32]

---

[28] Cf. Schaper, *Studies in Kant's Aesthetics*, 25, and L. W. Beck, *Essays on Kant and Hume* (New Haven, 1978), 167 f.

[29] Kant's talk of 'private validity' seems to be closely tied to a belief that someone insensitive to beauty would be egoistic. See §42, and *Kant's Gesammelte Schriften*, XXIV: 354, and *Anthropology from a Pragmatic Point of View*, tr. V. L. Dowdell (Carbondale, Ill., 1978), 147.

[30] See Gerold Prauss, *Erscheinung bei Kant* (Berlin, 1971).

[31] See David M. Armstrong, *Bodily Sensations* (London, 1962), 117.

[32] See above, n. 27.

Of course, it is likely that Kant is more interested in an implicit embedded judgment here, namely, 'this rose is fragrant'. But we can handle this judgment too without making any special distinction between private and general validity, for all we need is the general distinction between true and false judgment. We can say the rose is fragrant if and only if the rose really (phenomenally) is fragrant, and we can define 'fragrant' as we like for now, e.g. as pleasing (in an olfactory way) at least one normal person, or as pleasing most normal persons, or as pleasing all persons, etc.

We can now preserve Kant's contrast between 'sensual judgment' and other kinds of judgment without using his unfortunate terminology. Clearly there are some judgments that, although they are meant as universally valid, are still distinctive in that their *content* involves simply a claim about how things appear to *me* or are in *my* body. On the other hand, there are judgments that make broader claims either implicitly or explicitly in their content (e.g. '*x* is fragrant'; '*x* is pretty'), and Kant can and clearly does mean to classify aesthetic judgments here. But this still leaves aesthetic judgments in a quite unproblematic Kantian class; for most of our judgments are of this sort, and the fact that they are non-conceptual in the sense determined earlier is equally undisturbing. So the judgment that this rose is beautiful still would seem to require no *more* deduction than the judgment that the rose is fragrant—or for that matter, that it is here, fresh, small (an inch wide), etc.

2.3 A third proposal for trying to establish a distinctive need for deducing aesthetic judgments is to rely on the fact that Kant takes aesthetic judgment not to involve the determination of 'cognitive' qualities (§3.2). Unfortunately, any attempt non-circularly to determine Kant's criterion for cognitive judgments leads back into the difficulties of his general vagueness about particular judgments.[33] In the third *Critique* Kant twice shows awareness of the problem of the nature of particular judgments, but what he says is hardly sufficient. At one place he suggests that cognitive properties are distinguishable because they are 'determining', and this in turn is to rest on their following from the a priori features of experience that have already been derived (Introduction, VII: 5, cf. §57, Remark, I: 4). This statement is unsatisfactory given either of its natural interpretations. If it is taken to mean that particular properties are literally *derivable* from the a priori features, it does not follow from what Kant has argued so far and rather is absurd and in conflict with Kant's own general views (for he is not so rationalistic as to say that the specific properties of individual objects are sufficiently determined by his categorial framework). On the other hand, if it is taken to mean that judgments

---

[33] On this general problem see Robert Pippin, 'Kant on Empirical Concepts', *Studies in the History of Philosophy*, II (1979), 1–19.

involving such properties are merely in *accord* with transcendental analysis, then nothing yet rules out saying the same for beauty. In the second place where Kant broaches this issue, he indicates a more complex development of something closer to the first of these two alternatives. That is, in his Introduction he suggests a point that well could have become the dominant topic of the whole third *Critique*, namely that there may be some way to extend transcendental philosophy to give an a priori account of not only the fundamental principles of nature, but also the experience of some system of particular empirical laws (Introduction, V: 4). This line of argument, however, is in fact not taken very far by Kant, and it is unclear how it could ever reach the level of a deduction of a particular kind of phenomenal quality. It is thus still unclear why the beauty of a rose requires any *more* of a deduction than its size or fragrance.

The last considerations suggest a new version of the third proposal to the effect that what shows aesthetic judgments are distinct and non-cognitive is that they do not as such involve ascriptions of features involved in the empirical *laws* covering objects. Thus, we may judge that a rose has a particular size in accord with various laws—confirmed in prediction and explanation—that we take to cover the rose. The 'causal nexus' of the object involves certain law-like properties that we can take to be its 'primary' and cognitive ones. Since there do not appear to be such laws of beauty, the special need for a deduction here may seem finally established. Yet again there are serious questions, for according to Kant just how do we take a property to be objective on the basis of falling under a particular law—what is the procedure here? In response to this problem, about all one finds in Kant explicitly are mentions of simple observation, induction, and hypothesis testing. The particular conclusion that a rose is of a certain size and shape would thus rest on typical empirical grounds and would be a conclusion drawn from various observations and experiments. Of course, one could stress that beauty does not appear so open to experimental measuring procedures for the determination of applicable laws.[34] But in fact Kant does not stress this, and instead, when he talks about a judgment of beauty not being based on empirical grounds, he explains that primarily by saying that we don't properly make our aesthetic judgments by surveying and comparing the opinions of others (§33.2). Thus, once again the line of argument offered by Kant is quite inadequate to distinguish aesthetic from other particular qualities.[35] Here Kant's case rests merely on a sense in which what we mean by an aesthetic judgment is one determined through our own perception, and one could argue similarly that there are some non-aesthetic judgments

[34] See Schaper, *Studies in Kant's Aesthetics*, 25, 24, who goes so far as to say that here there is 'no established mode of verification', and correctness 'cannot be shown in the way in which the truth or falsity of an empirical judgment can be demonstrated'. It is not explained how this is really compatible with a belief in the validity of taste.

[35] Cf. ibid. 27, where Schaper emphasizes that taste is distinguished by resting on a 'stress on felt experience'—a fact that would hardly distinguish it from other objective perceptual attitudes.

(e.g. immediate observation reports) where non-reliance on a comparison of others' reports is also guaranteed as a matter of meaning.

It is unclear what reasons Kant himself had for employing this odd line of argument (though it may have something to do with the similar odd way in which he argues about non-conceptuality), and in any case it is not even evident that *he could* have so easily stressed the non-measurability and non-lawfulness of beauty. This is because similar features can attach to at least one non-aesthetic class of empirical qualities, namely the so-called secondary qualities. Kant was notoriously unclear about how to treat secondary qualities, and he appears to have changed his opinion just before the third *Critique*. Originally he held that qualities such as smell and taste do not *at all* attach to their purported object but are simply tied to observers and their bodies and vary with the supposed great variety in these bodies in the relevant respects (A28–9, B44, B70 n). Later he seemed to reject part of this view (by introducing a notion of 'objective sensation', §3.3) while still distinguishing primary and secondary qualities. However Kant exactly defines secondary qualities, he appears in trouble, for the most he says about the supposedly decisive features of measurability and lawfulness is that they (alone) directly cover the primary qualities, and this still would leave aesthetic properties not clearly distinguished from *all* properties that are at least usually taken to be cognitive.

Thus, the variations between Kant's earlier and later statements on secondary qualities may not matter too much. If he takes the early view and says that the qualities are sheerly subjective, he needs to explain the fact that people are necessarily at least *as* willing to say that all others should see a particular rose, in appropriate circumstances, as fragrant as to say that it is beautiful. Hence, whatever deduction is required for aesthetic taste would also have to be taken to be relevant to secondary qualities. On the other hand, if Kant takes the later view and says that, for example, a rose is objectively fragrant just as it is geometrically measurable, then the allowance of cognitive but not directly measurable properties makes the non-measurability of the aesthetic no longer a sufficient proof of its distinctiveness, and the special need for a deduction of taste is again unclear. Stated more concisely, the problem is this: even if secondary qualities are called subjective, Kant must allow they are as universally valid, and so (for all that can be said so far) are indistinguishable from aesthetic ones; and if they are rather called objective, their universality still is not explained (here at least) in the way that of primary qualities is, so again they are not demonstrably distinct from aesthetic ones.

One way to respond to this dilemma is to admit that a broad deduction is needed, so that what Kant offers as a deduction of taste can be taken to apply in some way to secondary qualities as well. This is in effect the response pursued above in Section 1, but at this point our duty is to consider whether some other way out is possible for Kant. There does seem to be an option available here, namely to develop Kant's later remarks in such a way that secondary qualities are to be understood as simply a particular complex of primary qualities (which qualities themselves may be, say, non-fragrant and colourless) in an object that is the cause and explanation of the effect in us of particular phenomenal quality impressions (such as of fragrance or color). Here the strategy is to give the universality of secondary qualities a type of objective correlate and explanation that actually has been used and accepted, whereas this is not the case for aesthetic qualities. Once again, however, what seems to be the obvious solution in fact involves considerable difficulties. The immediate difficulty is that it is unclear why one could not hypothesize that beauty also involves such an objectively based universal quality, *especially* since the very universality meant in aesthetic judgment would quite naturally call for such a hypothesis (cf. A821/B849). The fact that no laws of beauty have been discovered should be given some explanation, but this is not so hard to do. Here one can emphasize the functional and emergent nature of beauty, the fact that it can be applicable in situations with all sorts of material complexes. It should not be surprising if beauty has a special elusiveness, for it clearly involves a kind of functional satisfaction which, unlike that of most phenomenal qualities, can range over all kinds of sensations. As many different materials may constitute a taste, fragrance, or lustre, so also very many different fragrances, tastes, and/or lustres can constitute beauty, and thus the futility in the search for specific laws of beauty can be understood without special reasons for denying its objectivity. It is significant that there are many places where Kant himself recognizes that certain features might be quite objective (phenomenally) and yet, because of a special complexity, incapable of being brought under specific laws foreseeably describable by us (see e.g. his comments on history and psychology). Therefore, given Kant's own philosophy, and especially his acceptance of a universal validity in taste, there is still no clear reason why in principle there should be no objectivity in aesthetic as opposed to other (non-primary) qualities.

It must be admitted that this conclusion does go against Kant's own preference for speaking of the aesthetic as not objective. By now, however, this should no longer appear as a sufficient objection, for that tendency can be explained in terms of the oddities of the non-conceptuality argument (i.e. Kant's tendency to equate 'being in the concept of *x*' with 'being proved from that concept' or 'being part of the object *x, qua* thing in itself'), and it would in any case cause similar difficulties for the status of ordinary secondary qualities. Here much is often made of the fact that Kant speaks of beauty as 'only' 'intersubjectively' (*gemeingültig*) and not 'objectively' universally valid (*allegemeingültig*). But that discussion (§8.3 f.) does not invalidate our conclusion. For, although Kant does speak parenthetically of what may be contained in something's empirical concept, the examples of the 'objectively' universal that he gives have to do typically with pure concepts such as moral ones. And elsewhere he also indicates that ordinary secondary qualities are

2.4 There is a fourth and final proposal that must be dealt with if one is to preserve the conclusion that there are only relatively trivial senses in which Kant provides grounds for restricting talk of the aesthetic as objective. This proposal contends that taste is subjective because, as Kant repeatedly insists, it has to do with discrimination by a kind of pleasure, and pleasure is always a mere feeling and so not objective (§3.2). Here it can be responded that there is a genuine sense in which feeling is subjective, but this is inadequate to license any distinctive claim about taste. It is a fundamental of Kant's general philosophy that *whenever* we determine qualities a posteriori we must do so via intuition and thus via some sensation that is subjective at least in the sense that it *exists* in us. Thus, even when a tree is perceived as being really tall and green, there occur sensations that exist merely subjectively. So the fact that the kind of taste that Kant is discussing requires discrimination *by* something subjective does not entail that *what* is discriminated should be called subjective.

There are, of course, some understandable lines of thought that probably lie behind the fourth proposal. For example, if it were the case that these sensations themselves were somehow literally tall and green, they obviously could be said to be also more than subjective in that they would at least resembled intrinsic (phenomenal) objective qualities. Then it could be argued that, since objects do not have the quality of pleasure or its semblance themselves, the sensation of pleasure has a *special* subjectivity because of its not being even a resemblance of what is objective. However, this line of argument is surely inadequate, for *no* sensations literally resemble objects, and so the special nature of pleasure as opposed to other sensible qualities must lie in some other fact—and yet the only one that gets discussed directly by Kant is that it alone is not taken so *refer* to something in objects. But if we dismiss the odd requirement of resemblance, it is not yet clear why pleasure cannot have an objective reference.[36] So, although it certainly would be odd to think of beautiful things as themselves *feeling* pleasure, the most that need be asserted in an aesthetic judgment that, for example, picks out a tree as beautiful is that it is *somehow through* our feeling a kind of pleasure that the beauty (not the felt pleasure) of the tree is revealed.

Another understandable source of the fourth proposal would be the variability of feeling that Kant emphasizes, the fact that different persons exposed to the same object often have different feelings (§7.1). Here again one can counter with a similar claim about other sensible qualities: different persons exposed to the same

---

[36] Thus I differ again with Schaper, who says that aesthetic feelings are 'about' an object but then refuses to allow that they are 'a way of being aware of the features or qualities of something' (*Studies in Kant's Aesthetics*, 52).

object often experience quite different sensations of its spatiality—and yet we can agree that the object has objective spatial properties. Given all that Kant says, there remain ways in which one could account for the appearance of a special variability of pleasure without implying that pleasures cannot refer to some kind of objective property.[37]

In particular, it can be stressed (1) that 'pleasure' alone is obviously an extremely general and vague term (thus, it should not be surprising that 'I am undergoing pleasure' should be insufficient for making a very specific reference; as much could be said about the objective comment, 'I am having a bodily sensation'); (2) that, although there may be some objects that just as standardly give pleasure to normal humans as they standardly give impressions of a certain size and color, nonetheless, it is understandably and especially easy for such feelings of pleasure also to be stimulated by other causes and manipulations of the body even in the absence of the ordinary objects, whereas the stimulation of the size and color impressions, in the absence of the ordinary causes, is not *so* easy; and (3) that pleasure, or at least some kinds of it, is a relatively dispensable quality of our experience, for without it we can still carry out most of our acts and cognitions, just as people can get along relatively easily without any sense of smell (and thus the fact that smell is in this sense not necessary might lead some to *think* it is less real).

Given these considerations, it is unclear why the mere fact that pleasure involves feeling should automatically condemn it to revealing what is merely subjective. In ordinary circumstances some sets of pleasures are taken to be about as reliable indicators of the objective environment as many other sensory impressions (otherwise it is unimaginable how classical utilitarianism could have ever had much practical appeal). As Kant himself notes (§7.3), just as there is a way of learning what others will treat as red, or hard, or round, so also one can develop a sense for determining what will strike others as pleasant. (Kant says this sense provides a mere 'comparative' universality, but if that is the best we can have for any particular empirical claim, no special reasons appear to question its objectivity.)

It is true that this implies that not only aesthetic pleasure but also some of what Kant calls the pleasures of mere 'charm' and 'emotion' (§13) can escape from mere subjectivity. What this shows, however, is only that Kant's discussion of feeling alone lacks a clear concept of sensual interest, and thus by itself cannot found the needed distinction between ('non-conceptual') merely sensual reaction and genuinely disinterested aesthetic response. (And so the fact that my theory does not immediately distinguish these two need not matter either.) Kant makes no intrinsic distinction between these (e.g. by appealing to different felt qualia of

---

[37] Cf. R. Chisholm, *Perceiving* (Ithaca, NY, 1957), 138 f.; and Charles B. Daniels on 'pinching shoes' in 'Colors and Sensations, or How to Define a Pain Ostensively', *American Philosophical Quarterly*, 4 (1967), 235 f.

pleasure[38]), but at first simply takes the 'merely sensual' pleasures to be the ones that are so variable they cannot be taken to base a universal claim. This is surely inadequate, for if the notion of disinterest is to have epistemological value, it must provide means for *antecedently* singling out the judgments that can ('non-conceptually') make universal claims. Moreover, here Kant does not even have the escape of being able to say that the disinterestedness of a judgment is not supposed to be so much a justification for its universality as rather just a part of its meaning—for, as was pointed out before, interested judgments can also be universal. Thus, it must be something in the mere fact that a judgment is *sensually* interested that shows that it is unfit for universality. But since, as we have just seen, the only fact about a sensually interested judgment that Kant stresses here is its non-universality, we have come full circle, and the irrelevance suspected earlier in the notion of disinterest is now confirmed.

2.5 If neither disinterest as such nor any of the other proposals considered so far can help pick out aesthetic judgments, what can? The obvious strategy to follow here, given the conclusion that beauty can be treated as objective, is to find something in phenomenal objects themselves that would provide a basis for aesthetic pleasure as opposed to a response of mere charm or emotion. Kant suggests this move himself, but whereas he goes on to treat non-aesthetic feeling as sheerly subjective, we can rather allow even such feeling to reflect some kind of objective reference. In fact, a Kantian can admit some objectivity in all three kinds of experience that Kant fails to distinguish in enough detail: namely, the experience of sensual pleasure, of aesthetic pleasure, and of ordinary secondary qualities. The common bond here is the fact that all these experiences can be held to involve claims about how all others should directly experience a particular object (thus 'non-conceptually' and 'universally'). At the same time, fundamental distinctions can be maintained about these three types of experience. For example, the kinds of objective features that typically generate mere sensual pleasures can still be different from the kind that generates aesthetic ones. Kant himself has a famous candidate for the main feature here in his hypothesis that aesthetics judgments alone are due solely to an object's form (see §30.1, where Kant comes closest to explicitly treating beauty as objective). Furthermore, both groups of feeling responses can generally be distinguished from experiences of ordinary secondary qualities by noting how the former are less articulated and depend on the latter. It is usually because an object appears relatively rough, or colorful, for example, that one responds with the feelings that one does, and not vice versa. This fact fits in with the dispensability of feeling noted before: merely sensual or aesthetic reaction

---

[38] See Guyer, *Kant and the Claims of Taste*, 171. However, as R. E. Aquila has argued ('A New Look at Kant's Judgment of Taste', *Kant-Studien*, 70 (1979), 17–34), it could be allowed that there are reasons for positing some structural and phenomenological peculiarities in aesthetic pleasure.

can be founded in something quite objective and yet be distinct from 'merely perceptual' response, for it is quite imaginable for beings (e.g. robots) to have at least some sort of mere perceptual response to an object without having much feeling at all.

Even if a kind of objectivity is allowed to the whole range of experience, from ordinary secondary quality impressions through aesthetic pleasures to non-aesthetic pleasures, it would help to be able to say more about the distinctiveness of aesthetic as opposed to other feelings. Kant's own main suggestion here is that aesthetic response is a reflective response to form, either in the particular and dubious sense of delineation or the general sense of something that is simply there for all to see, whereas sensual response has to do with the 'matter' of each perceiver alone. Obviously, there remain difficulties with this suggestion, especially if some non-aesthetic pleasure claims can also make a claim about what all should experience. Nonetheless, these difficulties primarily affect the problem of *specifying a priori* just what it is that is to be considered objectively beautiful; they do not defeat the general idea that beauty is objective, or at least that it is best thought to be so by any Kantian who accepts that taste is universally valid. The important thing is that this belief is not threatened by any of the alleged features of aesthetic judgment that Kant himself stresses, namely, its disinterestedness, its non-conceptuality, its particularity, its non-cognitivity, its non-lawfulness, and its essential relation to feeling and pleasure. There are also indications that Kant had an awareness of the limits of transcendental philosophy here, for he says that aesthetics is a science only in so far as it merely explains a distinctive kind of judgment and the possibility of its validity (§34.2). Since in this case the kind of judgment happens to be particular and empirical, it should be no surprise that its proper instances are to be specified by ongoing practices rather than armchair legislation.[39]

---

[39] For an account of how for Kant the specific determination of beauty can involve the actual practice of criticism, see Robert Burch, 'Kant's Theory of Beauty as Ideal Art', in Dickie and Sclafani, *Aesthetics*, 688–703.

– 13 –

New Views on Kant's Judgment of Taste

The 1990s have already brought a host of important works on Kant's aesthetics. I will limit my observations here to just a few of these works, primarily in English, and even then I will focus only on how they approach one narrow set of issues: the conceptuality and objectivity of Kantian taste. (By 'taste', I will mean what Kant calls pure judgments of taste, and in practice I will focus almost entirely on assertions of beauty.) These issues have been at the center of my own contribution to the literature on Kant's aesthetics, and I approach them again because they seem to me to be central and still unresolved, even after their treatment this decade in some of the most impressive books ever dedicated to Kant's aesthetics.[1]

On this occasion my focus will be mainly on Hannah Ginsborg's contribution. Her book, *The Role of Taste in Kant's Theory of Cognition*, concentrates on precisely the issues that have been of central concern to me, and her essay 'Kant on the Subjectivity of Taste' develops her views further in terms of a direct critique of my own position.[2] Her expositions and objections are so well structured that I have found them to offer the ideal framework for reformulating my own views.

It may help first to indicate very briefly what my own position has been. Since Kant lists a number of necessary features of aesthetic judgment, one has to make a tactical decision right away about what to emphasize initially in one's own

---

[1] See my '*Kant and the Claims of Taste*, by P. Guyer', *New Scholasticism*, 54 (1980), 241–9; 'How to Save Kant's Deduction of Taste', *Journal of Value Inquiry*, 16 (1982), 295-302; 'Kant and the Objectivity of Taste', *British Journal of Aesthetics*, 23 (1983), 3–17 (the latter two essays are cited here as reprinted in Ch. 12 above); '*Imagination and Interpretation in Kant*, by R. Makkreel', *Man and World*, 25 (1992), 227–34. Very similar views, developed independently and almost simultaneously, appear in Anthony Savile, 'Objectivity in Kant's Aesthetic Judgment: Eva Schaper on Kant', *British Journal of Aesthetics*, 21 (1981), 364–9. Cf. also Anthony Savile, *Aesthetic Reconstructions: The Seminal Writings of Lessing, Kant and Schiller* (Oxford, 1987); Jens Kulenkampff, *Kants Logik des ästhetischen Urteils* (Frankfurt, 1978); Jens Kulenkampff, 'The Objectivity of Taste: Hume and Kant', *Nous*, 24 (1990), 93–100; and Jane Kneller, 'Kant's Concept of Beauty', *History of Philosophy Quarterly*, 3 (1986), 311–24.

[2] H. Ginsborg, *The Role of Taste in Kant's Theory of Cognition* (New York, 1990); and H. Ginsborg, 'Kant on the Subjectivity of Taste', *Kants Ästhetik/ Kant's Aesthetics/L'esthétique de Kant*, ed. H. Parret (Berlin/New York, 1998), 448–65. Ginsborg kindly shared a draft of her essay with me (the title of which is a direct contrast with my 'Kant and the Objectivity of Taste'), and I am greatly indebted to the stimulus of her work. I would also like to express my thanks to the other participants at the meeting in Cerisy-la-Salle (where this essay was first presented) for their help in innumerable ways.

approach. The main features that Kant lists are disinterestedness, universality, subjective purposiveness, and necessity. All of these characteristics are supposed to go together in taste, but when contemporary philosophers bother at all to defend one or the other, it is usually at the cost of the remaining features. In particular, the claim of universality, that judgments of taste can be properly taken to hold for others and not just for oneself, is often sacrificed even in some of the most careful and sympathetic interpretations. Given the disputed status of aesthetics, the claim of universality is clearly a very hard one to defend, but I still believe that it is where we need to start from in any attempt to understand Kant's own intentions. As long as one takes seriously the third *Critique's* talk of a *deduction* of taste, it surely appears that what Kant is primarily trying to do is to *justify* aesthetic judgments in general, which just is to explain how they can be universally valid. It may turn out here, as with his other deductions, that his explanations are not clearly compelling for everyone, but I take it to be a course of last resort to construct an interpretation that does not even have a chance of yielding the prime result that Kant was aiming to deduce. Hence, I will label as 'strong revisionists' any interpreters who undercut *from the start* the claim of universality, even if their works tie taste nicely to other aspects of reflective judgment or connect it very closely with such features as disinterestedness or subjective purposiveness. On the other hand, I will say that one is being a 'mild revisionist' if one proposes an interpretation that aims to show how Kant's universality claim can be defended roughly in the terms he proposed even while acknowledging that some of the other features (e.g. disinterestedness)[3] that Kant attaches to taste might have to be considered dispensable (unless they are given a stipulative definition that makes them fit; one could, for example, insist that a state is 'disinterested' precisely when and only when it allows universality). In addition, in the service of preserving compatibility with the intention of providing a deduction of taste, a mild revisionist account could introduce some features that seem even directly contrary to some of Kant's own explanations of the grounds of taste. In particular, while admitting that Kant frequently speaks of the non-conceptual and non-objective nature of taste, a mild revisionist could go on to propose that precisely for Kant's own purposes it would ultimately be better to say that taste is conceptual and objective.

Such a mild revisionism is worth exploring, I believe, because the main alternatives are, on the one hand, a strong revisionism that amounts to an empiricism which may be interesting in its own right but too quickly forfeits the right to call itself Kantian, and, on the other hand, an orthodoxy that holds on to the language of non-conceptuality and non-objectivity, but at the price of making the nature of Kantian taste unduly mysterious.

[3] Christel Fricke's analysis nicely indicates how some of these features are often independent of the others, for example how loose the connection is between disinterest and purposive form (*Kants Theorie des reinen Geschmacksurteils* (Berlin, 1990), 106).

Why would non-conceptuality and non-objectivity be mysterious here? The very simplest—and all too often rushed-over—reasons are these. First, taste is a matter of judgment for Kant, and it is also one of the basic doctrines of the *Critique of Pure Reason* that judgment requires concepts; hence, no matter how much some philosophers might regard taste as non-conceptual, one would naturally presume that for Kant, of all people, taste would have to be conceptual. Similarly with objectivity. Kant states that judgments 'must...allow of being universally communicated, for otherwise no agreement with the object would be owing to them'.[4] Such 'agreement' is precisely what one ordinarily understands by objectivity, and Kant's statement here is meant explicitly as both a general claim about judgment as such and a specific claim about aesthetic judgment. Moreover, if such judgments are taken to be objective, this would of course be the easiest way to understand how they could be universally valid.

Nonetheless, Kant does often speak of taste as non-conceptual and non-objective, and the orthodox line is to take these statements at face value. This language is regarded not as a complicated shorthand (as I propose), or a mystery, or an outright mistake, but as an indication of the intriguing notion that there can be a level of 'intersubjective validity' which exists between the sheer subjectivity of sensation and the sheer objectivity of concepts and inferences. For the orthodox, the notion of this level is to be taken not as a mere formal possibility, but as a crucial contribution to understanding the culmination of Kant's transcendental philosophy. It is to offer help in at least three problem areas. First, it is to provide the way to make sense of Kant's difficult statements about a subjective ground of taste; second, it is to provide an intrinsically attractive anti-rationalist account of the nature of aesthetic experience; and third, it is to provide a useful epistemic supplement to Kant's general theory of judgment by showing how our faculties can be 'fitted' for making valid claims independently even of their coming to typical objective judgments. These three virtues are all stressed in Ginsborg's book, and the third even determines its title: *The Role of Taste in Kant's Theory of Cognition*. Unfortunately, in order to focus here on her treatment of the issues of taste's conceptuality and objectivity, I will have to pass over many of the other important features of her study in order to stress the places where we differ rather than the many places where we agree. My concern at the moment is to exploit her work for the purpose of illustrating how perplexing it can be to hold on to the orthodox line. The aim is not to malign orthodoxy, but simply to provoke it to further clarifications. If it turns out that Kant can be defended after all without recourse to even a mild revisionism, that will be all the better for Kantians.

---

[4] Kant, *Critique of Judgment*, § 21, tr. from Ginsborg, *The Role of Taste*, 103: 'Erkenntnisse und Urteile müssen sich, samt der Überzeugung, die sie begleitet, allgemein mitteilen lassen; denn sonst käme ihnen keine Übereinstimmung mit dem Objekt zu'.

The perplexities of insisting on the non-conceptuality of Kantian taste come out especially clearly precisely because of some interesting special features of Ginsborg's account. In exploring the relation between pleasure and judgment, Ginsborg rejects the notion that Kant is at least implicitly relying on a distinction between aesthetic response and the judgment of taste, such that, as Paul Guyer has proposed, he is taking the judgment proper to come *after* the pleasure of taste, which itself supposedly succeeds in an 'unintentional' 'judgmental procedure', which is the harmony of the faculties in an aesthetic response.[5] Ginsborg proposes that we do not need such a complex analysis, and she stresses Kant's insistence in *Critique of Judgment* §9 that the pleasure in taste is the consequence rather than the source of aesthetic judging. Kant asks 'Whether in the judgment of taste the feeling of pleasure precedes the judging of the object, or the latter precedes the former', and he gives the reply, 'the ... [aesthetic] judging of the object ... is the ground of this pleasure in the harmony of the cognitive faculties'.[6]

This text does seem to indicate clearly enough that for Kant the pleasure in taste is not the source of judgment as such, but is its consequent—and if it were otherwise the universality thesis would obviously be all the harder to maintain. This is not an especially mysterious idea if one recalls that in his earlier work on morals Kant had spoken of how another feeling, namely respect, could be the consequence of one's acknowledgement of the moral law, an acknowledgement that is naturally understood as the judgment that the law is binding.[7] (Note also that making judgment fundamental here is compatible with allowing that after the occurrence of the pleasure that results from this judgment, there could also be all sorts of higher level judgments about the appropriateness of the first level judgment and its pleasure.)

Complications arise because, rather than resting with the solution that Kantian aesthetic judgment precedes aesthetic pleasure, Ginsborg repeatedly insists that they are 'one and the same.'[8] I suspect that she resorts to such an extreme view because of an unfortunate presupposition. Once one is strongly attached to the doctrine of the non-conceptuality of taste, it naturally seems attractive to draw aesthetic judgment close to feeling and thus not make it appear to be an independent intellectual act. However, Kant does not claim merely that in taste the pleasure

---

[5] Ibid. 4. I am abstracting from the question of whether she does justice to Guyer's account here. I also do not at all mean to question the value of distinguishing between Kant's terms 'Beurteilung', which is an immediate judging or 'estimation', and 'Geschmacksurteil', which is a linguistic achievement. Cf. Fricke, *Kants Theorie*, 3.

[6] *Critique of Judgment*, §9 ('Untersuchung der Frage: Ob im Geschmacksurteile das Gefühl der Lust vor der Beurteilung des Gegenstandes, oder diese vor jener vorhergehe'), tr. from Ginsborg, *The Role of Taste*, 3: 'Diese bloss subjektive (ästhetische) Beurteilung des Gegenstandes ... ist der Grund dieser Lust an der Harmonie der Erkenntnisvermögen.'

[7] In *Critique of Judgment*, §12, Kant reminds the reader of this discussion in the *Critique of Practical Reason* (Analytic, ch. 3).

[8] Ginsborg, *The Role of Taste*, 6.

does not precede the judging: what he says is that the judging must precede the pleasure. This is a priority thesis, not an identity thesis. Of course, the question can be pressed, how can one make a judgment about a pleasure if one doesn't already have it?[9] Here again, I believe the analogy with moral experience is helpful. The judgment that we ought to obey morality clearly precedes the feeling of respect, even if it happens always to be accompanied by that feeling, and even if it is about feeling in the sense that it entails the claim that others should react to the law just as one does oneself. But it is the mandated universal approval of the law, not the feeling as such, that is within the judgment proper about the law; similarly, the mandated universal approval of a beautiful object, but not the feeling as such, can be within an aesthetic judgment, even if from such a judgment it follows—as a causal effect in one's own case and as a normative claim for others—that there should come a certain kind of feeling.

Ginsborg comes very close to this position by saying that the judgment of taste does not claim 'the universal communicability of a prior feeling of pleasure', but rather claims 'its own universal communicability': 'in the first instance [I am] demanding not that others who perceive the object do so with pleasure, but simply that they agree with me'.[10] But then she adds, 'in the second place... a judgment of this kind is manifested in nothing other than a feeling of pleasure', and 'a judgment which claimed, self-referentially, its own communicability with respect to an object... could be nothing other than a feeling'.[11] She also says, 'the pleasure just is the judgment that [x is beautiful]', and 'the feeling of pleasure is itself the judgment of taste'.[12]

My difficulty here is simply with the identity thesis. Can't we say all that Kant wants and still allow that, as he also holds, judgment and pleasure are distinct? Ginsborg's main textual support is a passage which states that the 'subjective unity of the relation [of understanding and the imagination] can make itself known only through sensation'.[13] But a statement that x is 'made known' only through y is hardly an identity claim. In this case in particular, the sensation can be taken as that by which we get access to the 'unity' or harmony (and postulate it in others), and not literally as the harmony itself, since a sensation as such does not even contain the higher faculties of mind which define that harmony. Feeling and judging are distinct not only as particulars, in individual states of judging and feeling (which can, of course, be very closely linked, as above), but above all as different types: it is a fundamental doctrine of Kant's that judgments and feelings

---

[9] Cf. ibid. 4.
[10] Ibid. 23–4; cf. 32.
[11] Ibid. 24.
[12] Ibid. 36–7; cf. 71: 'the feeling of pleasure [is the state of mind]... in which I judge simply [!] that everyone who perceives that object should share my state of mind'.
[13] Translation from ibid. 36 (*Critique of Judgment*, §9: 'also kann jene subjektive Einheit des Verhältnisses sich nur durch Empfindung kenntlich machen').

as such have very different necessary structures—for example, only judgments can have truth value—and there is no point in jettisoning such a sensible doctrine needlessly here.

Ginsborg goes on to challenge the distinction from another end, by observing that aesthetic pleasure is not a mere given, and so it is like judgment in involving an attitude that we spontaneously develop.[14] But this doesn't help the identity thesis as such, for one can reject that thesis and still observe that, since aesthetic feelings are, as Kant says, dependent upon judgment, they can involve all the sophisticated features that Ginsborg invokes. (Similarly, one can insist that moral feeling is not 'mere sensation', but rather feeling consequent upon moral judgment, without having to collapse moral feeling and judgment into one another.) Once again, Ginsborg seems to be attracted to emphasizing feeling because she wants to draw taste away from conceptuality. She says, 'when we criticize someone's taste, we are not impugning their capacity to make correct inferences ... we are denying the appropriateness of those feelings in the first place'.[15] Kant makes similar statements, but they count against the conceptuality of taste only if one makes a caricature of the role of concepts. Inference is only one aspect of what one can do with concepts. One can also apply concepts originally to intuitions, for example in ordinary perception, or in what Ginsborg calls aesthetically perceiving 'the object in a certain way'.[16] To employ such a 'certain way' is precisely what is commonly called using a concept.

Often it is argued that such aesthetic perception cannot be conceptual because concepts are rule-governed, and this kind of perception does not consist in subsuming items under a rule. More recently, Wittgensteinian points about the limitations of determinate rules seem to have inspired some to argue that something like a non-conceptual aesthetic faculty must exist as a general precondition for the possibility of our employment of empirical concepts.[17] But this argument can be turned around; for what it rather appears to show is that the mere notion of rules gives us too naive a picture in general of what having a concept consists in. As Anthony Savile has argued, if one assumes that for concepts one must have a

> clear criterion of correct application ... [and if] this assumption is being used as way of fixing what is an empirical concept, then one might well be inclined to say that there are none. If, on the other hand, one wants to say with Wittgenstein that what quite generally makes the attribution of a predicate assertible is the readiness of people in light of all the circumstances to come to agree with one another in saying that the object is ϕ, there seems to be no reason why Kant's aesthetic judgments, which we make on the assump-

---

[14] Ginsborg, *The Role of Taste*, 29, 72.
[15] Ibid. 30.
[16] Ibid. 29.
[17] Ibid. 211; cf. Fricke, *Kants Theorie*, 170; and E. Schaper, *Studies in Kant's Aesthetics* (Edinburgh, 1979), 27, 50.

tion that others can come to agree with us, will not count as nearly objective as those that we are ready to recognize without hesitation as empirical.[18]

Savile jumps here to a conclusion about objectivity, but leaving that aside for now, his remarks show at least how one can turn considerations about determinate rules back into a defense of the conceptuality of taste. Perceiving something in a certain way can involve a concept even if it is not a matter of merely inferring from or subsuming under an already given concept.

What is remarkable is that, at the very moment Ginsborg stresses the judgmental nature of perception—both aesthetic and non-aesthetic—as well as the conceptual nature of 'ordinary' perception, she also alleges that this can help us to understand aesthetic perception as 'a judgment which makes a *non-conceptual* claim'.[19] Nothing that one antecedently understands about these terms or about Kant's philosophy (which by now has had a heavy effect on our antecedent understanding) would lead one to expect such a conclusion. The explanation for it can come only from the notorious fact that Kant himself does say that the beautiful 'pleases without a concept', and that aesthetic judgment does not amount to a cognition assigning a 'determinate property' to an object.[20] But I believe that none of this forces us to take Kantian taste to be non-conceptual in our common contemporary understanding of the term. We could rather say that, unlike morality or logic, taste is perceptual in part and not *merely* conceptual at base, and that it doesn't apply concepts in various special 'determinate' ways. Kant has, after all, a host of ways of speaking of properties that are not determinate; they can be 'indeterminate' items like the infinite, or the supersensible ground (which he says we are to understand as underlying the beautiful), or very general features like modalities and existence. They can be formal rather than limited to a specific kind of natural object. And even if they were to be said not to apply to a particular ordinary 'object' at all, not even to merely phenomenal objects, but simply to 'cognition in general' or to formal structures in relation to some general harmony of our faculties, there still would be some concept of them (e.g. the concept of these structures).[21] In this way the non-conceptuality doctrine is more radical than even the non-objectivity doctrine, and that is why I've begun the critique of orthodoxy in this order.

---

[18] Savile, 'Objectivity in Kant's Aesthetic Judgment, 364. Cf. Ch. 12 above, n. 27.

[19] Ginsborg, *The Role of Taste*, 30; cf. her conclusion, p. 219, about 'non-conceptual judgments'. (I leave aside the content of the astounding remark that 'the claim that there is such a thing as genuinely aesthetic experience is much less vulnerable to skepticism than the claim that we are capable of making conceptual judgments', as if it would be helpful to have two species of judgment, the conceptual and the non-conceptual.) Cf. also p. 205, where she speaks of claims to validity 'without the use of any concept', and defines the autonomy of taste in terms of independence from the 'understanding with its determinate concepts'.

[20] Ibid. 24.

[21] Cf. Ch. 12 above, Sections 2.2–2.3.

The orthodox might counter that the basic issue here should not be whether concepts can be *found* for what we approve in taste, for presumably everything that has any sense in the Kantian world can in principle come under some concepts—for example, there is at the very least, the concept 'what we approve in taste'[22]—but rather whether concepts are (perhaps all that is) used in *grounding* taste. But here again it would be very unfair to insist that the orthodox position fails only if it could be shown that our taste can be grounded on mere concepts. The opponent of orthodoxy here need not be a dogmatic 'teleologist', or a 'logicist' or a moralist, who presumes that some kind of mere analysis of essences is what reveals the beautiful. Note also that Kant's own difficult remarks about concepts are not limited to claims about how we come to know the beautiful. He says, 'aesthetic judgment [of subjective purposive form] does not base itself on any present concept nor does it furnish any such'.[23] This again can be taken to mean simply that what such judgment doesn't rest on or furnish is a particular natural kind of determining property of the 'perfection' of 'an' object. For, he goes on to say, the ground of taste is in 'the form of the object for reflection in general',[24] and in this way the aesthetic judgment 'determines the object in respect of satisfaction and the predicate of beauty'.[25] Unfortunately, Kant also says that this very determining happens 'independently of concepts'. But again, it is striking that he takes the trouble to indicate what he means in terms of very specific exclusions, and the whole cash value of his 'independence' claim can be spelled out in terms of these exclusions. His point is that there is no '*definite* concept' or '*definite* rule of cognition' here, that there is no reference to any concept that anywhere involves *design*, that the judgment is not occasioned by an intellectual 'designed' or '*intentional*' activity (*Critique of Judgment*, §9). If one were carefully to avoid these kinds of conceptualizations and say that taste, since it does involve predica-

---

[22] Cf. N. Wolterstorff, 'An Engagement with Kant's Theory of Beauty', in *Kant's Aesthetics*, ed. R. Meerbote (Atascadero, Calif., 1990), 113. Wolterstorff proposes that the following concept is central to Kant's analysis of taste: 'being a presentation of a sort such that there could be a determinate concept whose associated schema is a rule for the composition of distinct presentations of that sort... Let me call it the *aptness* concept. Kant... asserts that it is not itself a determinate concept... Nonetheless, it does, indeed, seem to be a concept' (115–16). Wolterstorff's analysis is a little more complex and subjective than I believe is necessary, but I find it congenial to the spirit of my approach, especially where I had earlier analyzed taste in terms of a 'particular harmonic response that [an] object is apt to produce for normal persons' (see Ch. 12 above, Section 1.3).

[23] *Critique of Judgment*, Introduction VII : 'ein ästhetisches Urteil... welches sich auf keinem vorhandenen Begriff vom Gegenstande gründet, und keinen von ihm verschafft'.

[24] Ibid.: 'bloss in der Form des Gegenstandes für die Reflexion überhaupt'. Fricke (*Kants Theorie*, 57-61) has an excellent account of what Kant might here mean with his talk of 'cognition in general'. She connects it with his discussion in §12 of the first *Critique* of the notions of unity, multiplicity, and completeness as conditions of cognition in general. Cf. Dieter Henrich, who picks up on Kant's more general, non-comparative use of the notion of reflection in *Aesthetic Judgment and the Moral Image of the World* (Stanford, Calif., 1992), 39.

[25] *Critique of Judgment*, §9: 'Nun bestimmt aber das Geschmacksurteil, unabhängig from Begriffen, das Objekt in Ansehung des Wohlgefallens und das Prädikat der Schönheit'.

tion and judgment and agreement with an object in a certain way, still cannot be wholly without what we understand by concepts, I cannot see how Kant himself would have differed except at the level of terminology. Given the arch-Leibnizian tradition he had to struggle against, it is only understandable that he might have gone a little overboard in discouraging talk of concepts.

So far, I have looked at Kant's exclusions and have abstracted from the fact that he positively characterizes the state 'without a *definite* concept' that underlies taste as a harmonious 'state of free play of the *cognitive* faculties'. He argues that since taste is universally valid this state must be universally communicable, for otherwise it could not be a cognition, i.e. a 'determination of the object with which given representations (in whatever subject) are to agree'. Thus, it is a cognition, although, just as it does not involve a 'definite' concept, it also involves only what is 'as if it were a definite cognition'. The operative contrasting notion for 'definite cognition' here is not 'non-cognition', but rather 'cognition in general': the free play of the cognitive faculties in taste consists in imagination and understanding agreeing 'with each other as is requisite for cognition in general' (*Critique of Judgment*, §9).

Another way to approach the conceptuality issue is thus to consider what is involved in the agreement or 'harmony' of faculties that Kant introduces here. Since it involves some validity and some cognition, and even an appropriate relation of our higher faculties, albeit of a very peculiar and general sort, it would seem only natural to construe this harmony as not entirely independent of concepts. Ginsborg reviews interpretations of this harmony which instead take it to be 'the non-conceptual recognition of purely formal features of the manifold'.[26] She rejects this approach not because of the non-conceptuality claim, but because she thinks the term 'purely formal' is unhelpful here for explaining what is meant by the harmony of faculties if it merely designates whatever it is that generates such a harmony.[27] I believe there are independent and instructive ways to fix the meaning of 'formal' here,[28] but the more important objection is that, as long as it is conceded that 'recognition' is involved, it appears especially odd to say that this is a 'non-conceptual' act. Ginsborg does not make this point, but she does quite appropriately go on to consider an interpretation proposed by Guyer which drops precisely this feature and takes the harmony of faculties to consist not in a synthesis of recognition but rather just in a relation of what Kant originally termed the prior syntheses of apprehension (in intuition) and reproduction (in imagination).[29] Here Ginsborg repeats the important and now

---

[26] Ginsborg, *The Role of Taste*, 56.
[27] Ibid. 57.
[28] Cf. Fricke, *Kants Theorie*.
[29] Ginsborg, *The Role of Taste*, 58. She cites Guyer's discussion (of the First Introduction for the *Critique of Judgment*, VIII, in *Kant and the Claims of Taste* (Cambridge, Mass., 1979), 85–6. Cf. R. Makkreel's critique of the notion of a pre-cognitive, pre-conceptual synthesis, *Imagination and Interpretation in Kant* (Chicago, 1990), 49–51, and the discussion in my 'Imagination and Interpretation in Kant', 231.

familiar objection that taking the harmony to be so elementary would make it omnipresent in a way that would appear to force Kant into the absurdity of regarding everything we perceive as beautiful.[30]

Another objection to this approach would begin with the point that Kant defines the harmony he is concerned with here as a relation of imagination and understanding, not of intuition and imagination. The reflective judgment of taste expresses this relation, yet not in terms of a 'concept ready for the given intuition' but in terms of a perceived 'relation between the two [higher] cognitive faculties'.[31] I take it again that such a complex perception is not really understandable without some use of concepts, and that Kant is best taken to mean not that taste uses no concepts at all, but that it essentially involves classifying of a very general and 'indefinite' sort. Ginsborg takes exactly the opposite strategy; rather than admit that the harmony involved with taste involves a synthesis that is clearly complex enough to require concepts, she proposes dropping the idea that the harmony involves a synthesis at all. Conceding that on Kant's mature view synthesis always brings conceptualization along with it, she contends that the harmony in taste involves only a singular representation, one that Kant stresses is judged without 'comparison' to others.[32] Thus taste supposedly remains free of synthesis and concepts. On my view, this strategy only illustrates once again the kind of difficult position that orthodoxy can force one into. Wouldn't it be much easier to concede that of course any perception of a specific relation of agreement between complex items—in this case, higher faculties of cognition—must involve some synthesis and some concept, even if it is brought together in one representation, and even if it doesn't involve a typical empirical and comparative process? If the harmony of the faculties and taste is as complex and judgmental as Kant proposes, how can it help but be synthetic and conceptual? On Ginsborg's own view, taste involves 'in a completely general form a claim to universal validity that is involved in a more determinate way in all empirical cognition'.[33] But claims that are universal and involved in all cognition do not become non-conceptual or lose synthetic character simply because they can be contrasted with some other claims that are more specific, empirical, and 'determinate'.

Dieter Henrich's recent interpretation has focused on precisely this point. He takes the harmonious play of the faculties in taste to involve an operation of the understanding's 'power of exhibiting concepts . . . by virtue of a feature distinctive of the exhibition [*Darstellung*] of concepts that are derived from perceptions in a

---

[30] Ginsborg, *The Role of Taste*, 65. Cf. Ch. 12 above, Section 1.3.
[31] Cited at Ginsborg, *The Role of Taste*, 58, from Guyer's citation, *Kant and the Claims of Taste*, 223, from the First Introduction for *Critique of Judgment*, VII: 'ein Begriff für die gegebene Anschauung bereit . . . Verhältnis beider Erkenntnisvermögen'.
[32] Ginsborg, *The Role of Taste*, 67.
[33] Ibid. 102.

general and formal way'. Here reflective judgment

compares the state of the imagination with the conditions of a possible conceptualization in general ... [but] one cannot even search for concepts unless one conceives [N.B.] of them already in light of the way in which they can be exhibited. But that amounts to saying that the ascent of reflective judgment from imagination toward understanding necessarily always already takes into account the way in which concepts are generally applied and thus exhibited.[34]

Henrich himself concludes that this is 'precisely how understanding as such enters the play *prior* to the acquisition of any particular concept',[35] but note that he has already spoken of how a 'conceiving' must take place here, so even on this kind of account it turns out that a kind of conceptualism is unavoidable.

The non-conceptualist can of course always proceed by using some very restricted stipulative notion of concepts and in that way claim that taste proceeds without any concepts, but this approach not only is strained but can have unfortunate consequences. Ginsborg argues that taste has a role in Kant's general theory of cognition because it illustrates a type of judgment *and* a non-conceptual level of mind that indicates a kind of validity that can make sense even in the absence of judgments of experience which make claims about objects distinct from us. The distinction between typical judgments of experience and judgments, like taste, that have to do with appearances is important, of course, but this does not make the latter kind of judgments and the states of mind that they require sheerly non-conceptual. It is true that 'to feel warmth on touching a stone is not yet to have a conceptual state of mind in which the property of warmth is ascribed to the stone',[36] but, contrary to what Ginsborg's interpretation would suggest, this is not because the judgment of perception 'I feel warm' is not conceptual—unless one arbitrarily assimilates all conceptualization to determinations of physical objects. The problem here is not simply one of terminology, for it can lead to the substantive mistake of suggesting that all states below the threshold of Kantian experience are much simpler than is the case. Thus, Ginsborg speaks of an 'assimilation that I am proposing between the way in which representations are represented in a judgment of perception and the way in which they are related in the subjective unity of representations'.[37] The latter unity is, on Ginsborg's own account, simply a sequence of inner sense, connected by some laws of association or perhaps just 'an unrepeated conjunction of representations in someone's mental history'.[38] Yet surely such 'subjective unity' is worlds away from Kantian

---

[34] Henrich, *Aesthetic Judgment*, p. 49. I abstract from Henrich's specific proposal here that the 'formal' way can be 'only' the 'unity and the precision of the *arrangement* of a perceived manifold in space and time'. Cf. Ginsborg's critique of similar proposals, *The Role of Taste*, 56.

[35] Henrich, *Aesthetic Judgment*, 49–50. Cf. Guyer, *Kant and the Claims of Taste*, 47, 104, 148, 152, 167–9, 219, 284–7.

[36] Ginsborg, *The Role of Taste*, 131.   [37] Ibid. 141–2.   [38] Ibid. 141.

judgments of perception or taste. A mere sequence of representations is not only not objective, not of 'experience'; as merely a 'sequence', it is not at the level of truth or judgment at all, and it lacks the elementary concepts and syntheses that Kant uses to distinguish our consciousness from that of brutes[39] even prior to any claim that there is knowledge of an external world. Precisely in order to save what is valuable in the idea that there could be a level of universal validity that need not involve determinations of actual physical objects, it is important not to assimilate judgments of appearances to a 'subjective unity' of mind, but rather to remember that these judgments are already conceptual states of mind—and giving up the non-conceptualist approach to taste makes this all the easier.

Within the conceptual domain, there is of course an important distinction between conceptual states in general and the specific higher-order acts of judgment that assert external objectivity, but one can hold onto this distinction and still go on to argue that in the end Kantian taste is best construed as involving not only conceptuality but also objectivity.

One motivation for objectivism is the way it can help respond to a serious problem noted earlier, namely that on first sight Kant's deduction of taste seems to license the conclusion that all objects are beautiful. If all that the deduction says is that taste is grounded on a harmony that is universally communicable because it is part of what is required for 'cognition in general', then it can seem that, since all objects meet these conditions for cognition, they must be said to be beautiful. On a non-conceptualist view this problem can appear especially acute, since in that case the conditions that are sufficient for something to be aesthetically approved are met even more easily because they do not even involve conceptualization.

Now, if it is added that harmony and taste do require concepts, and even concepts of a very sophisticated sort, the old problem about omnipresent beauty does not arise as immediately, and yet it still could happen that all objects we encounter might have to be said to be beautiful if they do meet the so-called 'extra' conceptual conditions for 'cognition in general'. But here it is important to note that Kant speaks not simply of a general harmony needed for cognition but also of 'one special proportion' of the cognitive faculties that some objects may generate more than others.[40] Objectivism comes in at this point, by urging that the natural way to develop the idea of this special proportion is to say that some objects have more of an aesthetic form than others, and that it is the perception of this form that is involved in the special proportion of taste. All this can take place in a way that is compatible with the harmony of faculties required for all cognition,

---

[39] Ginsborg is very concerned with precisely this distinction (ibid. 148, 197).

[40] Ibid. Cf. *Critique of Judgment*, §21; Fricke, *Kants Theorie*, 168; and see Ch. 12 above, Section 1.3. There are obviously many special problems with specifying such an objective form, but these problems do not amount to a transcendental refutation of the sheer possibility of valid judgments here. Cf. P. Guyer, *Kant and the Experience of Freedom* (Cambridge, 1993), 398, n. 14.

and thus taste can be universally communicable even if it involves more than meeting only the minimal conditions of communicability—just as a claim based on the perception of some empirical matter ('x is heavy') can be limited to some objects and yet also be universally valid.

I have elaborated this position elsewhere, and Ginsborg has responded to it in the new essay here that is the subject of my concluding remarks, but before I review that position it may help to indicate a difficulty with an alternative view. The problem is that, if one does not move to placing an emphasis on some kind of objective forms, it seems that all one is left with is trying to draw taste out of the bare experience of seeing that one's epistemic faculties are functioning harmoniously. Ginsborg puts her view this way: taste simply expresses 'our capacity to cognize whatever features of the world there may be',[41] and it is 'a judgment whose sole content is its claim to universal validity'.[42] Henrich has a somewhat similar proposal, namely that in taste 'the harmonious agreement of the cognitive powers arises, albeit in comparatively rare perceptual situations, from *nothing but* the fundamental constitution of the powers in question'.[43] The initial objection to such views is that, even if they could fit many of Kant's texts and avoid formal refutation, it is not clear how they connect with our ordinary specific notion of taste. That is, even if there is a special kind of judgment and feeling that one has when one's cognitive equipment is—and one realizes that it is—functioning neatly 'in general', why should that have anything to do specifically with the 'beautiful'? Why couldn't it be called merely a judgment of internal epistemic fitness, and left at that? Ironically, here the orthodox approach seems to drive Kant's aesthetics much more into the position of an intellectualization of taste than anything that is required by the doctrine that taste, in part, is essentially conceptual and objective.

The alternative of regarding taste as concerning specific qualities that are objective and distinctively aesthetic is, to be sure, not without its own problems. Ginsborg raises a series of considerations against taking this view to be compatible with good sense and the proper thrust of Kant's theory. Her first main point is that my account supposedly 'assumes that there are in fact psychophysical laws connecting certain complexes of primary qualities with certain kinds of pleasure in human beings'.[44] Here there seems to be some misunderstanding; for my real point is rather that 'non-lawfulness' is what is to be expected with aesthetic qualities (I speak of 'the futility in the search for specific laws' of beauty and its 'non-lawfulness'[45]), although I do say that one option for the objectivist is to

---

[41] Ginsborg, *The Role of Taste*, 161; cf. p. 202, 'immediate awareness of our capacity for empirical cognition'.
[42] Ibid. 171.
[43] Henrich, *Aesthetic Judgment*, 54.
[44] Ginsborg, 'Kant on the Subjectivity of Taste', 452.
[45] See Ch. 12 above, Sections 2.3 and 2.5.

consider secondary qualities in general as 'a particular complex of primary qualities',[46] and then to understand aesthetic qualities as analogous to secondary qualities. My strategy was dialectical, to argue that, even if one takes an ontologically reductive view of secondary qualities in general, beauty still can have a kind of objectivity (notwithstanding the futility of finding 'psycho-physical laws'); and if, on the other hand, one were to allow secondary qualities to have an ontological standing of their own—say precisely because of their 'non-lawfulness' (cf. my argument about 'non-measureable qualities'[47])—then the objectivist about taste has just as easy a time. My main point was simply that aesthetic features can still be said to be *at least as* objective as typical secondary ones, for all that Kant's arguments show.

In addition to the extreme 'pure' positions that traditional secondary qualities are ultimately mere complexes of primary qualities, or that they simply have an independent objective status, one could also propose a 'mixed' view that they are dispositional properties which combine objectivity and subjectivity. One might say, for example, that 'for an object to be red is for it to be the kind of thing which, under certain circumstances which we can specify as normal, arouses sensory impressions of redness'.[48] Precisely this position has been developed in some fascinating articles by David Wiggins and John McDowell, which came out shortly after my work,[49] and which I read as very congenial to it. As Ginsborg notes, 'The example of color serves for McDowell and Wiggins, as it does for Ameriks, to illustrate that a judgment which is based on human sensation or feeling can nonetheless qualify as objective.'[50] However, she sees their position as also very different from my own because they do not 'attempt to deny the dependence of colors on human experience'.[51] But even if I did not assert this dependence, I am also not at all forced to deny it. As a Kantian, one loves to find lots of things to be in some way dependent on human experience—and a Kantian can easily add that this still allows us to say that such things 'qualify as objective'. That's all the objectivism that the mild revisionist needs; if what is objective is *also* subjective in a non-idiosyncratic way, then that doesn't falsify objectivism. Nor does it falsify my initial point about colors, which was simply that, even if one were to take a very crude and non-'mixed' view of secondary qualities, this still wouldn't have to rule out objectivism about taste.

---

[46] See Ch. 12 above, Section 2.3.
[47] Ibid.
[48] Ginsborg, 'Kant on the Subjectivity of Taste', 455.
[49] See John McDowell, 'Aesthetic Value, Objectivity, and the Fabric of the World', in *Pleasure, Preference and Value*, ed. E. Schaper (Cambridge, 1983), 1–16; John McDowell, 'Values and Secondary Qualities', in *Morality and Objectivity*, ed. T. Honderich (London, 1985), 110–29; and David Wiggins, 'A Sensible Subjectivism?', in *Needs, Values, Truth* (Oxford, 1987).
[50] Ginsborg, 'Kant on the Subjectivity of Taste', 455.
[51] Ibid. 455.

There are other problems that Ginsborg presses against my view. She notes how Wiggins brings out the 'normativity' of aesthetic claims: 'if judgments of beauty are to be objective then the property they ascribe must be one of making pleasure appropriate, not merely one of causing it'.[52] This is an important point, but also one I would not at all want to deny, for I say that objective claims are about how one 'should directly experience a particular object', and about features that, because of their appropriate form, 'typically generate' certain responses.[53] Objectivism does not depend on claims about what 'most humans actually experience';[54] precisely because it emphasizes the forms of the objects themselves, it can easily allow things to be beautiful even if in fact humans are quite mixed up and oblivious to their beauty. Objectivism about taste isn't a theory about 'merely causal' relations, and yet it can point out, as Kant does in his philosophy in general, that beyond all the normative claims about harmony and form that we regard as legitimate, we can add that, precisely because we do regard these claims as legitimate, it is sensible also to presume that there are all sorts of relevant causal relations involved in our experiences.

None of these responses, however, touches what turns out to be Ginsborg's major critique of objectivism, namely that it denies the 'autonomy' that Kant ascribes to taste, i.e. the fact that every genuine judgment of taste 'demands that the subject judge for himself', and 'we insist on subjecting the object to our own eyes'.[55] For Ginsborg this means that Kantian beauty is subjective in even 'a deeper sense' than Wiggins and McDowell allow: 'It is subjective because its ascription to an object in any particular case depends on the sentiments of the particular human being making the ascription.' That is, 'Kant intends to rule out that I can judge of an object's beauty on the basis of anything except my own immediate experience.'[56]

The first way Ginsborg sees this position as conflicting with my objectivism is that she presumes that taste on my account *consists in* ascribing certain complexes of primary qualities to objects[57] or judging that these 'dispose' us to react in certain ways.[58] However, to rely on this point would be to confuse what taste itself is, on my account, with my philosophical explanation of what underlies taste. Taste itself is basically a perception of beautiful forms; unlike the philosopher, the subject making judgments of beauty need not know of or even think about such explanatory notions as primary qualities or physical dispositions.

---

[52] Ibid. 456.
[53] See Ch. 12 above, Section 2.5.
[54] Ginsborg, 'Kant on the Subjectivity of Taste', 454.
[55] Ibid. 452; cf. 460, and see also *Critique of Judgment*, §32 and §8; and Guyer, *Kant and the Experience of Freedom*, 281–4.
[56] Ginsborg, 'Kant on the Subjectivity of Taste', 461.
[57] Ibid. 452.
[58] Ibid. 458.

However, Ginsborg has another, deeper objection: namely that, if an aesthetic theory is committed to the existence of such underlying objective features, then, even if they aren't explicitly referred to in taste, *indirect* evidence about those features still *could* be brought in to ground one's judgment of taste, and this is contrary to Kant's principle that I must rely on my 'own eyes'. She also argues that for the objectivist 'the feelings of other people would provide reasons for me to judge one way or the other on the question of an object's beauty... because they would serve as evidence for the presence or absence of the pleasure-causing property'.[59] All this is objectionable because of Kant's well-known insistence that 'the approval of others can provide no valid proof for the judgment of beauty'.[60]

There are a number of issues to be distinguished here. If it is conceded that the question is not about how people actually proceed in taste—that is, if it is allowed that the objectivist by no means has to believe that in 'real life' one should aim at or ever could come up with causal analyses or surveys of other perceivers[61] that would supplant one's own direct aesthetic reactions—then the question is simply whether a judgment of taste could be warranted if, *per impossible*, one knew that the 'objective conditions' were satisfied even though one was not actually having any aesthetic 'experience'. Ginsborg denies precisely this possibility by saying: 'a claim that the mosque is beautiful implies that I have seen it myself... but it cannot make sense for me to judge that it is or is not beautiful if I have never experienced it'.[62]

At this point it could be that the issue has become a matter of mere words. One could certainly be permitted to reserve the term 'judgment of taste' for what by definition must be a direct perceptual judgment, but then it could be simply added that, although such judgments could always have an ineliminable significance, there could also be something else, which one can call a 'judgment of beauty', or aesthetic value, which would not itself have to be directly perceptual, but would pick out the very same individuals as proper judgments of taste. Analogously, one might argue that, no matter how science develops, observational statements cannot be totally replaced by theoretical statements, no matter how closely these might correspond or intersect—and yet the basic truths of science could still be picked out in terms of theoretical statements.

This terminological procedure saves the doctrine of the autonomy of taste in one sense, but not in a very interesting way. Ginsborg seems to have more in

---

[59] Ginsborg, 'Kant on the Subjectivity of Taste', 453.
[60] *Critique of Judgment*, § 33.
[61] Ginsborg is not entirely clear on this. At one point she implies that an objectivist would have to say 'the fact that a majority of humans felt pleasure in an object would compel me to judge that the object was beautiful' ('Kant on the Subjectivity of Taste', 462). But nothing in objectivism makes such an appeal to 'a majority' relevant.
[62] Ginsborg, 'Kant on the Subjectivity of Taste', 459.

mind, because she believes that here the situation with taste is fundamentally unlike that with color.[63] Even if one allows that colors have a necessary relation to human experience, everyone would at least on occasion concede that an object has a particular color without oneself making a direct experience of that particular object—and yet Ginsborg says that a judge of beauty could never make a parallel concession. Here, an analogy with pain (rather than color) may seem relevant; one could contend that to claim one is in pain just is to express and experience it directly oneself, and that nothing else, nothing objective, even seems to make sense as a warrant for the claim. This contention is certainly controversial, but even if it is allowed the crucial point remains that, although taste involves pleasure and pain, it is essential for Kant that it also (unlike what is supposed about pain here) involves universal validity. And, quite significantly, this means, in Ginsborg's own words, that judging something as beautiful entails being 'aware that one's present state of awareness is appropriate given one's current objective environment'.[64] But if the 'objective environment' is relevant at all, then how could it be in principle impossible to say that if a certain 'objective environment' is there then a certain aesthetic judgment is appropriate? Moreover, how can taste serve, as Kant surely intends it to, as some kind of sign of the fit of our cognitive faculties to our environment, our world, unless we take it not to vary quite independently of that world? This is all the objectivism that a mild revisionist needs, and so I would conclude that for these reasons it best fits Kant's ultimate intentions, even after all the arguments presented against it in the best new views on Kant's judgment of taste.

[63] Ibid.   [64] Ibid.

– 14 –

Taste, Conceptuality, and Objectivity

Contemporary interpreters, inside and outside of philosophy, tend to begin from their own very specific concerns and to follow traditional presuppositions as they struggle valiantly in attempting to exploit Kant's abstract remarks on taste. Usually preferring to bracket transcendental issues, they try to forge a connection with current debates on the fine arts concerning issues that are probably quite far from whatever Kant himself could have appreciated or had in mind in composing the *Critique of Judgment*. Despite these difficulties, Kant still seems relevant on practically any aesthetic issue of the day, and, amazing enough, no matter what basic perspective one tends to favor. On the one hand, Kant is often credited with having inaugurated the modern tradition of the autonomy of systematic aesthetics as such by strictly distinguishing pure judgments of taste from all other kinds of judgments, and by insisting that there is something in them that has an ineliminable a priori character. In this way, Kant appears to have opened up a new and inexhaustible realm for disciplined objective explorations (inspiring theoreticians such as Wellek and numerous neo-Kantians). On the other hand, for an even larger number of readers, Kant's 'Copernican Revolution', his idealistic terminology, his influential role as an inspirer and precursor of cultural revolutions such as romanticism and 'constructivist' theories in areas from mathematics to ethics, have all left him associated most closely with popular anti-objectivist movements, and with the thought that, if there is any knowledge at all in realms outside of natural science, it is of a very unusual kind, a kind that supposedly reflects a reality that we create rather than recognize (thus clearing the road for deconstruction).

My own view is that, when one takes a charitable, broad, systematic, and historical perspective on Kant's work,[1] at bottom there remains an unusual but still basically objectivist position, a position that is so deeply rooted that it applies even to the realms that are on the very opposite end of the scale from the 'hard science' that initially inspired Kant. I suspect that this underlying objectivism has been neglected largely for incidental terminological reasons, and because it

---

[1] This kind of historical orientation seems to me to be a special virtue of Canadian Kant scholarship in this century, and it is especially well exemplified in the careful studies of Pierre Laberge.

understandably seems so much more exciting to think instead of various ways in which Kant points toward subjectivism and the chaos of our own contemporary views. But it is also possible to see Kant as still very much a metaphysical objectivist 'across the board', as insisting on theoretical grounds for the reality of 'things in themselves', and as adding that we can actually determine, on rational and moral grounds, the most important features of ultimate reality, including numerous structures that map on to the beliefs of traditional religion (e.g. God, immortality, a kind of deeply satisfying purposiveness to history and the cosmos). And where, as often happens, the most we can make sense of is a metaphysics of nature rather than anything transcendent, there too a Kantian objectivism can be found that comes out 'across the board'.

All this tends to get lost sight of because of Kant's critical methodology and epistemology, his stress on the peculiar ways that these objective features are *discerned*, with all sorts of limitations on the methods favored by previous forms of dogmatism. He strongly criticizes views that concepts alone or intuitions alone are *sufficient* to determine reality, be it of a phenomenal or more than phenomenal kind. In this way Kant's approach contrasts so sharply with the empiricists and rationalists who preceded him, as well as with the positivists and romanties who succeeded him, that one can forget that his attacks concern their dogmatic models of *access* to reality and are not meant as a denial of objectivity as such. Similarly, since Kant is so fascinated by the paradigm of knowledge in Newtonian physics, it might at first appear that he dismisses 'objective' considerations for areas in which particular sensory inputs are crucial, such as in ordinary sense perception, or moral sensitivity, or aesthetic taste, or the discernment of particular organic forms. When he does turn to those domains, Kant naturally tends to stress the ways in which the special perceptions that they involve do not *of themselves* give us a determination or 'explanation' of the theoretical structure of the inner nature of things.[2] Nonetheless, the fact that access to these domains can require something particular and contingent on our part, something not deducible from pure concepts and/or pure intuitions alone, hardly means that they cannot be part of a process that reveals how matters 'really are', phenomenally if not noumenally. If Kant constantly insists that judgments in these areas do not 'determine' or 'constitute' 'things in themselves' or 'objects as such', one has to remember that even his favorite judgments, the foundations of physics, are also not entirely objective, but essentially reveal what is always *in part* also the 'subjective' nature of human cognition as such. All this suggests that for Kant *all* interesting forms of our 'disclosive' activity—the realms of mere cognition, and of will ('desire'), and of feeling—may be understood as a combination of subjectivity

---

[2] See R. Langton, *Kantian Humility* (Oxford, 1999). See my 'Kant and Short Arguments to Humility', in *Kant's Legacy: Essays in Honor of L. W. Beck*, ed. P. Cicovacki (Rochester, NY, 2000).

and objectivity, a combination that never destroys objectivity altogether. It is this complex perspective (which I will abbreviate simply as 'objectivist') that informs the following reflections that are aimed primarily at defending the neglected objective side of the story that can be told for even what might seem to be the most subjective of Kantian domains, the realm of taste.

In contemporary aesthetics, since at least the heyday of approaches dominated by Heidegger, Gadamer, and others, Kant's philosophy has been *criticized* as bearing special responsibility for an unfortunate 'subjective' turn.[3] More recent philosophers have agreed with this basic interpretive perspective even when they have gone on to *commend* Kant for supposedly accepting and stressing subjective components as primary for the treatment of taste.[4] In contrast to both of these approaches, I have argued elsewhere, as I will again on this occasion, that in the end Kant is best understood as presenting what 'we'—that is, current theoreticians using the standard terminology of our own era—should rather term an *objective* account of taste, an account that is intrinsically more plausible than the subjective positions usually ascribed to him.[5]

Some defenders of the subjectivist interpretations of Kant have also tended to stress, for closely related reasons, a *non-conceptual*, i.e. thoroughly intuitive, reading of his analysis, and against this trend I have also gone on to argue that Kantian taste is best understood in conceptual as well as objective terms.[6] Since there has still been some resistance to this line of interpretation, it seems only appropriate to mount yet another defense and elaboration of my 'objective–conceptual' view. This time, however, rather than repeat in detail the arguments made in earlier discussions, I will present only an outline of my position, while putting an emphasis on the *broader context* of Kant's work and on a clarification of some misunderstandings that appear to crop up repeatedly in *objections* raised against my reading of it. It should be emphasized that from the outset my interpretations always acknowledge that Kant himself writes frequently about judgments of taste as not being 'objective' or 'conceptual'; that is hardly a point that is being denied or forgotten. I see these passages, however, as a starting point for reflection, not as a final word. Kant says many remarkable things, for example that all spatio-temporal objects—raindrops and not only rainbows—are 'mere appearances', and the challenge for the interpreter is to put such statements in the best possible light while creating the least conflict with other parts of his writing.

---

[3] See e.g. John Fisher and Jeffrey Maitland, 'The Subjectivist Turn in Aesthetics: A Critical Analysis of Kant's Theory of Appreciation', *Review of Metaphysics*, 27 (1974), 726–51.

[4] See Hannah Ginsborg, 'Kant on the Subjectivity of Taste' in *Kants Ästhetik/Kant's Aesthetics/L'esthétique de Kant*, ed. H. Parret (Berlin/New York, 1998).

[5] See my 'How to Save Kant's Deduction of Taste', *Journal of Value Inquiry*, 16 (1982), 295–302, and 'Kant and the Objectivity of Taste', *British Journal of Aesthetics*, 23 (1983), 3–17.

[6] See my 'New Views on Kant's Judgment of Taste' in Parret, *Kants Ästhetik*, 431–47; and my 'On Paul Guyer's *Kant and the Experience of Freedom*', *Philosophy and Phenomenological Research*, 55, (1995), 361–7.

We need to find some sensible way to give the best expression of Kant's view, given common sense along with an appreciation for the most basic ideas of his philosophy as a whole and a sensitivity to our own natural ways of speaking now. On any interpretation of his philosophy, some terms are going to come out with a different meaning than one might understandably have supposed at first.

My original exegetical work was undertaken with the immediate purpose of seeking out the most productive way to begin to approach Kant's *deduction* of taste, and in particular of his paradigm, pure judgments of natural beauty. To take such an approach is not at all to deny that this deduction is only a small and not entirely representative part of Kant's aesthetics (let alone of aesthetics in general), and that Kant's aesthetic theory is not even the major topic of the book in which it is presented, the *Critique of Judgment*.[7] Nonetheless, the deduction of taste is the systematic heart of the work, the part that brings together all the central themes of his philosophy, and hence any reading of it should approach it from an informed perspective on how the third *Critique* fits into the larger issues of the Kantian philosophy as a whole. The remarks that follow will thus fall into three parts:

1. a preliminary section, which situates what I take to be the fundamental issue of the third *Critique* within the *general framework* of Kant's philosophy and its response to the distinctive questions of modern philosophy;
2. a core section, which reviews specifically how a reading of Kant's treatment of the *judgment of taste* as objective fits naturally into the overall project of Kant's transcendental philosophy as sketched in the preliminary section; and
3. a concluding section, which ties these general observations together with *responses to several recent criticisms* of the objectivist interpretation.

I

My general remarks in the first preliminary section, fall into three brief subsections: (1.1) an overview of some basic options within the era of modern philosophy; (1.2) a proposal about how to situate Kant's transcendental philosophy with regard to these options, and (1.3) an elucidation of an important new problem that arose for this era and that generated a special Kantian response.

1.1 Any very brief characterization of the whole period of modern philosophy obviously must be understood as meant with many implicit qualifications. Without any claim to originality, I propose that a helpful place to start in determining what is *distinctive* about modern philosophy is to focus on the remarkable phenomenon of *modern* science, and specifically on the new disciplines that arose with the Galilean revolution and the development of the exact science of

[7] See my '*Kant and the Claims of Taste*, by P. Guyer' (review), *New Scholasticism*, 54 (1980), 241–9.

Newtonian physics. This development by no means determined only one sort of possible philosophical reaction. I see three main lines of immediate reaction especially worth distinguishing: skepticism, scientism, and classical modern systematic metaphysics. The first two lines were encouraged by the very sharp contrast that arose between the highly theoretical and counter-intuitive 'scientific image' of modern physics, and the range of other widespread options, especially the 'manifest image' of common sense, the entrenched so-called common sense of the Aristotelian tradition, and the claims of primitive and radical empiricism.

1.1.1 It is well-known that the multiplicity of these images and the striking contrasts between them (combined with other cultural developments at this time, such as momentous religious conflicts and the new availability of ancient texts) led to a deep and influential concern with skepticism.[8] Even when, as in Descartes, the skeptical position was not at all presented in order to be endorsed, it hounded the modern era, at the very least until Hume—and precisely because the very rigor of modern thought disclosed more and more difficulties in finding non-question-begging philosophical responses to it. For my purposes, even philosophers who themselves are not at all skeptics (Rorty, Cavell, Stroud) can be seen as belonging to this group as long as they take—as so many have, even into the era of Wittgenstein—the fundamental function of modern philosophy, at least heretofore, to reside in nothing less than providing a refutation of or continual confrontation with skepticism.

1.1.2 A second option, which grew ever more popular in the aftermath of Hume, was to turn away from the frustrating issue of skepticism, while accepting a sharp contrast between modern science and other images of reality, but at the same time taking this to signify nothing other than the sheer error of all non-scientific perspectives. On this 'scientistic' option, as it has been developed by radical naturalists, philosophy is to become little more than philosophy of science, a codification of technical knowledge accepted largely without question from ongoing scientific disciplines.[9]

1.1.3 Familiar as these options have become, especially in our own time, most of *classical* modern philosophy seems to have taken a third and quite different course. In rationalism and empiricism alike—in Descartes, Leibniz, Spinoza, as in Berkeley and (much of) Hume and Mill, among others—what one finds in fact is not primarily a mere concern with skepticism or anything like a proto-Quinean scientistic physicalism. What one finds is rather the construction of intricate and massive 'systems of the world', each set out with many of the *formal* features of the new highly systematic sciences of the Newtonian era, but with ontologies—e.g. of

---

[8] See e.g. Richard Popkin, *The History of Skepticism from Erasmus to Descartes* (New York, 1964); and Edwin Curley, *Descartes against the Skeptics* (Cambridge, Mass., 1978).

[9] A sophisticated variation of this view is discussed in Michael Friedman, 'Philosophical Naturalism', *Proceedings and Addresses of the American Philosophical Association*, 71 (1997), 7–21.

monads or other special substances or all-encompassing impressions—determined ultimately by philosophers alone, and ultimately in considerable contrast to the 'furniture' that the scientists of the era took themselves to be discussing. Only with the decline of phenomenalism (and of traditional idealism), and the growing anarchy of metaphilosophical developments after the second World War, has this remarkable option moved away from the center of the philosophical stage.

1.2   Where does *Kant's* transcendental philosophy fit in among these options? One could *try* to align him with any one of the three paths that have been noted—the battle against skepticism, or the mere articulation of modern science, or the development of a pure philosophical ontology. In fact, many contemporary Kant interpretations have fixed on one or the other of the first two approaches, i.e. the extremes of taking Kant to be basically a respondent to the skeptic (cf. Strawson, Wolff) or an apologist for the Newtonian science of his time (Körner and after). I have often argued against these popular interpretive strategies,[10] and I would contend more positively now that it is most useful to think of Kant's transcendental approach as introducing a unique *fourth* basic option in response to the fundamental challenge set by the rise of modern science.

Like other options, the Kantian transcendental option accepts as its starting point a *sharp apparent* contrast between common sense and modern science. However, what Kant goes on to propose is that, instead of focusing on trying to establish with certainty (against skepticism) that the objects of common sense exist, let alone that they have philosophical dominance; or, in contrast, on explaining that it is only the theoretical discoveries of science that determine what is objective, one can rather work primarily to determine a *positive philosophical* relation *between* the frameworks of our manifest and scientific images.[11]

This is, I believe, how the basic propositions of Kant's first *Critique* can be best understood. That book defends principles involving philosophical concepts, such as causality and substance, that are to be taken, in different ways, as necessary framework presuppositions relevant *both* for ordinary empirical judgments (so that we can, for instance, say that a boat is moving a certain way, in objective space and time, only if we place it in relation to some general and 'transcendentally' necessary principles of experience), as well as for the fundamental axioms of modern physics, as Kant goes on to try to show in detail in his *Metaphysical Foundations of Natural Science*. Kant's investigations can thus be seen as aimed at clarifying the basic meaning and metaphysical presuppositions of Newtonian

---

[10] See my 'Kant's Transcendental Deduction as a Regressive Argument', *Kant-Studien*, 69 (1978), 273–87. I would distinguish this point from the fact that of course Kant was highly concerned with the Humean skepticism specifically about 'reason'.

[11] These images are emphasized in Wilfrid Sellars' very Kantian and very aptly titled *Science, Perception, and Reality* (London, 1963). For more details, see ch. 2 of my *Kant and the Fate of Autonomy* (Cambridge, 2000).

axioms, and yet, since his transcendental arguments first provide a ground for causality at all, they do not (unlike 'scientism') simply take the objective truth of the scientific principles themselves as an absolute first premise. On this strategy, one also does not attempt to introduce a special philosophical ontology for the natural world (there is a complication here, for I also think that Kant is committed to more than what is 'natural'; but that complication can be abstracted from in this context), i.e. a 'new system'—to use a Leibnizian phrase that Kant employed in his own early career—that competes with the entities posited by science itself. Instead, one tries to explain how the peculiar objects of modern science can cohere with the ordinary sensible judgments that we make, as well as with whatever metaphysical commitments are unavoidable for us. In the end, particular statements about houses and boats are to be considered as backed up epistemically by reference to items that are instances of general laws covering in an exact way all sorts of theoretical entities, entities that one is not expected to be able to perceive directly—as Kant noted with respect to small particles and magnetic fields (*KrV*, A226/B273). The whole framework of these entities is to be taken not to replace but merely to provide a precise ground of explanation for (while also remaining dependent upon) the everyday objective judgments that we make about the macro-objects of ordinary perception.

Kant's approach here remains 'transcendental' because it speaks primarily not about objects as such, but about our a priori *knowledge* of objects, that is about the general principles that are necessary if we are to have any empirical knowledge at all—and that are also claimed to be necessary for the new exact mathematical sciences that are taken to underlie all such knowledge. For example, transcendental philosophy does not itself supply a geometrical specification of objects, but it does argue for principles that 'make intelligible' an a priori link between geometrical science and the objects of experience. In this way Kant's philosophy is unique in focusing on a position that lies 'in between' the domains of ordinary empirical judgment and theoretical science; and, while it accepts both domains as legitimate, it takes neither as absolute by itself but rather aims to articulate the philosophical principles they need to share in order to be jointly understandable and acceptable. Sensory observation, scientific theory, and philosophical interpretation are thus all intertwined in a systematic process of reflective equilibrium.

1.3 Whatever the immediate attractions of this Kantian option, there is an obvious new problem that must be faced by all philosophies that take very seriously the precise theoretical perspective of modern science. The problem is that, even if we were to go so far as to assume an easy fit between experience and one exact scientific framework of mathematics and physics (an assumption much more questionable now than two centuries ago), there remains a cluster of prestigious disciplines that do not seem limited to that austere framework. There are, for example, the disciplines of psychology, of chemistry and biology, of anthropology and history ('social science'), and also, somewhere along the line, the assertions of fields such as aesthetics and philosophy itself. In all these areas, highly respected authorities claim to have attained considerable knowledge, and yet the judgments that constitute their disciplines obviously cannot in any plausible way be translated or directly transformed into the language of either actual physics or elementary common sense—or even the constitutive principles of Kant's mediating Transcendental Analytic.

1.3.1 For a long time the most influential philosophical way of reacting to this difficulty was dominated by the positivist presumption that there is no deep significance in holding on to the autonomy of domains less exact than physics—or, in the case of the tradition from Hume to Mill and Mach—less exact than a psychological theory of sensations designed precisely to model the latest physics. To be sure, for various heuristic and practical purposes, disciplines other than physics (and its exact correlates) might be allowed to continue, but the common presumption was that they gained their ultimate theoretical value solely from their eventual ground (whether or not it could ever be achieved in a 'reduction') in a truly 'hard' foundational science. When the laws of physics came to be taken in a less mechanistic and more dynamic manner, or for a time were even transposed into psychological laws, this only underscored rather than undercut the hegemony of the form of modern physics. Descartes' philosophical disinterest in manifest empirical qualities such as color (regarded as too 'confused' to be a 'true' idea in the ultimate science) was an indication of the attitude that was to be typical of most scientific philosophers throughout the modern period. In the end, the account of the domain of commonsense judgments, and of all disciplines that were not expressed with the exactness of physics, was little more than a theory of error. (This kind of attitude can still be seen in current accounts, for example in philosophies of mind that take explanations couched in commonsense language to have the status of nothing more than a scientifically immature and philosophically irrelevant 'folk psychology'.)

1.3.2 There are endless complications in this story, but for our purposes the first point to note is that initially Kant's philosophy can *seem* to fall right into its general dismissive pattern. But the crucial second point here is that Kant's approach is actually quite distinctive and has aspects that make it both worse and better than the typical modern system. On the one hand, there is the embarrassing fact that sometimes Kant is extreme about an allegiance to physics and physics alone. His textbook on natural science explicitly excludes all psychology and even chemistry (because he did not see that it had developed its own precise quantitative explanations[12]) from the domain of genuine science, and thus it appears to turn its back on the remarkable rise of two of the major cognitive

---

[12] See Michael Friedman, *Kant and the Exact Sciences* (Cambridge, Mass., 1992), esp. ch. 5, III.

developments of his time. On the other hand, and more importantly, it is clear that, as Kant moved beyond the core principles of the understanding in the Transcendental Analytic even in his first *Critique*, he focused more and more on special non-mathematical ideas of reason (and at first he suggests something like such ideas for methodological features of even physics as well), which he argued we really need in order to make intelligible the vast realm of objective claims about our environment that we cannot hope to demonstrate from physics alone, since, as he puts is, there could *never* be 'a Newton' for even 'a blade of grass'.[13]

Thus, at the same time that Kant criticized claims made on behalf of the *rigor* of fields such as psychology and chemistry, he also argued that they are governed by fundamental, and not merely empirical, 'regulative' principles that we should never expect to be replaced by the 'constitutive' claims of any physics that humans could actually develop. It is important to see that Kant always insisted on an objective place for such principles even for disciplines that he came to criticize strongly precisely with regard to their *exact* scientific status. In Kant's schoolbook tradition, psychology, for example, was presented confidently as a science, in both empirical and rational forms, just as, in what appear to be older parts of the first *Critique*, Kant himself speaks of a distinct science of mind fully parallel to that of body (A846/B874). By the time of the *Metaphysical Foundations* (Introduction), however, he denied that psychology was a genuine science (primarily because it seemed not properly quantitative)—and yet he never took back his claim that the 'idea' of 'unity' provides for a basic regulative principle that *we must* always use when *objectively investigating* the mind as such. He insisted that we reason in an entirely proper and inevitable fashion here as long as we do not inflate this idea of the mind's unity—even of the 'necessary unity of apperception'—into an *absolute* ontological claim at *either* the level of nature or beyond. I take him to mean not that there are no objective truths here, but rather that we cannot be *certain* about what they are, and we cannot foreclose the possibility that (unlike the case for 'constitutive' structures) there could be hidden underlying structures of a form that we could never theoretically determine (e.g. invisible 'splits' in mental 'substance').

A similar perspective can be found in Kant's remarks on all the other disciplines that fall 'in between' elementary common sense and physics and the constitutive transcendental principles underlying both domains. Psychology is hardly the only example here; the *Critique of Judgment* is focused largely on the claim that biology is *forever* to be governed by a 'regulative' idea of purposiveness. At the same time that Kant restricts all 'constitutive' claims about organisms as purposive, he also insists that in 'reflectively' judging about them, as we constantly must—given the

---

[13] *Critique of Judgment*, §§75, 77.

remarkable objective but particular and contingent structures that we have actually 'seen', and our constant need to make cognitive empirical progress—we cannot proceed otherwise than by thinking in purposive terms, by seeing them '*as if*' they have a unity that is a ground and not only an effect of their parts. It turns out that his main restrictions against asserting 'constitutive' purposes in living things mainly concern matters that scientists would never worry about —e.g. the remote possibility that a hidden 'mechanism' of an ultimately non-material sort (since Kant denies that mere matter itself could ever explain life) might be responsible for animals, and the desire to block any dogmatic *theoretical argument* (as opposed to mere rational and practical belief) that we can see how a spiritual being is actually guiding the purposive structure of living nature.[14]

For anthropology, the interpretive disciplines,[15] and history, Kant introduces the similar (but only similar) idea of a 'pragmatic' or moral purposiveness that provides for a distinctive unity in the study of human beings. Just as, for all that we theoretically 'know', blind mechanism and not genuine purposiveness might be the ultimate truth about living beings as such, so too an amoral structure and pointless end might be the ultimate truth about the history of the human race— and yet in neither case, supposedly, can a rational human judge 'really think' in such terms. In the case of human history, we can even realize that the purposive structures we are most interested in are generated not so much from heuristic scientific considerations as from hope in a destiny pleasing our own noblest ambitions—and yet for Kant this remains a common and *rational* hope, answering to an interest even more compelling than that of scientific systematicity and reflecting a structure that is even more fundamental.[16]

Kantian aesthetic theory can be seen as one more development along this line, a line where pure ideas such as unity, purposiveness, and morality are presented as rationally inescapable in very specific contexts even while their technically 'non-constitutive' status is repeatedly noted. For Kant, a naturally beautiful object is to be thought of (*a*) as 'purposive *without* a purpose', i.e. precisely as not designed beforehand; and yet (*b*) as especially 'fitting' our faculties, and 'disinterestedly' pleasing, i.e. apart from mere moral or sensory grounds; and yet, (*c*) such an object is still to be taken as truly purposive *for all of us*; and (*d*) as actually and even

---

[14] With these careful qualifications, no wonder that Kant has been argued to be a crucial inspiration for important 'non-reductive' biologists such as Cuvier. On Kant and biology, I have benefited from recent work by Hannah Ginsborg, Paul Guyer, and Michael Letteney.

[15] On Kant's notion of interpretive judgments, see R. Makkreel, who prefers not to use the term 'objective', but notes that for Kant, 'Like a reflective judgment, an authentic interpretation...is [an] intersubjectively valid mode of cognition [*Erkenntis*] "for us" (human beings as such)' ('Gadamer and the Problem of How to Relate Kant and Hegel to Hermeneutics', *Laval theologique et philosophique*, 53 (1997), 163). Makkreel is interpreting *Critique of Judgment*, §90.

[16] Notes from Kant's metaphysics lectures even contain a statement that such 'moral belief is as unshakable as the greatest speculative certainty, indeed even more certain' (*Lectures on Metaphysics/ Immanuel Kant*), ed. and tr. Karl Ameriks and Steve Naragon (Cambridge, 1997), III. XXIX: 778.

'necessarily' pleasing in a pure way. The remarkable fact is that these claims, whatever their limitations (and whatever the general difficulties in all talk of 'merely regulative' principles) are clearly taken by Kant to have a 'universal' standing, a claim on all other humans as such, that is as 'solid' in its own way as the objective assertions in other 'in between' fields such as psychology or even biology, where one also proceeds to make legitimate public claims about the sensible world that are not fully exact, or certain, or clearly ontologically absolute.

II

These preliminaries provide the essential context for beginning to approach the core issue of Kant's specific account of paradigm *aesthetic* judgments. In general, aesthetics appears as a maverick field, not easily connected, without distortion, with other parts of systematic philosophy. Yet, in embedding his discussion of aesthetic judgments in a *Critique of Judgment* concerned with many other issues, Kant admirably attempted to defend the autonomy of aesthetic judgments while at the same time giving them an explicit positive relation to other important kinds of similar judgments within his mature account of knowledge. One should not allow difficulties with Kant's views concerning particular sciences to obscure the main point that was just made about Kant's unique underlying intentions, that he obviously did not at all want simply to condemn to error the whole diverse realm of judgments that are commonly accepted but less than 'exactly' scientific. Rather, the whole point of a *Critique of Judgment* is to explain how, despite the special significance of the laws of physics and the constitutive principles underlying them, there remains an extensive and ineliminable role that philosophy can outline for various basic types of judgment of a more commonsense level, including those that concern legitimate particular claims in the empirical domain. As long as aesthetic judgments are like these claims, in being genuine judgments and not mere passive impressions or acts of will, it is only natural to expect that, given Kant's very definition of judgment as a combination of concepts, they should also be conceptual in some sense (and in that sense convey some sort of objective content).

Similarly, Kant's decision to offer a 'deduction' of judgments of taste suggests that there is something objective to be 'deduced', i.e. validated. Moreover, although aesthetic judgments are not themselves a priori, Kant says they are in some sense 'pure', and so they can even be given a transcendental deduction. Such a deduction typically involves saying (*a*) that there is a distinctive class of presumably legitimate judgments; and (*b*) that there is some kind of 'pure'—hence 'transcendental'—story to be told about the ground of these judgments, especially since they claim to have some kind of universal validity. Because of the very centrality of the notion of presumed legitimacy here, it seems evident to me that, among the four 'moments' of taste ((a)–(d) above) that Kant claims, it is most appropriate to stress from the start the underlying insistence that taste is meant as 'universal'. The three other moments—concerning the disinterestedness, subjective purposiveness, and necessity of taste—are all significant, but Kant's point in including them in a discussion leading to a transcendental deduction is lost if the relevant judgments are not even thought as valid, as 'holding for all' in the proper context, and as being in this core sense objective and not merely subjective.

This kind of objectivity need not conflict with saying that there is also some sort of 'subjectivity' present here. Kant at times makes statements about a kind of subjectivity in our paradigmatic moral and theoretical judgments as well, and yet, by current standards, his views in these areas surely count as fundamentally objective (as holding for at least all spatio-temporal rational agents). The common Kantian 'subjectivity' here is innocent enough and points simply to these judgments' having an essential relation to our sensibility in general, in contrast to judgments that are meant 'super-objectively', i.e. for contexts, such as logic, that are thought of independently of all relation to this sensibility. This kind of so-called 'subjectivity' does nothing to introduce empirical relativity or to call into question the universal validity of these judgments. On the contrary, it is precisely because, for Kant, there are paradigm aesthetic judgments that are presumed from the start to hold for *all* subjects who are basically like human beings, that he thinks a special deduction of them is needed. As long as this universality is presumed, it does not seem to me that his view should be taken as involving a restriction that would conflict with what nearly all of *us now* would ordinarily mean in saying a claim is 'objective'.

This is, nonetheless, a highly controversial issue because there happen to be many places where Kant can *seem* to mean just the opposite of this, and even to say expressively that judgments of taste are not 'objective'. Elsewhere I have given explanations of how the peculiarities of the background of these complicating statements can still allow us to take them in a way that does not require giving up the objectivist interpretation that seems so natural in a transcendental context. Rather than repeat that whole story, in my third and concluding section I will simply confront a series of objections that have been made even after these explanations. But first, it may help to fill out some of the positive ways in which an objectivist approach to these judgments can allow Kant's discussion of aesthetics to fit in nicely with other parts of his system.

A typical Kantian aesthetic judgment asserts that a particular natural object x, e.g. this flower, is beautiful. The surface structure of such an assertion certainly seems to involve both an object (x) and a concept ('beautiful'). Moreover, Kant makes clear that the assertion is meant 'universally', i.e. such that one precisely does not mean that it *merely seems* to some particular person, or even to an entire community, that something has a particular aspect. What the judgment *means* is rather that, even though the object is particular and empirical, the aesthetic quality of the object is 'universally' valid, i.e. valid for any human being with the standard sensory equipment and related faculties. In this way, although of course not in all other ways, the judgment is *like* other basic kinds of judgment at the center of Kantian transcendental investigations—for example, 'this boat is moving down the stream', or 'my consciousness is in some "determined" state at time *t*', or 'this extent of matter has such and such location and dimensions', or 'this particular person should be helped'. In surface structure, an aesthetic judgment thus shares the particular and objective form had by other starting points in transcendental considerations. Of course an aesthetic characterization of an object is not the same thing as a geometric, or kinematic, or moral consideration of it. This much is not hard to see from the simplest reflection on what we or Kant could mean by the concept of the 'beautiful'. Nor is the concept here a concept of logic or of bare sensation, although it does need to involve the logical and sensory dimensions as well. In these ways beauty is a concept that is *like* all those in the whole field of whatever goes beyond the merely subjective but falls short of the exactly scientific as well as the realm of that which altogether transcends the sensible. It is a concept taken to be valid for some particular sensible objects in a way that all ('normal') humans with common sense have the capacity to accept.

The distinctively transcendental theme here arises when one recalls that Kant wants to add that, even in judging particular contingent and empirical objects (cf. *KrV*, § 19), there is always a component of universality and necessity that requires a 'pure' explanation, a reference to some not entirely empirical aspect of our faculty of representation. Thus, Kant stresses that, in addition to an ineliminable component of sensation, even empirical geometrical judgments require a component of pure intuition, while empirical physical judgments require (in addition) a component of pure understanding, and concrete moral judgments require a component of pure practical reason, i.e. pure will. Similarly, Kant will argue that aesthetic judgments arise from sensations of empirical objects but require the pure component of a special harmony, a striking harmony of the faculties of understanding and imagination.

This is a 'special' harmony in that it goes beyond the minimal fit required for us to be able to have empirical knowledge at all. Sometimes it is thought that, because of this kind of reference to harmony in aesthetic judgment, Kant is absurdly committed to saying that all sensible objects would have to be beautiful because in a sense their cognition also always requires some harmony. I have argued against this objection elsewhere;[17] the main idea behind the response can be illustrated in terms of the following rough analogy. Imagine that every actual

---

[17] See my 'How to Save Kant'.

car can be said to have a lowest and a highest operable gear. Note that this feature of having a minimum and a maximum is not a property that a car simply has, but is one that it necessarily has—although of course the particular gears, like the car itself, are matters of contingency. Whenever the car moves, it must move with at least its minimal gear, and some cars need not ever have, or actually reach, any higher gear. Somewhat similarly, Kant believes that each cognizable object can be known to be minimally harmonious with our faculties, and yet some might, and others might not, involve an even higher, a 'most favorable' and aesthetic, harmony, one that reflects a fundamental balance of our higher faculties (when properly stimulated by perception). This is only an analogy, but it suffices, I believe, to meet the concern that there is some immediate absurdity in Kant's notion of aesthetic harmony. It also points to a specific way in which there can be a harmony that can concern empirical objects and yet be indicated in a pure way, somewhat as in the Anticipations of Perception the feature of a 'degree' of the real in appearance is empirical in its detail and yet specifiable a priori as a fundamental possibility. Note also that, although on this theory the relevant objective feature is originally 'picked out' perceptually, i.e. without explicit reflection, it can still make sense to 'back up' or check these judgments by trying to discern if they really are appropriate, i.e. have arisen from the proper 'pure' sources (the aesthetic form of the object, and not its mere sensory material or intellectual form).[18] In this way Kant's theory can reflect 'realistic' commonsense presumptions about aesthetic judgment that correspond to similar presumptions about judgments concerning other sensible qualities, without falling back into an empiricism or 'noumenalism' about taste.

One fact that makes matters complex here is that, although we might express our typical spatial, temporal, and moral judgments also in entirely pure modes, i.e. general rules that abstract from (but do not transcend) all sensible particulars, Kantian aesthetic judgments can never be abstract and are always directly about concrete particulars. The 'pure harmony' here is not something for which, as with pure intuition, or pure concepts of the understanding, or pure practical reason, we can imagine drawing up a possibly empty field. In that sense, beauty has an inescapably concrete quality—but it can still be objective, and it can still require a pure component. Typically, the pure component in a transcendental Kantian story involves an isolatable a priori concept, as in pure examples of moral or

---

[18] It is in this way that I believe one can escape the dilemma of interpretations (that I associate, respectively, with Guyer and Ginsborg) that tend to the extremes of either placing Kantian aesthetic judgments basically in a later reflective judgment about one's psychological history, or stressing an immediate experience in which the judgment is collapsed into an identity with a feeling of pleasure. I believe that, like Moore and other 'realists', Kant allows (with a recognition of relevant disanalogies) basic aesthetic and ethical 'experience' to have a similar three part structure of immediate 'perceptual' judgment, consequent 'pure' feeling, and explicit reflection. For some further details, see the works cited above in nn. 5 and 6.

geometric necessity, but in aesthetics there seems to be no such isolatable quality. And yet it is not entirely misleading for Kant to bring in the notion of the a priori here. Even if 'beauty' itself is not an a priori concept like substance or duty or infinity, it can happen that there are particular empirical objects which, to be fully intelligible in the way that we actually judge them, require an a priori specifiable—e.g. 'most favorable'—balance of the mind's most basic faculties. Such a capacity is consistent with no human being actually appreciating beauty (because of various distractions), just as Kant's theory of pure intuition is, as it should be, consistent with the existence of beings who might not ever get so far as to work out a geometry.

In defending Kant's notion of aesthetic harmony as having a defensible place in his general objective and transcendental scheme, I by no means want to suggest that this notion is sufficient to provide a general account of what we regard as distinctive and most interesting about aesthetic value. Kant himself moves quickly from this abstract level to more concrete discussions about different kinds of aesthetic value (dependent, sublime, etc.), different sorts of aesthetic ideas, and important relations to other aspects of our life, especially morality. Admittedly, these discussions go only so far, and Kant's quaint presumptions about natural beauty or simple ornamental forms can seem both too thin and too naively universalistic to capture what is significant for us in aesthetics, especially in the complex new art forms of romanticism and after. But all aesthetic theories have severe limits, and there is no way to do justice to Kant on these issues without giving his whole theory a much longer hearing than is possible in this context. While these qualifications should not be minimized, it is enough for my purposes if some headway can be made in simply finding some consistent and interesting *starting* points in his account.

III

So much for the exposition of some of the systematic benefits of the position that Kantian aesthetic judgments are objective and conceptual. I turn now to several common and recently restated objections to this position: three objections to the conceptual aspect, and four to the purely objectivist aspect.

3.1 A first objection stresses the conjunction of Kant's saying that concepts in general involve *rules* (*KrV*, A106) and that taste cannot be determined by rules.[19] The objection also notes that concepts are general representations, and therefore express 'universal' rules, whereas taste, on Kant's account, is focused on claims about particular cases.

---

[19] Paul Guyer, 'Moral Anthropology in Kant's Aesthetics and Ethics: A Reply to Ameriks and Sherman', *Philosophy and Phenomenological Research*, 55 (1995), 380 (hereafter: 'Reply').

TASTE, CONCEPTUALITY, AND OBJECTIVITY

3.1.1   My own view is that, properly understood, all this can be granted without harm to the conceptualist interpretation. One simply has to go into some detail about various roles for terms such as 'rule' and 'universal'. While Kant deserves credit for stressing the notion of a rule precisely in order to get away from primitive theories that a concept can be understood in a crude empirical or Platonist way, as merely a particular impression (or association set) or supersensible Form, he also clearly understands that in general the rule-like guiding power of our concepts cannot be reduced to a formula-type rule. This is why he stresses that in our actual use of concepts definitions are very rarely to be found, and a mysterious faculty of the imagination involving schemata must always be used. In this way he anticipates a Wittgensteinian insight, namely that, while having a concept seems like 'following a rule', we should not presume that a possession of *prior explicit* rules fully captures what it is to have genuine control of a concept—even in supposedly clear mathematical cases. Nonetheless, there remains an important sense in which every basic concept that we can actually use involves a 'universal rule' simply because it must be taken to be able to apply to a multiplicity of possible cases. The conceptualist's point is that the same thing can be said about 'beauty', that it makes no sense for us to presume there are legitimate Kantian judgments of taste and then go on to say that we do not think that there are several instances of beauty. As long as there are a number of such instances, there are several items that we are all supposed to acknowledge as having something truly in common (viz. having a form that normally generates a special harmony in us), and in that sense there is a 'universal rule' present after all.

It is almost as if those who think there is problem here are supposing that for Kant using concepts is always a matter of mechanically *deducing* a particular from a general premise. But this is precisely the opposite of what should be expected in a situation like this where taste is characterized as a matter of reflective rather than determinative judgment. Furthermore, the model of deducing something from an antecedent rule rarely fits what we find with *any sensory* concepts—and the sensory context is precisely the relevant one for Kantian aesthetics. When we come to see something as having a certain color, or when we tell someone to look for 'red' objects, there is also no *antecedent* informative general rule that we can state either. We simply expect that people have a capacity for seeing things in a normal way—like *this!*—and roughly the same thing happens when a Kantian expects others to see what appears beautiful. We should not assume that formulae found in academic manuals, or in reports of social preferences, should be our guide in basic judgments of sense or taste. Kant's saying especially negative things about rules in the context of aesthetics can be explained as deriving largely from the fact that there was a serious misconception in his time that involved giving credence to such specially formulated rules. To criticize *such* rules in taste is not to reject all that we now can charitably enough understand by rules and concepts (and their natural objective import).

3.1.2   A second kind of objection, closely related to the first, stresses Kant's explicit disinterest, for example in judgments about beautiful flowers, in concepts such as those formulated by a botanist.[20] Again, the conceptualist can easily enough reply that to say that concepts are essential to Kantian taste is not at all to say that all sorts of concepts must play a role. In aesthetics Kant can and does easily enough dismiss (as irrelevant) scientific concepts, and also the kinds of philosophical and teleological concepts about perfection that other aestheticians of his era had stressed. This hardly shows that aesthetic judgment does not require a concept at all. Moreover, since such judgment clearly involves sensory perception, and presumably some understanding of what is perceived in terms of the ordinary sensory concepts (e.g. red, bright, etc.) that the aesthetic instances supervene upon, there obviously are always many relevant general concepts involved in any particular judgment of taste. Again, the fact that one cannot formulate the concept of the beautiful in an informative way ahead of time, as a botanist might be able to formulate what she is looking for when going out to search for specimens, is no more of a mark against there needing to be a basic concept present here than against there also being concepts for 'red' or 'blue'—or even for 'good' and 'pleasant'.

3.1.3   A third and related way that a conceptualist reading of Kant has been criticized is by drawing attention to Kant's claim in his account of aesthetic Ideas that 'no definite concept' can be 'adequate' to such an Idea.[21] It is true that Kant stresses there is no 'definite' rule here such that an Idea 'determines' how it is to be illustrated. The whole notion of an aesthetic 'genius' is the notion of someone who can creatively fashion remarkable exemplars of Ideas without relying on a stock formula. Once more, all this can be granted—and it even helps explain part of why Kant speaks so often of taste as not involving a 'definite' concept. In fact, most of our uses of concepts are rather indefinite, but there is a special indefiniteness about beauty that no doubt involves the fact that we find more and more instances of it that surprise us in all sorts of ways (even putting aside, as Kant does here, the variability of cultural contexts). But all this does not mean that any particular instance is ever properly appreciated in a way that goes beyond concepts *altogether*—any more than happens with mathematical or philosophical discover-

---

[20] Guyer, 'Reply', 380–1: '...and the empirical concepts that may naturally present themselves in *conjunction* with a beautiful object, such as the botanist's concept of the flower as the reproductive organ of the plant, are declared to be irrelevant to the aesthetic judgment on it'.

[21] Ibid. 381: 'In all these cases [involving an Idea] the aesthetic response is essentially a response to the harmonious relation between some concept and the perceived form of the object either exemplifying or expressing that concept, where, however, the appropriateness of the fit between the thought and form cannot itself be seen as being completely determined by any rule; thus, again in Kant's sense, the aesthetic judgment itself remains non-conceptual even if the object to which we are responding is in some sense at least partially intellectual.'

ies. The fact that creating or discovering such instances in the aesthetic case necessarily involves concrete intuitive activities as well may explain why one naturally tends not to stress the conceptual element. But to be a conceptualist is not to say that concepts always dominate and distinguish taste, any more than that they distinguish perception as such; it is only to say that, in some indefinite way or other, they have to be present, given that there must be judgment, and especially judgment of a kind that is meant to reflect something upon which all others can agree.

3.2 This leaves only the objections and replies directly to the objectivist aspect of my interpretation, which happen to overlap in several ways with the points just discussed.

3.2.1 A first objection picks up on the fact that my interpretation sees judgments of taste fundamentally as a kind of ordinary, particular, empirical judgment, and then notes that such judgment seems not to have a 'high' enough rank in Kant's system to call for a deduction. Since, as I have also stressed on occasion, the *Critique of Pure Reason*, especially in its paradigmatic transcendental deduction, focuses on features that necessarily have an a priori and universal scope, e.g. categories such as causality, it might seem inappropriate to think that a transcendental deduction of taste could focus on what is empirical and restricted.[22] My counter here is simply that this is what makes the third *Critique* especially interesting, that it finally places explicit focus on the context of particular empirical judgments, for which there surely can also be some kind of Kantian transcendental story, especially for judgments of an irreducible type that make a distinctive claim to universal validity and involve a special ('pure') reflective interaction of faculties. Moreover, given examples such as the Refutation of Idealism, there is plenty of reason to believe that interesting Kantian arguments can begin from a particular contingent premise and not aim at concluding to a universal 'law'.

3.2.2 A very closely related second objection claims that, insofar as Kant has a transcendental interest in the area of sensible judgments as such, this must have to do with their *spatio-temporal* form, *rather* than with qualitative aspects such as beauty.[23] There is a twofold response available for this worry. First, in fact Kant suggests that the validity of aesthetic judgments is tied to their involving a perception of qualities that happen to track an especially harmonious form of spatio-temporal relations in the objects perceived. From the general perspective of

---

[22] Ibid. 382: 'As Ameriks himself has argued, Kant's primary concern in the constructive argument of the *Critique of Pure Reason* is to demonstrate the a priori validity of the categories.' See also below n. 23.

[23] Ibid. 383: 'Kant's own discussion of secondary qualities in the "Transcendental Aesthetic" expressly distinguishes the epistemological subjectivity of judgments about secondary qualities from the ontological subjectivity but epistemological objectivity of judgments about spatio-temporal form, thus implying precisely that he does not hold any high opinion about the objectivity of empirical perceptual judgments (see A28–9, B44). So ordinary empirical judgments do not seem to hold as high an epistemological rank in Kant's mind as Ameriks supposes.'

aesthetics, this may seem to be a regrettably narrow feature in Kant's account, but it does show that he is aware of and interested in ways of tying his account of taste to other aspects of his standard transcendental story even while maintaining a focus on particular empirical judgments. A second response to the objection would contend that, even if Kant can and does find it easier to make transcendental arguments in respect of spatio-temporal qualities rather than other features of perception, there is still no clear reason why his account could not naturally be extended into a transcendental story of how taste is related even to qualitative aspects of color, sound, etc., because of various essential relations within the relevant 'quality spaces'.

3.2.3 A third objection consists in contending that an interpretation of taste as an instance of typical objective *empirical* judgment makes it impossible to argue, as Kant wants, for an a priori principle here.[24] To this objection one can reply by referring to the many features noted earlier concerning the general context of the third *Critique* and indicating that Kant's main interest in this era has to do primarily with finding ways of establishing *framework* principles, i.e. special forms of reflective judgment, for *many* realms of common empirical judgment—e.g. in biology and other quasi-teleological domains. Moreover, it can be argued (as I have in earlier work) with respect to taste in particular that the Kantian theory of a harmony of faculties essential to aesthetic judgment can be presented as a pure and transcendental story—similar, for example, to his story of the origins of the moral feeling of respect—and thus not as a matter of mere empirical psychology.[25]

3.2.4 A fourth and final worry about the objectivist interpretation concerns the fact that in taste Kant seems to be much more concerned with necessity, and thus with a more *significant degree of 'intersubjective validity'*, than is the case with respect to ordinary empirical judgments. Here again a response can be built on the specific account given earlier of the harmony of the faculties in taste. Precisely because an aesthetic harmony is supposed to involve a special kind of 'best' fit, one can see how Kant can regard taste both as about empirical qualities and also as involving special features that can still have a more than merely empirical specification.[26] They can involve a special significance, a 'peak experience', that

---

[24] Ibid.: 'The burden of proof that Kant takes on in the case of aesthetic judgments is to show that a prima facie purely subjective response in fact rests on an a priori principle adequate to insure their universal validity. Kant makes no such claim about ordinary empirical judgments.'

[25] See above n. 18.

[26] Guyer, 'Reply', 382, reconstructs my reading of Kant's deduction of taste (in the earlier papers cited above) as concluding, 'all that the deduction of judgments of taste has to show is that such judgments call upon the same cognitive capacities as other empirical judgments, the objectivity of which is not in dispute'. This reconstruction misses my key point that, although there are generic 'cognitive capacities' common to taste as to other perceptions, aesthetic situations are in addition marked by the triggering of a specific sensitivity in us to a kind of 'harmony' generated by beautiful, and only beautiful, forms (under standard circumstances). That is the point that saves the deduction.

has systematic relations to other basic human capacities, and that one would not have to assume is a matter of mere chance, or unindicative of some deep source of agreement within human beings in general.

There is much more to be said about the positive details—and the aesthetic limitations—of an objective and conceptual reading of Kant's account of taste, but for the reasons just given I conclude that, rather than being damaging, the most recent objections to the account are helpful in bringing out various ways in which, according to this reading, the third *Critique* provides a valuable filling out of Kant's general doctrine of judgment.

INDEX

Abicht, J. H. 184 n. 81
Adams, R. M. 17 n. 25
affection 100, 151–2, 156–7, 208
Allison, H. E. 1, 2 n., 23 n. 32, 42, 44–5, 68 n. 7, 73–5, 76 nn. 45 and 48, 78, 80, 83 n. 87, 89 n. 131, 98–9, 104–6, 109–10, 136, 142 n. 16, 212–25, 236 n., 245 n. 22, 272 n. 20
Analogies 9, 25, 125, 129, 130, 134, 142, 215 n. 8, 216, 260
Anscombe, G. E. M. 276
Antinomies 30, 70, 75, 107–11, 115–23, 136, 166–8, 180, 228, 233, 253
Apel, K.-O. 47 n. 55
appearances 33–8, 91, 94
apperception 15–16, 54–66, 85, 151, 259
Aquila, R. E. 68 nn. 8–9, 73, 79 n. 62, 80, 64, 81 n. 73, 83–4, 86 n. 102, 88 n. 123, 305 n.
  argument from 171–2, 254, 256
  argument to 172–3, 176, 254, 256
Armstrong, D. M. 139, 298 n. 31
Atwell, J. 200 n. 17
Aune, B. 194, 197
autonomy 6, 45–8, 173–5, 179 n. 67, 210, 221–62, 313 n. 19, 322, 324

Bartuschat, W. 67 n. 4
Batscha, Z. 67 n. 3
Baum, M. 78, 86 nn. 104 and 114, 92 n. 143
Baumgarten, A. 118–33, 155 n. 42, 272
Bayle, P. 123 n.
beauty 15–17, 37, 46, 285–343
Beck, L. W. 43, 67 n. 1, 68 nn. 7 and 10, 77 n. 50, 80 n. 64, 81 n. 71, 82 n. 83, 87 n. 119, 88–96, 102 n., 113 n., 121 n. 11, 126 n. 26, 142 n. 15, 145, 162, 164 n. 15, 169 n. 32, 178 n. 67, 185–8, 190 n. 116, 191, 214, 215 n. 8, 219 n. 15, 226 n. 3, 232, 298 n. 28
Becker, W. 85 n. 95, 176 n. 58, 177
Beiser, F. 120 n. 10, 282 n.
Bencivenga, E. 99
Benedikt, M. 68 n. 8
Bennett, J. 1, 41, 51, 55, 57, 72–3, 85, 123 n. 15, 143 n. 18, 178 n. 67
Benson, P. 204 n. 24, 205 n. 29
Berkeley, G. 6, 25, 80, 135, 141, 328
Bieri, P. 71 n. 21, 85 nn. 94–5, 88 n. 122
Bilfinger, G. B. 124
Bird, G. 56, 69, 77 n. 53, 80, 103
Bittner, R. 67 n. 3, 171 n. 40, 184 n. 81, 232 n., 255 n. 3
Bondeli, M. 47 n. 56
Bossart, W. 88 n. 123, 92 n. 139
Brandom, R. 47 n. 55
Breazeale, D. 8 n. 8, 13 n., 282 n.
Brittan, G. 67 n. 5
Broad, C. D. 83, 86 n. 101, 87 n. 121, 89 n. 128
Brouillet, R. 91
Bubner, R. 85 n. 94
Buchdahl, G. 68 n. 7
Burch, R. 306 n.

Carl, W. 102 n., 142 n. 15
Carrier, D. 292 n.
Cassam, Q. 12 n. 20
categories 7, 12, 28, 32, 51, 54, 59, 62–4, 66, 78, 90–5, 98, 116, 141–2, 217, 297, 341
causality 9, 22, 36, 44, 52, 60, 65–6, 68, 79, 88, 90–1, 100–1, 115, 132, 134, 146, 153–4, 157, 210, 215, 217–18, 221–4, 232–45, 252–62, 276–7, 294, 302, 321
Cavell, S. 24, 328
character 216, 220
Chipman, L. 72 n. 24

INDEX

Chisholm, R. 16 n., 135, 139, 288 n. 9, 304 n.
Churchill, W. 226 n. 2
Cicovacki, P. 102 n., 142 n. 15, 325 n.
circular argumentation 170, 173, 190
Clark, G. 113 n.
Cohen, H. 1
common ground 22–5
common sense 5–10, 18, 20, 29, 127, 327, 337
concurrence 155 n. 42
Copernican turn 28–9, 35, 99, 102, 106, 268, 271, 324
Cramer, K. 67 n. 3, 85 n. 94, 184 n. 81, 255 n. 3
Crawford, D. W. 285 n. 1, 290, 291 n. 19
Crusius, C. 264–6, 272
Curley, E. 328

Daniels, C. 304 n.
Descartes, R. 6, 14, 26, 48, 328, 331
Giovanni, G. di 92 n. 139
Dickie, G. 292 n., 295 n. 26
Dowdell, V. 298 n. 29
Dryer, D. 68 n. 7, 71 n. 21, 72 n. 26, 92 n. 139
Duchesneau, F. 68 n. 7, 87 n. 119
Dummett, M. 98
Duncan, A. R. C. 190 n. 116, 191 n. 117

Einstein, A. 30
Elliot, R. K. 285 n. 1, 290 n. 16
Englehardt, P. 191 n. 119
Engstrom, S. 11 n. 16, 263 n.
Enskat, R. 67 n. 5
Erdmann, B. 124 n., 133 n. 46
Erhard, J. B. 11
essence theory 148
Euclid 87
experience 5–22, 28–32, 44, 54–7, 60–5, 75, 86–7, 103, 110, 146, 216, 230, 260, 287 n. 8, 289, 306

fact of reason 176–7, 184–5, 189, 213, 220, 228, 249–62, 276

fatalism 165
Feder, J. G. 135
Fichte, J. G. 6, 26, 136
Findlay, J. 24 n. 36, 85 n. 95
Fink-Eitel, H. 75 n. 44
Fisher, J. 326 n. 3
Fleischacker, S. 230 n.
Fleischer, M. 191 n. 119
Fløistad, G. 200 n. 15
Förster, E. 102 n., 226 n. 1
Frank, M. 11 n. 15
Franks, P. 11 n. 16, 282 n.
freedom 7, 16, 21, 24, 27, 31, 34, 36–9, 44–5, 82, 145 n. 27, 149, 155 n. 42, 156 n. 43, 157, 161–92, 203, 207, 211–62, 291 n. 20
  argument from 171–2, 254, 256
  argument to 171–3, 176, 254, 256
Fricke, C. 308 n., 312 n. 17, 318 n. 40
Friedman, M. 12 n. 19, 41 n. 48, 99 n. 6, 215 n. 8, 328 n. 9, 331 n.
Frierson, P. 282 n.
Funke, G. 72 n. 22, 73 n. 29, 74 n. 37, 81 n. 71, 82, 136 n. 4, 227 n. 5

Gadamer, H.-G. 326
Garve, C. 135
Geiger, I. 280 n. 37
geometry argument 53, 142
George, R. 81 n. 71
Gerhardt, V. 232 n.
Gersh, S. 12 n. 20
Ginsborg, H. 46, 307–23, 326 n. 4, 333 n. 14, 337 n.
Gochnauer, M. 80 n. 64
God 7, 23–4, 29, 31, 39, 71, 73–6, 80–2, 101, 114, 116, 120, 125–32, 153–6, 165, 179 n. 67, 210, 265–70, 325
good will 37, 44, 155, 193–210, 224
  general capacity view of 193, 199–201
  particular intention view of 193–8
  whole character view of 193, 201–11, 216, 220
Gotterbarn, D. 74 n. 37

INDEX

Gram, M. 61 n. 11, 67 n. 6, 79, 82, 88 n. 123
Greene, T. M. 191 n. 122
Gregor, M. 2 n., 226 n. 1, 256 n. 4
Griffiths, A. P. 88 n. 122
Guyer, P. 1, 2 n., 42, 46, 71 n. 21, 72 n. 26, 86–9, 92 n. 140, 93 n. 148, 94, 98–9, 101 n. 9, 103 n. 14, 104–5, 107–110, 112 n., 116 n. 4, 117 n. 7, 122 n. 13, 129 nn. 36 and 38, 136, 145 n. 27, 226 n. 1, 263 n., 285–306, 310, 315 n. 29, 318 n. 40, 321 n. 55, 333 n. 14, 337 n., 338 n., 340 n. 20 342 n. 26

Hacker, P. 86 n. 111
Harbison, W. 202 n. 20
Hare, J. 278 n. 29, 282 n.
harmony 17, 22, 102, 106, 118–20, 124–7, 132, 149, 269, 280, 290–3, 311–18, 336–7
Harrison, R. 57, 89 n. 125
Hartmann, K. 85 n. 95
Heath, P. 240 n., 263 n.
Hegel, G. W. F. 6, 44–5, 103, 137, 198, 212–14, 222–5
Heidegger, M. 35 n. 42, 326
Heidt, S. 47 n. 55
Heimsoeth, H. 82
Heinze, M. 120 n. 9, 123 n. 14
Heller, T. C. 263 n.
Henrich, D. 2, 41, 43, 63 n. 12, 86 nn. 99–100, 89 nn. 125 and 128, 90–2, 98, 161 n. 2, 162, 171 n. 40, 184 n. 81, 185 n. 88, 186 n. 93, 189–91, 227 n. 4, 256 n. 4, 314 n. 24, 316–17, 319 n. 43
Henson, R. 204, 207
Herbert, F. von 11
Herder, J. G. 128
Herman, B. 21 n., 204–7
Herz, M. 100, 142
Hintikka, J. 53 n., 67 n. 6, 68 n. 6, 71, 72 n. 22, 73 n. 29
Hoaglund, J. 72 n. 23

Höffe, O. 194 n. 4, 211, 221 n. 16, 226 n. 1
Hölderlin, F. 31
Honderich, T. 320 n. 49
Horstmann, R. P. 67 n. 5, 71 n. 21, 78, 85 n. 94, 86 n. 104, 92 n. 143
Hossenfelder, M. 86 n. 103, 93
Hudson, H. H. 191 n. 122
Hume, D. 6, 20 n., 25–6, 29, 65, 87–90, 260–1, 264–9, 280, 328, 331
Humphrey, T. B. 61 n. 10, 67 n. 5, 113 n., 142 n. 16
Hurley, S. 151
Hutcheson, f. 264–7

Ilting, K.-H. 177 n. 64, 189 n. 110
immaterialism 6
immortality 7
interaction 25–33, 42, 120, 124–34
interpretation 1, 47–8

Jacobi, F. H. 20, 25, 29, 79
Johnson, M. 288 n. 15
Jones, H. 194 n. 3, 199, 200 n. 15
judgment 5–16, 28, 43, 47, 64, 66, 71, 78, 86, 91–7, 151, 174, 178, 207, 227–9, 243, 247, 267, 275–8, 286–8, 294–323, 318, 336–343

Kain, P. 274 n. 25, 278 n. 29, 282 n.
Kalter, A. 68 n. 9
Kant, works cited
    Anthropology from a Pragmatic Point of View 298 n. 29
    Critique of Judgment 2–4, 20–2, 47, 67, 236, 285–343
    Critique of Practical Reason 2–4, 16, 20, 22, 43–5, 161–92, 197, 213, 220, 243 n. 20, 249–62, 270
    Critique of Pure Reason 2–4, 8, 16, 43, 162, 166, 180, 188, 227–30, 250–62, 293, 332
    Groundwork of the Metaphysics of Morals 1–3, 43–5, 82, 161–206, 213, 226–48, 250, 280

– 347 –

INDEX

Kant, works cited (*cont.*):
  Inaugural Dissertation (*Selected Pre-Critical Writings and Correspondence with Herz*) 9 n. 9, 102, 104, 112, 113 n., 126–7, 132, 149–50, 153
  Lectures on Metaphysics/Immanuel Kant 6 n., 119 n. 8, 125, 143 n. 18, 154 n. 40, 155 n. 42, 162, 165 n. 20, 166 n. 22, 168, 171, 176 n. 58, 180 n. 71, 227 n. 5, 270 n. 13, 275 n., 333 n. 16
  Lectures on Philosophical Theology 113 n.
  Living Forces 144
  Metaphysical Foundations of Natural Science 117, 143 n. 16, 182, 329, 332
  Metaphysics of Morals 193 n., 207
  'Moral Mrongovius II' 194, 197, 200 n. 17, 202, 207–8, 210, 219, 271–2
  'Moral Vigilantius' 240 n.
  Nova Dilucidatio 113 n., 124–5, 132
  Observations on the Beautiful and the Sublime 203
  Physical Monadology 145
  Prolegomena to Any Future Metaphysics 9, 40 n., 61, 83, 101, 163, 167 n. 26, 168
  'Reflexionen' 92, 154 n. 40, 162, 166, 168, 176 n. 58, 202, 234 n.
  Religion Within the Boundaries of Mere Reason 193 n., 197 n. 9, 201, 207 n. 31, 208–9, 220
  'Review of Schulz' 163, 164 n. 15, 168–9, 171, 186
  'Von einem neuerdings erhobenen vornehmen Ton in der Philosophie' 184 n. 81
  What Real Progress Has Metaphysics Made in Germany since the Time of Leibniz and Wolff? 113 n., 114 n., 117–19
Kaulbach, F. 184 n. 81
Kerferd, G. 113 n.
Kierkegaard, S. 276
Kitcher, P. 10 n. 11, 67 n. 5, 106
Kneller, J. 307 n. 1

Körner, S. 61 n. 10, 64 n., 88 n. 122, 329
Korsgaard, C. 194, 197 n. 9, 199 n. 14, 200 n. 17, 226 n. 1, 245 n. 22, 246 n., 262 n., 268 n. 10
Kraft, B. 226 n. 1
Krausser, P. 81 n. 71
Krüger, L. 71 n. 21, 85 n. 94, 189 n. 106
Kulenkampff, J. 67 n. 4, 285 n. 2, 307 n. 1

Laberge, P. 67 n. 2, 68 nn. 7 and 10, 87 n. 119, 324 n.
Lachièze-Rey, P. 76
Langton, R. 6 n., 17 n. 25, 42–3, 138–57, 325 n.
Larmore, C. 46, 274–82
Laywine, A. 112 n., 145 n. 27
Lazzari, A. 47 n. 56
Lehmann, G. 73 n. 29
Leibniz, G. 6, 14, 25–6, 39, 107, 112–13, 116–18, 126, 127 n. 33, 129–30, 141, 144–5, 147, 151, 153, 216, 272–3, 297, 328, 330
Letteney, M. 333 n. 14
Lewis, C. I. 90 n. 132, 93
Lewis, D. 139
Lewy, C. 83 n. 85
Locke, J. 40, 139
Louden, R. B. 198 n., 202 n. 20
Loux, M. J. 139
Lucas, H. C. 128 n. 34

Mach, E. 331
MacIntosh, J. J. 61 n. 10, 67 n. 6
MacIntyre, A. 223 n. 18
Mackie, J. L. 68 n. 9
Maier, J. P. 1 n.
Maitland, J. 326 n. 3
Majer, U. 67 n. 5
Makkreel, R. 11 n. 17, 307 n. 1, 315 n. 29, 333 n. 15
Malebranche, N. 25, 126–7, 130, 141
Maluschke, G. 78 n. 57
Marc-Wogau, K. 285 n. 2
Martin, G. 72 n. 24

– 348 –

INDEX

Marty, F. 68 n. 10
Marx, W. 78 n. 57
Matthews, H. E. 73–4, 77 n. 52, 79
McDowell, J. 32 n., 35 n. 40, 320–1
McGinn, C. 155 n. 43
Meerbote, R. 71, 87 n. 121, 220
Meier, G. F. 119 n. 8
Melnick, A. 70, 77–8, 88 n. 122, 91 n. 135, 107 n. 21, 123 n. 15
Mendelssohn, M. 139
Menzer, P. 197 n. 9, 201 n. 18, 203 n. 21
metaphysical deduction 28, 53, 64
Mijuskovic, B. 59 n., 86 n. 109
Mill, J. S. 328, 331
Mittelstrass, J. 81 n. 71
modesty 5–8, 15, 41
Moore, G. E. 337 n.
moral conversion 209–11
moral law 15, 16, 45, 161–92, 214, 254, 257, 269–70
moral realism 45, 135, 246 n., 268, 273–5, 281
Moran, D. 12 n. 20
Morgenbesser, S. 67 n. 5
Morrison, J. C. 135 n. 3
Morrissey, B. 68 n. 7, 87 n. 119
Murphy, J. G. 68 n. 7, 199, 200 n. 16

Nagel, G. 103
Nagel, T. 215
Naragon, S. 112 n., 119 n. 8, 143 n. 18, 227 n. 5, 270 n. 13, 333 n. 16
Nelson, L. 189 n. 106, 189 n. 110
Newton, I. 8–10, 21, 30, 39, 87, 107, 116, 128, 146, 332
Nietzsche, F. 48
non-conceptuality 296–8, 309–13, 326
noumena 7, 24 n. 36, 34, 80–4, 107, 115, 117, 130, 155 n. 43, 178, 179 n. 67, 181, 185, 212, 215, 217–18, 261, 269, 274, 297

O'Connor, D. 211 n.
O'Neill, O. 213 n. 3

Osborne, H. 295 n. 25
Ouden, B. den 273 n. 23
Owens, D. 255 n. 2

Paralogisms 14, 89, 115, 120, 122 n. 13, 167–8, 180, 182–3, 219, 243, 259, 269, 286
Parret, H. 307 n. 2, 326 n. 6
Parsons, C. 67 n. 5
passivity argument 141, 152, 175, 181
Paton, H. J. 1, 43, 162, 172, 189–93, 195–6, 200
Patten, S. C. 68 n. 9, 86 n. 117
Penelhum, T. 61 n. 10, 67 n. 6
philosophy of mind 44
Pippin, R. B. 68 n. 8, 78 n. 57, 103 n. 15, 236 n., 282 n., 299 n.
Plantinga, A. 27 n., 156 n. 43, 260 n.
Planty-Bonjour, G. 128 n. 34
Popkin, R. 328 n. 8
Posy, C. 107 n. 21, 123 n. 15
Prauss, G. 2, 16 n., 42, 63 n. 12, 67 n. 2, 73, 75 n. 44, 76–9, 87 n. 121, 89 n. 131, 90, 93–8, 161 n. 1, 185 n. 88, 186 n. 89, 211, 213 n. 3, 227 n. 4, 232 n., 234 n., 236 n., 298 n. 30
principle of coexistence 145
principle of succession 145
Putnam, H. 98–9, 102, 135

qualia 97, 304
Quinn, P. 211, 274 n. 25

Ragland, C. P. 47 n. 55
Rawls, J. 21 n., 45, 135, 213, 226 n. 1, 256 n. 4, 268 n. 10, 282 n.
Reath, A. 256 n. 4
receptivity 141, 147, 152 n. 36, 153
Refutation of Idealism 14, 17–21, 89, 125, 145 n. 27, 259
Regan, D. H. 278 n. 30, 279 n. 35
regressive approach 4, 8–21, 29–33, 41–4, 51–66, 257
Rehberg, A. 255 n. 3

Reiner, H. 191
Reinhold, K. 6, 13, 135–8
relation argument 150 n. 32
representation 7–8, 11–15, 19, 28, 52–66, 91, 100–2, 137
Rescher, N. 81 n. 71, 83 n. 86
restraint argument 125–134, 153–6
Reuscher, J. 113 n.
Riedel, M. 81 n. 71, 177 n. 64
Ritter, J. 184 n. 81
Robinson, H. 155 n. 43
Rohs, P. 89 n. 128, 93 n. 149
Rorty, R. 12, 57 n., 85 n. 98, 98, 129 n. 36, 135, 328
Rosenberg, J. 88 n. 122
Rossvaer, V. 200 n. 15
Rousset, B. 76

Savile, A. 307 n. 1, 312–13
Schacht, R. 223 n.
Schaper, E. 64 n., 86 n. 113, 88 n. 123, 103 n. 14, 296 n., 298 n. 28, 299 n., 303 n., 312 n. 17
Schelling, F. W. J. 6
Schmucker, J. 68 n. 10, 184 n. 78, 185 n. 88, 272 n. 20
Schneewind, J. 45, 128 n. 36, 129 n. 36, 135 n. 1, 240 n., 263–74, 279
Schönecker, D. 47 n. 56, 226 n. 1, 241 n. 18
Schultz, J. 119, 135 n. 3, 168
Schwaiger, C. 278 n. 29
Schwan, A. 86 n. 99, 161 n. 2, 227 n. 4, 256 n. 4
Schwemmer, O. 249 n.
Sclafani, R. 292 n., 295 n. 26
Scott-Taggert, M. 67–8, 82
secondary qualities 320–1, 341 n. 23
Seebohm, T. 136 n. 4
Seidl, H. 74 n. 37
self-consciousness 13–14, 16, 55–6, 59, 86–92, 182
self-knowledge 3, 14, 116, 122, 152, 182–3
self-legislation 172, 201, 242, 244, 246 n., 271, 274–82

Sellars, W. 1, 16 n., 34, 41 n. 48, 68 nn. 6 and 9, 79, 88 n. 122, 97–8, 227 n. 4, 329 n. 11
sensation 15, 288, 298, 303–6, 311–2, 336–7
Seung, T. 278 n. 29
Shaftesbury, lord 264–5, 269
short argument to idealism 136–57
Silber, J. 191
Singer, M. 191
skepticism 7–12, 17–19, 41, 44, 56, 61–2, 65–6, 85–90, 138, 141, 264–74, 286, 289, 328
Skinner, Q. 129 n. 36, 263 n.
Smilansky, S. 255 n. 2
Smith, G. W. 86 n. 105
Smith, N. K. 1, 2 n., 63 n. 13, 73 n. 29, 113 n.
Smith, W. 68 n. 7
Solomon, W. D. 161 n. 1
Sophocles 280
Sorrell, T. 205, 207 n. 35
Sousa, M. 263 n.
Spinoza, B. 6, 20 n., 24–6, 126, 131, 145, 328
spiritualism 6
Stamm, M. 282 n.
Stark, W. 119 n. 8
Stegmaier, W. 67 n. 4
Stern, P. 211 n.
Stern, R. 11 n. 18
Stevenson, L. 85 n. 96, 86 n. 108
Stine, W. 88 n. 122, 89 n. 129
Strawson, P. F. 1, 12, 41, 51, 55–6, 61, 85, 98, 139, 141, 142 n. 14, 329
Stroud, B. 56 n. 5, 85, 86 nn. 101 and 110, 328
Strube, C. 77 n. 50
Stuhlmann-Laeisz, R. 67 n. 5
Sturma, D. 14 n. 23
subjective objects 95, 97
subjective validity 96
substance 139 n. 12, 145, 150 n. 31, 167
Suppes, P. 67 n. 5

INDEX

taste 4–7, 22, 46, 285–323, 334–43
Taylor, C. 88 n. 122
temptation 206, 208–9
things in themselves 6, 17, 22–4, 29–35, 39–43, 69–84, 103, 113, 121, 136–57, 214 n. 6, 217, 325
Thomas Aquinas 6
Thompson, M. 68 n. 6
Tieftrunk, J H. 136 n. 4
Tlumak, J. 89 n. 125
transcendental affinity 65–6, 89
transcendental deduction 5–14, 28, 41–3, 51–66, 68, 84–98, 308, 327, 334
transcendental idealism 5–13, 18–44, 54, 65, 68–84, 98–111, 134–57, 167, 181–2, 214–15, 221, 230–1, 250
Tuschling, B. 128 n. 34

Ulrich, J. A. 120 n. 10

Vaihinger, H. 51 n.
Van Cleve, J. 13 n., 17 n. 25, 24 n. 36, 68 n. 7, 89 n. 127, 139 n. 12
Velkley, R. 2
Vossenkuhl, W. 103 n. 14

Wagner, H. 92 n. 139
Walford, D. E. 113 n.
Walker, R. C. S. 67 n. 2, 68, 80–1, 88 n. 122, 89 n. 128, 91, 92 n. 138, 93 nn. 148 and 150, 103, 129 n. 37
Walsh, W. H. 81–3, 86 n. 116
Washburn, M. 68 n. 9, 183 n. 77
Watkins, E. 10 n. 13, 25 n., 112 n., 145 n. 27
Weldon, T. D. 61 n. 10

Wellbery, D. 263 n.
Wellek, R. 324
Werkmeister, W. H. 79 n. 61
Westphal, M. 73 n. 30
White, I. 68 n. 6
White, M. 67 n. 5
Whiting, J. 263 n.
Wick, W. 186 n. 89
Wiehl, R. 85 n. 94
Wiggins, D. 320–1
Wilkerson, T. 68 n. 6, 79–80, 85 n. 97, 86 n. 112, 88–9
will 171–2, 190, 238, 242, 245
Willaschek, M. 249 n.
Williams, B. 98
Williams, T. C. 189 nn. 106 and 110
Wilson, K. D. 68 n. 6, 80 n. 64, 81 n. 73
Wilson, M. D. 80 n. 64
Wiredu, J. E. 67 n. 5
Wittgenstein, L. 27 n., 48, 98, 312, 328, 339
Wolff, C. 118–19, 126, 129, 272
Wolff, R. P. 41, 55, 59, 90 n. 132, 189 n. 110, 190 n. 116, 196 n. 7, 197 n. 10, 202 n. 19, 329
Wolterstorff, N. 102–3, 135, 314 n. 22
Wood, A. 36 n., 44–5, 46 n. 53, 47 n. 55, 68 n. 10, 72 n. 26, 104, 113 n., 117 n. 7, 198 n., 203 n. 22, 212–25, 245 n. 22, 258 n., 259 n. 8, 281 n. 41, 282 n.
Wundt, M. 121

Zemach, E. 89 n. 126
Zöller, G. 142 n. 16
Zwenger, T. 47 n. 56